Basic Wills, Trusts, and Estates for Paralegals

This is dedicated to all my wealthy friends
and relations who I trust will remember me
generously in their wills

Summary of Contents

Contents *vii*
Preface *xv*
Acknowledgments *xvii*
Introduction *xix*

Chapter 1 General Overview of Estate Planning and Estate Administration 1
Chapter 2 Sources of Property 21
Chapter 3 The Laws of Succession 49
Chapter 4 Trusts 63
Chapter 5 Wills 111
Chapter 6 Estate Planning for the Elderly 155
Chapter 7 Estate Administration 187
Chapter 8 Taxation 231
Chapter 9 Comparison of Estate Law in the Different Jurisdictions 255
Appendix: Forms 261

Glossary *357*
Index *367*

Contents

Preface *xv*
Acknowledgments *xvii*
Introduction *xix*

CHAPTER 1: GENERAL OVERVIEW OF ESTATE PLANNING AND ESTATE ADMINISTRATION **1**

Chapter Overview 1
Estate Planning 2
Estate Planning Strategies 4
Gifts 4
Title Transfers 5
Trusts 6
Life Insurance 6
Wills 7
How to Make an Effective Estate Plan 8
Situational Analysis 9
Estate Administration 11
Situational Analysis 15
Chapter Summary 16
Key Terms 17
Case Studies 18
Exercises 20
Analytical Problem 20

CHAPTER 2: SOURCES OF PROPERTY 21

Chapter Overview 21
Types of Property 22
Real Property 23
Concurrent Ownership 24
Tenancy in Common 24
Joint Tenancy 25
Tenancy by the Entirety 27
Community Property 28
Tenancy in Partnership 28
Life Estates 29
Leaseholds 31
Other Interests in Real Property 32
Mortgage 32
Easements 32
Liens 33
Elective Share 33
Personal Property 35
General Tangibles 35
Intangibles 36
General Intangibles 36
Intellectual Property 39
Claims and Benefits 40
Situational Analysis 42
Chapter Summary 43
Key Terms 44
Case Studies 46
Exercises 47
Analytical Problem 48

CHAPTER 3: THE LAWS OF SUCCESSION 49

Chapter Overview 49
Intestate Succession Defined 50
How Intestate Succession Works 51
Situational Analysis 54
Intestate Administration 55
The Effect of the Laws of Succession 57
Situational Analysis 58
Chapter Summary 59
Key Terms 59
Case Studies 60
Exercises 62
Analytical Problem 62

CHAPTER 4: TRUSTS 63

Chapter Overview 63
Trust Requirements 65
A Trustor 65
Trust Property 67
A Valid Trust Purpose 68
A Trustee 70
A Beneficiary 75
Types of Trusts 78
Express Trusts 78
Implied Trusts 80
Special Situation Trusts 82
Spendthrift Trusts 82
Short-Term Trusts 83
Supplemental Needs Trusts 83
Totten Trusts 84
Marital Deduction Trusts 84
Life Insurance Trusts 85
Creation of the Trust 85
Inter Vivos Trusts 86
Testamentary Trusts 87
Restrictions on Trusts 87
Statute of Uses 87
Rule Against Perpetuities 88
Investments and Roles of the Parties 90
Restrictions on Trust Purpose 91
Termination of Trusts 92
Tax Considerations 94
General 94
Short-Term Trusts 95
Generation Skipping Transfers 96
Drafting a Trust 97
Situational Analysis 102
Chapter Summary 103
Key Terms 104
Case Studies 107
Exercises 108
Analytical Problem 109

CHAPTER 5: WILLS 111

Chapter Overview 111
Testamentary Capacity 112
Age 112
Mental Ability 112

Intent 114
Fraud 114
Menace 114
Undue Influence 115
Temporary Incapacity 116
Will Provisions 116
Surviving Spouse 116
Antenuptial Agreements 117
Omitted Children 117
Advancements 118
Charitable Gifts 118
Ademption 118
Lapsed Gifts 119
Abatement 119
Drafting a Will 120
Preparation 120
Clauses 122
Executing a Will 131
Witnesses 131
Execution 132
Self-Proving Wills 133
Miscellaneous Instruments 134
Nuncupative Wills 134
Holographic Wills 134
Statutory Wills 135
Living Wills 135
Power of Attorney 135
Changing the Will 136
Amendment Through Codicils 136
Amendment Through Operation of Law 137
Revocation 138
Will Contests 139
Sample Will and Accompanying Documents 142
Situational Analysis 149
Chapter Summary 150
Key Terms 150
Case Studies 152
Exercises 153
Analytical Problem 154

CHAPTER 6: ESTATE PLANNING FOR THE ELDERLY 155

Chapter Overview 155
Health Care and the Elderly 156
Medicare 156

Medicaid 159
Related Health Care Documents 160
Guardianship 161
Income Maintenance 164
Social Security 165
Supplemental Security Income 166
Veterans' Benefits 166
Private Pension Plans 167
Plans Funded by the Individual 167
Plans Funded by the Individual's Employer 168
Ethical Concerns 168
Situational Analysis 169
Chapter Summary 170
Key Terms 171
Case Studies 172
Exercises 174
Analytical Problem 174
Social Security Form 175

CHAPTER 7: ESTATE ADMINISTRATION 187

Chapter Overview 187
The Preprobate Process 188
Death Certificate 188
Exhibit 1. Death Certificate 190
Petition to Open Safe Deposit Box 191
Exhibit 2. Petition to Open Safe Deposit Box 192
Petition to Search 193
Exhibit 3. Petition to Search 194
Petition for Guardian ad Litem 195
Petition for Family Allowance 195
Petition for Interim (Preliminary, Temporary) Letters 195
Probate Administration 196
Exhibit 4. Informal Proceeding Forms 197
Petition for Letters of Administration 204
Exhibit 5. Petition for Letters of Administration 205
Petition for Letters Testamentary 206
Exhibit 6. Petition for Letters Testamentary 207
Notice and Waivers of Notice 209
Exhibit 7. Notice and Waivers 210
Probate Hearing 216
Letters 216
Exhibit 8. Orders and Letters 218
Estate Administration 220
Exhibit 9. Final Accounting 223
Chapter Summary 226
Key Terms 227

Case Studies 228
Exercises 229
Analytical Problem 230

CHAPTER 8: TAXATION 231

Chapter Overview 231
Federal Tax Law 233
Federal Tax Forms 234
SS-4: Application for Employer I.D. Number 234
Form 706—United States Estate and Generation Skipping Transfer Tax Return 234
Form 706 Schedules Relating to Assets 236
Schedule A: Real Estate 236
Schedule B: Stocks and Bonds 237
Schedule C: Mortgages, Notes, and Cash 239
Schedule D: Insurance on Decedent's Life 239
Schedule E: Jointly Held Property 240
Schedule F: Other Miscellaneous Property 241
Schedule G: Transfers During Decedent's Life 241
Schedule H: Powers of Appointment 242
Schedule I: Annuities 242
Form 706 Schedules Relating to Deductions 243
Schedule J: Funeral and Administrative Expenses 243
Schedule K: Debts of the Decedent 243
Schedule L: Net Losses During Administration 244
Schedule M: Bequests to Surviving Spouse 244
Schedule N: Qualified ESOP Sales 244
Schedule O: Charitable, Public, and Similar Gifts and Bequests 244
Form 706 Schedules Relating to Credits 245
Schedule P: Credit for Foreign Taxes Paid 245
Schedule Q: Credit for Tax on Prior Transfer 245
Schedule R: Generation Skipping Transfer 246
Schedule S: Excess Retirement Accumulations 246
Form 1041—Fiduciary Income Tax Return 246
Form 1040—U.S. Individual Income Tax Return 246
Situational Analysis 247
Chapter Summary 247
Key Terms 249
Case Studies 249
Exercises 251
Analytical Problem 253

CHAPTER 9: COMPARISON OF ESTATE LAW IN THE DIFFERENT JURISDICTIONS 255

Chapter Overview 255
Chapter Summary 259
Exercises 259

APPENDIX: FORMS 261

Glossary *357*
Index *367*

Preface

Basic Wills, Trusts, and Estates for Paralegals is designed as an introductory text for students in paralegal programs. Its purpose is to provide a basic understanding of the legal principles involved in estate work. This book will provide all the information that a legal assistant will need to know in order to assist in the preparation and completion of all documents incident to an estate practice. It is not intended to be a seminal thesis.

Because estate law is primarily state statute oriented, a comparison study of all the state statutes has been included as the final chapter of this book. Throughout the work specific reference is made to particular jurisdictions to highlight important or interesting aspects of particular state law. However, reference should always be made to the law of the jurisdiction in which the parties reside or own property.

Jeffrey A. Helewitz

August 2005

Acknowledgments

I have been extremely fortunate to have had the kind assistance of several people in the preparation of this project. I would like to pay particular thanks to two former students, Wendy Shomer and Regina Norman, who generously provided succinct and helpful criticism of the work in progress. Words cannot express my gratitude to these two intelligent women.

I wish to thank all of the people at Little, Brown and Company who were involved in the production of the first edition and the team at Aspen Publishers. All of them have been unflaggingly cheerful, humorous, and encouraging.

One final thank you goes to the reviewers. Their careful efforts in reviewing the manuscript, and the many thoughtful comments and suggestions that resulted, are greatly appreciated.

Introduction
or
A Fable of Four Families

Once upon a time in the not too distant past there lived four families of diverse ethnic, cultural, racial, and economic backgrounds who, by circumstances too strange to tell, all wound up at the same law firm for advice with respect to their estates. This book relates the odyssey of these four families as they tread the rocky path of estate planning and administration.

Who are these families?

First, there is the **Jones** family. Loretta Jones is a 23-year-old single mother who lives in the city in a one-bedroom apartment that she shares with Evan, her five-year-old son. Ms. Jones is a secretary who is going to school part-time in the evenings, studying to become a paralegal to make a better life for herself and her son. Evan is in kindergarten every weekday morning, and after school Ms. Jones' mother, Aida, looks after him until Loretta comes home from work or school. Evan's father, Jason Leroy, lives in another city and occasionally sends Loretta some money for his son. Loretta's main concern is that, should anything happen to her, Evan would be looked after and his education would be provided for.

The **Bush** family lives in the same city as Loretta and Evan, but their circumstances are entirely different. Oscar and Hyacinth Bush have been married for almost 24 years and have one child, Byron, who is away at the state university. Oscar works for the city government, and Hyacinth takes care of their two-bedroom apartment. Oscar's parents are deceased and he has no siblings. Hyacinth has two sisters: Fern, married to Barney Potts, and Fleur Laplante, who is single. Hyacinth's aged and slightly senile father, David, lives with Fern and Barney in a nearby city. Fern and Barney have one child, a married daughter Rose, and one grandchild,

Rose's daughter Davida. Oscar and Hyacinth want to make sure that there is enough money to see that Byron can complete his education and that they can enjoy a comfortable retirement.

The **Lears** are an elderly couple living in the suburbs. Dr. Kingston Lear is a partner in a small medical practice in the city. Donna Lear is a homemaker, active in several charities. The Lears have three grown daughters. Regina was divorced and has two children from her first marriage, Matthew and Mark Hahn. She also has two children from her current marriage to Leonard Dodger, named Mary and Margaret. The Lears' second daughter, Grace, is unmarried and works overseas with the U.S. State Department. Her legal residence is still with her parents. Cornelia, the third daughter, is married to a doctor in partnership with her father and has one son, Anthony. Cornelia also has custody of Regina's two sons. Their father, Joseph Hahn, will have nothing to do with them and rarely pays the child support he is supposed to pay pursuant to the divorce decree between him and Regina. Regina's second husband, Leonard, doesn't like Matthew and Mark and physically abused them. Cornelia went to court and was awarded guardianship of the two boys. At the present time Regina and Leonard are suing Kingston and Donna for title to the house in which Regina and Leonard live. The house was originally purchased by Kingston and Donna as an investment, but after her divorce the Lears let Regina live in the house. When Regina remarried she and Leonard stayed in the house, claiming that the house was theirs, and the family is now involved in a bitter lawsuit over title.

The Lears have a much more complicated situation than the Joneses or the Bushes. The Lears have many valuable assets, have children and grandchildren to look after, and are in the middle of litigation with one of their children. They want to make sure that their grandchildren, Matthew and Mark, are protected and cared for, that Regina and Leonard do not wind up with the house, and that the other children and grandchildren are treated fairly when the Lears die.

Finally, there is Tom **Poole**. Tom is in his mid-thirties, is unmarried, and owns a cooperative apartment in the city. Tom, like Oscar, works for the city, and has managed, by extreme frugality, to acquire a sizable amount of cash and blue chip stocks. Both of Tom's parents, Lottie and Simon, are living, and Tom has an older brother, Ken, who is also unmarried. Tom's brother makes a good living, and his parents, although retired, are fairly affluent. Tom wants to increase the size of his assets so that he will have a comfortable retirement and also wants to see that, in case of death, his estate goes to his friends rather than to his family who does not need his money.

These four families—Loretta Jones and her son Evan, Oscar and Hyacinth Bush, Dr. and Mrs. Lear, and Tom Poole—will be the ships we will guide through the murky waters of estate planning and administration to the golden shore of property distribution.

Basic Wills, Trusts, and Estates for Paralegals

1 General Overview of Estate Planning and Estate Administration

CHAPTER OVERVIEW

The purpose of this chapter is to provide a general overview and introduction to the concepts of estate planning and estate administration. For most people the word "estate" conjures up visions of mourners in black, bleak cemeteries, and sometimes, wicked stepparents who have control over all the family money. Few, if any, of these visions are true or accurate.

Estate planning is essentially a branch of financial planning. Its purpose is to help the individual acquire and accumulate assets so that all of his or her financial needs and desires during life can be met. The appropriate distribution of these assets on the person's death is merely one aspect of overall estate planning. Rather than being concerned with a person's demise, the estate planner is actually involved with a person's life. If a person has no assets, there is nothing to distribute after death. The estate planner attempts to help the client to have assets sufficiently substantial so that there is a need to plan the distribution of these assets on death.

Estate administration, on the other hand, concerns the distribution of a person's assets after death. One who administers an estate will be involved with passing title to property from the deceased to his or her heirs, according to the wishes of the decedent or the provisions of the state statutes; seeing that all taxes are paid; and insuring the orderly conclusion to the person's legal life. In other words, estate planning helps a person acquire assets during life, and estate administration helps distribute those assets upon the person's death.

This chapter will discuss the various approaches that can be used for the proper planning and administration of an estate, the courts and statutes that are involved in both the planning and administration of the estate, and the role of the legal assistant with respect to the foregoing.

Estate Planning

Estate planning can be defined as the method whereby a person accumulates, manages, and disposes of real and personal property during his life and after his death. The primary function of effective estate planning is to meet the short- and long-term financial needs of the client and to see that the client's particular concerns can be met after his death. Although all estate planning is concerned with the acquisition of property with the least possible negative tax consequences, each person's financial plan will of necessity be different because of each person's unique financial needs.

Lawyers and financial planners are involved in creating an estate. The financial planner, usually certified, is conversant with all types of potential investments that can provide either capital growth or income. In order to see that the investment objectives designed by the financial planner are met, the attorney is involved in the preparation of all legal documents pertaining to these investments. In each case, the legal assistant aids in gathering the information necessary to create the estate plan.

The first questions to be answered with respect to estate planning are: What are the client's current assets? Family situation? Financial goals? In order to be effective and appropriate, the estate plan must take into consideration all of these factors.

If a client has few assets, the first objective is to devise a method whereby he or she can accumulate some property. This requires a detailed analysis of all of his or her income and expenses and a determination of how much of that income is disposable. **Disposable income** is that income a person has after paying all taxes and expenses for a given period (a week, a month, etc.). It is only this money that can be used to acquire assets; the rest of the income is being used to support his or her current life. If a person has no disposable income, it becomes necessary to create a budget so that some income, however little, can be saved. Conversely, if a person has a great deal of disposable income, it is necessary to see that the income is appropriately invested so as to meet the future financial needs of the client.

EXAMPLES:

1. Loretta Jones has a very modest salary. At the end of the month, after paying rent, utilities, food, tuition, and so forth, she has very little left as disposable income. Loretta needs to find out whether there is some way she could better manage her money so as to accumulate some savings.

2. Tom Poole spends very little of his actual income. At the end of the month he has several thousand dollars left. Tom needs to find appropriate investments for his disposable income to make it productive, that is, to produce more income or growth.

Each person's family situation helps determine his or her financial needs. The financial needs of a couple who is retired with grown children are entirely different from those of a single mother with a young child. Estate and financial planning is concerned with assuring that the financial needs of the client's family can be met: providing for the education of a young child, purchasing a first home for a young couple, and assuring a worry-free retirement.

Finally, the financial wishes of the client must be taken into consideration. It may be well to provide for needs, but most people would like to see their hard work result in more than just basic necessities. Vacations, buying a first or second home, purchasing a car or boat, and so on, are all worthwhile and psychologically necessary ingredients of each person's estate plan. These financial dreams or desires can be grouped into short-term goals, mid-term goals, and long-range plans. A trip at the end of the year is a short-term goal; buying a first home within five years is a mid-term goal; and paying for a child's education is a long-term goal. All of these goals must be identified before an effective estate plan can be created.

EXAMPLE:

Oscar and Hyacinth want to buy a vacation home that they can also use for their retirement. They would like to buy the home when Byron graduates from college. This is a mid-term goal, because Byron is already at university and will probably complete his education in the next few years.

It is beyond the scope of this book to discuss in detail all of the potential investment strategies that are available. That would be more appropriate to a treatise directly concerned with finance and investment. However, several financial strategies that are of particular concern with respect to estate planning should be noted.

When a long-term strategy has been devised for the client, it is necessary to see that this plan can still go forward even if the client dies. This is why the family situation is important. Most peoples' financial plans involve persons other than themselves—spouses, children, other relations, and friends—and as a part of financial planning the professional must make sure that a person's financial wishes for others can continue even after his or her death.

This endpoint of financial planning—what to do on death—raises two problems: (1) keeping the person's assets intact without having them diminished by taxes, and (2) identifying the most effective method of insuring that the decedent's wishes are carried out with respect to transferring his or her property after death.

Many tax considerations are involved in planning an estate. The taxing authorities get involved during life (by taxing income and transfers of large amounts of property as gifts) and after death (by taxing the estate of a decedent). Good estate planning keeps the tax consequences to a minimum. Income taxation and state estate taxation are beyond the scope of this text, but a few words must be mentioned at this point with respect to federal estate and gift taxation. (A more detailed discussion appears where appropriate throughout the text and specifically in Chapters 3, 6, and 9.)

Only property that the decedent owns at the time of death is taxable (plus some property transferred within three years of death, under certain circumstances discussed in Chapter 8). This property is divided into two broad categories: **nonprobate assets**, which is property that passes directly from the decedent to another person without court authorization but by operation of law, and **probate assets**, which is property that must be transferred by order of the court. Both nonprobate and probate assets may be taxed, but if the decedent's assets have been properly managed prior to death, the estate may be able to reduce its tax burden. Certain strategies can be employed, depending on the client's particular circumstances, to divest the client of some of his or her property during life.

EXAMPLE:

Five years before his death, Dr. Lear gives his home to his daughter Grace as a gift, even though he and Donna continue to reside in the home. On Kingston's death, because title belongs to Grace, the house is not part of Kingston's probate assets—he did not own the home when he died. However, his estate still may owe taxes on the value of the house. See Chapter 8.

Estate Planning Strategies

Gifts

The most common method whereby a person transfers property during life is as a **gift**, which is a transfer of property by a **donor** (giver) to **a donee** (recipient) without **consideration**. In other words, it is a transfer in which the donor gives, but does not receive, something of value. All property transferred by outright gift (in which the donor did not retain any interest) is owned by the donee and is not part of the donor's estate. However, the Internal Revenue Service imposes a tax on property transferred by gift. A donor may transfer, tax free, up to $11,000 worth of property per donee per year. Gifts above this amount, except for gifts to spouses, to charities, or for tuition or medical care, must be reported to the IRS on Form 709. No tax is due on these gifts until the total amount exceeds the maximum size of an estate that may pass tax free because of the Unified Tax Credit (Chapter 8). In 2001, the maximum amount that could pass estate tax free was $675,000. In 2002, the amount increased to $700,000; in 2004, $1.5 million; in 2006, it became $2 million; and in 2009, $3.5 million. In 2010, there will be no estate tax, but in 2011 the tax may revert back to the 2001 levels. When the donor dies, the gifts reported on Form 709 are deducted from the dollar exemption permitted for the year of death. This tax exclusion means that a person may transfer much of his estate while he is alive and be able to see the recipients enjoy the property. (The amount of the gift exclusion is doubled if the gifts are made jointly by husbands and wives.) Many states impose a gift tax; for information regarding state taxation, see Chapter 9.

EXAMPLE:

When Kingston transferred title to the house to Grace, he paid a gift tax on the transfer. In this manner Grace received the house "tax free."

Title Transfers

Another strategy that can be employed to minimize estate taxation is to hold title to property in multiple ownership, such as a **tenancy by the entirety** or a **joint tenancy**. The specifics of these types of ownership will be discussed in detail in the next chapter, but for the moment its import is that, with certain types of multiple ownership, upon death the property passes immediately to the surviving owner. If certain legal steps are taken when title to the property is created, a portion of this property may be excluded from the client's taxable estate, and the surviving owner acquires the property immediately upon the client's death.

EXAMPLE:

Cornelia and her husband hold title to their house as tenants by the entirety. When her husband dies, as the surviving tenant, title to the house immediately passes to Cornelia. See Chapter 2.

Trusts

Establishing a trust has become a fairly common method of transferring property while alive so as to avoid estate taxation on death. Trusts will be fully discussed in Chapter 4, but for now be aware that, if properly drafted, a person can transfer his or her property while he or she is alive to a trust that is considered a separate legal entity, and so, upon death, the property is owned by the trust and not the decedent. Recently, the **living trust** (a trust established by a person that takes effect during his or her life) has become a popular strategy for estate planning. Be alert to the fact that creating a trust may have its own tax consequences, and, depending upon how the trust is created, it may still be considered part of the decedent's taxable estate, especially if the decedent continued to benefit from and/or control the property in the trust.

Living trusts may only be beneficial for persons with a comparatively large estate. Note also that there are drawbacks to a person divesting himself or herself of property during lifetime, most notably the lack of control of the assets.

EXAMPLE:

In order to provide an income for their grandchildren, Kingston and Donna put a large sum of money into a trust, using the income from the trust to support Matthew and Mark. The trust stipulates that when Matthew and Mark become adults they will receive the money that remains in the trust.

Life Insurance

One of the most effective methods of leaving a fairly large amount of nonfederally taxable property is by the purchase of life insurance. Provided that the insured names a specific **beneficiary** of the policy (the person who is to receive the proceeds on death of the insured), the proceeds of the policy pass immediately to the beneficiary upon proof of the insured's demise and are not considered part of the decedent's assets. If, however, the insured retained **incidents of ownership** (that is, the right to change the beneficiary, pledge, borrow, or assign the policy), then the proceeds of the policy are considered part of the insured's estate and are fully taxable. See Chapter 8. Life insurance remains an excellent method for a person with few assets to leave his heirs well-provided for.

Several different types of life insurance policies are available on the market today. **Term life insurance** is life insurance that is purchased at a relatively small premium but has no cash value (meaning that it cannot be surrendered for money), and the premium is increased every five or ten years as the insured ages. **Whole life insurance** policies have a cash surrender value representing the amount of premiums the insured has already paid and may be borrowed against. A **cash surrender value** means that the insured can cancel the policy and receive money at any time specified in the policy. The premiums for whole life are very high, but never increase as the insured ages.

Two other types of insurance policies are also fairly popular. **Limited payment life insurance** is a policy that has very high premiums, but the insurance is fully paid up in a relatively short period of time. With this type of policy the insured does not have to make life-long payments and has property rights in the policy when the premiums are paid. **Endowment policies** are insurance policies that are paid up in a set period of time (usually 25 years), at the end of which time the proceeds are paid to the insured, if alive, or to the named beneficiary if the insured is deceased. Both of these types of insurance policies carry very high premiums and are therefore most appropriate for persons with considerable disposable income.

Wills

Last, but definitely not least, estate taxation can be avoided or minimized and the person's wishes can be carried out by having a properly drafted will. A **will** is a written document that, if certain statutory requirements are met, disposes of a person's property upon his or her death according to the wishes stated in the will. One of the greatest tax advantages that can be effected by a will is a **marital deduction**. Under current law, all property left by a deceased to a surviving spouse as a marital deduction passes to the spouse tax free, regardless of the size of the estate. This tax advantage is only available to legally married couples and does not avoid taxation of that property upon the eventual death of the surviving spouse.

To qualify as a marital deduction, the property does not have to be transferred outright to the spouse. For example, favorable federal tax treatment is conferred on **Qualified Terminable Interest Property trusts (QTIPs)**, in which the spouse has the income of the property for life, but on the death of the spouse the property passes to other persons named in the trust. For a full discussion of this topic, see Chapter 5.

EXAMPLE:

Barney, in his will, leaves all of his property to his wife Fern as a marital deduction. When Barney dies, all of his property goes to Fern, tax free.

In addition to the marital deduction, estates valued up to the lifetime exemption pass free of federal tax, even if there is no will. Does this mean that a person who has an estate of less than that amount does not need estate planning or a will? No. Even though the property may pass tax free, it is still important to see that the property goes to the people chosen by the client to receive the property, with as little legal confusion as possible. To this end, estate planning is always recommended.

How to Make an Effective Estate Plan

Estate and financial planning are merely methods of taking control of one's finances, so that present and anticipated financial needs and desires may be met and that property acquired during life can pass to those persons and institutions the decedent wishes to benefit on his or her death. Although estate planning is typically arranged by a financial planner or an attorney, the legal assistant plays a crucial role in gathering all of the important family and financial data the professionals will need to consider when drawing up a plan. Much of this information is the same information that will be needed in drafting a will.

The primary area of concern is the family situation of the client. As demonstrated by the four families of our situational analysis (below), each person's situation is different. Loretta Jones is young and has a small child to support and educate, whereas Tom Poole is single with no current or presumptive dependents. Loretta must plan for the future of her son in terms of basic needs, but Tom is free to indulge in personal desires. Every paralegal working in the estate field, as a first step, should determine the family situation of each client.

The second category of information that must be gathered is the present financial status of each client. This means ascertaining a person's income and its source (salary, interest, dividends, etc.), and all of his or her current assets. An **asset** is property that has a monetary value that is owned by an individual. Examples of assets are jewelry, savings accounts, cars, homes, and the like. Each asset should be categorized as **real property** (buildings, land, fixtures, and air and ground rights) or **personal property** (all nonreal property, such as jewelry and cash). This financial itemization is not only important for estate planning, it is crucial in the drafting of a person's will and eventually in administering the estate. Also, one cannot decide where one is going until the starting point is known, and this determination of current assets establishes that starting point.

The next step involves planning for the accumulation of money and assets for the future. This is the work of the lawyer or financial planner, but the legal assistant may become involved in the drafting of legal documents associated with the accumulation of these assets, such as drawing up a contract for the purchase of a home or an employment contract for a client who accepts a better paying job. How these assets are accumulated depends on the risk aversion of the client. **Risk aversion** means the degree of risk a person is willing to endure in order to secure a return on his or her investment. For example, a **certificate of deposit** (a long-term interest bearing bank account) is government insured, and so has almost no risk, and consequently a small interest rate; a publicly traded corporate stock may have a greater rate of return, but the company may go bankrupt, leaving the investor with nothing. Therefore, the appropriate investment for each person is dependent upon the degree of risk of losing that investment he or she is willing to take.

The accumulation of assets must have some purpose, namely to meet the client's current and long-term financial needs. For example, Loretta Jones has a short-term need to be able to move to a larger apartment in a better neighborhood, or perhaps buy a house, and a mid-term need to pay for her son's education and medical expenses. In the long-term, she would like to travel and have a comfortable retirement. The Bush family is older and their son is almost grown. Their immediate goal is to see that Byron can complete his education, and they would like to purchase a vacation home. Eventually, they would like to insure a comfortable retirement that includes several trips each year. However, since each family is in a different financial situation and time of life, the appropriate method of accumulating assets to meet these goals will vary.

Finally, as the culmination of this plan, it is necessary to see that, should something happen to the client, the client's survivors could continue to live in the manner the deceased would wish. To this end, it may become necessary to draft various legal documents to insure the continuation of the client's general financial plan, such as a will, a trust, guardianship papers, and so forth.

SITUATIONAL ANALYSIS

How would the foregoing discussion of estate planning affect our four families?

Loretta Jones

Ms. Jones, at the present time, has very little disposable income. As previously stated, disposable income is that income a person has after meeting all current expenses; it is also referred to as **discretionary income**. Loretta is not well paid and is going to school at night. She is responsible for a five-year-old son. In these circumstances, probably the best plan for Loretta would be to purchase term life insurance. With term life insurance the premiums are low, especially because of Loretta's age, but the proceeds of the policy can be large enough to assure that Evan can be taken care of financially should something happen to Loretta. Provided that Loretta does not name her own estate as the beneficiary of the policy and she relinquishes all rights of ownership, the proceeds of the policy will pass directly to Evan and not be considered part of Loretta's taxable estate. This means that the entire proceeds will go to Evan tax free. In this fashion

Loretta can leave Evan several hundred thousand dollars at her death tax free, far more than she could accumulate at the present time with even the most severe of savings plans.

However, Evan is only five years old. A five-year-old is incapable of handling hundreds of thousands of dollars. Therefore, Loretta should create a trust into which the insurance proceeds are placed for Evan's benefit. Someone with more maturity will manage the funds in order to produce an income to support Evan until he is an adult. A full discussion of trusts will appear in Chapter 4.

Finally, because Evan is a minor, he will need someone to be his legal guardian to raise and be legally responsible for him if Loretta dies. Although Evan's father is alive, he lives in another city and has little contact with Evan. Loretta's mother, Aida, currently takes care of Evan, and it would seem likely that Loretta would wish her mother to be Evan's guardian. Therefore, Loretta will need, at the very least, to draw up guardianship papers or perhaps a will that includes a guardianship provision. Because Evan's father may complain that guardianship of his son is being given to someone else, it would be best to try to work out this problem as soon as possible.

Oscar and Hyacinth Bush

The Bushes are older than Loretta and are in better financial shape. Their son is already at university and is no longer a minor. Their financial goals are to buy a vacation/retirement home and to have a comfortable retirement. Also, as a government employee, Oscar has a substantial pension and retirement plan, and the government provides him with a life insurance policy. Under these circumstances, the Bushes can assume some risk in their investments in order to achieve their goals. In their case it must be determined first how Oscar's pension plan works. Are the payments sufficient to support a retirement they would enjoy? Would Hyacinth still receive benefits as Oscar's widow? Once Byron finishes school, the money the Bushes spend on tuition can be used to purchase their vacation home, but how should they hold title? If they are tenants by the entirety, each spouse will automatically acquire the property on the other's death, but when the survivor dies it will be taxable. Might it make sense to put title in Byron's name, or in the name of all three of them as joint tenants, so that the house will eventually pass to Byron with the least amount of negative tax consequences? This question with respect to title will be discussed in the next chapter.

Hyacinth has an elderly father. If anything happens to her, she may want to make sure that some property is used to help support him so that the entire burden does not fall on Fern. Hyacinth may want to establish a living trust now, providing a small income to her father for his life, and then have the money either revert to her or go to her son when her father dies.

Finally, to minimize estate taxes and to provide gifts for Fern, Barney, Fleur, Rose, David, and Davida, the Bushes need to create a will.

Kingston and Donna Lear

The Lears have a quite complicated family situation. Financially, the Lears are very well off, and because they are elderly, their financial desires are primarily concerned with providing for their children and grandchildren. Because of the current problem with Regina and Joseph, not only do the Lears need to settle the title to the house the Hahns are living in, but they also want to make sure that Regina and Joseph do not benefit from the Lears' deaths. However, the Lears do want to provide for their grandchildren and also see that their unmarried daughter has some financial security. This is a multi-dimensional problem that must be addressed from several different angles.

Because the grandchildren are minors, the Lears should establish some trusts for the grandchildren's benefit, keeping the capital out of the grandchildren's hands until they are adults. By proper draftsmanship, the Lears can make sure that the grandchildren are provided for, and that the grandchildren eventually receive the capital.

To provide for Grace, the Lears may want to transfer title to their house to her, or to put it into a joint tenancy. In this manner, when they die, the house will not be part of their probate assets, and consequently out of the reach of Regina. (See the section on will contests in Chapter 7.)

The Lears' main concern is that Regina and her husband will attempt to get as much of their estate as possible. Even if they have a will, and omit Regina, as their child, Regina may be able to challenge the will. Even if she doesn't win, the court costs will diminish the Lears' estate. By transferring as much property as possible while they are alive, when they die there will be little left as probate assets. To achieve this end the Lears will have to take several different steps that will be discussed later in the text.

Tom Poole

Tom is probably in the most enviable financial situation. As a government employee he is guaranteed a decent salary and pension, and because his family is well off he does not have to worry about providing for anyone but himself. Therefore, Tom is in a perfect position to take advantage of some riskier investments in order to accumulate assets. Nonetheless, because Tom wants selected friends to inherit his property, it is necessary for Tom to execute a will that will distribute his assets to those friends and family according to his wishes. If Tom does not have a will his parents will most probably inherit his property, which is not Tom's wishes. In the context of estate planning, Tom is in the most straightforward situation.

Estate Administration

Eventually no matter how careful, good, religious, and charitable a person is, he or she will die. Whereas estate planning is concerned with the acquisition of property when a person is alive, estate administration is concerned with the distribution of that acquired property once the person is dead.

Estate administration is governed by state statutes. Every jurisdiction has its own statute to cover the orderly administration and disposition of a person's estate. For a comparison of the different statutes, see Chapter 9. Each state has created a special court that has jurisdiction over a decedent's assets. These courts have what is referred to as **probate** authority, meaning that they are empowered to probate, or prove, a document to be a person's last will and testament, and to oversee the administration of a decedent's estate. A decedent's assets must be administered under the auspices of this court, regardless of whether the person died with a will. The paralegal's function will be to assist the attorney to see that a person's estate is properly administered according to the state statute and the dictates of the appropriate court.

During the estate planning phase, the client is alive and directly responsible for all of the decisions made with respect to his or her property. Once a client dies, the function of continuing the client's wishes is handled by a person, or persons, known generically as the **personal representative**, who is the person designated by the court to see that the decedent's property is distributed either according to the provisions of the will or according to the provision of state statute if there is no will.

A person who dies with a valid will is considered to have died **testate** (with a will or testament). The person designated in the will to be his or her personal representative is known as the **executor** (masculine) or **executrix** (feminine). If the will fails to name a personal representative, or the person so named cannot, for any reason, fulfill the functions of a personal representative, the court will appoint someone to be the personal representative. This court-appointed personal representative of a testator is known as an **administrator cum testamento annexo** ("with a will attached").

EXAMPLE:

In his will Tom appoints his brother Ken to be his executor. At Tom's death, Ken has moved to Europe and is not available to administer the estate. The court then appoints Tom's father, Simon, to be the administrator CTA to replace Ken, who cannot fulfill the functions of a personal representative.

A person who dies without a valid will is considered to have died **intestate** (without a will). In these circumstances, the court will appoint a personal representative known as the **general administrator** (masculine) or **general administratrix** (feminine). Should the general administrator fail, for any reason, to complete the administration of the estate, the court will appoint a successor administrator known as an **administrator de bonis non**.

EXAMPLE:

David Laplante dies without a will. Hyacinth, as his eldest daughter, asks the court to be his administratrix. Because Hyacinth is David's next of kin, the court appoints her to be the general administratrix.

Whether called an executor or administrator, the person is a personal representative, meaning that he or she is representing the interests of the decedent. The personal representative stands in the place of the decedent for seeing that the decedent's wishes are carried out, either by will or by statute, and as such is considered to be a **fiduciary**. A fiduciary is a person who is in a position of trust, and consequently is held to a *higher standard of care* than that of "ordinary" care. The personal representative has three main functions to fulfill with respect to the administration of an estate:

1. Collect, preserve, and manage the assets in the estate.
2. Settle and pay all claims against the estate
3. Distribute the remaining assets to the heirs of the estate according to the will or the state statute

Generally, personal representatives hire lawyers to help them perform their functions, and the attorney delegates many of these responsibilities to the legal assistant. In this manner many paralegals act as the assistant to the personal representative under the supervision of the attorney.

In order for a person to have the legal authority to act as a decedent's personal representative, he or she must be given the authority by the appropriate court.

All estate administration starts with a petition to the appropriate state court. In this petition a prospective personal representative requests the court to grant him or her the authority to act as the executor or administrator. The petition must be filed in the state in which the deceased was **domiciled**—the decedent's legal home and permanent residence. A person may have many residences but only one domicile. A decedent's domiciliary state has the primary jurisdiction over his estate, and each state determines whether a person is domiciled within its borders. All other states in which the decedent owned property have **ancillary**, or secondary, jurisdiction, limited only to assets located in that state.

EXAMPLE:

Oscar and Hyacinth buy their vacation home in a neighboring state. When they die, that state has ancillary jurisdiction over the vacation home and its contents. The state in which they primarily reside has domiciliary jurisdiction.

There have been problems in determining a person's domicile in situations in which a deceased owned several homes and lived in each one several months each year. It is important during the estate planning stage to determine and substantiate a person's domicile. Such planning will avoid problems later.

The appropriate **venue** for filing the petition is in the court located in the county in which the decedent was domiciled. "Venue" refers to the physical location of the courthouse; even though the court is a state court, it has locations in every county, and the petition must be filed in the correct county.

Accompanying the petition must be a copy of the **death certificate**. Court officials are a cautious group and will not believe a person is dead even if you throw the body on the desk. The only proof they accept is a certified death certificate from the government that constitutes the official statement of death.

If the deceased died testate, the petition must also include the *original* of the will. Copies will not be accepted except in very limited and unusual circumstances. If the decedent died intestate, the petition must affirmatively state that no will exists. The details of the petition and its accompanying documents will be discussed in Chapter 7. Usually, the petition is filed by the person named in the will as the executor or by a close relative who wishes to be appointed the administrator.

When the petition is filed, the court typically sets a hearing date, at which time anyone having an interest in the estate—family members, creditors, persons named in the will—can come in to **contest**, or challenge, the petition. It is the obligation of the petitioner to notify all of these people that a petition has been filed and that a hearing date has been set. If no one challenges the petition, the court will order the petition granted.

When the petition is granted, the petitioner must file an oath of office with the court, promising to fulfill his or her functions faithfully. Bond may be required to be posted to insure the faithful performance of the petitioner's duties. At this point the court will issue a document known as **letters**, which is the court order authorizing the personal representative to administer the decedent's estate. If the decedent died testate, the letters are called **letters testamentary**; if the decedent died intestate, the letters are termed **letters of administration**. These letters are proof that the personal representative is authorized to administer the deceased's assets. Bankers and brokers will not release the decedent's assets without letters.

EXAMPLE:

Hyacinth, as her father's administratrix, goes to his bank to get the money he had in a savings account. Before the bank will turn over the funds, it requires a copy of Hyacinth's letters of administration, proving the court's order of Hyacinth's authority to dispose of her father's assets.

Once the letters are issued, the personal representative starts the process of collecting the assets, paying the debts, and distributing the property of the decedent. When the estate is fully distributed, the personal representative may also be required to file an accounting with the court to prove that the estate has been properly administered. For the particular requirement of each state, see Chapter 9.

Working under the direction of the attorney, the paralegal will complete the petition for the court, see to the sending of notices to interested parties, and collect the letters from the court (see Chapter 6). He or she will locate the assets of the decedent, discover the addresses of all beneficiaries of the estate, and check all claims against the estate. The paralegal is responsible for assisting in the preparation of all of the tax returns incident to the estate (see Chapter 8) and is charged with obtaining releases from everyone who receives property from the estate. If the deceased owned property in several jurisdictions, the paralegal will assist in the establishment of ancillary administrations in all states other than the domiciliary state. Most important, the paralegal will deal directly with the decedent's family and beneficiaries, explain the entire estate administration process to them, and mollify them until they actually receive their gifts (which is only after all taxes and debts have been paid). More than any other area of law, estate work affords the legal assistant direct and constant client contact and court work.

Several states permit a more simplified administrative process, known as a **summary proceeding** or **informal administration**. These simplified proceedings are usually only permitted for very small estates. (A list of the states that permit such proceedings appears in Chapter 9.) These proceedings require less paperwork and are much more streamlined. Typically, a **formal administration** can take a year or more, just in paying debts and taxes.

SITUATIONAL ANALYSIS

Loretta Jones

Even though Loretta has a modest estate, this does not mean that she does not need a will to assure that her wishes are carried out after death. If Loretta dies intestate, Evan, as her only child, would inherit everything. But Evan is only five years old: Who would manage the money for him, who will raise him, and who will get the letter from the court to see that the property is distributed to him? Loretta needs a will, most probably naming her mother as executrix and guardian of Evan.

Oscar and Hyacinth Bush

The Bushes need a will, if for no other reason than to take advantage of the marital deduction. Also, if they do acquire that vacation home, and it is purchased in another state, they will have to decide who will administer that property. They will also have to substantiate which state is their domiciliary state. Finally, because Hyacinth wants to make some provisions for her father and to leave some small gifts to her sisters and nieces, a will would be the most effective method of seeing that her wishes are carried out.

Kingston and Donna Lear

The Lears definitely need a will. They want to make sure that their daughter Regina will not acquire any of their property, they want to leave substantial gifts to their grandchildren, and they want to make sure that Grace gets their home, which is still her legal residence. Cornelia is well settled and financially secure, and so does not need the Lears' assets, except for some sentimental gifts. Without a will, the Lears' property would be divided equally among their three daughters—definitely not their wish.

Tom Poole

As noted above, Tom wants his friends to inherit his property rather than his family. Without a will, his parents get everything. A properly drafted will shall insure that the bulk of his estate will go to his friends, while still leaving some assets to his parents and brother. Also, he may wish to designate a friend as his personal representative, rather than his brother or a parent, who would typically be approved for that function by the court should Tom die intestate.

CHAPTER SUMMARY

The difference between estate planning and estate administration is primarily the difference between asset accumulation and asset distribution. While a person is alive she can make her own decisions with respect to the disposition of her assets, but after her death, someone must fulfill this function for her.

Estate planning requires an analysis of a client's family situation, current assets, and projected financial desires. A financial planner or attorney generally assists in the creation of an appropriate estate plan that will enable a client to accumulate property during life and see that it is distributed after death with the least possible tax burden and in accordance with the decedent's wishes.

Estate administration is concerned with seeing that all of a decedent's assets are properly accounted for, that the decedent's debts are paid, and that the remaining assets are distributed according to the wishes of the deceased. The paralegal is responsible for assisting in every phase of both estate planning and administration.

ESTATE PLAN ↓	Paralegal gathers information about the client's family, present assets, and financial desires. Assists in the preparation of legal documents that help accomplish the client's goals: contracts, trusts, wills, etc.
CLIENT DIES ↓	Paralegal helps prepare petition for the court, discusses the administration process with the family, and assists personal representative.
PETITION FILED ↓	Paralegal files petition and accompanying documents, notifies interested parties, obtains letters, locates assets and debts.
ADMINISTRATION ↓	Paralegal helps value and categorize assets, scrutinizes claims, obtains receipts and releases for all payments, assists in the preparation of all tax returns, and maintains contact with family and beneficiaries.
CLOSING ESTATE ↓	Paralegal assists in preparing a final accounting of the distribution of the estate.

Key Terms

Ancillary administration: Estate administration in a state in which decedent owned property other than his domiciliary state.

Administrator de bonis non (DBN): Personal representative appointed by the court when a previous administrator fails to complete the administration.

Administrator cum testamento annexo (CTA): Personal representative appointed by the court when the will fails to name an executor or the named executor fails to complete the administration.

Beneficiary: Person who inherits property under a will; recipient of insurance proceeds.

Certificate of deposit: Long-term bank savings account.

Discretionary income: Disposable income.

Domicile: Legal home.

Donee: Recipient of a gift.

Donor: Person who gives a gift.

Endowment policy: Short-term life insurance policy in which proceeds are paid to the insured, if alive at the end of the term, or to a beneficiary named in the policy if the insured is deceased.

Estate administration: Process of collecting assets, paying debts, and distributing a person's assets after his death.

Estate planning: Process of helping a person accumulate assets during his life and allocate them on his death.

Executor(trix): Personal representative named in a will.

Financial plan: Strategy to help a person acquire assets.

Formal administration: Estate administration including all notices and a hearing.

General administrator: Personal representative appointed by the court for an intestate.

Incidents of ownership: Retaining rights to property, such as the ability to sell the property, benefit from the property, etc.

Informal administration: Estate administration for small estates, permitted in some states.

Intestate: Person who dies without a valid will.

Joint tenancy: Title to property held by more than one person with a right of survivorship.

Letters of administration: Court order authorizing a personal representative of an intestate to administer the estate.

Letters testamentary: Court order authorizing a personal representative of a testate to administer the estate.

Living trust: Trust created to take effect during a person's life.

Marital deduction: Estate tax advantage for property given to surviving spouse—it passes tax free.

Personal representative: Fiduciary responsible for administering a decedent's estate.

Probate: To prove a will is valid.

Qualified terminable interest property (QTIP): Property given to surviving spouse that qualifies as a marital deduction even though the spouse's interest is not absolute ownership.

Risk aversion: Degree of risk a person is willing to undertake in selecting an investment.

Summary proceedings: Abbreviated administration permitted in some states for small estates.

Tenancy by the entirety: Joint ownership of property for legally married husbands and wives, with a right of survivorship.

Term life insurance: Life insurance in which premiums increase periodically, the insured has no cash surrender value, and the face amount decreases over time.

Testate: Person who dies with a valid will.

Venue: Physical location of the appropriate court.

Whole life insurance: Life insurance in which premiums and face amount remain constant and the insured has property rights in the policy.

Will: Document used to dispose of a person's property after death.

Case Studies

1. Do the continuing installment payments of lottery prize money paid to a decedent constitute probate or non-probate assets?

A man won $2 million in a state Super Jackpot lottery, and the payments were to be made in 20 equal installments of $100,000. The man had failed to pay property taxes on his residence, and the state had sent him a notice to quit. One day there was a fire and explosion at the residence, and the man eventually died as a result of injuries caused by the explosion. The explosion injured several other persons and also caused property damage to other people's property, all of whom came to sue the estate. The man died intestate, survived by his wife and several children who received the installment payments. The family claimed the continuing payments, and the state and other creditors claimed the proceeds. The court held that, according to the lottery's provisions, the payments are to be paid directly to a winner's heirs in case of the winner's demise prior to complete payment, and as such they were non-probate assets outside of the estate and safe from creditors' claims. *Michigan Basic Property Ins. Assn. v. Ware*, 1998 Mich. App. LEXIS 15.

2. Can the heirs under a will mutually agree to disregard the testator's wishes so as to have the property pass as though the deceased died intestate, thereby bypassing estate and tax laws?

In *Anderson v. Commissioner of Internal Revenue*, 56 T.C.M. 78 (1988), the decedent, while in the hospital prior to death, indicated a wish to revise his will, but lapsed into a coma before the new will could be drawn up. All of the relatives who inherited under the will agreed to refrain from probating the will so that the property would be distributed according to the law of intestate succession, which would be in accord with the deceased's expressed wishes. The state law permits heirs to agree that a valid will should not be probated, but the Internal Revenue Service is not bound by such laws and found that, for estate tax purposes, the property would be considered as if it had passed under the provisions of the valid will that the hairs failed to probate. The decedent could not avoid either death or taxes!

3. Guardianship, like conservatorship, may have a direct effect on a person's estate planning. Once a person has been deemed incapable of managing his or her affairs, and a guardian or conservator has been appointed by a court of competent jurisdiction, questions may arise with respect to the guardian's ability to effect a change in the incapacitated person's estate plan. Also, just because a person is deemed incapacitated does not mean that he or she is incapable of executing a valid will. For a full discussion of the effect of guardianship on a person's estate planning options, see *Estate of Mann*, 184 Cal. App. 3d 593 (1986).

4. A wealthy man died owning two homes in two neighboring states. As he aged, he spent more and more time in what was originally his vacation home, until by the date of his death he spent approximately six months each year in each home. In attempting to establish domiciliary and ancillary jurisdiction for the estate, each of the states claimed domicile. After lengthy court battles, the end result was that each state determined that he was domiciled in its jurisdiction, and the estate was doubly taxed. *In re Dorrance Estate*, 170 A. 601 (N.J. Prerog. Ct. 1934), and *In re Dorrance Estate*, 163 A. 303 (Pa. 1932).

How would you go about documenting a person's domicile to distinguish it from his other residences and thus avoid a situation like the Dorrance estate?

EXERCISES

1. Check your own state statute to see whether your state permits informal or summary proceedings. What, if any, limitations does the state impose on these proceedings? What is your opinion of these streamlined proceedings?
2. Create a questionnaire you would use to gather information necessary to devise an appropriate estate plan for a client.
3. Obtain copies of a term life insurance policy and a whole life insurance policy and compare the two for appropriateness for a particular client situation.
4. Discuss, in your own words, the functions a paralegal performs with respect to estate planning and estate administration.
5. Discuss several alternatives to wills that can be used to distribute a person's assets. For each alternative, indicate the type of estate for which it would be beneficial or detrimental, and explain why.

ANALYTICAL PROBLEM

A gay couple wishes to create an estate plan that will protect the survivor from claims of the deceased partner's family. What options are available to see their wishes are carried out?

2 Sources of Property

CHAPTER OVERVIEW

Before an effective will or estate plan can be created, it is necessary to determine exactly what property the client currently owns.

All property is divided into two broad categories: real and personal. **Real property** consists of land and anything permanently affixed to the land such as a home, garage, office building, and so forth, including air and ground rights. **Personal property** is all non-real property. Typical examples of personal property are cars, jewelry, books, furniture, stocks, and cash. Also included as personal property are rights that a person might acquire, such as the right of exclusive ownership of an artistic work he created (see below).

One of the primary functions performed by a paralegal with respect to creating an estate plan, drafting a will, or administering an estate, is to ascertain exactly what property the client possesses and to describe that property in clear, legally sufficient words so that it can be properly identified and distinguished from similar property the client may own or possess. In order to accomplish this task, the paralegal should develop a **tickler**, or checklist, of all of the different categories of property. This tickler can be used as a questionnaire for the client so that all of his assets can be determined. Additionally, it is a good idea to have the client document his proof of ownership — this will enable the paralegal to help determine the property's value and to discover whether in fact the client actually does have a right to the property. It is amazing that many people do not actually know how they acquired their assets, or do not realize that property they have always considered as theirs actually belongs to someone else. A person can only dispose of property in which he or she has a disposable interest or ownership.

Once the property has been discovered and described, it can then be used as the basis of developing an estate plan and a will. Spending time at the beginning to gather all of the necessary information will save countless hours later on, especially during the administration of the estate, because all of the documentation necessary for the orderly distribution of the client's assets will already be on hand.

This chapter will discuss the various types of property that a person may own, and how that property should be described in order to distinguish it from similar property.

Types of Property

As stated above, all property is divided into the two broad categories of real and personal property. Regardless of the type, all property is acquired by purchase, gift (either during life or as the result of someone's death), happenstance, or employment. The method of acquisition determines the right or title the client has to the property, and it is imperative to determine the client's title in order to determine what he or she may do with the property. Simply because a person has control over a piece of property does not mean that he or she has the right to dispose of it.

EXAMPLE:

Fern borrows Hyacinth's pearl necklace to wear for a special occasion. Fern may possess the jewelry, but she does not have the right to give the necklace away. The pearls belong to Hyacinth, and Fern merely has the loan of the jewelry that she must return to her sister. This type of arrangement is known as a **bailment**, in which one person has the right to possess another person's property.

If the property was acquired by purchase, there usually will be some written documentation of the sale. A writing is usually required for the sale of goods valued at over $500 and when dealing with an interest in real estate. Real property can only be **conveyed**, or transferred, by deed or will; a writing is mandatory to pass title to realty. This documentation can be used not only to determine ownership, but also to determine value for the purpose of taxation. See Chapter 8.

Gifts are not always documented by a writing, but for expensive items it is always a good idea to have the client indicate from whom it was received. This will help describe the property later on.

EXAMPLE:

On his birthday Tom Poole received a gold rope chain from his parents. Two years earlier he had bought a gold rope chain for himself when he was on vacation. The chains are of different lengths and weights, but they are both gold rope chains. If Tom wants to leave one of the chains to his brother, by describing the chain as the one he received from his parents it can be distinguished from the other chain which he might want to leave to someone else.

If the property in question is real estate, the transfer, even if by gift, will be recorded. All real estate transactions that transfer title to the property must be recorded in the county recorder's office of the county in which the property is located. If the transfer was a gift while the donor was alive, a deed of transfer will appear in the county record book; if the gift came about by will, the will itself will be recorded, as well as a deed from the estate. The county record book not only indicates how the property was acquired, but also the specific type of title the owner has (see below).

When a person receives property as a condition of employment, such as stock options or contributions to a pension plan, the transfer is usually documented by the employer in pay slips, employment contracts, or employment handbooks. Many times clients don't even realize that they have acquired property because of their employment, and it is necessary to obtain a copy of the client's pay records to discover whether the client has rights to property of which the client is unaware.

Finally, and much less frequently, a person simply has property whose origins are totally hidden. The client may have found a watch in the street, for example, or may simply have acquired property over the years without being able to remember how he or she came to possess the items. These pieces of property simply must be appropriately described and, if valuable, be appraised.

The total sum of all of the above-acquired property constitutes a person's assets. **Assets** are property or rights that are owned and disposable by the client. Once all of the assets have been accounted for, the client can then indicate what he or she wishes done with the property.

Real Property

Title to all real property is generally referred to as an **estate**, and falls into two major categories: A **freehold estate** is any realty that a person owns absolutely for an uncertain duration; a **leasehold** is any realty that a person holds for a specified period of time, usually documented by a rental agreement or a lease.

EXAMPLES:

1. Donna and Kingston purchased their home many years ago. They bought their home outright, and therefore have a freehold (i.e., it is theirs for their lives, and life is of uncertain duration). They have the right to dispose of it upon death or during their lifetimes.
2. Loretta rents an apartment in the city. She has a two-year lease on the apartment. At the end of the two years she no longer has any right to the apartment under her current title. This is a leasehold estate because it ends at a specified time, and Loretta's rights are established by contract with the owner.

Before discussing all of the different rights and methods of ownership a person may have in real estate, it is necessary to offer some brief definitions of the most common terms associated with transferring rights to realty. A **conveyance** is any transfer of title to real property from one person to another. A **deed** is a document signed by the parties that transfers title to real estate. A **tenancy** is the right to hold real estate. **Title** is the right of ownership or possession in property.

The highest form of ownership that a person can have in real estate is known as a **fee simple**. This is the largest estate possible and represents an absolute and undivided interest in the real property. A person who holds property in fee simple has the right to transfer the property during life or at death, and creditors of the owner can attach the property to satisfy claims because it is owned absolutely by the fee holder. It is also called a **tenancy in severalty** if only one person holds title to the property.

Concurrent Ownership

Tenancy in severalty represents sole ownership in fee in the property. However, there are many situations in which more than one person holds title to the property. This multiple ownership of property is known as **concurrent ownership** and there are five types of concurrent ownership possible in the United States.

Tenancy in Common

A **tenancy in common**, one of the oldest forms of multiple ownership of property, dates back to feudal times. In a tenancy in common, two or more persons own separate but undivided interests in property. Each tenant in common has the right to sell, give, or will his or her portion of the title away, and the person who subsequently acquires this portion of the title becomes a tenant in common with the other tenants. There is no right of survivorship in the remaining tenants. The only requirement to create a tenancy in common is that each tenant has an equal right of possession. It does not have to be an equal title—one co-tenant could have a greater interest than the other.

EXAMPLES:

1. Hyacinth and Fern inherited the house Fern lives in from a favorite aunt as tenants in common. Because Hyacinth didn't need the property, Hyacinth gave her right to the house to Fleur. Hyacinth and Fern were tenants in common, acquiring the title by will. When Hyacinth gave her interest to Fleur, Fleur became the tenant in common with Fern.
2. In the above example assume the aunt left the house equally to all three nieces. When Hyacinth conveyed her interest to Fleur, Fern and Fleur were still tenants in common, but Fleur had rights to two thirds of the property (her own third plus Hyacinth's), Fern having the right to just one third.

Joint Tenancy

A **joint tenancy** is also an old form of multiple ownership of property, but it is much more complex than a tenancy in common. In order to create a joint tenancy, all of the joint tenants must acquire their title with what are known as the Four Unities: title, time, interest, and possession. What this means is that the joint tenants must have received their rights to the property by the same conveyance, at the same time, and have been given equal rights with respect to title and possession by the conveyancing instrument.

EXAMPLE:

In her will, Hyacinth's aunt specifies that her nieces will inherit the property as joint tenants. In this instance, Hyacinth, Fern, and Fleur are joint tenants, because they have all acquired the property at the same time (the aunt's death) by the same conveyance (the will), were given the same title (joint tenants), and were given equal right to possession and title (specified joint tenants).

Joint tenants have equal rights to the use, enjoyment, and control of the property, but none is considered to be the outright owner of any particular part of the whole; they own the property collectively. The joint tenants are considered an ownership unit, unlike tenants in common who are considered individually. If a joint tenant's interest in the property is conveyed to an outsider, the result is a division of title to the property into a tenancy in common in which one tenant in common is an individual and the other tenant in common is a joint tenancy. In this way the title to the property is **partitioned** into two forms of ownership.

EXAMPLE:

Hyacinth, Fern, and Fleur own their aunt's house as joint tenants. Hyacinth decides to give her share of the house to her son Byron. After the conveyance, the resulting title is a tenancy in common with Byron as one tenant in common, and Fern and Fleur collectively as the second tenant in common. However, Fern and Fleur still hold their title to the tenancy in common as joint tenants.

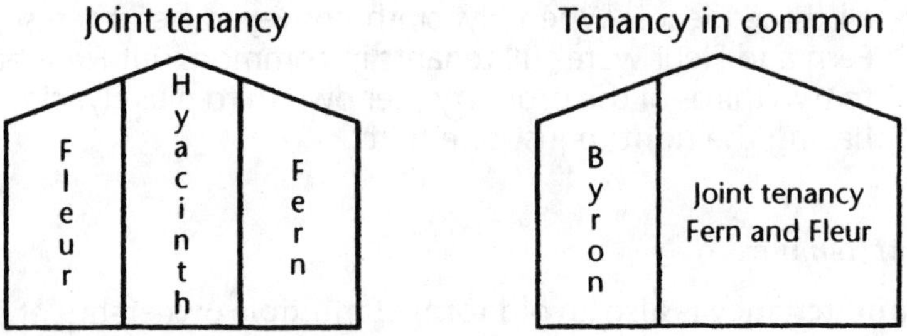

This may appear confusing, but it has important ramifications with respect to what rights the tenant has in the property. A joint tenancy automatically creates a **right of survivorship** in the remaining joint tenants. This means that a joint tenant's portion of the property will automatically devolve on the surviving joint tenants at his or her death. A joint tenant's interest cannot be disposed of by will; if the interest isn't transferred during the joint tenant's life he or she has no control over its disposition on death. Eventually, if no lifetime transfer is made of the property, the longest living joint tenant winds up owning the entire property as a tenancy in severalty.

Consequently, a client who holds title as a joint tenant cannot dispose of his interest in the property by a will; it will automatically pass to the surviving joint tenants. Because of this limitation on transferability, unless specified, when property is conveyed to more than one person the law generally assumes it to be a tenancy in common. Joint tenants who wish to change title to the property without transferring their interests permanently to a third person will typically use a convention known as a **straw man**. In this situation, the joint tenants unite to convey the title to an outsider, who then immediately conveys the property back to the joint tenants, but this time the conveyance specifies that title is to be held as tenants in common. In this manner each co-owner can alienate his or her interest without confusing the title. (A straw man may also be used to change a tenancy in common to a joint tenancy.)

EXAMPLES:

1. When Hyacinth and her sisters inherit the property as joint tenants, they convey the property to their father who in turn conveys it back to them as tenants in common. In this fashion the property is owned by three separate persons, each of whom can convey her interest as a tenant in common. When Hyacinth gives her share to Byron, now Byron, Fern, and Fleur are each tenants in common for one third of the whole. In this instance, if Fern should die her interest would not automatically pass to Fleur, which would have happened in the previous example.
2. The three sisters do nothing with the title to the property, but remain as joint tenants. In Fern's will she leaves her interest to her granddaughter Davida. When Fern dies the title passes equally to Hyacinth and Fleur; Davida gets nothing. As a joint tenant Fern was incapable of passing her interest by her will.

Tenancy by the Entirety

A tenancy by the entirety is a form of joint tenancy created *only for legally married husbands and wives.* Under tenancy by the entireties, when one spouse dies, the property automatically passes to the surviving spouse. Also, neither spouse may alienate his or her interest during life without the other's consent. Additionally, the law considers that each spouse contributed equally to the acquisition of the property, so that only one-half of the value of the property is considered to be part of the deceased spouse's taxable estate. (See Chapter 8.) Unless specified otherwise, when husbands and wives acquire property it is usually considered that they hold title as tenants by the entirety, but it is always a good idea to specify the title in the conveyance as well. Note that not all jurisdictions permit tenancies by the entirety, and in those states married couples will hold title as joint tenants.

EXAMPLE:

Loretta manages to save enough money to put a down payment on a small house. On the deed she puts down Jason Leroy and herself as tenants by the entirety. They are not. Because Loretta and Jason are not married, they cannot be tenants by the entirety, and on her death all of the property is considered part of her taxable estate. Additionally, in this instance, there is confusion as to how the title actually is held, and this should be cleared up during the phase of estate planning so that Loretta can be sure that her son inherits all of her property.

Unfortunately, many people have no idea exactly how they hold title to property if there is more than one tenant. Many times siblings inherit property, or friends purchase property together, and unless they are legally sophisticated, they just assume that they own the property "together," without understanding the legal ramifications of the different types of title. Whenever a client indicates an interest in real estate, it is always the best policy to get a copy of the conveyance from the county recorder's office. Never rely on the client's understanding of title. In this fashion, the paralegal can discover exactly the type of title the client has, and if any changes are necessary, as with Loretta above, the attorney can arrange the change prior to making any disposition of the property for the client.

Community Property

Nine jurisdictions in the United States have **community property** for all property acquired by a married couple during the marriage. This title will automatically be applied by law unless the couple specifies a different type of title. This ownership is automatic by law in these states, but may be changed by specific agreement of the couple themselves. With community property, one-half of the property acquired during the marriage is considered to be owned by each spouse, and only that half may be conveyed; the other half is the property of the other spouse. On death, one-half is the property of the survivor, the other half can be conveyed by the deceased spouse's will. The jurisdictions that have community property are indicated in Chapter 9.

Tenancy in Partnership

A **tenancy in partnership** is a special category of multiple ownership of property that was created for business situations. As the name would indicate, this form of ownership is available for businesses that operate as a general or limited partnership, and it has some attributes of both a tenancy in common and a joint tenancy. For estate purposes, its import lies in the fact that any property held in tenancy in partnership automatically passes to the surviving partners, but the heirs of the deceased partner are entitled to the value of the deceased partner's interest in the property. In other words, the factory would pass to the surviving partners, but the deceased partner's widow would be entitled to the cash value of her husband's share.

EXAMPLE:

Tom's father is a partner in a small accounting firm. The partnership owns the building in which it operates, valued at $300,000, and Simon has two partners. When Simon dies, the surviving partners get his interest in the building, but must pay Lottie $100,000, the value of Simon's share in the property.

If the client is involved with property held in tenancy in partnership, it is a good idea to make sure that the partnership maintains life insurance on the partners so that the heirs of a deceased partner can be paid off without having to sell the partnership assets.

Title to property should always be specified in the conveyance. Make sure that title is clear and accurate before attempting to make any disposition of the property.

Life Estates

Up to now we have discussed situations in which the person with title may have rights to pass title to the property upon death. However, there is another category of freehold estate in which the holder's rights terminate automatically on death, and the holder has absolutely no right to transfer his interest by will.

A **life estate** is an interest in property that a person has only for his or her life. If the life estate is tied to the life of another, it is a **life estate pur autre vie**. All rights and title terminate on the death of the life in question, and the conveyance that created the title may also indicate to whom title eventually passes.

EXAMPLE:

In his will, David Laplante leaves a small summer cottage he owns to Hyacinth for life, because she always wanted a summer home, then to his granddaughter Davida. Hyacinth has a life estate, meaning that her interest in the property lasts only for her life, and on her death the title to the house automatically passes to Davida.

The person who acquires title after the death of the life tenant is known as the **remainderman**. The remainderman may hold title in any manner specified by the original conveyance.

EXAMPLE:

David leaves the summer house to Hyacinth for life, then to Davida for life, then outright to Davida's children. In this case both Hyacinth and Davida have life estates, and Davida's presumptive children eventually will acquire the property as tenants in common, assuming Davida has more than one child. A tenancy in common is presumed because no specific title was mentioned in the will (remember, the law presumes a tenancy in common if there is a multiple ownership). If Davida has only one child, that child will inherit a tenancy in severalty.

Although she has a life estate, Davida's enjoyment of her interest is delayed until Hyacinth's death; Davida is a *successor life tenant.*

The life tenant's interest exists like a full ownership, except that a life tenant cannot use the property in a manner that would diminish its value to the remainderman. For instance, if the property had oil on it, the life tenant could extract the oil for normal use and exploitation, but could not leave the remainderman with just the wasted land.

Although the life tenant cannot dispose of the property upon death—it automatically goes to the remainderman—transfer of title while he or she is alive is permitted. The person who acquires the interest of a life tenant is considered to be a **life tenant pur autre vie** (a life tenant for someone else's life). A life estate pur autre vie may also be created by the grantor in the original conveyance, for example, to Hyacinth for the life of Fleur.

EXAMPLES:

1. Hyacinth transfers her interest in the summer cottage to Byron. Byron is a life tenant pur autre vie; his rights terminate not on his death or a specified time, but on the death of Hyacinth, the "life" in the life estate.
2. Byron is killed in a car accident. In his will he leaves his interest in the summer cottage to his Aunt Fleur. Fleur is now the successor tenant in a life estate for the life of Hyacinth. Fleur's interest terminates on Hyacinth's death.

A life tenant pur autre vie, unlike the life tenant himself, may have rights that can be transferred on death. Because the life tenant pur autre vie's interest exists as long as someone else is alive, it is possible that the life tenant pur autre vie will predecease the measuring life, in which case there is still an interest that can be passed.

When dealing with a life estate pur autre vie, always examine the conveyance to determine what rights may be passed on the death of the life tenant pur autre vie.

Life estates may be changed if all of the life tenants and remaindermen join to create a new type of ownership. For example, if Hyacinth wanted Davida to own the house outright, she could simply transfer her interest to Davida, who would then have a tenancy in severalty by the joining of the life estate with the remainder interest. Or, they could both join to convey the property outright to a third person who would thereby acquire full ownership. Once again, the paralegal must examine all of the documentation incident to the title to provide the attorney with information so the attorney can offer advice as to what can be done with the property and determine what the client's wishes are with respect to the disposition of the property.

Leaseholds

Real property that is not held in a freehold estate is usually held as a leasehold. A **lease** is a contract in which the person with a transferable interest in real estate will permit another to use that property, for specified purposes, for a period of time in consideration of a fee paid to the owner. The person with the transferable interest is the **landlord** or the **lessor**; the person who contracts for the use of the property is the **tenant** or the **lessee**, and the fee is typically referred to as **rent**.

If the client is the tenant of a lease of real property, he or she may have the right to transfer the lease to third persons. This is all dependent upon the terms of the lease itself, and the contract must be analyzed to determine whether the tenant can pass his or her interest. Usually the successor tenant will be responsible for the payment of the rent. If the lease is a commercial one, the lease itself may exist for ten or more years, meaning that the client-tenant may have a valuable asset that can be passed on at death.

EXAMPLE:

Tom's brother Ken owns a small manufacturing company. He has a ten-year lease on the commercial premises at a modest rent, and the lease can be transferred by Ken. When Ken dies, eight years remain on the lease, and current rentals are three times the rent Ken was paying. This is a valuable interest in real estate that Ken can leave in his will — the right to use the property for another eight years.

On the other hand, the client may be the landlord of a leasehold. In this case the landlord will have two separate interests that can be left in a will. First, as the owner of the property, subject to any of the limitations discussed above, the landlord can will the title to the property itself. Second, as the landlord, he or she may will the right to receive the rental income to someone different than the person to whom the property is left. This must be fully discussed with the client before drafting a will.

Other Interests in Real Property

There are four other interests that must be discussed in relation to title to real estate.

Mortgage

A **mortgage** is a security interest taken by a **mortgagee** from the person who is purchasing the real estate, known as the **mortgagor**. The interest is guaranteed by the real estate itself; if the mortgagor fails to repay the loan the mortgagee can **foreclose** on the property, thereby acquiring title to the realty. When the mortgagor dies, the property is still subject to the interest. Consequently, whenever a client wills real estate, the paralegal must discover whether there is a mortgage on the property, and if so, whether the client wants his or her heir to take the property subject to the mortgage. This would mean that the heir not only gets the property, he also gets to pay off the mortgage as well. Or the client can indicate that the property will pass free and clear, stating that his estate will pay off the outstanding mortgage on the property. It is always a good idea to have a client invest in mortgage insurance that will pay off the mortgage on his death so that the mortgage does not become a responsibility of his heirs.

If the client is the mortgagee, another situation arises. Nowadays, with an increase in owner financing of homes, a client may have sold his previous house and have become the mortgagee himself in order to consummate the sale, reduce his taxes, and produce an income. When he dies, he can leave the right to receive the mortgage payments, and the incidental right to foreclose, to an heir. Therefore, even though a client no longer owns real estate, he may still have a valuable interest in real estate that the paralegal must discover and discuss.

Easements

An **easement** is a right of passage over or use of someone else's property. Easements can come about merely by usage over a period of time, or by actual agreement between the property owner and the easement holder. Whenever real estate is conveyed it is conveyed subject to any easements that attach to it, which might limit the use to which the property can be put. Many easements appear on the title to property in the county recorder's office; others exist only by the common law. The paralegal must discover whether any easements exist with respect to a given piece of property, and then determine what, if anything, the client wants to do about the situation.

EXAMPLE:

The summer cottage Hyacinth and her sisters inherited from their father is adjacent to a main road. Behind the house there is another cottage whose only access to the road is over a small strip of land on the sisters' property. This right of passage was recorded in the county office when the developer built the houses. The sisters own the property subject to the easement; they cannot construct a wall that would prevent the neighbor's access to the road. The easement holder has rights over the sisters' property.

Liens

Real estate may also be subject to various liens. A **lien** is a right to property acquired by a creditor of the property owner. Typical liens are those held by the government for nonpayment of taxes and those held by workers who helped construct the property but were not paid for their work. Mortgages and judgments against the property are also liens. The paralegal must determine whether there are any liens on the real estate that will create problems of title and ownership, and see that the liens are cleared. If liens are not cleared, creditors could attach and sell the property in order to satisfy the debt.

EXAMPLE:

Hyacinth and her sisters are stunned to find out that their father hadn't paid his real estate taxes on the summer cottage for over five years. The county has put a lien on the house, and the sisters must come up with the back taxes or the county will sell the house at public auction to satisfy its claims.

Elective Share

Finally, if the property owner is survived by a spouse, the spouse is given certain rights to the property. Historically, a widow was automatically entitled to a life estate in one third of the real property her husband owned during the marriage. This right was known as a **dower** (hence the terms "dowager" and "dower house"). A widower's right was known as **curtesy** and included a life estate in all of the wife's property if they had a child born alive. Today, surviving spouses of whatever gender are entitled to a portion of the deceased spouse's estate known as a **statutory share** or **elective share** or **forced share**. This right cannot be defeated unless it is specifically waived by the survivor—even if the deceased spouse attempts to pass the property away from the surviving spouse by will. Therefore, before any property can pass to other persons, including children and grandchildren, the surviving spouse must be given his or her portion of the estate. Additionally, for tax and administrative purposes, a surviving spouse in some states is entitled to a **homestead exemption** for real estate that was the couple's primary residence. These factors must be taken into consideration when drafting a client's will.

One last word concerning real property. Many people purchase their residences or offices as **condominiums (condos)** or **co-operatives (co-ops)**. Generally, condominium ownership is similar to a tenancy in common, whereas co-ops are, in fact, not considered real property but personal property. The rationale for having co-ops considered personalty is the fact that the purchaser only acquires **shares** in a corporation, and the share entitles the holder to the use of a particular unit or portion of the real estate. Furthermore, the owner of shares in a co-op cannot freely transfer his or her interest: The underlying agreement among the shareholders restricts transferability, and consequently the agreement itself must be analyzed to determine whether the shares may be transferred, and to whom. Many states now have statutes specifically regulating condominiums and cooperatives, and the specific state statute in question must be checked.

EXAMPLE:

Tom has the opportunity to buy his apartment as a co-op. Although it may make good financial sense in his situation (why rent if he can afford to buy?), the co-op agreement states that the co-op board of shareholders has the right to approve any transferee of Tom's shares, and he may only freely transfer his interest without board approval to his spouse or children, not friends, as Tom desires. In this instance, such a purchase may not meet Tom's financial and estate needs.

Take note that anything that is permanently affixed to a building may be considered real property, not personalty. These items are called **fixtures**. Examples of fixtures include chandeliers, carpeting, and bathroom sinks.

Be aware that even though these various titles to property are generally discussed as part of real property, personal property is subject to the same titles.

The best advice that can be given when dealing with a client's real estate, of whatever degree or description, is to check all documentation associated with the property. Do not trust the client's recollection or beliefs; it is safest to have proof of right and title, and then any problems incident thereto can be corrected. Forewarned is forearmed!

Personal Property

Generally, all nonreal property is considered to be personal property. Personal property is divided into tangible and intangible property. **Tangible** property is anything that can be touched and/or moved, and its value is intrinsic to the item itself. **Intangible** property is that personal property that itself may have little monetary value, but it is representative of something of value. Intangible personal property is sometimes referred to as a **chose in action**.

EXAMPLES:

1. Loretta inherited a 14K gold cross from her grandmother. The cross is tangible personal property because it has a specific value itself.
2. Grace, the Lears' daughter, maintains a savings account in a local bank. The amount in her account is printed on a savings account passbook. The passbook is an intangible; it represents Grace's right to her funds in the bank.

If the object itself has little value but represents a right to something of value, it is an intangible.

General Tangibles

A primary duty of a paralegal after determining the client's real property interests is to discover the client's personal assets. Most people are only superficially aware of their property. Because they see and use the property everyday they tend to overlook it. The legal assistant should have the client make an itemized list of all of his tangible property. The list should contain a detailed description of each item, an indication of its value, and, if possible, should be photographed. Obviously, items of little monetary value can simply be grouped as "household goods" or "used clothes"; items that are more valuable to the client, either monetarily or sentimentally, must be delineated. Some general categories that the legal assistant might wish to consider would be arts, antiques, jewelry, furs, cars, electronic equipment, and collectibles. The items should be identified in such a way that there will be no confusion in determining which item was meant in case the client has several of a specific type of property.

EXAMPLE:

Donna Lear wants to leave some of her oriental rugs to her daughters Grace and Cornelia. In her will she leaves Grace her embassy size blue Kashan that she herself inherited from her great-aunt, and Cornelia is given two Kashan rugs, one 5×7 feet and the other 10×12. Both were purchased by Donna on trips to Europe. If the items weren't specifically described, it would be impossible to determine which rug goes to which daughter.

Once the general tangibles have been categorized, the paralegal must see to it that the property is properly insured. One of the responsibilities incident to both estate planning and estate administration is to preserve the client's assets. Insurance is not only the best way to protect the property from loss, but the value on the insurance policy may be used for the purpose of estate taxation. (See Chapter 8.)

Intangibles

Intangible property can be further subdivided into general intangibles, intellectual property, claims and benefits, and business property. Each of these categories will be discussed in turn.

General Intangibles

General intangibles include such items as certificates of deposit, stocks, and bonds. Savings and time accounts are typical of the intangible property many people have, but it is necessary to have a list of all of these accounts, including the number of the account and the name of the bank. Many people keep these items secret, even from their closest family members, and when they die their funds may be lost to their heirs because no one knew the accounts existed. It is a good practice to have clients keep all of their financial records in fire-proof boxes in their homes or offices. On the clients' deaths their heirs will then have access to all documents necessary to gather the decedent's assets.

EXAMPLE:

Loretta is putting a small amount of money away each week in a savings account. She doesn't want Jason to know about the account, and so she keeps the account a secret. When she dies, her mother and son may not be able to get the money, which would have been Loretta's wish, because even they did not know the account existed.

Corporate **stock** or **shares** are documents that represent the owner's, or holder's, percentage interest in the company that issued the stock. Either these shares are traded in the open market (the New York Stock Exchange, the American Stock Exchange, NASDAQ, the Chicago Board of Trade, etc.) or are **closely held** meaning that the shares are only owned by a few people. In either event, these shares are known as **securities** and have a value represented by the value of the company that issued the shares. Shares that are publicly traded on the open market have values that fluctuate each day; the value, or selling price, is reported in the newspaper. Closely held stock, on the other hand, is not publicly traded, so its value must be determined each time the shareholder wishes to transfer these shares. Additionally, most closely held companies restrict the transferability of their shares, meaning that the shareholder may not have the right to sell, give, or leave by will the share to whomever he or she wants.

EXAMPLES:

1. Many years ago Kingston purchased Xerox stock in the open market. If he wishes to leave the shares to his wife on his death, the value of the shares can be determined by looking at its selling price in the local newspaper. Because the stock is publicly traded, Kingston can leave the shares to whomever he wishes.
2. Kingston is also a shareholder in a medical corporation. Kingston is a doctor, as are all of the other shareholders. The corporation is known as a Professional Corporation, meaning that all of the shareholders must be licensed to perform the professional services for which the company was organized (in this instance, medicine). When Kingston dies, he cannot leave his shares to Donna because she is not a doctor. Under a written agreement the shares will revert to the corporation, which will have to pay Kingston's estate the estimated value of the percentage of the company represented by Kingston's shares. (See Chapter 8.)

Bonds are issued either by companies or the government, and are evidences of indebtedness. In other words, the bond holder lends money to the issuer for a set number of years, and during the period of the loan the bondholder receives interest on the loan. At the end of the period, the bondholder gets the loan money back. Bonds are generally publicly traded like stock; however, with bonds the client has the possibility of leaving the interest payments to one person, but willing the amount of the loan (the **face value**) to someone else who will receive the money at the termination of the loan period (**maturity date**). Bonds are **secured investments**, meaning that the debtor corporation or government has set aside some property that the bondholder can attach in the case of default. If a corporation issues a bond that does not have some secured property attached to it, it is called a **debenture**.

EXAMPLES:

1. Kingston, as part of his investment strategy, purchased some government bonds ten years ago. The bonds were 30-year bonds, meaning that there are still 20 years left before Kingston gets his loan back. During all 30 years Kingston is receiving interest on his loan. In his will he can leave the interest payments to one person, but the face value of the bond to someone else who will have to wait until the maturity date to get the money.
2. Tom has purchased a corporate debenture because the interest rate was very good. Just like Kingston in the example above, Tom can split the debenture into its interest and principal component parts in his will. However, because the debenture is not secured, if the company goes bankrupt, Tom may lose most or all of his investment, or his heir would receive nothing. Because of the risk, the interest rate he receives is higher than it would be if the security had been a bond.

Bonds and debentures are deemed to be debt securities in the same way stock is considered to be equity securities.

Promissory notes are loans evidenced by a document indicating interest payments and a pay back date. They are similar to bonds and debentures except that they are issued for a shorter period of time. With respect to estates, the client could either have been the lender or the borrower. If she was the lender, she has an asset that can be left in a manner similar to that of bonds discussed above. If, on the other hand, she was the borrower, her estate has a debt that must be repaid.

EXAMPLES:

1. Oscar lent his brother-in-law Barney $10,000 to start a business, evidenced by a promissory note. The interest payment is five percent for five years. This is an asset Oscar can leave in his will.
2. In order to make a down payment on his co-op apartment, Tom borrowed $10,000 from his parents, evidenced by a promissory note indicating a five-year loan at an annual interest rate of five percent. This is a debt of Tom's that his estate must pay at his death.

As discussed above, a mortgage is a security interest taken on the purchase of real estate, secured by the realty itself. If the client has given a mortgage on his property, it is a debt of the estate; if the client has financed the sale of his own property by taking a mortgage from the buyer, this is an asset of the client's that he can leave in his will.

Intellectual Property

Intellectual property is any property that was created by a person to which he has exclusive use. Intellectual property falls into three categories: copyrights, patents, and marks.

Copyrights are governmental grants to the author of a writing or the creator of a work of art. A person who creates a book, a poem, a sculpture, and so forth, automatically has a common law right to the exclusive use of the work. However, in order to document and protect this right, the work can be statutorily copyrighted with the federal government in Washington, D.C. Once copyrighted, the author or creator has an exclusive right to use the copyrighted property for his or her life plus 70 years. This means that the owner of a copyright can leave that right in his or her will. Depending upon the length of life of the recipient of the right, it can be further passed on for 70 years after the death of the creator. At that point it is in the public domain.

EXAMPLE:

Grace is writing a book about her experiences as an American woman working abroad for the U.S. government. When completed, Grace will copyright the work. When Grace dies, she can leave her copyright to whomever she wishes.

The monetary value of a copyright comes from the owner's licensing of that right. A **license** permits the licensee to use the copyrighted work, paying the owner of the right a fee for the use. As a typical example, a book is copyrighted by the author, and the publisher is licensed to print and sell that book, paying the author a fee known as a **royalty** for the use.

If the client has licensed a copyright, once again there are two assets that can be passed on — the copyright itself and the licensing fee.

A **patent** is a governmental grant of exclusive use of an invention given to the inventor. The patent must be registered with the U.S. Patent Office in Washington, D.C., and the exclusive right is only good for a period of 20 years, at which point it passes into the public domain. Not unlike a copyright, a patent can be licensed to produce an income to the patent holder, and in this instance the patent holder also has two assets that can be passed on — the patent and the licensing fee.

A **mark** is the exclusive right to use a name, symbol, or group of words that signify a particular product or service, distinguishing it from similar products and services. If the item is a product, the mark is called a **trademark**; if the item is a service, the mark is called a **service mark**. An example of a trademark is "Pepsi-Cola." An example of a service mark is "CBS." Marks are typically associated with business and business property.

Marks are registered with the federal government, and the government grants the owner the exclusive right to use the mark for ten years. The mark may be renewed for unlimited ten-year periods, but if not renewed, the owner loses his rights. Additionally, if the owner permits someone to use the mark without his authorization, the donor will also lose the exclusive right to the mark.

EXAMPLE:

Loretta's mother, Aida, operates a small business out of her apartment, making a special spaghetti sauce. Aida has trademarked her sauce's name "Aida's Own." The mark (as well as the recipe) can be left to Loretta in Aida's will, or she could sell her rights to a competitor who wants to buy her out.

Not only must the paralegal discover whether the client has rights to intellectual property, but he or she must ensure that the asset is protected. Also, if the client is the licensee of someone else's property, the client may be able to leave the right to license the property to a third person. The legal assistant must obtain a copy of the licensing agreement to help the attorney determine what rights the client may have.

Claims and Benefits

The client may be entitled to several types of claims and benefits. These must be analyzed to determine whether they represent assets that may be passed on.

Annuities and Pensions. An **annuity** is a fixed sum of money paid to the recipient at fixed intervals. Social Security is an example of an annuity. Many people purchase annuity insurance policies to guarantee them an income when they retire or reach a certain age. A **pension** is a form of a retirement annuity paid to former employees by employers. In each instance these rights to the income are the result of a specific contract, which means that the paralegal must obtain a copy of the client's contract to help the lawyer determine what rights the client may have.

Many people assume that their retirement and/or annuity income will continue to be paid to their survivors, but this is not always the case. The contract will specify whether survivors have any right to the income.

EXAMPLE:

When Oscar retires he is entitled to both Social Security and a pension. When he dies, the government will continue Social Security payments (albeit reduced) to Hyacinth as the widow, but under his pension plan Oscar's pension income terminates at his death. To protect Hyacinth, Oscar has purchased a private annuity from an insurance company that will pay income to both Oscar and Hyacinth, and the survivor, for life.

Powers of Appointment. A **power of appointment** is the right of a person to nominate a successor beneficiary. For example, Kingston could leave his house to Donna for life, and give Donna the power to decide who will get title on her death, Cornelia or Grace. Most people acquire powers of appointment through another person's will or trust and many times are unaware of the fact. (Trusts are discussed in Chapter 4.) The legal assistant must use detective and analytical skills to discover whether the client does have a power of appointment, and if so, how he or she wishes to exercise the power. Powers of appointment aren't typical, but they are by no means unusual.

General Debts. Any money or property owing to the client is an asset that can be left by will. Some debts are actually evidenced by documents, such as bonds, debentures, and promissory notes. The paralegal must ascertain whether the client is a creditor, and if so, document that fact for the efficient administration of the estate.

Wrongful Death. An action for the **wrongful death** of a person caused by the negligent or intentional act of another can be maintained by the decedent's estate. Wrongful death actions can become a valuable asset of the estate, and may be specifically left to named beneficiaries. Although this is not an asset the client may enjoy during life, it may provide an enormous sum to the value of his estate on the client's death.

EXAMPLE:

Tom has to fly to Honolulu on business. If the plane crashes en route, caused by the negligence of the airlines, Tom's estate has a claim against the airline for wrongful death. In his will Tom can specify that, should he die by any means that would give rise to an action for wrongful death, the proceeds of any such action should go to his mother Lottie.

Business Property. Many people operate small businesses, either as their main source of income or as a sideline. All property associated with the business that a person operates himself or herself (a **sole proprietorship**) may be left in a will. This will include the tangible property of the business—machines, paper, computers—as well as its intangibles. In addition to the property discussed above, a business may have some additional kinds of intangible property. **Accounts receivable** represent the money due from customers for products or services sold. These accounts are intangible assets that may be left by the sole proprietor. **Goodwill** is the reputation in the community the business has generated. When the business is sold, the goodwill represents an intangible asset to which a dollar amount will be attached as part of the total selling price. Never forget to include goodwill as a business asset. Lastly, there are **prepaid expenses**. Any business expense for which the owner has prepaid, such as insurance, labor, and so forth, are assets to which the business is entitled. The people who received the prepayments are debtors of the business, and must either provide the goods or services that were prepaid or return the unused prepayment.

SITUATIONAL ANALYSIS

Loretta Jones

Loretta has no real property, but she does possess both tangible and intangible personal property. Her grandmother's gold cross is her most treasured possession. In addition to the cross, she has a slim gold chain that she wears with the cross, and gold hoop earrings. Her television and stereo are not new and have little current value. Loretta's employers have a pension plan for their employees, and in Loretta's situation her minor child would be entitled to some benefits until he reaches the age of 18 (a contract provision of the plan). It is necessary that whomever Loretta selects as Evan's guardian be aware of this income that can be used for his support.

Aida may have a very valuable asset in her spaghetti sauce recipe and trademark. She may want to see whether she could develop this into a larger business, or sell the rights for a substantial profit and income.

The Bush Family

Hyacinth is a co-owner with her sisters in the house her aunt left them. The exact title must be determined and arrangements made to insure that the property will be passed on according to the sisters' wishes. Additionally, the lien on her father's house should be cleared and provisions made for the easement over the property.

Oscar is the promissee of a promissory note from Barney, and provisions should be made for leaving this asset. Also, Hyacinth should be familiar with the terms of Oscar's annuity.

In addition to what has already been mentioned, the Bushes have other personal property that must be itemized and described.

The Lear Family

The Lears have a very complicated real estate problem. Their daughter Regina and her husband are presently occupying a house owned by the Lears, and Regina is claiming the property as hers. The Lears must institute a court action immediately to **quiet title** (get a definite decree indicating ownership). If that is not done immediately, the Lears may lose their claim to the house.

Presently, Kingston and Donna hold title to their home as tenants by the entirety. However, they want Grace to inherit the house immediately upon their deaths. They may consider changing title to a joint tenancy with Grace. This should be discussed with the attorney and their accountant.

Kingston owns stock in a professional corporation, which means the corporation must pay his estate the value of the shares on Kingston's death—he cannot alienate the shares. Because there is no market value for the shares, the paralegal should determine whether the shareholders have an agreement with respect to the value of the stock, and if not, see that one is created to make sure that the family receives full value for Kingston's interest. Kingston also has to decide how to dispose of his bonds.

Grace is writing a book which should be copyrighted when completed.

In addition to the preceding, the Lears own quite a few valuable pieces of personal property and have numerous bank accounts. The paralegal must spend a considerable amount of time with the Lears to catalog all of their personal property.

Tom Poole

Tom is contemplating buying a co-operative apartment. The agreement must be analyzed to determine what rights Tom has with respect to transferring the shares. Tom also has some debentures that should be considered when devising his estate plan. Tom has a savings and checking account, a CD, and various other items of personal property that have to be itemized, valued, and considered in creating his will.

CHAPTER SUMMARY

One of the most important functions of a paralegal with respect to estate planning is to work with the client to discover and categorize all of the client's assets. The easiest way to accomplish this task is to devise a tickler that will take into account all of the various types of property a person may own. The most important categories are:

Real Property	*Personal Property*	
	Tangibles:	*Intangibles:*
Description	Cars	Bank accounts
Title	Electronic equipment	Intellectual property
Mortgages	Jewelry	Stocks
Easements	Furs	Bonds (debentures)
Liens	Arts and antiques	Business property
Leases	Collectibles	Insurance policies
	Furnishings	Pension plans
	Household effects	Annuities
		Promissory notes
		Licenses

Be sure that each item is properly described, and that there is some document of ownership and valuation

Key Terms

Accounts receivable: Money owed to a business from customers for property or services sold.
Annuity: Periodic payments of fixed sums of money.
Bond: Evidence of indebtedness secured by a specific piece of property, paying interest until the loan is repaid.
Chose in action: One form of intangible personal property.
Closely held: Privately owned corporation.
Community property: Method of holding title to property acquired during marriage; each spouse owns one half of the property.
Concurrent ownership: Fee estate held by two or more persons.
Condominium: Type of ownership of real estate with some attributes of a tenancy in common.
Conveyance: Transfer of real estate.
Co-operative: Type of interest in realty evidenced by owning shares; considered personal property.
Copyright: Government grant of exclusive use of artistic and literary works given to the creator.
Curtesy: Old form of widower's right in property of deceased wife.
Debenture: Unsecured evidence of indebtedness similar to a bond.
Deed: Document specifying title to real estate.
Dower: Old form of widow's right in property of deceased husband.
Easement: Right of access over or use of another person's land.
Elective share: Forced share.
Estate: Right in real property.

Face value: Amount appearing on a bond or debenture; amount of the loan.
Fee: Estate in real property.
Fee simple: Highest form of estate.
Fixture: Property attached to buildings considered to be real property.
Foreclosure: Right of mortgagee to seize and attach real estate for nonpayment of the loan.
Forced share: Current right of surviving spouse to a portion of deceased spouse's property.
Freehold: Estate in land for an indefinite period.
Gift: Method of acquiring property whereby the recipient gives no consideration.
Goodwill: Intangible asset of a business based on the business' reputation.
Grantee: Recipient of real estate.
Grantor: Transferor of real estate.
Homestead exemption: Estate property not subject to creditors' claims.
Intangible: Personal property that represents something of value but may have little intrinsic value itself.
Joint tenancy: Method of multiple ownership of property with right of survivorship.
Landlord: Person who leases real estate.
Leasehold: Tenancy in real estate for a fixed period of time.
Lessee: Tenant.
Lessor: Landlord.
License: Grant of use of intellectual property given by the holder of the exclusive right to the property.
Lien: Creditor's attachment of real and personal property.
Life estate: Tenancy for a period of a person's life.
Life estate pur autre vie: Tenancy for the life of another person.
Mark: Exclusive right to use a name or symbol that designates a service or trade.
Maturity date: Date on which debtor repays the bond or debenture.
Mortgage: Security interest on real estate.
Mortgagee: Person who gives a mortgage to purchase real estate.
Mortgagor: Person who takes a mortgage to purchase real estate.
Partition: Method of dividing the interests of multiple owners of real estate.
Patent: Government grant of exclusive use of a scientific invention given to the inventor.
Personal property: Property that is movable and or intangible, not real property.
Power of appointment: Authority to select a successor beneficiary.
Promissory note: Evidence of indebtedness.
Prepaid expense: Right to receive goods or services previously paid for.
Quiet title: Action to settle title to real estate.
Real property: Land and anything permanently affixed to the land.
Remainderman: Person in whom legal and equitable titles merge.

Rent: Fee paid by a tenant to a landlord.
Royalty: Fee paid by a licensee to the holder of a copyright.
Secured interest: Creditor's right to specific property which has been set aside to satisfy the creditor in case of default.
Securities: Contractual, proprietary interests between an investor and a business, evidenced by stocks, bonds, etc.
Share: Stock; portion of a corporation owned by an investor.
Sole proprietorship: Business owned by one person.
Statutory share: Forced share of the decedent's estate.
Stock: Evidence of ownership in a corporation.
Straw man: Method of changing title held by multiple owners.
Tangible property: Personal property that is moveable or touchable.
Tenancy: Right to real property.
Tenancy by the entirety: Joint ownership of property between legally married couples.
Tenancy in partnership: Multiple ownership of property by business partners; property passes to surviving partners, heirs of deceased partner receive the value of the deceased partner's interest in the property.
Tenancy in common: Multiple ownership of property in which each co-tenant owns a divisible portion of the whole.
Tenancy in severalty: Ownership in real estate by just one person.
Tickler: Checklist or deadline reminder system.
Title: Evidence of ownership or possession of property.
Wrongful death: Action to recover for the willful or negligent death of a person.

Case Studies

1. Can a life estate be created in personal property that, by its nature, is consumable?

Two parents willed a sum of money to one child for his life, the remainder to go to his sister upon his death. There was no provision limiting the son's use of the funds; he was not restricted to using just the income on the earnings. In these circumstances the court held that no life estate was created. Although life estates may be created in personal property, the life tenant must have some limitations placed on the property's use, especially if the property in question is depletable, such as cash. *Quandel v. Skene*, 321 N.W.2d 91 (N.D. 1982).

2. Does the concept of community property expand to personal property as well as real estate, and if so, can this title be defeated by the actions of the couple?

Texas is a community property state, and its law presupposes that all property acquired by a married couple during marriage is community property. A widow was questioning whether a $40,000 certificate of deposit, placed in a joint account, was considered community property or a joint tenancy. The court held that the CD constituted community property, and that without a written declaration by the couple specifying their intention to partition the title into a joint tenancy, the property remains community property. Merely placing the funds in a joint account does not constitute sufficient evidence of a desire to change the title. As a consequence, the widow received $20,000 as her community property share, but had to divide the remaining $20,000 with her husband's children from a previous marriage. If the court had found a joint tenancy, all $40,000 would have gone to the widow as the surviving joint tenant. *Tuttle v. Simpson*, 735 S.W.2d 539 (Tex. 1987).

3. Can the claim of a surviving spouse pursuant to state community property law be defeated by the deceased spouse opening up Totten Trust accounts for the benefit or their children?

A man opened up ten Totten Trust accounts with community property funds. One of the accounts named the wife as the beneficiary, and the other nine were opened up for the benefit of the couple's nine children. At his death, the funds in the children's accounts totaled $131,500, and the funds in the wife's account amounted to $38,500. The wife claimed one-half of the $131,500 as community property, and the court agreed. An inter vivos transfer to a bank account in trust for a non-spouse, even for the benefit of the couple's children, cannot defeat the surviving spouse's interest in one-half of the community property. Happy Mother's Day! *Estate of Wilson v. Bowens*, 183 Cal. App. 3d 67 (1986).

4. What would be the effect of an agreement between a husband and a wife that a bank account would be held as a tenancy by the entireties? When a wife's creditor attempted to garnish the account, the husband asserted the account was held as a tenancy by the entireties. The court said the agreement alone was insufficient to create that title; other factors must also be considered. *Morse v. Kohl, Metzger, Spotts, P.A.*, 725 W.2d 436 (Fla. App. 1999).

EXERCISES

1. Create a detailed tickler that can be used to discover all property owned by a client. Indicate all of the information necessary to identify and determine rights to this property.
2. Complete the tickler created in the first exercise to itemize all of your own property. The best way to understand the difficulties is to prepare one for yourself.
3. Go to your county recorder's office and check the chain of title for the building you live in.
4. Check your state's statute to determine whether there is a specific enactment for co-operatives and condominiums.
5. Obtain and analyze the shareholder's right to transfer his interest in a co-operative apartment. These documents can be obtained in a law library or through the Internet.

ANALYTICAL PROBLEM

In California, a community property state, a widow questions whether a $100,000 certificate of deposit placed in joint names is community property or a joint tenancy. There is no document covering the account, and the children of the husband's first marriage challenge the widow's claim. Assess the claims of the widow and the children.

3 The Laws of Succession

CHAPTER OVERVIEW

Before a will is drafted or an estate plan is established, it is necessary to determine the persons who are the client's closest relatives. Not only does this help the client focus on an appropriate estate plan, but it may also indicate whether a will is even necessary.

Every state, *by statute*, has indicated who will inherit a person's property if the person dies without a valid will. Without exception, these inheritors are those people who are the most closely related to the decedent. The assumption behind these laws is that most people would prefer their property to descend to their nearest and dearest rather than to wind up in the hands of strangers.

These intestate heirs are the persons who have the right to petition the court to be appointed the decedent's personal representative, and all intestate takers must be notified of the decedent's death and the administration of the estate. Furthermore, if a person dies with a will, these same intestate heirs have the right to challenge the document presented to the court as the last will and testament of the decedent. If the document is found invalid for any reason, the decedent is deemed to have died intestate and the intestate heirs may acquire the property.

The administration of an intestate estate generally follows the same procedures as the administration of a testate estate. The same probate court has jurisdiction, and the same administrative requirements are necessary, but for the necessity of proving a document to be the decedent's last valid will.

With respect to the laws of succession, it is the duty of the paralegal to gather all of the requisite family data from the client for the attorney to use in the preparation of the will and/or the administration of the estate.

Intestate Succession Defined

Interstate succession is the process by which a state statute determines who acquires a decedent's property, and in what proportion, if the decedent dies without a valid will. The intestate succession laws are designed to insure that a person's property stays within that person's family. If a person dies without any blood relations who can be located, his or her property will go to the state in which the property is located. This is known as **escheating**.

The intestate succession laws, or **laws of succession**, or **laws of descent and distribution**, follow the general principle that a person's property should pass by blood relationships, known as **consanguinity** (relationship by blood). The only exception to the rule of consanguinity with respect to the laws of succession is that a legal spouse is always considered to be the nearest relative of a decedent. A married couple are considered to be a single unit. Persons related to a decedent by marriage instead of blood (spouses excepted) are considered to be related by **affinity**. Under the laws of intestate succession, relatives by marriage are not entitled to a person's property (with a will a person may leave property to whomever he or she desires, but that is not the case if the person dies intestate). Persons who are connected with a decedent by neither blood nor marriage are not considered at all under the laws of succession, no matter how close the emotional relationship may be.

Historically, illegitimate (nonmarital) children were not entitled to inherit from either parent. Later, these children were permitted to inherit from their mother and their mother's family. Today, nonmarital children may also inherit from their father and their father's family provided that the paternity of the child has been established and acknowledged or the parents marry after the birth of the child. Each state has enacted provisions for determining paternity for the purpose or inheritance. The requirements for each jurisdiction must be individually checked.

EXAMPLES:

1. Hyacinth has a husband, a son, a father, two sisters, a niece, and a grandniece, all living. Although each of these persons is related to Hyacinth by blood, her husband, Oscar, is considered to be her closest relative under the laws of succession.
2. Fleur is related to her sister Fern by blood, and if Fleur dies intestate Fern is one of her intestate heirs. Fleur is related to Barney by

marriage—he is married to Fern, Fleur's sister. If Fleur dies intestate, Barney has no claim against her estate because he is not an intestate heir.

3. Loretta has a mother living, Aida, and a son, Evan, fathered by Jason Leroy. Both Aida and Evan are intestate heirs of Loretta, but Jason has no legal relationship to Loretta either by blood or marriage. Take note, though, that Evan is an intestate heir of Jason because he is Jason's son.
4. When Jason dies, under his state law Evan is considered an intestate heir because Jason had acknowledged paternity during his life.

The intestate takers of a person's estate are categorized by the type of property they inherit. If the decedent left real property, the intestate taker is called an **heir**. If the decedent left personal property, the intestate taker of the personalty is called a **distributee**. For simplicity's sake, most intestate takers are generically referred to as heirs.

How Intestate Succession Works

The theory of intestate succession is very simple—the closest blood relatives, that is, **next of kin**, inherit the decedent's property. However, it is not always so simple to determine who is the "closest blood relative." To determine "closeness," the law uses a concept known as **degrees of separation**. Simply put, this means the law calculates how many generations the deceased is removed from the intestate claimant. The fewer the number of generations, the nearer the intestate heir.

In counting degrees of separation, the law works in two directions. The primary direction is **lineal**, or in a straight line from the decedent. Lineal relations are those persons who are the direct ancestors or descendents of the deceased. An **ancestor** is a person from an earlier generation, and a **descendent** is a person from a later generation. For example, all lineal ancestors, or **ascendents** have the word "parent" as part of their title when claiming kinship to the decedent (e.g., parent, grandparent, great-grandparent). Lineal descendents are the **issue** or offspring or "children," of the deceased, and are called children, grandchildren, great-grandchildren, and so on.

The second direction used by the intestate succession laws to determine degrees of relationships is **collateral**, or nonlineal. This category includes all blood relatives who are not directly ascending or descending from the deceased, such as siblings, aunts and uncles, cousins, and so forth.

EXAMPLES:

1. Davida has three lineal ascendent generations living: her mother, Rose; her grandparents, Fern and Barney; and her great-grandfather, David. All these persons have the word "parent" in their title in relation to Davida.
2. Aida has two lineal descendents living; her child, Loretta, and her grandchild, Evan. Both Loretta and Evan have the word "child" in their title in relation to Aida.
3. Tom Poole has two lineal ascendents and one collateral relative living. His parents, Lottie and Simon, are his lineal ascendents, and his brother, Ken, is his collateral relative.
4. Anthony Montague, Cornelia's son, has several collateral relatives: his aunts, Grace and Regina; and Regina's children, his cousins, Matthew, Mark, Mary, and Margaret. Note that even though Regina's children are from two different fathers, they are still Anthony's collateral relatives because they are related to him through Regina, his blood aunt. If Joseph Hoch, Matthew and Mark's father, has a child by another marriage, that child would not be a blood relative of Anthony's because Joseph is not his blood uncle, but the child would be a collateral blood relative of Matthew and Mark, Joseph's sons.

All relationships, for the purpose of the laws of succession, are determined *only* by blood relationships. People may have blood relatives in common who are not blood relatives of each other: Relations from the mother's and father's sides are not related to each other, as exemplified above with Anthony, Matthew, and Mark.

In order to determine the degree of closeness, a generational family tree must be drawn. Once completed, the degree of separation is determined by counting how many people separate the relatives in question. For example, Lottie and Simon, as Tom's parents, are related to Tom in the first degree—they are the first blood relatives encountered on Tom's family tree. Ken, Tom's brother, is related to Tom in the second degree. How? By counting how many people separate Tom from Ken. First go up to Tom's parents (1), then go down to Ken (2). Ken is related to Tom through Lottie and Simon.

Degrees of separation are counted by determining how the blood has passed from the decedent to the relative in question. For lineal relations, the degrees of separation are very easy to determine—just count up or down. Parents are one, grandparents are two, children are one, grandchildren are two, and so forth. Note that ascendents and descendents may both be related in the same degree to the decedent.

The calculations become more complicated in determining the degrees of separation for collateral relatives. To perform the computation, count the number of generations up to the first blood ancestor the decedent and the collateral relative have in common, then count down to the relative in question. The total indicates the degrees of separation.

EXAMPLE:

To determine the degrees of separation between Byron and Davida, count up to the first blood lineal ascendent both share, who is David, then count down to Davida. Byron to Hyacinth (1), Hyacinth to David (2), David to Fern (3), Fern to Rose (4), Rose to Davida (5). Byron and Davida are relatives in the fifth degree. See the family tree diagram below.

Always bear the following in mind when attempting these calculations: (1) *adopted children* under most statutes are considered blood relatives of the adopted family; (2) persons related only by marriage are not considered at all for the purpose of intestate succession; (3) relatives of *half-blood* are only blood relatives if the person in question is related through the blood parent. Different state statutes indicate the proportion of the estate a half-blood may inherit.

One interesting sidelight to the intestate succession laws is that the actual physical body of the decedent is considered the property of the decedent's next of kin (closest blood relative), who has the authority to dispose of the corpse.

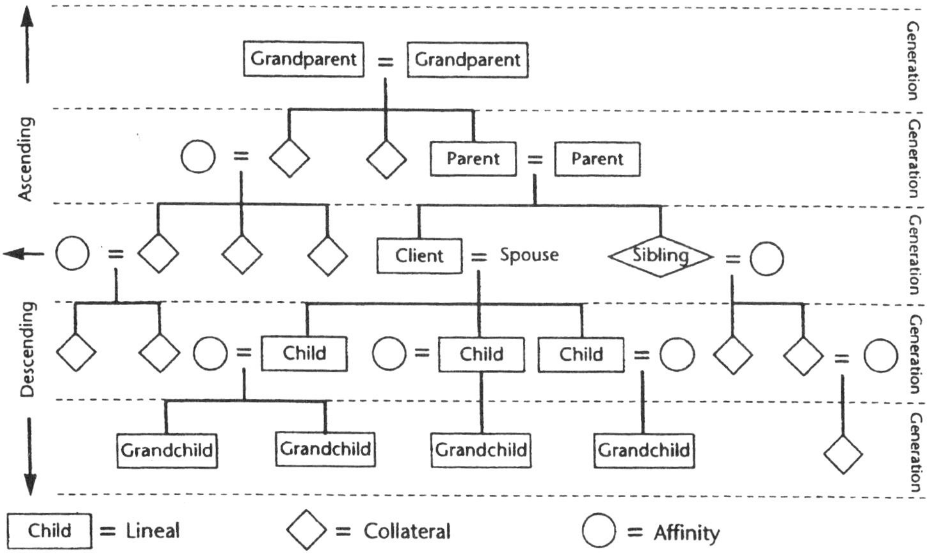

SITUATIONAL ANALYSIS

The following represents the family trees of our four families. Similar family trees should be created for every client to determine degrees of separation.

Loretta Jones

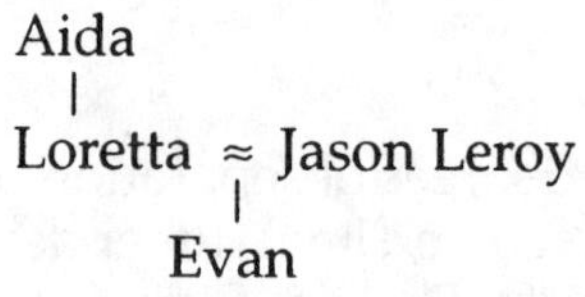

Jason Leroy is a blood relative only of Evan; otherwise all relationships are lineal. Both Aida and Evan are related to Loretta in the first degree.

The Bush Family

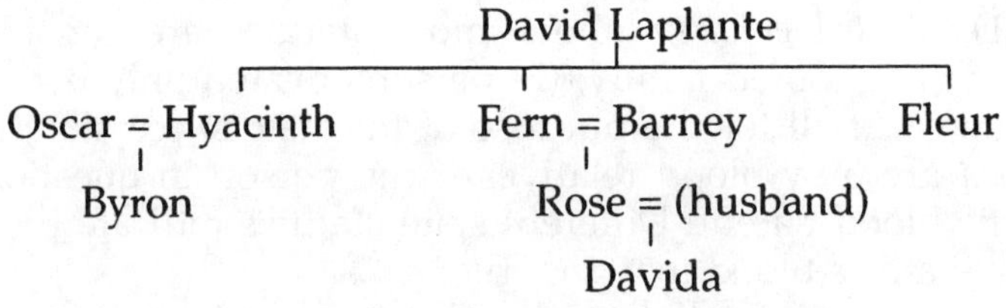

This family tree indicates four generations in the Bush family descending from David Laplante. Note that Oscar, Barney, and Rose's husband are only blood relatives of their children—they are not considered intestate heirs of any other members of the Laplante family (except their spouses).

The Lear Family

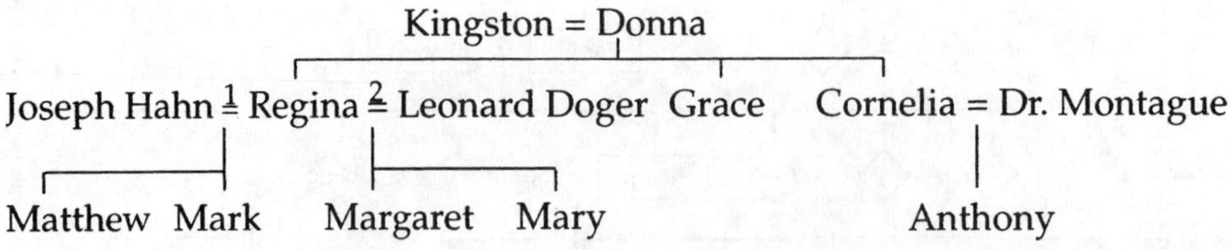

Joseph Hahn is only a blood relative to Matthew and Mark. Because he and Regina are divorced he is no longer an intestate heir of Regina, whereas Leonard, her current husband, is. Dr. Montague is only an intestate heir of his wife and son. Neither Dr. Montague, Joseph Hahn, nor Leonard Doger are intestate heirs of Kingston and Donna. Matthew and Mark are half-blood brothers to Margaret and Mary, only having one parent in common: Regina.

Tom Poole

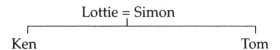

Lottie = Simon

Ken Tom

Intestate Administration

Intestate administration generally follows the same procedures as testate administration, except that (1) there is no will to follow and (2) the personal representative is called an **administrator**. (See Chapter 7.) The primary differences lie in who petitions to be appointed the personal representative and in how the property is distributed.

Generally, the intestate heir in the closest degree of separation to the decedent is the person who will petition to be appointed the personal representative. If the decedent is survived by a spouse, that spouse is typically appointed. If there is no surviving spouse, or he or she does not wish to fulfill the function, usually adult children will be appointed. Because the closest blood relative has the greatest claim on the estate, it is that person the court typically appoints.

Once the personal representative has been affirmed by the court and has been issued letters of administration (see Chapter 1), the personal representative must determine who are the intestate heirs.

The general rule is that persons of a closer degree take the property in preference to persons of a further degree. In other words, if the closest relative is related in the third degree, she will cut off all claims of persons related in the fourth degree and further.

EXAMPLE:

If David Laplante dies without a will, his heirs are his three daughters, all of the first degree, his two grandchildren of the second degree, and a great-granddaughter of the third degree. Because his daughters are living, they divide up the estate among themselves, cutting off claims of the persons related by a greater degree of separation.

Intestate heirs are grouped by degrees of separation into **classes**. All relations of the first degree create a class, all relations of the second degree create a class, and so forth. As soon as one person is found alive in any class, that class determines the proportionate distribution of the estate. There are three methods used to determine intestate distribution: (1) per capita, (2) per stirpes, and (3) by representation.

Once the closest class with a living member is ascertained, it must be determined how many people originally existed in this class. This means that even if persons predeceased the decedent, their existence at one time is taken into consideration for the purpose of intestate administration. The decedent's estate is evenly divided among all of the people who originally existed in this closest class of which at least one member is still alive. All members of the class who are alive at the date of death of the decedent take their portion **per capita**—equally to each person in his own right. For members of the class who predeceased the intestate, the other two methods of distribution—per stirpes or by representation—apply. **Per stirpes**, which translates as "by representation," provides that the portion that would have gone to the predeceased per capita class member be distributed to that person's issue in equal shares. Should the predeceased member have no issue, the per capita class is considered never to have included that person. Per stirpes distribution mandates that the estate descends lineally to the issue of the predeceased per capita class member.

Recently, many jurisdictions have enacted statutes that provide for distribution **by representation**, which in this context is not meant to be the translation of per stirpes. With this representative method, the estate is distributed in equal shares to all members of the per capita class. If there are any predeceased members, that person's portion is pooled together with the portions of other predeceased per capita class members and their collective issue shares that pool equally.

The difference between per stripes and by representation distribution is that, with the former, the property descends lineally, whereas with the latter, members of each generation share equally, more of a horizontal distribution. By representation distribution means that the portion of the estate a person receives is dependent upon his or her generation, not his or her ancestor.

EXAMPLES:

1. David Laplante dies intestate. Hyacinth, Fern, and Fleur are the members of the class related by the first degree. Because they are alive, they cut off claims of persons of further removed generations.
2. Assume that Hyacinth and David die together in a car accident. Fern and Fleur are still related to David in the first degree, but the class originally contained three people (Fern, Fleur, and Hyacinth). For the purpose of intestate administration, the class is considered to have three persons. Fern and Fleur each inherit one-third of David's estate per capita (in their own right), and Byron, as Hyacinth's heir, inherits the last third of David's estate per stirpes, representing his deceased mother's interest.
3. Assume Byron was also in the car with Hyacinth and David. In this instance Fern and Fleur would each inherit one-half of David's estate. Because Byron is also deceased, he cannot take Hyacinth's portion per stirpes, and so that third is divided between Fern and

Fleur. Why doesn't Oscar inherit as a surviving spouse? Because he is not a blood relative of David's, and it is David's estate that is being distributed. In order to take per stirpes, the representative must also be related by blood to the decedent.

Under almost every statute, the surviving spouse will take before any blood relative except children, and lineal descendents have preference over ascendents and collateral relatives. However, every state statute must be individually analyzed. See the Appendix for specific state examples.

The Effect of the Laws of Succession

The primary purpose of the laws of succession, also referred to as **the laws of descent and distribution**, is to provide for the orderly distribution of an intestate's assets to his or her closest blood relations. However, the intestate succession laws have several other effects.

First of all, the laws of descent and distribution indicate who will inherit a person's estate if he or she has no will, and in what proportion. For example, in New York a surviving spouse takes the first $50,000 of an estate, plus half of the remainder, the other half going to the issue by representation. Also, many blood relatives may be disqualified from inheriting for various reasons, depending upon the provisions of the statute. For the purpose of estate planning, it is important for a client to understand who will get his or her property if there is no will. In certain circumstances the intestate result may satisfy the client; in other situations this realization may convince the client of the necessity of a last will and testament.

Second, as will be discussed in Chapter 5, one of the requirements to make a valid will is that the testator have **testamentary capacity**, the legal ability to execute a will. One element of testamentary capacity is knowing who your closest relations are, legally if not emotionally. The intestate succession laws state quite affirmatively who are a person's nearest relations.

Third, by realizing who will inherit under intestacy, it may become apparent that a will is necessary, even if the same people will inherit. A will can designate how and to whom each piece of property will go, can take into consideration the age, mental and physical condition, and financial need of each heir, and, very importantly, can take advantage of tax benefits (Chapter 1).

Fourth, and by no means least, the intestate succession laws indicate who has the right to challenge a person's will in court. This can influence not only whether a person decides to have a will, but what disposition to make in the will to forestall relatives from challenging its validity.

This is not to say that a will is a perfect solution in every situation. Having a will opens up a person's assets to the scrutiny of the court and the judicial bureaucracy. It can involve a great deal of time and expense, especially if the document is challenged in court. Nevertheless, the important consideration is that a person make a knowing and intelligent choice with respect to the distribution of his assets on his death, and to do this he must understand the laws of succession.

On a positive note, nowadays it is very rare that a person (read paralegal) must actually do the calculations to determine the degrees of relationship. Most of the forms that have to be filled out for the probate court have a section dealing with the intestate succession, and the petitioner simply has to fill in the form, which already does all of the counting. Most statutes provide that the order of distribution is to the spouse and children or issue, then to parents, siblings, and grandparents, and finally to descendents of the grandparents. (See Chapter 7 and the Appendix.) However, it is still necessary to know who a client's relations are and what their relationship is to the client; gathering such information is the responsibility of the legal assistant.

SITUATIONAL ANALYSIS

Loretta Jones

Under the intestate succession laws, Loretta's property would go to her only child, Evan. However, Evan is a minor and is not capable of handling money or rearing himself. In her situation Loretta should have a will because of Evan's age. If Evan were an adult, a will might not be necessary.

Oscar and Hyacinth Bush

If either Oscar or Hyacinth dies, his or her estate would be divided between the survivor and Byron. This means that no provision would exist for other relatives. Nevertheless, if the estate is under the tax-free limit, intestacy might be a viable alternative for them, unless Hyacinth wants to make some provisions for her father, sisters, and nieces.

The Lear Family

If the Lears do not transfer their property while they are alive, they certainly need a will. Without a will, Cornelia, Grace, and Regina would inherit equally. Because the Lears are having problems with Regina and do not want her to receive any of their property, but do want to provide for their grandchildren and other daughters, a will becomes a necessity. In this instance the laws of intestate succession would directly contradict the Lears' wishes.

Tom Poole

Under most laws of intestate succession, Tom's parents would inherit all of his property. Because Tom wants his property to go to friends, in this case a will is also necessary. Remember, friends have absolutely no rights under the intestate succession laws; the only way a friend can inherit is if the decedent leaves the friend property pursuant to a will.

CHAPTER SUMMARY

The laws of succession determine who inherits a person's property, and in what proportion, if a person dies without a valid will. Although these laws serve to protect the interests of blood relations with respect to a decedent's property, they do not take into consideration the heir's age or needs nor the wishes of the decedent. Furthermore, the laws of descent and distribution only deal with property distribution and make no accommodation for certain tax advantages that might be applicable.

One of the first functions to be performed by the legal assistant with respect to estate law is to determine the client's family situation. This entails discovering all of a client's relations, and using this information to create a family tree. The family tree highlights who are (and implicitly, who are not) a person's intestate heirs, which can be determinative in the decision to draft a will. It can be quite a surprise to the client to discover that he is not the intestate heir of a favorite, and wealthy, aunt because she is only related to him by marriage.

Not only is this family information useful to the attorney in drafting a will, but it is necessary for the orderly administration of the estate once the client has died. All intestate heirs must be notified if a will is submitted to probate, and each has the right to challenge the validity of that will. Additionally, mentioning relatives in a will is an indication of the testator's testamentary capacity, one of the requisite elements of a valid will.

If a person has no intestate heirs and does not dispose of his property by will, all of his assets will escheat to the state. This is another reason why most people would prefer a will to intestacy.

Key Terms

Administrator: Personal representative of an intestate.
Affinity: Relationship by marriage.
Ancestor: Relative of a previous generation.
Ascendent: Lineal ancestor.
Collateral Relative: Nonlineal blood relations.
Consanguinity: Relationship determined by blood ties.
Class: Group of persons of the same degree.
Degrees of separation: Number of generations a person is removed from the decedent.

Distributee: Intestate inheritor of personal property.
Escheat: Process by which the state inherits property of an intestate who has no heirs.
Heir: Intestate inheritor of real property.
Illegitimate: Born out of wedlock.
Intestate succession: Persons who are entitled to inherit property of a person who dies without a will.
Issue: Direct lineal descendents.
Laws of descent and distribution: Statutes indicating a person's intestate heirs.
Laws of succession: Statutes indicating a person's intestate heirs.
Letters of administration: Court orders authorizing the personal representative of an intestate to administer the estate.
Lineal relation: Blood relatives directly ascending or descending.
Next of kin: Closest intestate blood relation.
Nonmarital children: Children born out of wedlock.
Per capita: Equally to each person in his or her own right.
Per stirpes: Taking property by right of representation.
Testamentary capacity: Legal ability to execute a will.

Case Studies

1. Does the fact that a parent abandoned a child prevent that parent from inheriting that child's estate under the laws of intestate succession?

When her son was two years old a woman divorced her husband and from that time forward failed to provide any financial support for the son, nor did she show any interest in or display any love or affection for the child. At age 15 the son was killed in a car accident, and the son's estate settled a claim against the wrongdoer for over half a million dollars. At this point the mother reappeared to claim her intestate rights. The court held that the applicable statutory law that disqualified intestate heirs only referred to persons who are convicted of murdering the deceased and persons who abandon spouses. The statute was silent with respect to abandoning one's children and therefore the mother was entitled to inherit one-half of the son's estate. *Hortarek v. Benson*, 211 Conn. 121 (1989). What is your opinion of this case? Does your state statutory law provide for a similar result?

2. Can the father of a non-marital child inherit from that child under the law of descent and distribution if paternity was never lawfully acknowledged?

A man acknowledged the paternity of a non-marital child by executing an "Affidavit of Paternity for Child Out of Wedlock" before a notary public, but he never actually filed the affidavit with the appropriate state agency. The state law requires such a filing as lawful proof of paternity.

Consequently, the father was precluded from inheriting from the estate of the child. Note that the law of intestate succession can affect the rights of a parent to inherit as well as that of a child. *Estate of Morris*, 123 N.C. App. 264 (1996).

3. Esther O'Handlen died intestate, leaving no surviving spouse, issue, parent, sibling, or offspring of siblings. Under the Illinois statute of descent and distribution, in these circumstances the intestate's property is required to pass per stirpes to the intestate's grandparents or their issue.

Esther's grandfather married twice, and had children from both unions. The surviving relatives were Esther's full-blooded aunt plus several descendents of Esther's grandfather by his other marriage (half-blood relatives of Esther). The probate court divided Esther's property into two moieties (halves), one going to the descendents of Esther's grandmother, the other going to the descendents of her grandfather. Esther's half-blood relations challenged this division, claiming this improperly discriminated against relations of the half-blood; under the court's ruling the full-blooded aunt received one-half of the estate as the descendent of Esther's grandmother, and then shared with the half-blood relations as a descendent of Esther's grandfather. The appellate court affirmed the decision of the trial court.

Descent and distribution is statutorily governed, and the statute determined the distribution by dividing the property into halves to be divided among the issue of each grandparent. The statute does not discriminate because each heir received an equal portion depending upon his or her relationship to the deceased. The statute would only discriminate if it awarded different shares to persons related in the same degree. *In re Estate of O'Handlen*, 571 N.E.2d 482 (Ill. 1991).

Do you agree with the decision of the court? Why?

4. A man murdered his mother and brother. The mother died testate, but the brother died without a will. The children of the convicted murderer claimed their father's portion of the intestate uncle's estate. The sister of the deceased protested, claiming that under the so-called "Slayer's Statute" (see Chapter 5) a murderer is prohibited from benefiting from the estate of the victim, and, as a matter of public policy, the prohibition should extend to the murderer's issue as well. The court disagreed. In its reasoning the court stated that the murderer's minor children were in no way responsible for the death of their uncle, and the Florida descent and distribution statute provides for the distribution of an intestate's estate to sibling or siblings' issue per stirpes. Although the murderer cannot benefit, his children may still claim his share by representation, taking, in this instance, one-half of the estate, the remaining one-half going to the children's aunt. *In re Estate of Benson*, 548 So. 2d 775 (Fla. Dist. Ct. App. 1989).

Do you agree with the court's decision? If a slayer statute is to have any effect, shouldn't the murderer's heirs be excluded from benefiting as well? Couldn't the murderer be considered to be benefiting indirectly?

EXERCISES

1. Create your own family tree.
2. Using your family tree, indicate all persons who are related to you by the fourth and fifth degrees.
3. Using your family tree, indicate all persons who are related to you by affinity.
4. Locate your state statute dealing with the laws of descent and distribution. Under your state statute, if you died intestate today, who would inherit your property?
5. Discuss the circumstances in which the laws of succession would make it more or less important to have a will.

ANALYTICAL PROBLEM

A client comes to your office with the following set of facts: He was placed for adoption when he was an infant and is now 25 years old. With the knowledge of his adoptive family, he has sought out his natural parents, and has made contact with his natural mother. Unfortunately, his natural mother has just died, leaving no will and no other issue. The client wants to attempt to inherit by intestate succession. Advise the client according to your state's statutory and case law.

4 Trusts

CHAPTER OVERVIEW

As discussed in Chapter 1, one of the primary objectives of creating an estate plan is to make sure that a person's property will be maintained and used for a purpose consistent with the property owner's wishes. One popular method of achieving this goal is to create a trust, either while the person is alive or as part of the person's will. The concept of the trust has existed for thousands of years, and was originated by the ancient Romans. After several centuries of decline, the trust was revived during the feudal period, and today is a fairly typical legal relationship found in all sorts of circumstances.

A **trust** is a fiduciary relationship in which property is transferred from the **trustor**, the creator of the trust, to one or more persons, known as **trustees**. The trustees hold the **legal title** to the property, subject to fiduciary duties imposed by the trustor, to hold and use the property for the benefit of another individual, called the **beneficiary** who holds the **equitable title**.

The trust itself is considered a legal entity in its own right, with the trustee and the beneficiary each holding a portion of the complete title to the property. This relationship between the trustee and the beneficiary is *not* like the relationship of joint tenants or tenants in common in which each tenant owns a portion of the property itself; in a trust, the property is owned by the trust, but each participant holds a portion of the *title*, not a portion of the property.

The purpose of a trust, originally and currently, is to see that property is appropriately managed and its income disbursed to persons whom the trustor wishes to benefit from the property. A trust is not limited to the life of any one person, and may continue to provide benefits for several generations beyond that of the trustor himself. It is a method whereby a person may maintain control over his or her property even from the grave. Trusts can be created during the trustor's life by having the trustor transfer the property while alive, known as an **inter vivos or living trust**. They may also be created as part of a testamentary disposition in a person's will (a **testamentary trust**).

There are several benefits to creating a trust rather than making an outright gift of the property to the beneficiary:

1. The beneficiary may not be capable of managing the property, either because of age or infirmity, and by having a trustee manage the assets, the trustor would be assured that the property will produce an income for the beneficiary.
2. Because the trust can be multigenerational, the trustor can make sure that the assets will still exist for several generations and not be spent by the first generation beneficiary, leaving nothing for later generations.
3. By placing property in trust during a person's lifetime, that property is not considered owned by the person at death (with some exceptions discussed later in this chapter and in Chapter 8), and therefore is not taxable or subject to the claims of intestate heirs.
4. If the trustor normally provides support for another person or dependent, by placing property in trust sufficient to produce the income the trustor typically gives to the dependent, he will have shifted the income tax burden to the trust and the beneficiaries, which may have more advantages, tax-wise, than paying taxes on the income and taking a small deduction for the dependents.

EXAMPLES:

1. Loretta wants to make sure that Evan will have money to support himself should she die. If Evan received the money from Loretta's life insurance, as a minor he would be incapable of managing the funds. If Loretta establishes a trust for Evan with the proceeds of the life insurance, she can select a trustee who is knowledgeable in money management to make sure that Evan has an income.
2. Oscar, in his will, leaves all of his assets in trust for Hyacinth, to provide income to support her for life, and on her death the income is to go to Byron for life. At Byron's death, the property will be divided among Byron's children. In this manner neither Hyacinth nor Byron can squander the assets, and Oscar can be assured that his prospective grandchildren will inherit his property.
3. Kingston and Donna transfer the bulk of their property in trust while they are alive. They make themselves the beneficiaries of the trust so that they can still enjoy the income from their assets, but

at their deaths the property goes to their grandchildren. When they die, this property would probably not be federally taxable because they do not own it on their deaths—it is owned by the trust. Additionally, should Regina attempt to challenge their wills or claim an intestate share of their estates, she would fail: Because Kingston and Donna have divested themselves of the assets, it is not owned by them at death and consequently there is no property for Regina to acquire.

4. Fern and Barney contribute to the support of David. At their income level, the taxes they pay on the income they use to support David is not offset by the dependency deduction. By using a trust, David still receives an income, on which he may have to pay taxes, but at a lower rate than Fern and Barney, and Fern and Barney have reduced their income which will reduce their taxes and may change their tax bracket.

Trusts may be created for any lawful purpose, and must be created by means of a written instrument. This chapter will detail all of the different types of trusts, the requirements necessary to create a valid trust, and restrictions on trusts. It will also provide instruction on how to draft a trust. A paralegal may be called upon to gather all of the information from the client necessary to create the trust, draft the initial trust (whether as its own document or as part of a will), and be required to interpret trusts to determine the rights and liabilities of a given client.

Trust Requirements

There are five requisite elements for the creation of a valid trust:

1. a trustor
2. trust property
3. a valid trust purpose
4. a trustee
5. a beneficiary

Each of these elements will be discussed in turn.

A Trustor

The trustor is the person who initially owns the property and who is the creator of the trust relationship. In order to be able to create a trust, the trustor must own a transferable interest in property. This may mean outright ownership in fee, or it could be a tenancy or any other title that permits the title holder to convey the property to a third person.

The term "trustor" is generic, as is **creator**, referring to the person who establishes a trust. Specifically, however, the law does distinguish titles dependent upon the nature of the property used to create the trust. If the property transferred is real estate, the trustor is known as the **grantor**. If the property transferred is personal property, the trustor is called the **settlor**.

The trustor does not have to be a natural person: Any legal entity capable of owning and transferring property may be the creator of a trust. The only requirement is that the trustor must have a transferable interest and have the legal capacity to enter into a legal transfer of the property.

EXAMPLES:

1. Tom wants to put the shares of his co-op apartment in trust. Under the cooperative agreement, Tom may not transfer his shares except to specifically designated individuals. In this situation, Tom cannot create a trust because he does not have the legal right to transfer the shares.
2. Cornelia wins $50,000 in her state lottery. She takes the money to her bank to establish a trust to provide an income for her son, Anthony. Cornelia has a transferable interest in the cash and therefore may establish a trust with these funds.
3. Cornelia's husband, Dr. Montague, purchased a small apartment building for investment purposes. He places the deed to the building in trust in order to provide an income for Anthony. Because the property transferred is real estate, Dr. Montague is referred as "the grantor."
4. Grace Lear has acquired several government bonds over the years. In order to help support her nephews, Matthew and Mark, she places these securities in trust, using the income for the nephews' benefit. Grace is a settlor because the trust property is personalty.
5. Ken Poole owns a small manufacturing corporation, and he wishes to establish a trust to provide some benefits for his employees. The corporation, as a legal entity, is capable of holding and transferring title to property, and therefore is legally capable of creating a valid trust.
6. At her birth, Davida's aunts get together and set up a bank account in Davida's name. Although Davida, as a minor, is legally capable of owning property, she is legally incapable of transferring the property: She lacks what is known as *contractual capacity*. Consequently, Davida may not be the creator of a trust.

Trust Property

Almost any transferable property can be made the subject of a trust agreement. Transferable property includes all real estate and tangible and intangible property, including choses in action. The only type of property that could not be the subject of a trust would be such items as government pensions, tort claims, and any other interest or item to which attaches a restriction on transferability.

Additionally, as a general principle, only property that is capable of producing an income may be the subject of a trust. If a person places in the trust personal property that is not income-producing and does not indicate that the property may be sold to purchase income-producing property, the "trust," in reality, simply becomes a custodial arrangement.

EXAMPLES:

1. Tom, as a government employee, will eventually be entitled to both a government pension and Social Security. Under the terms of his pension agreement, his interest cannot be transferred; the actual income can be transferred once it is in Tom's hands, but the right to receive the income cannot be made the property interest of a trust.
2. Rose inherited a very valuable pearl necklace from her grandmother, David's deceased wife. Rose wants to ensure that Davida eventually inherits the jewelry, so she creates a trust for Davida, placing the jewels in trust, permitting Davida to use the jewels after she attains a certain age, and eventually giving the necklace to her outright. This is not a trust, because the trustee is merely maintaining non-income-producing property for Davida. It is a bailment with certain restrictions placed on the bailor.

Trust property is classified according to the nature of the property. If real property is placed in trust, it is referred to as the **corpus**, or body, of the trust. If personal property, other than cash, is placed in trust, it is called the **res**, or "thing." If cash is used as the trust property, it is generally referred to as the **principal**. However, the term "corpus" is usually used generically for all trust property.

EXAMPLES:

1. Kingston places a $100,000 corporate bond in trust to produce an income for his grandchildren. The bond is referred to as "the trust res" because it is personal property.

2. Simon places the deed to a small apartment building he owns in trust to produce an income for himself and Lottie. The apartment building, as realty, forms the corpus of the trust.
3. Hyacinth places $25,000 in trust to produce an income for her father, David. The $25,000 in cash represents the principal of the trust.
4. Cornelia and her husband create a trust using an office building they own, some corporate stock, and $10,000 in cash as the basis of the trust property. In this instance, with mixed trust assets, the property is generally referred to as "the corpus," or simply "the trust property."

In order for the trust to be validly created, the trust property must be legally and sufficiently described, in existence, and owned by the trustor at the date of creation of the trust. In other words, a trust cannot be created from anticipated property or property over which the trustor does not have a current transferable interest. However, these items may be *added* to the corpus of a trust that already exists. (See below for a description of a life insurance trust.)

EXAMPLES:

1. Loretta wins the state lottery for $500,000, with payments to be made in 20 yearly installments. Loretta can only create a trust once she has the first installment in hand, and the trust would be limited to just the amount of that payment. She cannot create a trust with her anticipated $500,000.
2. Loretta creates a small trust for Evan. In her life insurance policy she indicates that the beneficiary of the proceeds of the policy is to be the trust that she has previously established. This is perfectly valid. Property is being added to the trust as the property becomes transferable.

A Valid Trust Purpose

As stated above, a trust may be created for any lawful purpose. A trust will not be valid if it violates any civil or criminal law. Many people use trusts to provide income to family members or themselves, as well as for charitable purposes. Also, to take advantage of the marital deduction for estate taxes, many persons establish a trust for the surviving spouse for life, with the assets to go to other persons on the spouse's death. This is known as Qualified Terminable Interest Property (QTIP), previously mentioned.

EXAMPLES:

1. Oscar and Hyacinth convey $50,000 to a trust to provide an income for Byron. This is an example of a valid trust to benefit a family member.
2. Tom Poole uses his corporate stock to establish a trust to provide a scholarship for needy students at his alma mater. This is an example of a valid trust established to serve a charitable purpose of the creator.
3. In his will, Barney establishes a QTIP trust to provide Fern with an income for life, and, on her death the property is to go to Rose. This trust serves to provide an income for a family member as well as taking advantage of estate tax benefits for marital deductions.
4. A construction company president approaches Oscar, telling Oscar that the company will set up a trust fund for him and his family if he will see to it that the construction company is awarded all government contracts for the next two years. This trust would be invalid because it is a violation of the law, both civil and criminal.
5. An extremist group approaches Grace, offering to place one million dollars in trust for her if she will get them access to the U.S. embassy for the purpose of placing a bomb in the building. This trust is invalid as a violation of criminal law.

In order for the trust to be valid, not only must the purpose of the trust be lawful, but the purpose must be specifically stated in the trust instrument itself. A trust cannot be enforced if its purpose is unclear or incapable of being ascertained. Also, the trust purpose must impose certain duties for the trustee to perform. If the trustee has no function other than custodial ones, the trust is considered passive, and the property is deemed to be owned outright by the beneficiary.

EXAMPLE:

Loretta takes $15,000 of her first lottery installment to her local bank and puts the money in trust for Evan. Although Loretta's purpose may appear discernible, she has, in fact, not indicated one. Does Evan get the income, is it a custodial account until he reaches majority, or is the money to be used for his education? And what is the trustee to do with the funds? To be valid, the trust *must* clearly state a trust purpose and impose duties on the trustee.

A Trustee

A trustee is the person (or persons) given the legal title to the trust property, along with certain duties and obligations to perform in order to carry out the wishes of the trustor (the trust purpose). A trustee is a **fiduciary**; that is, a person who, because of his position of trust, is held to a higher standard of care than ordinary care, the usual legal standard. As a fiduciary, not only must the trustee use general ordinary, reasonable skill and prudence in the management of the trust assets, but he or she must meet certain other obligations as well:

a) The trustee must not delegate the performance of the trust duties. As a fiduciary trustee is required to act personally for the benefit of the trust and the beneficiary.
b) The trustee must be loyal to the trust and the beneficiary, and not benefit personally from the management of the trust assets. Although trustees are permitted fees in payment for their performance (either specifically stated in the trust instrument or as set by statute as a percentage of the income produced by the trust), they are prohibited from **self-dealing** (making a personal profit at the expense of the trust).
c) The trustee is required to maintain accurate records and accounts of his or her management of the assets, and these accounts must be given to the beneficiary.
d) The trustee is required to take possession of the trust property and to make it profitable. It is considered a breach of fiduciary obligation if the trustee does not make the trust assets profitable.
e) The trustee must see that all debts of the trust are paid, such as fiduciary taxes (see Chapter 8), and must collect all monies or property owing to the trust.

In addition to the foregoing, as the holder of the legal title to the trust property, the trustee is obligated to preserve, protect, and defend the corpus of the trust, which is the primary attribute of holding legal title. And the trustee must fulfill the specific duties detailed in the trust instrument.

EXAMPLES:

1. Dr. Montague is made the trustee of the trust Kingston and Donna establish for the benefit of their grandchildren. As a potential investment, Dr. Montague decides to invest in real estate for the trust. Once he locates the appropriate property, he buys it for $10 per acre for himself. Dr. Montague cannot sell the property he owns to the trust for $15 per acre, making a profit on the deal. As a trustee he is required to be loyal to the trust and make investments for the benefit of the trust, not himself.

2. Rose establishes a trust for her daughter, Davida, and makes Fleur the trustee. The trust is to provide an income to support Davida until she is 25 years old, at which time she is to receive the corpus outright. At her 25th birthday, Davida discovers that Fleur has kept no records of the trust and there is no money left. Fleur is liable to Davida for breach of fiduciary obligations.

3. Dr. Montague uses a major brokerage firm to buy and sell securities for the trust for which he is the trustee. His broker embezzles the trust funds, but because the broker was a school friend of Dr. Montague, the doctor does not want to prosecute. This is a breach of trust. The embezzler owes the stolen funds to the Trust, and as trustee, Dr. Montague is obligated to recover the money.

Any individual who is capable of taking, holding, and owning property is capable of being a trustee, and this includes the trustor, who may make himself the trustee of the trust he or she establishes. Additionally, the courts require that the trustee have contractual capacity (i.e., the ability to enter into valid contracts and thereby administer the trust). A trustee can be a natural person or corporation. Municipal governments can only be trustees for charitable trusts, not for trusts that serve a private purpose of the trustor. The U.S. Government cannot be a trustee of any trust because of **sovereign immunity:** the legal inability of the government to be sued without its consent.

Most states have statutes governing who may, or may not, be a trustee or fiduciary, and as a general proposition, these follow the same guidelines as those for persons who may be appointed personal representatives of a decedent (see Chapter 9). Typically, nonresident trustees may serve, but usually they are required either to appoint a resident to serve as cotrustee or to post a bond with the court and to agree to submit to the court's juriduction. Aliens resident in the United States usually can serve, but the individual state statute must be checked.

EXAMPLES:

1. When Loretta establishes her trust with the lottery winnings, she decides to appoint Jason Leroy as the trustee. Jason has moved out of state. In order for Jason to serve, the state requires that he appoint a resident cotrustee, and he selects Aida. Now both Jason and Aida are the trustees of the trust.

2. Tom Poole uses his corporate stock to establish a scholarship for needy students. Tom appoints the city government as the trustee because his alma mater is a city-run university. In this instance, the municipality may serve as trustee because it is a charitable trust.

3. Not trusting Jason, Loretta, when told Jason cannot serve as trustee, chooses to appoint the municipal government as the trustee instead. In this case the government cannot serve because the trust was created for a private, noncharitable purpose—the support of Loretta's son, Evan.

If the trustor appoints more than one person to serve as trustee, the cotrustees are deemed to hold the property (and the obligations) as joint tenants. As indicated from the prior discussion in Chapter 2, this means that each trustee has a right of survivorship, so that if one dies or is removed, the survivor remains as the trustee, absorbing the powers and obligations of the former cotrustee.

EXAMPLE:

Loretta finally decides to have both Jason and Aida serve as cotrustees. If Jason should be killed in a car accident, Aida, as the survivor, becomes the sole trustee of the trust. On the other hand, if Aida were to die, Jason, as an out-of-state trustee, might be required to appoint a replacement for Aida.

A trustee only becomes obligated to the trust once he or she makes a positive act with respect to the trust, such as accepting title to the property or starting to administer the trust. If a person does not wish to be a trustee, the person may either make a formal resignation of the position or simply fail to act with respect to the trust. Obviously, the law favors a formal rejection over a failure to act.

EXAMPLE:

After Loretta's trust is established, one year goes by during which time Jason makes no attempt to administer the trust, and never responds to Aida's requests for action. Jason's failure to act constitutes grounds for his removal as trustee, constituting a rejection of the position.

A person who has affirmatively accepted the position of trustee is not only subject to the obligations discussed above, but is now also potentially liable to the beneficiary of the trust.

The trustee is liable to the beneficiary for any loss in value to the trust property occasioned by the trustee's mismanagement. To avoid this consequence, many trusts specify (or the trustee decides to invest the trust property in) investments that appear on the **legal list**. The legal list is a statutory list of "low risk" securities that a trustee may invest in without being charged with mismanagement. The list consists of government-backed securities and blue-chip stocks and bonds. Take note, however, that merely investing in the legal list is not enough. The trust's funds must be invested in several different securities to minimize risk, and the law imposes a duty on the trustee to make the trust funds as profitable as possible, which may require investments outside the legal list.

The trustee may also be sued by the beneficiary for damages resulting from a breach of loyalty and for the trustee's failure to recover trust funds wrongfully taken by third persons. Examples would be Dr. Montague's purchase of the real estate for his own benefit and his failure to prosecute the embezzler, discussed above. Further, the beneficiary can seek **specific performance** from the court, ordering the trustee to fulfill his trust obligation should he or she fail to act, or, conversely, seek an **injunction** to stop the trustee from engaging in a prohibited act.

EXAMPLE:

The Lears' trust requires the trustee, Dr. Montague, to use the income from the trust to pay for the education of the Lears' grandchildren. Dr. Montague does not believe Mark is bright enough to warrant spending money on school, even though Mark has been accepted by a college. Mark, as the beneficiary (see below), can go to court for specific performance to have Dr. Montague expend the money for the trust purpose—his schooling.

The beneficiaries have the right to go to court to have a trustee removed. Generally, there are eight grounds that can be the basis for an action to remove a trustee:

1. Lack of capacity. If the trustee lacks contractual capacity, the trustee will be unable to administer the trust, and therefore should be removed.

2. Breach of trust. Any time a trustee violates a fiduciary obligation it is grounds for removal.

3. Refusal to give bond when required. If the court and/or statute requires the trustee to post a bond, and he or she fails to do so, he or she may be removed. See Chapter 8.

4. Refusal to give accounts. Not only must the trustee maintain accurate accounts of the trust property, but the accounts must be given to the beneficiary. If the trustee refuses to give the accounts to the beneficiary, he or she may be removed.

5. Conviction of a crime. The trustee who commits and is convicted of a crime, either of moral turpitude that would make it appear that he or she is unsuitable to be a trustee or one that results in incarceration, can be removed.

6. Showing favoritism to one beneficiary. The trustee must treat all beneficiaries equally, according to the terms of the trust. Favoring one beneficiary gives grounds to the unfavored beneficiaries for the trustee's removal.

7. Long absence. If the trustee is away for a long period of time, making it difficult for him or her to administer the trust, the trustee can be replaced. Remember, the trustee is under a duty of personal responsibility and may not delegate his or her duties. Note, however, that because of modern technology a trustee may still be able to perform his or her duties even if he or she is absent from the state for a long period.

8. Unreasonable failure to cooperate with cotrustees. Because cotrustees are joint tenants, they must act collectively. If one of the cotrustees *unreasonably* fails to cooperate, it is impossible for the trust to be administered. Take careful note of the fact that the unwillingness to cooperate must be *unreasonable*; if the trustee is not cooperating because he does not believe the proposed actions are in the best interests of the trust, grounds for removal may not be present.

EXAMPLES:

1. Aida, several years after the trust is created, becomes senile and incapable of caring for herself. She can, and should, be removed as a trustee for lack of capacity.
2. Prior to the termination date of the trust, Davida realizes that Fleur has not been keeping adequate records of the trust funds. Davida can go to court to have Fleur removed as trustee for breach of fiduciary obligation.
3. The court requires Jason, in addition to appointing a resident cotrustee, to post a bond to assure the faithful performance of his duties. Jason doesn't put up the money, and therefore can be removed as trustee.
4. Dr. Montague does keep accounts of his trust, but he refuses to let Mark, one of the beneficiaries, have access to the records. Mark has grounds to have Dr. Montague removed as trustee.
5. Jason is involved in a hit-and-run accident, killing a small child. After trial, Jason is put in jail. Jason cannot fulfill his function as trustee from the prison, and consequently, can be removed as trustee.
6. Although Dr. Montague refuses to pay Mark's college tuition, he is using the trust income to pay for the education of his son, Anthony, and Mark's brother, Matthew. Because Dr. Montague

is favoring some beneficiaries over another, Mark, the disfavored beneficiary, can sue to have Dr. Montague removed as trustee.

7. Aida sells her spaghetti sauce recipe to a major food manufacturer for a substantial sum of money. As a treat, she books a trip around the world on a luxury liner. The trip will last one year. Because she will be away for a long period of time, she can be removed as trustee because she will be unable to manage the trust funds during the period of her absence.
8. Despite repeated requests from Aida, Jason fails to respond or participate in any trust activity, stalemating investments. Jason can be removed for failing to cooperate, unreasonably, with his cotrustee, Aida.

In addition to his or her liability to the beneficiary, the trustee is personally liable for any personal negligence that results in injury to third persons.

EXAMPLE:

Part of the corpus of the Lears' trust is a small apartment building. Dr. Montague, as trustee, fails to maintain the building, and a tenant is injured by falling plaster. Dr. Montague is personally liable because his negligence caused the injury.

Because trustees are subject to stringent obligations and responsibilities, it behooves the trustor to choose a trustee very carefully, and a potential trustee should be extremely confident of his ability to fulfill the fiduciary obligations before accepting the position.

A Beneficiary

Every valid trust must have a beneficiary or **cestui que trust** who is clearly identified, specifically by name or by class. Any person who is capable of taking title to property may be a beneficiary. Unlike the trustee, the beneficiary does not need to possess contractual capacity.

If the trust names more than one person as beneficiary, the beneficiaries are considered to hold the property as tenants in common, meaning that each one has a divisible, separate interest in the trust property. Note the difference between being cotrustees (joint tenants) and cobeneficiaries (tenants in common). When the beneficiaries are identified by class, and that class can be added to, each beneficiary's interest as a tenant in common may be reduced, or **divested** by the addition of other beneficiaries to that class.

Unless prohibited by the trust or by statute, a beneficiary may freely alienate his or her interest in the trust. This means that the beneficiary's interest may be given away or sold, or be subject to the claims of his creditors. The situations in which a beneficiary is incapable of alienating his interest will be discussed below.

EXAMPLES:

1. When Loretta creates the trust, she is doing so for the benefit of her son, Evan. Evan is the beneficiary. Even though Evan is a minor lacking contractual capacity, he is capable of owning property, and therefore may be the beneficiary of a trust.
2. The trust established by the Lears was created for the benefit of their grandchildren. Currently they have five grandchildren — Matthew, Mark, Mary, Margaret, and Anthony — and each grandchild is a tenant in common entitled to one-fifth of the trust income. The term "grandchildren" used in the trust is an example of a beneficiary designated by class — an identifiable group.
3. The Lears' trust indicates it is for the benefit of their grandchildren. At present there are five people in this group, but if Grace has a child, that child, as a grandchild, is also entitled to benefit from the trust, and the five portions are now divided into six.
4. The trust created by Loretta is to be used to help support Evan until he attains the age of 25. On his 21st birthday Evan buys a car, but cannot meet the car loan payments. The bank may attach Evan's interest in the trust.

The trust instrument itself may not only identify the beneficiaries of the income generated by the trust, it may also indicate a point in time when the trust will terminate, and who will receive what remains in the trust corpus at that termination date. This person, who receives the corpus of the trust upon termination, is also a beneficiary, but his interest, and enjoyment, is postponed. Legally, this person is referred to as the **remainderman**, meaning he or she receives the remains of the corpus when the trust ends. If the remainderman happens to be the trustor, this remaining interest is referred to as a **reversion**, or **reversionary interest**, meaning that the corpus reverts to the trustor (the original title-holder).

EXAMPLE:

In Loretta's trust she states that the trust is to provide support for Evan until he attains the age of 25, at which point whatever is left in the trust is to be given outright to Loretta and Evan in equal portions. In this scenario, Evan is not only the beneficiary for the income of the trust, he is also the remainderman for 50 percent of the corpus, and Loretta is the trustor with a reversionary interest in the other 50 percent of the remaining corpus.

The beneficiary has the **equitable** or **beneficial title** to the trust property, giving him or her the right to enjoy the trust property subject to any limitations imposed by the trustor ("for his education only"). It is not a free and total enjoyment of the corpus.

EXAMPLE:

Under the terms of his mother's trust, Evan only has the right to the income of the trust to be used for his support. Evan cannot get his hands on the bulk of the assets because his enjoyment is limited to income only during the term of the trust.

To recap, in order for there to be a valid and enforceable trust, there must be a trustor who holds a transferable interest in property that is capable of being transferred, who, by written instrument, transfers title to a trust, giving named trustees the legal title to the property (to preserve, protect, and defend the trust corpus) along with specified duties to perform for the benefit of named beneficiaries, who have the equitable title (enjoyment of the corpus) subject to limitations imposed by the trustor. A typical example of a trust would be as follows:

A mother has two children: a daughter, who is 11, and a son, who is 10. The mother goes to her bank's trust department and deposits $500,000 with the bank, subject to a written trust agreement provided by the bank. Under the agreement, the bank is named as trustee and is given the obligation to invest the money to produce an income to pay for the educational expenses of the children. If in any one year the income is greater than the educational expenses, the excess is to be added to the corpus; if the income is insufficient to meet the educational expenses, the trustees are authorized to **invade the corpus** (use the trust funds) to meet the expenses. When the youngest child shall attain the age of 25, the trust is to terminate. At the termination, each child is to receive $100,000 outright, the American Cancer Society is to receive $100,000, and, if there is anything left over, the remainder of the corpus goes back to the mother.

Under this situation, the trust can be broken down as follows:

Trustor:	Mother, with a transferable interest in $500,000
Trust purpose:	to provide for the educational expenses of the children
Trust property:	$500,000
Trustee:	the bank, a corporate trustee

Trust duties:	To invest the money, produce an income, and expend the income on the children's education. Trustee also has discretion to invade the corpus if the income is insufficient to meet the expenses.
Beneficiary:	son and daughter, income beneficiaries for educational expenses only
Beneficial enjoyment:	educational expenses
Termination:	in 15 years when son reaches 25
Remainderman:	Son: $100,000 Daughter: $100,000 American Cancer Society (charitable remainderman): $100,000
Reversionary interest:	mother, for whatever is left

This trust may be considered a **discretionary trust**, also called a **sprinkling** or **spray trust**, because the trustee has the discretion to allocate the income among the beneficiaries; the trust does not specify that each beneficiary receives an equal share. These types of discretionary trusts may give rise to actions against the trustee based on favoritism mentioned above.

Types of Trusts

Now that the general requirements for creating a trust have been discussed, it is time to classify different types of trusts. There are slight differences in the general requirements detailed above depending upon the nature of the trust created. Generally, trusts can be considered to fall into three broad categories: (1) express trusts, (2) implied trusts, and (3) special situation trusts.

Express Trusts

An express trust is any trust that is created by the deliberate and voluntary actions of the trustor, evidenced by a written document. As already mentioned, a trust may be formed for any valid purpose. An express trust is classified according to the purpose for which it was created. A **private trust** is any trust established to serve the personal interests of the trustor. As indicated above, such private purposes usually are for the support of family members.

Conversely, a **public** or **charitable trust** is designed not to benefit private individuals, but to benefit the public at large under the broad concept of charity. The requirements to create a valid public trust are precisely the same requirements necessary for creating a private trust, but, in addition, the law imposes certain other requirements. First, the trustor must specifically indicate an intention to create a public trust, that is, a charitable purpose must be specified in the creating document. Second, the public must benefit from the operation of the trust, not just certain private individuals. And third, the beneficiaries must be an indefinite class. An **indefinite class** is a group that does not contain specifically identified individuals, but rather is composed of a broad spectrum of persons who meet the description of the class.

EXAMPLES:

1. When Loretta won the lottery and created her trust, her purpose was to provide for the support and education of her son. This furthers a private purpose of the trustor.
2. Kingston and Donna are placing their assets into trust to serve two distinct purposes: (1) they want to assure that their grandchildren will have an income that can provide for their educations, and (2) they want to try to keep their assets out of the hands of Regina and her husband. By placing assets in trust, and designating a specific purpose to benefit their grandchildren, the Lears have established a valid private trust.
3. When Tom created a trust to provide scholarships for needy students at his alma mater, he created a valid public trust. His specified purpose was to provide scholarships (an educational purpose generally considered charitable) and the beneficiaries were an indefinite class described as students at the university who demonstrate financial need. Any student meeting the financial criteria of the trust would be considered a beneficiary, and consequently the class of beneficiaries is indefinite because the beneficiaries are not limited to specific persons.

As stated above, a municipality may be the trustee of a public trust but is precluded from being the trustee of a private trust. Additionally, unlike private trusts, which are required to terminate at a specified time (see below), public trusts are permitted to exist indefinitely.

As a special subset of charitable trusts, there are **charitable remainder annuity trusts** in which the income goes to a private person and the remainder goes to the charity, and **charitable remainder unitrusts**, in which the private person receives a percentage of the income (required to be at least five percent), with the remainder of the income going to a charity. These types of trusts are hybrids, serving both public and private purposes.

EXAMPLE:

Donna establishes a trust with an insurance company as trustee in which her daughter, Grace, receives an income for life, and upon Grace's death the corpus is distributed outright to the city museum. This is an example of a charitable remainder annuity trust.

One consequence of the perpetual existence of public trusts is that the charitable purpose for which the trust was created may cease to exist. For example, if a trust is established to provide money for research to find a cure for AIDS, the purpose for which the trust was created would terminate once a cure was found. What happens to the trust at that point?

Rather than return the trust corpus to the trustor or his heirs, the courts have decided that, provided a valid public purpose has been stated in the trust instrument, the trust will continue as a public trust, providing benefits for a purpose as near as possible to the original purpose specified by the trustor. This doctrine is known as **cy pres**, meaning "as near as possible." Therefore, in the situation just posited, if a cure for AIDS was found, the court might decide that the trust would continue to provide money to research a cure for cancer, a charitable purpose close to the original purpose of the trust. The doctrine of cy pres can only be applied if a general charitable purpose is stated by the trustor, and the court will determine the successor public beneficiary of the trust if the trustor has not given that responsibility to the trustee.

EXAMPLE:

Ken Poole is an avid runner, and he creates a trust to maintain a running path in his favorite city park, with the city as the trustee. Several years after the creation of the trust, the discovery of underground toxic waste forces the city to close the park and rezone its use. Rather than terminate the trust, the city continues Ken's trust to maintain a different running path. The general public purpose of the trust was to provide recreational running paths for the public, and the general purpose can still be accomplished even though the specific purpose no longer exists.

Remember, the doctrine of cy pres is only applicable to public trusts; it can never be applied to a private trust.

Implied Trusts

An implied trust comes about not by the deliberate and voluntary action of a trustor, but by **operation of law**. Operation of law means that a specific action is automatically given a legal consequence by the law rather than by the desire or action of the parties themselves. Implied trusts are imposed because of the presumed intent of the parties.

There are two categories of implied trusts: resulting trusts and constructive trusts. A **resulting trust** comes about because of the perceived or inferred intent of a property owner. With a resulting trust, the law assumes that the parties in question are holding the property in trust for someone else, even though there is no specific declaration to that effect.

There are three generally recognized resulting trusts. In a **purchase money resulting trust**, the law presumes that the person who actually pays for the property owns the property, and that anyone who happens to have possession of the property is holding the property "in trust" for the owner. The second type of resulting trust is a **failed trust**. This trust is one that cannot, for any reason, be enforced. In this situation, the trustee is deemed to be holding the corpus in trust for the trustor, to whom the property is eventually returned.

The last category of resulting trusts is the **overendowed trust**. An overendowed trust is one in which the income is greater than is necessary to accomplish the trust purpose. If the trustor did not specify what is to be done with the excess income (as was done in the trust example discussed above with the mother with two children to educate), the law presumes the trustee is holding the excess income in trust for the settlor until the settlor claims it. As can be seen, the rationale of the resulting trust is that property is always held for the true owner.

EXAMPLES:

1. Grace, living overseas, sends Donna some money to buy electronic equipment for her that she cannot find abroad. Grace asks Donna to hold the items until she can send for them. Even though the equipment is in Donna's possession, it belongs to Grace, who paid for it. Donna is considered to be the trustee of the equipment, holding it for Grace's benefit.
2. When Loretta creates her trust, she inadvertently neglects to specify the purpose for creating the trust. Because one of the requisite elements of a valid trust is missing, the trust cannot be enforced and has "failed." If Loretta does not correct the error, the trustee is considered to be holding the corpus in trust for Loretta, the settlor.
3. Loretta cures the defect of her trust by stating that its purpose is to provide for the support of Evan until he attains the age of 25. Unfortunately, Evan is killed by a hit-and-run driver two years later. Because there is no longer a beneficiary, the trust cannot be enforced, and fails. Once again, the property is being held in trust for Loretta until she claims the funds.

The other kind of implied trust, the **constructive trust**, is a trust created by the courts of equity to right a wrong. Whenever anyone acquires title to property unlawfully or unfairly, he is deemed to be holding the ill-gotten gains in trust for the true owner. The concept is a legal fiction used to maintain title to the property in the true owner.

EXAMPLES:

1. Fleur arrives home one evening to discover that her apartment has been burgled. If the police ever find the criminal, the burglar is presumed to be holding Fleur's property in constructive trust for Fleur. Fleur is the true owner, and the burglar never acquired legal title to the property.
2. Dr. Montague is finally persuaded to prosecute the stock broker who embezzled the trust funds. Once again, because the broker acquired the funds illegally, he is considered to be holding the funds in constructive trust for the trust.

Special Situation Trusts

This category of trusts is a catch-all used to include various types of trust situations.

Spendthrift Trusts

A **spendthrift trust** is a private trust in which the trustor specifies that the beneficiary's interest in the trust may not be attached by creditors. This is usually done in situations in which trustor is afraid that the beneficiary will squander his or her interest away. Although declaring a trust to be "spendthrift" means the beneficiary will receive the income interest, it does not preclude the beneficiary's creditors from ever attaching the property. Once the money is in the hands of the beneficiary, the creditors can attach it. Sometimes, to protect the beneficiary, the trust will indicate that the income may only be expended to pay the beneficiary's rent, utilities, and so forth, so that the trustor can be assured that the beneficiary will be housed; in this instance the beneficiary never actually handles the income.

EXAMPLE:

Fern and Barney want to establish a trust for Rose, but are afraid that Rose, a compulsive shopper, will run through the income before she ever receives it. Therefore, Fern and Barney stipulate that the trust is a spendthrift trust, with the income to be used to pay Rose's rent and food bills. This will protect Rose from herself and guarantee her maintenance.

Short-Term Trusts

Short-term, or **Clifford**, trusts are trusts that are created for a short period of time. People create short-term trusts for various reasons: to establish a child in business, to provide annual charitable gifts for a period of time, to provide college tuition payments, and so forth. Provided that the trust meets all of the requirements of every other trust, the time element does not effect the trust's validity. However, and most importantly, under the federal tax laws, reversionary trusts, are subject to negative tax consequences, as will be discussed later in this chapter in the section on tax considerations. Be aware, though, that if the time frame indicated in the trust is indefinite, such as for a person's life, it is not subject to the tax consequences of a short-term trust. The reason is that the duration of the trust in these circumstance is indefinite and could have continued beyond ten years and a day. The tax laws for short-term trusts only operate when the limited time period is definite.

EXAMPLES:

1. Hyacinth establishes a small trust to provide some income for her elderly father for his life. Even though David dies three years after the trust is created, it is not considered a short-term trust because it was established for an indefinite period — David's life.

2. Donna is very active on the board of her city's museum, and she always gives the museum large yearly donations. Rather than having to remember to write out a check, Donna creates a small trust to make payments to the museum for the next five years. This is a short-term trust, subject to the federal tax consequences mentioned before. Even though this trust lasts longer that the one created by Hyacinth in the preceding example, Donna's trust has a specified, finite duration of only five years, whereas Hyacinth's was for the indefinite period of David's life.

Supplemental Needs Trusts

Trusts may be established, not to provide general income to a beneficiary or to provide for fixed expenditures, but to provide for "supplemental needs," that is, medical expenses above what is reimbursed or paid for by insurance and health care programs. These trusts provide funds for extraordinary expenses that may be incurred by the beneficiary, but do not provide regular income distributions if no such extraordinary need exists.

Totten Trusts

Totten trusts are bank accounts people open in their own names "in trust" for someone else. These are not true trusts, because there is no trust purpose, no trustee, no immediate beneficiary, and the creator has total control over the funds. On the account holder's death, the funds remaining in the account pass to the person named on the account as the beneficiary. Remember, these are not true trusts, and the funds may be subject to the claims of the creditors of the person who opened the account.

EXAMPLE:

Aida opens a small savings account, saying that the account is in trust for her grandson, Evan. Aida has total control over the account, and may add to or withdraw from the account at will. This is a Totten trust.

Marital Deduction Trusts

A marital deduction is a tax advantage permitted to legally married couples in which any property left to a surviving spouse may pass tax free as a marital deduction (Chapters 1, 5, and 8). This tax benefit applies not only to outright gifts to the surviving spouse, but may also be accomplished by the creation of several different types of trusts. The benefit to creating a trust that qualifies as a marital deduction is that the spouse receives the benefit of the income, but the decedent can be certain the property will remain intact and can be passed on to other persons after the death of the surviving spouse. In all these situations the surviving spouse must have a life interest in the trust.

A **Qualified Terminable Interest Property (QTIP) Trust** is a federal tax provision in which a trust may be created by will for a surviving spouse, giving the spouse a life interest in all of the income of the trust. On the survivor's death, the property will pass to other persons indicated in the trust. Not only must the trust meet the general requirements of trust law, it must also meet the specific requirements of 2056(b)(7) of the Internal Revenue Code.

An **A-B Trust**, or **credit shelter trust**, comes about when the testator creates two separate trusts. The surviving spouse has a life interest in the income from the first trust, and at death, the corpus passes to the second trust. The second trust also gives the spouse a life interest, but at death, this second trust continues and provides benefits to other beneficiaries. What is the purpose of this double trust? Depending upon the size of the estate, it may be possible to have the entire estate pass tax-free to persons other than the surviving spouse. For example, if the decedent's estate is valued at $1 million in year 2001, $675,000 can go tax-free to anyone, and the marital deduction is unlimited (Chapter 1). By having two trusts, each worth 500,000, one would qualify for the marital deduction, and the other would be under the taxable minimum. When the spouse dies, the $500,000 in the first trust is also under the taxable minimum, so that the entire estate may pass tax-free to other persons, such as grandchildren. If only one trust had been created, originally there would be no taxes because the property would pass as a marital deduction, but on the spouse's death the estate would be taxed—in this instance, on the amount over the tax-free limit. The A-B trusts avoid this consequence. Note that the use of a credit shelter trust is not limited to marital deductions, but may be used in many circumstances to minimize taxes.

Additionally, the decedent may leave the surviving spouse a life estate in the property with a power of appointment to select among named successor beneficiaries on the spouse's death. In this instance, the marital deduction still applies, but the surviving spouse must pass the property to specified persons on death—it is not automatic.

Life Insurance Trusts

In a life insurance trust, the insured specifies the beneficiary of the policy to be a trust that is already in existence, created by a separate document. The policy does not create the trust, but the proceeds add to the corpus of an existing trust.

A life insurance trust is an example of a **pour-over trust** in which a testator, in his will, leaves property to a trust that had been created while he was alive. This testamentary gift "pours over" into the existing trust, adding to its corpus.

A life insurance policy may also be used to fund an inter vivos trust, even though at the time of creation the funds are a future right. When the insured dies the insurer pays the funds into the trust. This is an exception to the general rule that a trust must be funded with existing property when it is created.

EXAMPLE:

When Loretta takes out a life insurance policy, she names as the beneficiary a trust she has already created at her bank for Evan's benefit. This is a pour-over life insurance trust.

All trusts will fall into one of the preceding categories.

Creation of the Trust

To be enforceable, a trust must be created by a written document. Although there is an exception for trusts of personal property for extremely short durations (mere possession of the property creates the trust), for the purposes of estate law, a writing will be necessary. Trusts are categorized by the type of writing that creates the trust.

Inter Vivos Trusts

Inter vivos trusts, or living trusts, are created and take effect during the lifetime of the trustor. A trustor establishes the trust by having a **declaration of trust**, or a **trust instrument** prepared that details all of the trust requirements discussed above. Simple trust instruments are sufficient for creating a trust of personal property. If the corpus of the trust is real estate, the trust must be created by a **deed** or **conveyance of trust** that is filed in the county recorder's office in the county in which the land is located. An example of a written trust instrument appears below in the section on drafting trusts.

EXAMPLES:

1. When Loretta goes to her bank to create a trust with her lottery winnings, the bank's trust department had a Declaration of Trust form already prepared. Loretta merely gives the bank the details of the trustee's duties and the names of the beneficiary and remaindermen. Once the declaration is signed and the money conveyed, the trust is created.
2. When the doctors decide to create the real estate investment trust, they have a trust instrument drawn up specifying the details of the trust, and then execute a Deed of Trust in order to give legal title to their trustee. The deed of trust is recorded in the county where the shopping center is located.

No specific words are necessary to create a trust, provided that the intention to create a trust is clear on the face of the document. Many law form books provide sample trust instruments, and several states, such as California, have **statutory trusts** (trusts that are created by following a form detailed in the state's code itself).

An inter vivos trust may be either **revocable** or **irrevocable**. A revocable trust is one in which the trustor retains the ability to terminate the trust, whereas with an irrevocable trust the trustor has relinquished the right to end the trust, and the trust terminates by its own provisions.

EXAMPLE:

Leonard Doger, Regina's husband, creates a trust for the benefit of his daughters, Mary and Margaret. Leonard retains the power to revoke the trust. If the girls displease Leonard, he has the power to cut off their trust income by revoking the trust.

Testamentary Trusts

As the name would indicate, a testamentary trust is created under the terms of the last will and testament of a testator. Many testators create trusts in their wills in order to provide income gifts to beneficiaries over several generations, or to establish a charitable fund. Also, as previously mentioned, a trust may be used for the purpose of providing a marital deduction for a surviving spouse, while still guaranteeing other persons will receive the assets at the death of the spouse. All of the requirements to create a trust still apply to testamentary trusts; the only difference is that the writing creating the trust is a will rather than a simple trust instrument, and the will must meet all of the requirements established for wills. The words used to create the trust are identical to inter vivos trusts.

EXAMPLE:

In his will, David Laplante creates a trust of his assets for the purpose of providing an income to Fern for life, then to Rose for life after Fern's death, and finally to have the assets go outright to Rose's children who survive her. This is an example of a testamentary trust because David created the trust by his will; had he made the exact same provisions by a declaration of trust while alive it would be an inter vivos trust.

Remember, a trust can be created separate from, or as part of, a will, depending upon the needs of the client. Note the concept of pour-over trusts discussed above.

Restrictions on Trusts

In order to understand the restrictions that are placed on trusts it is important to be conversant with some of the legal history of trusts.

Statute of Uses

Although trusts existed thousands of years ago under Roman civil law, the modern interpretation of trusts dates from the feudal period in England. The feudal form of a trust was called a **use**. The lord could place title in the land in the use for the benefit of himself, his son, his grandson, and so on. Uses were regulated by a law called the **Statute of Uses**, which declared that no use was valid unless it imposed active duties on the trustee. This meant that the trustee could not merely be a caretaker, but must have fiduciary obligations to fulfill as well. Passive uses were deemed void. Consequently, title could be held up only as long as the trustee had active functions to perform.

Modern law still requires that a valid and enforceable trust impose active duties on the trustee. When the trust is created, in specifying the trust purposes, the trustor must also indicate the duties of the trustee.

EXAMPLE:

In the trust created by Kingston and Donna for their grandchildren, they impose the duty on Dr. Montague, as trustee, to make the trust property productive, and to use the income to pay for the education of their grandchildren. This is an active trust.

Rule Against Perpetuities

To avoid tying up title to property indefinitely, a corollary to trust law was enacted. The **Rule Against Perpetuities** states that all interests must vest, if at all, within 21 years after the death of the lives in being, plus the period of gestation. If all interests do not vest within this time period, the entire trust is deemed invalid and fails.

What does this mean? *Vesting* means having an enforceable right; "all interests" means all current and future beneficiaries. Thus all current and future beneficiaries must have a legally enforceable right in the trust within the stated period of time or the trust fails.

The measuring stick for the requisite period is a life in being. Any person living and named in the instrument creating the trust is a life in being, and all potential or future interests must vest within 21 years after the death of the last living life in being (plus the period of gestation). The interests that must vest are those of the beneficiaries who are not yet alive when the trust is created; if they were alive they would be lives in being. Therefore, what the Rule is concerned with is the rights of the future, or "after-born," generation of beneficiaries.

The Rule applies whenever any interest, in theory, may not vest within the period; the actual facts of the particular people involved are irrelevant. For practical purposes, the Rule will come into play whenever a trustor names as beneficiaries a class rather than specific persons, and that class is capable of being added to after the trust comes into existence.

EXAMPLES:

1. David creates an inter vivos trust in which the income from the corpus goes to his children for life, then to his grandchildren for life, then outright to his great-grandchildren at

his grandchildren's deaths. This trust violates the Rule Against Perpetuities.

At the time the trust is created, David has three daughters, two grandchildren, and a great-granddaughter. However, Fleur is not yet married. What if Fleur has a child one year after the trust is created? Her child is David's grandchild, but is not a life in being, having been born after the trust was established. Assume all of the family is killed in a car accident, except for Fleur's child. Under the trust, this grandchild is entitled to the income for life, after which the corpus goes to any of David's great-grandchildren then living. If Fern's child lives for seventy years, his child, the great-grandchild, would not have a vested interest until after the period specified by the Rule. Fleur's child is after born, not a life in being, and his child's interest will not vest until after his death, which could easily be more than 21 years after the deaths of the lives in being.

In addition, David could still have another child after creating the trust. This child is also not a life in being, but its grandchild has rights that also may not vest until well after the statutory period.

2. In the same situation as above, David's trust now states that income is to go to Hyacinth, Fern, and Fleur for life, then to Byron and Rose for life, then to Davida. In this instance the Rule has not been violated. Every person is a life in being, and there can be no later-born beneficiaries because the beneficiaries are named individually and not by class.

The facts of the situation are not as important as the theoretical aspect. Under the law, an 80-year-old woman is deemed capable of bearing children, even though medically this is extremely unlikely. (This is known as the **Doctrine of the Fertile Octogenarian**.) The Rule Against Perpetuities is extremely complex, and even lawyers have trouble understanding and applying it. For practical purposes, the following guidelines should be kept in mind:

1. Whenever a trust mentions "grandchildren" by class rather than by specific name, the Rule may be violated.
2. Whenever the trust delays an interest until someone attains an age greater than 21 years, the Rule may be violated unless that person is named and alive at the date of the creation of the trust.
3. Whenever any class may be added to, however unlikely that may rationally appear, the Rule may be violated.

To avoid problems, when drafting a trust limit beneficiaries to no more than two generations removed from the trustor, and only impose age restrictions on persons alive at the date of the creation of the trust or to age 21. Take note that many jurisdictions have enacted special provisions called **salvage doctrines** that avoid these common law problems that violated the rule. These doctrines help preserve trusts. Each state's statute must be individually scrutinized.

The two preceding restrictions have a historical basis for trusts; there are other restrictions of more modern provenance.

Investments and Roles of the Parties

Because of the fiduciary obligations imposed on the trustee to make the corpus productive, and the personal liability of the trustee for diminution of the corpus, most states have enacted a *legal list of investments*, such as blue chip stock and government securities, that can be invested in by the trustee so as to avoid potential liability. These investments are considered extremely secure, and provided the trustee does not overinvest in just one security, he or she can avoid liability by adhering to the list. The trustor can specify that investments be limited to the legal list or can specify any other investment desired. If the trust instrument does not limit the potential investments for the trustee, the trustee is generally considered to have discretion in deciding the appropriate investments.

Although parties to a trust may play many roles, there is a prohibition against the trustee and the beneficiary being the same person. The purpose of the trust is to divide title to property into its legal and equitable components and give those component titles to different people. If the same person has both titles, by definition, there is no trust. There is an exception if there is more than one trustee (one of the trustees may also be a beneficiary), but in no event may all of the trustees and beneficiaries be the same persons. To be valid, at least one other person must have an interest in the trust, even if it is only future or remainder interest.

Aside from that limitation, the trustor may be the trustee, or the beneficiary, as well.

EXAMPLES:

1. In order to safeguard their assets from Regina's clutches, Donna and Kingston place all of their assets in trust and appoint a trust company as trustee. The trust makes them the beneficiaries for life, then gives the assets outright to their grandchildren then living. This is valid because Donna and Kingston are the trustors and beneficiaries; the trustee is a separate individual.
2. Loretta, instead of having the bank's trust department act as trustee of the trust she creates, makes herself the trustee for the trust she establishes for Evan's benefit. Loretta is both the trustor and the trustee, and the trust is valid.

Restrictions on Trust Purpose

Finally, there are certain restrictions placed on the purpose for which the trust is created. Certain purposes are considered contrary to public policy and invalidate the trust.

1. Trusts based on an illegal agreement. If the purpose for which the trust is created is illegal, the trust itself will be unenforceable.

2. Trusts in restraint of marriage. If the purpose of the trust is to induce someone not to marry, the trust is unenforceable. Take note that not every trust concerning marriage is invalid. If the purpose of the trust is to induce the beneficiary to marry a particular person, to marry within a particular religion, or to postpone marriage until attaining one's majority, the trust will be enforced.

3. Trusts used to induce religious conversion. If the purpose of the trust is to induce the beneficiary to convert to a different religion, the trust is invalid as contrary to public policy.

4. Trusts that exclude beneficiaries who have contact with specific family members. Some families are involved in internecine battles and some trustors want to keep other family members away from the persons with whom they are feuding. The law deems it contrary to public policy to create a trust that punishes beneficiaries for having family contact, because such provisions promote family disunity.

5. Trusts used to defraud creditors. A person is precluded from placing his property in trust so that his creditors cannot attach his assets. This acts as a fraud on creditors, and therefore is against public policy (as well as many state laws).

EXAMPLES:

1. Being totally disgusted with Regina and her husband, the Lears contemplate finding a hit man to do away with them. The Lears plan to pay the hit man by setting up a trust in his favor. This trust would be invalid because it is based on an illegal agreement.

2. The Lears discover that Grace has become infatuated with a fortune hunter and plans to marry him. The Lears approach the man and tell him they will make him the beneficiary of a trust that will provide him with an income as long as he does not marry Grace. This trust would be unenforceable.

3. Aida, having made money on the sale of her spaghetti sauce recipe, approaches Jason and tells him she will set up a trust in his favor if he marries Loretta and "makes an honest woman of her." If Jason (and Loretta) agree, this would be a valid trust because it promotes, doesn't restrain, marriage.

4. Before her marriage, Rose converted to her future husband's religion, and she is now raising Davida according to its tenets. David wants his granddaughter to practice his religion, and creates a trust to which Rose and Davida will be the beneficiaries if they convert back to David's religion. This trust is unenforceable.

5. Because of all the trouble they are having with Regina and her husband, the Lears state in their trust that any grandchild who has contact with Regina or Leonard will lose his or her interest in the trust. This trust is unenforceable, even though Regina may in fact be despicable.

6. After winning the lottery, Loretta goes on a wild spending spree and is now aware that she won't have any money left if she pays her bills. She creates a spendthrift trust with herself as beneficiary in order to retain her winnings. This trust is invalid because it is an attempt to defraud her creditors.

In summary, there are five major categories of restrictions placed on the creation of a valid and enforceable trust. These restrictions are:

1. The trust must be active, imposing active duties on the trustee.
2. The trust cannot violate the Rule Against Perpetuities by existing for an unreasonably long time.
3. The trustor can specify investments for the trustee that may involve reference to the legal list for safety's sake.
4. All the trustees and beneficiaries cannot be the same person(s).
5. The purpose for which the trust is created cannot be illegal or contrary to public policy.

Termination of Trusts

Private trusts are prohibited from existing in perpetuity. At some point in time the trust must terminate, at most within the period of time permitted by the Rule Against Perpetuities. Generally, all private trusts terminate in one of six ways:

1. A trust will terminate by completing its purpose. Every valid trust must state a purpose for which it is created. Once that objective has been accomplished, the trust terminates because there is no further reason for its continuance.
2. A trust will terminate if its purpose is illegal or impossible to attain. The law will not countenance a trust formed for an illegal purpose. If it is determined that the objective of the trust violates laws or public policy, the trust terminates.

Additionally, if the purpose for which the trust was established becomes impossible to attain, the trust is considered terminated and the corpus is either held by the trustee in an implied trust for the trustor or is distributed to the named remainderman.

3. A trust will terminate in accordance with its own terms. The trust instrument itself may establish a particular point in time at which the trust terminates. This would be true even if the purpose for which the trust was established still exists.
4. A trust will terminate if it is revoked by the trustor. A trustor, when creating the trust, may retain, for himself the right to revoke the trust. This provision is perfectly valid, although it may engender some negative tax consequences (as will be discussed in the following section). If the trustor did retain the power to revoke, exercising that power terminates the trust.
5. A trust will terminate when the legal and equitable titles merge in the same person. As discussed above, the purpose of a trust is to divide title to property into its component parts of legal and equitable titles, and to give those titles to two separate persons. Consequently, if the same person holds both the legal and equitable titles, by definition there no longer is a trust.
6. A trust can terminate at the request of the beneficiaries. In certain circumstances, if *all* of the beneficiaries agree, a trust may be terminated and the proceeds distributed to the remainderman. However, take careful note that *all* of the beneficiaries must agree. If there are presumptive beneficiaries not yet in existence, their interests must be represented by a guardian ad litem, and if any beneficiary is unwilling to terminate the trust, the trust will continue.

EXAMPLES:

1. Hyacinth establishes a trust to provide an income to her father for life, then the corpus is to be given outright to Byron. When David dies, the trust terminates, and the trust property is given to Byron as the remainderman.

2. Grace is approached by a foreign terrorist group and asked to help them gain entrance to the U.S. embassy, for which a trust has been set up for Grace's benefit. The trust is invalid because the objective of the trust is illegal. The corpus is held in an implied trust for the trustor.

3. Loretta establishes a trust in her will to provide an income to support Evan until he reaches the age of 25, at which time the corpus is to be divided equally between Evan and Aida. Evan dies in a car accident at age 16; it is impossible to provide support for him for the next nine years. Accordingly, the trust is terminated and all of the proceeds go outright to Aida as the surviving remainderman.

4. In the trust Donna established for the city museum, Donna stated that the trust would continue to make payments to the museum for ten years and one day, at which time the trust would terminate and the corpus would revert to Donna or her heirs. In this instance the trust itself indicates a termination date even though the museum could still need the money after that date.
5. Feeling a little guilty about Regina, the Lears decide to create a small spendthrift trust for her benefit, in case her husband stops supporting her. However, because of the strained relations, the Lears retain a power to revoke the trust. Regina and her husband go to court to sue the Lears, and the Lears revoke the trust.
6. David creates a small trust to provide an income to his unmarried daughter, Fleur. In the trust instrument, David makes himself and Fleur cotrustees, with Fleur as the sole beneficiary. Because there is a cotrustee, the fact that Fleur is both trustee and beneficiary does not invalidate the trust. However, David dies suddenly, and there is no provision for the appointment of a successor cotrustee. In this situation, Fleur is the only trustee and beneficiary, and so the legal and equitable titles have merged in one person, Fleur, and the trust is terminated.
7. In their wills, the Lears establish a trust to provide an income to their children for life, then their grandchildren until the youngest attains the age of 21, at which time the corpus is to be divided equally to their issue then living. Because this is a testamentary trust, all of the Lear children are in existence when the trust is created, but the class of grandchildren can be added to if Regina, Grace, or Cornelia have more children, and the Lears' further issue are as yet undetermined. In order to terminate this trust, all of the living children and grandchildren must agree, and also get the approval of a guardian ad litem to represent the interests of the unborn grandchildren and issue.

   Query: Why was the trust set up in this fashion?

Once a trust is terminated, its corpus is either distributed to the remainderman named in the trust, or reverts back to the trustor or the trustor's heirs.

Tax Considerations

General

A trust is considered to be a legal entity, and consequently it is responsible for paying income taxes on the income it generates that is not disbursed to trustees or beneficiaries. A trust's income is federally taxed at the highest possible individual income tax rates (see Chapter 8) and files its own returns, known as **fiduciary returns**. However, not all of a trust's income is taxable to the trust. Trustees are permitted to receive a fee for the performance of their duties, and the fee is deductible as an expense from the trust's gross income. The trustee is individually responsible for paying income taxes on the fees received for the management of the trust.

The beneficiary, like the trustee, may be liable for income taxes that might be due on distribution, depending upon the individual income tax situation of the beneficiary (some distributions may be considered tax free gifts to the beneficiary) and the nature of the trust.

The difference between the income generated and the income disbursed represents the trust's taxable income.

EXAMPLES:

In the trust established by the Lears for the benefit of their grandchildren, the gross income from the trust for the year is $100,000. Dr. Montague, as trustee, receives a fee of $5,000; the trust distributes $80,000 to the grandchildren for the purpose of paying their educational expenses. In this tax year, the trust has taxable income of $15,000, Dr. Montague has earned income from the trust of $5,000, and there may be a gift or income tax due on the distributions to the grandchildren.

Short-Term Trusts

Short-term trusts, or Clifford trusts, are not necessarily taxed in the same manner as a general trust. Because the corpus of a short-term trust reverts to the grantor at the termination of the trust, the IRS has established certain tax rules with respect to these trusts.

Many people attempted to reduce their individual tax burden by transferring property to a trust from which they still benefited. The thought was that the trust, as its own tax entity, would pay taxes on the income that presumably would reduce the tax burden of the trustor who would otherwise be responsible for the taxes on that income.

Under current IRS rules, if the trust is established with a reversion in the grantor, the trustor is liable for the taxes on the trust income. This is known as the **Duration Rule**. There may also be gift tax liability on the income distribution.

In addition to the duration requirement, the IRS has determined that the trustor is liable for the taxes on the trust if any of the following applies:

1. the trustor retains the power to revoke the trust
2. the income from the trust may (not must) be used for the benefit of the trustor or the trustor's spouse (**Recapture Rule**)

3. the trustor retains the power to control the beneficiary's enjoyment of the trust income (**Enjoyment Control Rule**)
4. the trustor retains control that *may* be exercised for his own benefit (**Administrative Control Rule**)
5. the trust income can be used to pay insurance premiums for the trustor or the trustor's spouse (**Premium Payment Rule**)

EXAMPLE:

David sets up a short-term trust to provide an income for his grandchildren, and makes himself the trustee with the power to determine how much of the income, if any, each grandchild will receive in any given year. Because David has retained the power to control the grandchildren's enjoyment of the income, he is liable for the taxes on the trust's income.

Although a person may have valid reasons for establishing a short-term trust, such as to support an elderly relative, finance annual charitable gifts, or establish a child in business, the trustor should be aware of the tax consequences if the trust is for too short a duration or if the trustor retains too much control or enjoyment over the trust income.

Generation Skipping Transfers

Probably the most complex area of tax law concerned with trusts deals with generation skipping transfers. A **generation skipping transfer** is a transfer of property into a trust or otherwise in which the beneficiaries or transferees are two or more generations removed from the trustor. An example would be a trust established to benefit the trustor's children and grandchildren—the grandchildren are two generations removed from the trustor. Most trusts are created in order to provide income for future generations, but a tax consequence of these trusts was that, as a separate entity, the trust existed for several generations and the government lost revenue from potential estate taxes that would be due as each generation died (see Chapter 8). In order to recapture this "lost" revenue, the generation skipping transfer tax was established in the 1980s by the U.S. Congress.

The generation skipping transfer tax is very complicated, and subject to a variety of its own rules and regulations far too complicated for the purpose of this text. For the paralegal, however, a few of the general rules should be borne in mind whenever called upon to draft a trust in which the beneficiaries are several generations removed from the trustor.

1. There is a $1,000,000 exclusion for gifts benefiting the trustor's grandchildren.

2. There must be two or more generations of beneficiaries in the trust in order for the rules to apply.
3. The tax's purpose is to tax the property as beneficiaries of each succeeding generation benefits from the trust.
4. The generation skipping transfer tax can be avoided if the trustor pays a gift tax when the trust is created.
5. The tax on the corpus is due as each generation succeeds to the benefits.
6. The trustee is liable for payment of the taxes.
7. All taxes are computed on actuarial tables representing the generation's expected interest in the trust.
8. For the purpose of the imposition of the tax, anyone with a power of appointment is considered to be a beneficiary of the trust.
9. The tax is imposed only once per generation.
10. The tax may be imposed even if the beneficiaries are not related to the trustor if the trust exists for multiple generations.

This is a fairly complex area of tax law that is more appropriate for accountants or persons involved with fiduciary accounting on a regular basis. The legal assistant should be aware of the potential tax consequences of these transfers, and that he or she obtain guidance from the attorney or accountant working with the client.

Also, remember that because a trust is a taxable entity, it must obtain a Taxpayer Identification Number from the IRS as soon as it is formed (Chapter 8).

Drafting a Trust

Now that most of the legal formalities surrounding the creation, operation, and termination of a trust have been discussed, it is time to draft a simple trust. By using the following outline for guidance, the legal assistant will be able to draft a simple trust, either inter vivos or testamentary.

Name of the Trust. Although not legally necessary, it is always a good idea to give some name to the trust in order to distinguish it from other trusts the trustor may create. The trust may simply be captioned "Declaration of Trust" or form a clause in a will. A name is also appropriate, such as "The Lear Family Trust."

Appointment of a Trustee. One of the most common errors in drafting a trust is, unbelievably, that the instrument will neglect to name someone as trustee. Even if all of the other provisions are correct, a court could not enforce a trust without a trustee. Therefore, always make sure that a person, or persons, is named. Remember, too, that the trustee must have contractual capacity, and may be required to post a bond depending upon individual state laws. For example, in the Lears' trust, the instrument states, "We hereby appoint Dr. Montague to serve as Trustee of the trust herein established."

Trust Purpose. Always make sure that the purpose of the trust is specified. Use terms that are clear and precise, and be sure that the purpose does not violate any laws or public policy as mentioned above. The Lears' trust states, "The purpose of this trust is to generate income that is to be used to defray the educational expenses of our grandchildren."

Powers of the Trustee. Although the trustee, under law, has the general power to manage the trust property, a well-drafted trust will specify the powers the trustee will have in addition to general powers. This provision may also give the trustee a certain degree of discretion with respect to investments and distribution of income; it may also limit the trustee's powers to very specific functions. For example:

> Without limiting his general powers, the Trustee is hereby authorized to sell, lease, or otherwise dispose of any part of any real or personal property, at such time and upon such terms as he may deem best; to invest the assets of the trust in such securities and properties as he, in his discretion may determine, whether or not authorized by law for investment of these funds; and to retain for any period any investment made or property held by me, no matter how speculative.

The preceding is a short form of a trustee's powers clause, giving the trustee broad discretion. The clause may be more limiting, particularizing investments or limiting investments to the legal list. Much more complex powers clauses may be used as well. An example of a detailed powers clause appears in the next chapter in the section on drafting wills (the same clauses are appropriate to trustees and personal representatives), and form books available in every law library will include several examples of these clauses, as well as state statutes that provide for statutory trusts. However broad, narrow, or complex the powers clause, make sure the trust has one!

Trust Property. Remember that a trust can only be established with transferable property that is in existence and in which the trustor has a transferable interest, except for the life insurance trust discussed above. When drafting the trust, be very specific in detailing the property and describing it in its correct legal terminology.

Beneficiary. Always name a beneficiary in the trust. This is not as important if the trust is a charitable or public trust. If no beneficiary is named in a private trust, it will fail and the corpus will be held in a resulting trust for the trustor. The beneficiary can be individually named — "our grandchildren Matthew, Mark, Mary, Margaret, and Anthony" — or indicated by class — "our grandchildren." The first example is exclusionary, limiting the beneficiaries to those persons named, and the second is inclusive, including grandchildren now living plus those who are after-born.

Power of Appointment. Although unnecessary, a trust may indicate a person (either the trustee, beneficiary, or a third person) who has a **power of appointment:** the ability to name a successor beneficiary.

By including a power of appointment, the power holder can take into consideration the financial needs of the beneficiaries and thereby distribute benefits to those most deserving. For example, "At the termination of the trust, my Trustee shall distribute the corpus of the trust to whomever of my grandchildren he deems needy, and in such proportion as he deems warranted." This is a form of a power of appointment.

Termination. A well-written trust should indicate its termination, either by the life of the beneficiary, a specified number of years, or the occurrence of a specified event (e.g., "This trust shall terminate upon the death of my last living named beneficiary," "This trust shall exist for a period of ten years plus one day," or "This trust shall continue until my son marries or attains the age of twenty-five, whichever comes first").

Remainderman. Finally, every private trust should indicate who is to receive the corpus at the termination of the trust. If no remainderman is named, the corpus reverts to the trustor or his heirs. For example, "At the termination of the trust, the corpus is to be equally divided among all of my issue then living per capita."

Signature. Have the instrument signed by the trustor and witnessed or notarized.

To summarize the preceding, the following would be an example of a trust established by Loretta:

The Evan Jones Trust

I, Loretta Jones, by this Instrument of Trust, hereby establish the Evan Jones Trust.

I hereby appoint the __________ Bank of __________ to act as Trustee of the Trust. Without limiting the Trustee's general powers, I authorize my Trustee to sell, lease, or otherwise dispose of any part of my real or personal property, at such time and upon such terms as it may deem best; to invest the assets of the Trust in such securities and properties as it, in its sole discretion, may determine, whether or not authorized by law for investment of trust funds; and to retain for any purpose any investment made or property held by me, no matter how speculative.

I hereby hold my Trustee harmless for any diminution in value of the Trust not caused by its willful, deliberate, or negligent action, or for any loss not due to a breach of its fiduciary obligations.

As compensation for its services as Trustee, the Trustee shall receive a fee equal to five percent (5%) of the gross income generated by the Trust.

I have this day deposited the sum of $ ______ (Dollars) in the Trustee Bank as the corpus of the Trust herein established.

The Trustee shall invest the corpus, make it productive, and use the income so generated to defray the expenses of raising and educating my son, Evan Jones, the Beneficiary of this Trust. The Trustee shall disburse the income periodically, but in no event less frequently than four times per year, to the legal Guardian of my son, Evan Jones, and shall receive from said Guardian records of how said income has been dispensed. Should my son require more money for his support than is generated by the Trust, the Trustee, in its sole discretion, may invade the corpus for such purpose. Should the income in any year be greater than is necessary for my son's support, the Trustee shall add the excess income to the corpus.

This Trust shall terminate when my son, Evan Jones, attains the age of twenty-five, or marries, whichever comes first. At the termination of the Trust, the Trustee shall distribute the corpus of the Trust then remaining to my son, Evan Jones. Should Evan Jones die before the termination of this Trust, the Trust shall terminate on his death and the corpus then remaining shall be distributed outright to Evan's issue; should Evan die without issue, the corpus shall be distributed to my heirs at law, per stirpes.

IN WITNESS WHEREOF I have hereunto set my hand and seal this ____________ day of ____________, 20____.

/s/ ______________________________
Loretta Jones, Trustor

[witnessed and/or notarized]

The following is an example of a charitable remainder annuity trust created by the Internal Revenue Service as a sample.

Rev. Proc. 2003-53

SAMPLE INTER VIVOS CHARITABLE REMAINDER ANNUITY TRUST—ONE LIFE

On this ___ day of ___, 20___, I, ___ (hereinafter "the Donor"), desiring to establish a charitable remainder annuity trust, within the meaning of *Rev. Proc. 2003-53 and §664(d)(1) of the Internal Revenue Code* (hereinafter "the Code"), hereby enter into this trust agreement with ___ as the initial trustee (hereinafter "the Trustee"). This trust shall be known as the ___ Charitable Remainder Annuity Trust.

1. *Funding of Trust.* The Donor hereby transfers and irrevocably assigns, on the above date, to the Trustee **[*6]** the property described in Schedule A, and the Trustee accepts the property and agrees to hold, manage, and distribute the property under the terms set forth in this trust instrument.

2. *Payment of Annuity Amount.* In each taxable year of the trust during the annuity period, the Trustee shall pay to [*permissible recipient*] (hereinafter "the Recipient") an annuity amount equal to [*a number no less than 5 and no more than 50*] percent of the initial net fair market value of all property transferred to the trust, valued as of the above date (that is, the date of the transfer). The first day of the annuity period shall be the date the property is transferred to the trust and the last day of the annuity

period shall be the date of the Recipient's death. The annuity amount shall be paid in equal quarterly installments at the end of each calendar quarter from income, and to the extent income is not sufficient, from principal. Any income of the trust for a taxable year in excess of the annuity amount shall be added to principal. If the initial net fair market value of the trust assets is incorrectly determined, then within a reasonable period after the value is finally determined for federal tax purposes, the Trustee shall pay to the Recipient (in the case of an undervaluation) or receive from the Recipient (in the case of an overvaluation) an amount equal to the difference between the annuity amount(s) properly payable and the annuity amount(s) actually paid.

3. *Proration of Annuity Amount.* The Trustee shall prorate the annuity amount on a daily basis for any short taxable year. In the taxable year of the trust during which the annuity period ends, the Trustee shall prorate the annuity amount on a daily basis for the number of days of the annuity period in that taxable year.

4. *Distribution to Charity.* At the termination of the annuity period, the Trustee shall distribute all of the then principal and income of the trust (other than any amount due the Recipient or the Recipient's estate under the provisions above) to [*designated remainderman*] (hereinafter "the Charitable Organization"). If the Charitable Organization is not an organization described in §§170(c), 2055(a), and 2522(a) of the Code at the time when any principal or income of the trust is to be distributed to it, then the Trustee shall distribute the then principal and income to one or more organizations described in §§170(c), 2055(a), and 2522(a) of the Code as the Trustee shall select, and in the proportions as the Trustee shall decide, in the Trustee's sole discretion.

5. *Additional Contributions.* No additional contributions shall be made to the trust after the initial contribution.

6. *Prohibited Transactions.* The Trustee shall not engage in any act of self-dealing within the meaning of §4941(d) of the Code, as modified by §4947(a)(2)(A) of the Code, and shall not make any taxable expenditures within the meaning of §4945(d) of the Code, as modified by §4947(a)(2)(A) of the Code.

7. *Taxable Year.* The taxable year of the trust shall be the calendar year.

8. *Governing Law.* The operation of the trust shall be governed by the laws of the State of ___. However, the Trustee is prohibited from exercising any power or discretion granted under said laws that would be inconsistent with the qualification of the trust as a charitable remainder annuity trust under §664(d)(1) of the Code and the corresponding regulations.

9. *Limited Power of Amendment.* This trust is irrevocable. However, the Trustee shall have the power, acting alone, to amend the trust from time to time in any manner required for the sole purpose of ensuring that the trust qualifies and continues to qualify as a charitable remainder annuity trust within the meaning of §664(d)(1) of the Code.

10. *Investment of Trust Assets*. Nothing in this trust instrument shall be construed to restrict the Trustee from investing the trust assets in a manner that could result in the annual realization of a reasonable amount of income or gain from the sale or disposition of trust assets.

SITUATIONAL ANALYSIS

The Jones Family

Unfortunately, when the alarm clock went off Loretta woke up and realized that she did not win the lottery discussed throughout this chapter. Does this mean that she does not need to establish a trust? The answer is no! Because Loretta has the responsibility of raising a child, she should create a trust to provide for Evan's support. With the proceeds from the life insurance policy she purchased as part of her estate plan (discussed in Chapter 1) poured over into this trust, she can feel secure that Evan will be taken care of. Also, because the trust is in existence when she dies, the insurance proceeds will probably go into the trust tax free.

The Lear Family

Because of the problems the Lears have with Regina and Leonard, they might consider creating a living trust. They can place most of their assets into this trust and make themselves its beneficiaries: They can therefore still enjoy the income from their property for their lives, then have the trust continue to provide benefits for their grandchildren. In this manner they still have the use of their assets, and at their deaths, because the property is held by the trust, it is neither part of their taxable estate (with certain exceptions discussed in Chapter 8) nor subject to any potential claims by Regina. They will be divested of ownership of the property while still being able to enjoy that property while alive and provide for its distribution on their deaths.

The Bush Family

Because Byron is already an adult, the Bushes do not have to worry about supporting a minor child. However, as part of a tax strategy, they may want to include a trust for the surviving spouse, such as a QTIP, in their wills. In this manner they can benefit from the tax exclusion for marital deductions and still see that the property will be intact for their issue when the survivor dies. This will be discussed in more detail in the next chapter.

Tom Poole

Tom really has no need to create a trust. If he still feels charitably inclined, he may create a public trust for scholarships at his university in his will, or he could simply make a testamentary gift to an existing scholarship fund of the university's. Remember, trusts are not beneficial or necessary for every person. Each person's financial and familial situation must be considered to determine whether a trust is indicated.

CHAPTER SUMMARY

A trust is a legal entity created by a person with a transferable interest in property who is known as the trustor. The trust holds the property in which the title to that property has been divided into its two component parts: legal title and equitable title. The legal title is held by the trustee, who has the obligation to preserve, protect, and defend the trust property and to see that its income is disbursed according to the wishes of the trustor. The equitable title is held by the beneficiary, who has the right to enjoy the trust property subject to any limitations imposed by the trustor.

A trust may be created for any legal purpose, either private, serving the personal wishes of the trustor, or public, providing a charitable benefit to the public at large. In order for a trust to be enforceable, not only must it have a valid purpose, but it must contain property (real or personal) capable of producing an income, a trustee, and a beneficiary. The trustor may also be the trustee or the beneficiary.

Trusts must be created by written documents. If the trust is created during the life of the trustor, the trust is an inter vivos, or living, trust, and is created by a Declaration of Trust or Deed of Trust and takes effect during the life of the trustor. If the trust comes into existence at the trustor's death, it is a testamentary trust established by the last will and testament of the trustor.

Trusts fall into three general categories: express, implied, and special situations. An express trust comes about by the deliberate and voluntary action of the trustor and may be created for any legal purpose, private or public. An implied trust comes about not by the actions of the trustor but by operation of law. There are two types of implied trusts: resulting trusts, in which property is held for the benefit of the property owner without the existence of an express trust, and constructive trusts, which are imposed by the courts of equity to right a wrong. Special situation trusts are trusts that are established for particular purposes, and are a subdivision of express trusts, such as business trusts, short-term trusts, spend-thrift trusts, and so forth.

The trustee must have contractual capacity and be given active duties to perform—passive trusts are not enforceable under trust law. The trustee is a fiduciary, and must be loyal to the trust and the beneficiary, making sure that the trust is profitable.

Private trusts may not exist in perpetuity. The longevity of a trust is determined by the Rule Against Perpetuities, which states that all interests must vest, if at all, within 21 years after the death of a life in being, plus the period of gestation. A trust may terminate by accomplishing its purpose, by being incapable of accomplishing its purpose, or at the end of a period specified by the creator. At its termination, the legal and equitable titles merge into one person (or persons) known as the remainderman, who acquires full ownership of the property. If the remainderman is the trustor, the remaining interest is called a reversion.

Trusts are subject to various tax laws. Generally, a regular trust is liable for income taxes on all income produced by the trust not otherwise distributed as expenses or as income to the beneficiaries. The trustee is obligated to see that all trust income taxes are paid. The trustee is also liable for income taxes on the income he or she receives for managing the trust. The beneficiaries may be individually liable for any tax due on the income they receive from the trust.

Income generated by reversionary trusts (trusts that are formed with a reversion in the grantor) may be the tax responsibility of the grantor, especially if the grantor receives a benefit from the operation of the trust.

Any trust that provides benefits to persons two or more generations removed from the trustor is known as a generation skipping transfer, and, if the trustor does not pay a gift tax when creating the trust, the trust must pay taxes each time a new generation becomes entitled to benefit from the trust.

When drafting a trust, the legal assistant must be sure to cover all of the following areas:

1. name of the trust
2. appointment of the trustee
3. trust purpose
4. powers of the trustee
5. trust property
6. beneficiary
7. power of appointment
8. termination
9. remainderman
10. signatures

Each client's family and financial situation must be individually analyzed to determine whether a trust would be an appropriate devise to meet his particular needs.

Key Terms

A-B trusts: Credit shelter and marital deduction trusts.

Administrative Control Rule: Tax rule for short-term trust making the trustor tax liable if he retains administrative control over the trust.

Beneficiary: Person who has equitable title to a trust.

Cestui que trust: Beneficiary.

Charitable trust: Trust created for a public, charitable purpose.

Charitable remainder annuity trust: Trust in which the income goes to a private person and the remainder goes to charity.
Charitable remainder unitrust: Trust in which a private person receives a percentage of the income, the rest and the remainder going to charity.
Clifford trust: Short-term trust.
Constructive trust: Implied trust used to right a wrong.
Conveyance of trust: Method of transferring realty to a trust.
Corpus: Trust property.
Creator: Trustor.
Cy pres: Doctrine permitting changes in the operation of a public trust.
Declaration of trust: Instrument creating an inter vivos trust.
Deed of trust: Method of transferring realty to a trust.
Discretionary trust: Trust in which trustee is given broad powers of discretion with respect to investments and distribution of income.
Divested: Losing a legal right.
Duration Rule: Tax rule stating trusts that exist for less than ten years and a day, or the life of the beneficiary, make the grantor tax liable.
Enjoyment Control Rule: Tax rule for short-term trusts making the trustor tax liable if he may enjoy the income from the trust.
Equitable title: Title giving the beneficiary the right to enjoy the trust property subject to limitations imposed by the trustor.
Express trust: Trust created by the voluntary and deliberate act of the trustor.
Failed trust: Trust that terminates because its objective cannot be accomplished.
Fertile octogenarian: Doctrine stating a person is capable of bearing children until death.
Fiduciary: Trustee, a person held to a standard of care higher than ordinary care.
Fiduciary returns: Tax returns filed by trustees and executors.
Generation skipping transfer: Trusts that benefit persons two or more generations removed from the trustor are subject to special tax rules.
Grantor: Person who creates a trust with real estate.
Implied trust: Trust created by operation of law.
Indefinite class: Group identified by general characteristics, a charitable group.
Injunction: Court order to stop performing a specified act.
Inter vivos trust: Trust taking effect during the life of the trustor.
Irrevocable trust: Trust that cannot be revoked by the creator.
Legal list: Statutorily approved investments for fiduciaries.
Legal title: Title held by the trustee giving the holder the right to preserve, protect, and defend the trust property, subject to duties imposed by the trustor.
Operation of law: Actions having certain legal consequences regardless of the wishes of the parties involved.

Overendowed trust: Resulting trust with income greater than is needed to accomplish the trust purpose.
Premium payment rule: Tax rule for short-term trust making the trustor tax liable if the trust can be use to pay the trustor's insurance premiums.
Pour-over trust: Property being added to the corpus of a separate trust.
Power of appointment: Legal right to select successor beneficiary.
Principal: Trust property of cash.
Private trust: Trust designed to fulfill a private purpose of the trustor.
Public trust: Charitable trust.
Purchase money resulting trust: Resulting trust in which person holds property for thc benefit of the person who paid for the property.
Qualified terminable interest property (QTIP): Property left to a surviving spouse under a trust that qualifies for a marital deduction.
Recapture Rule: Tax rule taxing the trustor of a short-term trust.
Remainderman: Person in whom legal and equitable titles merge.
Res: Trust property consisting of personalty.
Resulting trust: Implied trust in which the trust property reverts to the trustor.
Reversion: Legal and equitable title merging in the trustor.
Reversionary interest: Remainder interests of a trustor.
Revocable trust: Trust in which the trustor retains the power to revoke.
Rule Against Perpetuities: All interests must vest, if at all, within 21 years after the death of a life in being plus the period of gestation.
Salvage doctrines: State statutory rules used to save trusts from violating the rule against perpetuities.
Self-dealing: Breach of fiduciary obligation in which trustee makes a benefit for himself instead of the trust.
Settlor: Trustor who creates a trust with personal property.
Sovereign immunity: Legal inability to sue the government.
Specific performance: Court order to perform a specific act.
Spendthrift trust: Trust designed to prevent the beneficiary from alienating his interest.
Spray trust: Discretionary trust.
Sprinkling trust: Discretionary trust.
Statute of Uses: Feudal law concerned with trusts.
Statutory trust: Trust provided by specific state statute.
Testamentary trust: Trust created by a will.
Totten trust: Bank account "in trust for" a third party.
Trust instrument: Document creating a trust.
Trustee: Person who holds legal title to trust property.
Trustor: Creator of a trust.
Trust property: Property held in trust.
Use: Feudal term for a trust.
Vested: Moment at which a person has an enforceable right.

Case Studies

1. Constructive trusts are created by the court when the court perceives that an injustice has taken place. In *Latham v. Father Divine*, 209 N.Y. 23 (1949), the plaintiffs, non-distributee heirs of the deceased, argued that the provisions of the deceased's will leaving all of her property to Father Divine should not be carried out because the deceased indicated an intent to change her will but was prevented from executing the new will by associates of Father Divine, who caused her death. The woman had gone to an attorney to have the new will drawn up, but died under mysterious circumstances before the new will could be executed. The plaintiffs were to receive a large bequest under the non-executed will. The court concluded that the executed will in favor of Father Divine should be probated, but, because of the wrongdoing on the part of Father Divine's associates, the proceeds should be held in a constructive trust for the cousins. This case presents several interesting applications of the concept of a constructive trust granting relief to beneficiaries of an unexecuted will.

2. Before a court will impose a constructive trust, the proponent must be able to demonstrate that he or she is seeking this remedy with "clean hands": is not guilty of any wrongdoing him or herself.

In *Taylor v. Fields*, 178 Cal. App. 3d 653 (1986), the long-term lover of the decedent attempted to establish a constructive trust over the property owned by the decedent based on a promise he had made to her in return for sexual favors. In denying her claim the court stated that one who seeks equity must have clean hands, and therefore it refused to enforce an agreement in which the parties were in pari delicti.

3. One of the primary obligations of a trustee is to see that the trust produces an adequate income to meet the purpose for which the trust was established. Although this may sound simple enough, that is not always the case. For instance, what is the duty of a trustee if the income is greater than is necessary to meet the trust's obligations? The courts have held that even if a trustee has managed funds so well that there is an excess, he is not excused of his obligation to make the trust productive if he simply permits that excess to accumulate. It is still considered a breach of a trustee's fiduciary obligation if he does not invest the excess to produce even greater income. *In re Consupak*, 87 B.R. 529 (Bankr. N.D. Ill. 1988).

Not only is the trustee bound to make the corpus productive, but he may be personally liable if his mismanagement causes a loss to the corpus. In *Jones v. Ellis*, 551 So. 2d 396 (Ala. 1989), the trustee was also the director of a corporation, and he invested all of the trust funds in the stock of the corporation for which he was a director. As the value of the corporation diminished, so did the value of the trust corpus. The court held that a trustee is held to a fiduciary standard of a prudent investor, meaning that he must be as concerned with trust funds as he is with his own. And, if there is a choice to be made by a person who is both a trustee and a director, the duty as trustee prevails. Consequently, investing all of the funds of a trust in just one security, and maintaining that security as the value of the security diminishes, is a breach of trust for which the trustee is personally liable.

The trustee may be liable if he causes the trust to make too much or too little income. You can't win either way!

4. In order for a trust to be valid and enforceable, the trustee must be given active duties to perform.

In *Board of Co-operative Educ. Serv. v. County of Nassau*, 137 A.D.2d 476, 524 N.Y.S.2d 224 (1988), the U.S. Government conveyed a sum of money to the Board to be used for educational purposes in the county for a 25-year period. At the end of the 25 years, the Board no longer had any active obligation under the original agreement, and the county sued to obtain the funds. In its decision, the court held that when a once-active trust becomes passive, that is, the trustee no longer has any active duty to fulfill, the trust is considered terminated and the corpus either reverts to the settlor or belongs to the beneficiary outright.

When drafting a trust, be sure the trustee has some duties to perform.

5. Is an inter vivos revocable trust valid if the creator is both the trustee and the beneficiary with a remainder going to a third person at the creator's death?

Under historical trust law a trust will fail if all of the trustees and all of the beneficiaries are the same persons. However, under modern interpretation, as long as some other person has any interest in the trust, regardless of how vague or remote, the trust will be held valid. In *Farkas v. Williams*, 5 Ill. 2nd 417 (1957), a man created a revocable inter vivos trust with himself as trustee income beneficiary and a friend as the remainderman. During his life he made several changes in the trust property and treated it as his own. At his death both his estate and the remainderman claimed the trust corpus. The court held that even though the decedent had exercised virtual total control of the trust during his life, the friend, as remainderman, did have an interest in the trust and therefore the trust was valid and the property passed out of the decedent's estate. How would this decision affect a person's estate plan?

EXERCISES

1. Draft a trust for Kingston and Donna Lear based on the situational analysis discussed up to this point. Assume that they want to establish the trust to pay for their grandchildren's educations, and then have the corpus distributed equally to the grandchildren at some point in time when they are all adults. The Lears want to place publicly traded stocks and bonds in the trust, valued at $387,000, plus $100,000 in cash.
2. Discuss in your own words the requirements to create a valid trust.
3. Go to the internet and find examples of trusts. Does your state have a statutory trust? If so, compare it to the examples you have found. Which do you prefer? Why?

4. What factors would determine whether a person should create a testamentary or inter vivos trust? Discuss in detail.
5. How can you avoid violating the Rule Against Perpetuities and being subject to the generation skipping transfer tax?

ANALYTICAL PROBLEM

Your client wishes to create a trust to provide scholarships for students of a particular religion at a private school. Do you see any problems with this scheme? Create a trust designed to accomplish the client's purpose.

5 Wills

CHAPTER OVERVIEW

A will is one of the most formal legal documents that exists in the modern legal system. Because the will represents the wishes of a person no longer living, the law requires a great deal of formality to assure that the document does, in fact, truly represent the desires of a person who can no longer speak for himself.

All of the information that has appeared in the previous chapters now coalesces into the final aspect of estate planning: the will. Although every will is different, depending upon the family and financial situation of each testator, certain standard clauses appear in almost every will, and a certain order and methodology is incident to preparing most wills. This chapter will detail all of those standard provisions and provide guidance for the paralegal to assist him or her in the preparation of a last will and testament.

Not only are there certain formalities incident to drafting the will, there are strict standards required to execute, or finalize, the instrument. If these formalities are not adhered to, the will may not pass the scrutiny of the probate court. Additionally, even if a will is properly drafted and executed, the testator may have engaged in some act or activity that has the effect of revoking or amending the will.

Any person who is named in any will executed by the testator, as well as all intestate heirs of the deceased, has the right to challenge the validity of the instrument presented to the probate court as the last will of the decedent. It is the function of the lawyer and the legal assistant who drafted the will to make sure that the legal formalities have been met so that the will can withstand these challenges, or, if the attorney one of the challenging heirs, to see that sufficient evidence and ntation validates the challenge.

In addition to formal, written wills, which represent the bulk of the documents presented for probate, many jurisdictions permit less formal instruments under special circumstances that also may represent the last wishes of a decedent. Recently, many jurisdictions have also approved documents known as **living wills**, which indicate a person's wishes with respect to life termination in the event of the person becoming incapacitated with no reasonable expectation of recovery. All of these items must be discussed with the client and prepared by the attorney and paralegal for the client's signature.

Testamentary Capacity

The primary requirement necessary for a person to be permitted to execute a valid will is that the person have **testamentary capacity**. Testamentary capacity represents the legal ability, pursuant to the state statute, for a person to execute a will, and it has three major areas of concern: age, mental ability, and intent.

Age

Every state statute indicates a minimum age for a person to be permitted to execute a valid will. See Chapter 9. The majority of states indicate the minimum age as 18 years old, and a few states permit minors (persons younger than 18) to execute a will if they are married or in military service. It is necessary to check each state's statute to determine the age requirement for testators.

EXAMPLE:

Anthony Montague wants to execute a will to provide for the disposition of his baseball card collection. Anthony is 16 years old. Because of his age, Anthony is statutorily incapable of executing a will.

Mental Ability

The mental ability of the testator to execute a will is probably the most important statutory requirement with respect to the execution of a will. Generally, testamentary capacity means the ability of a person to know the nature and extent of one's property and the natural bounty of one's affections. Simply stated, this means that a person must know what property he or she owns and who his or her nearest relatives are. This is one of the main reasons why the client is asked to provide information with respect to his or her property (Chapter 2) and his or her family tree (Chapter 3). By having this information at hand, it can be incorporated into the terms of the will to demonstrate the client's testamentary capacity. The law does not require that the will specify all of the property owned by the testator, nor is the testator required to leave property to his or her relations (except to a spouse, in most jurisdictions). The law merely wants to make sure that these assets and persons were considered when the will was drawn up.

EXAMPLES:

1. David Laplante is getting up in years and his memory isn't what it used to be. When he goes to a lawyer to have a will prepared, he forgets that he has a daughter named Fleur. If the will is drafted under these circumstances, it may be easy to prove that David lacked testamentary capacity, because he could not recall the "natural bounty of his affection"—his child.
2. Regina executes a will in which she leaves a diamond necklace to her daughter Mary. Regina has never owned a diamond necklace. On its face, the will indicates a lack of testamentary capacity because Regina was giving away property she has never owned.

Take careful note of the fact that the mental ability of the testator is only pertinent for the moment at which the will was signed, and only relates to the testator's knowledge of his or her assets and relations; it is not as high a standard as contractual capacity. The law looks to this finite moment in time to determine testamentary capacity. The person's mental state *before or after* the signing does not affect the person's capacity *at the moment* of execution, but may only be evidence of his or her mental state at that period. Therefore, even persons who are mentally deficient, who would normally lack "capacity" as it is generally thought of, may still have the legal ability to execute a will. Remember, the testator only has to know the nature and extent of his or her property and the natural bounty of his or her affections!

EXAMPLE:

Lottie's cousin, Myron, has severe delusions in which he hears the voice of Joan of Arc telling him to save France from the EEC. However, Myron knows exactly what property he owns and who his relations are, and he executes a will accordingly. Even though Myron has a mental problem, he still possesses testamentary capacity.

Intent

The element of intent requires that the testator freely and voluntarily execute the will. This means that the testator cannot be forced into signing the document, nor can the testator be under some disability that would take away his or her free will. One of the most typical challenges to the validity of a will is that the person did not execute the will voluntarily. Generally, intent concerns four main areas:

Fraud

Fraud means that the person signing the will was induced to sign by another person who intentionally misled the signatory with respect to what was being signed, either in the nature of the document or the provisions it contains. If fraud can be proven, the will is invalid, because the testator was not signing what he thought he was signing.

EXAMPLES:

1. Regina goes to her parents and says that, in order to keep peace in the family, she is willing to sign away any claims she may have in the house where she is living. Regina brings a document that she says is her release, and she has her parents sign as accepting the release. However, one of the pages the Lears sign is a will in which the Lears purport to leave everything they own to Regina. If that "will" is introduced to a probate court, it would not be accepted as valid because the Lears did not knowingly sign a will—they were lied to by Regina.
2. Grace decides that, traveling as much as she does for work, she should have a will, and she goes to a lawyer she finds in the yellow pages. The lawyer drafts a will for Grace which he says is written exactly according to her direction. Later, it is discovered that the lawyer has worded the provisions in such a manner that he, and not Grace's family, is the primary beneficiary. The will is invalid—Grace was defrauded into believing the provisions were as she had stated.

Menace

Menace means that the testator was forced, coerced, or threatened into signing the will. Any document signed under duress is not considered valid because the signatory lacked the requisite intent to sign.

EXAMPLES:

1. Regina's husband goes to Kingston with a prepared will. Doger tells Kingston that if Kingston does not sign the will in which everything Kingston owns is left to Regina, he, Doger, will physically abuse Mary and Margaret, Kingston's granddaughters. Kingston signs the will. The will is invalid—Kingston was forced to sign under emotional duress.
2. Regina's husband goes to Grace with a prepared will that states that she leaves everything she owns to her "beloved sister, Regina." Doger coerces Grace into signing the will by threatening to expose her "lurid" past to her employers, which will destroy her security clearance and get her fired. The will is invalid because Grace was threatened into signing it—it was not executed of her own free will.

Undue Influence

Undue influence, unlike menace, occurs when a person who is in a position of trust with the testator uses that close relationship to convince the testator to draw a will in a particular fashion. Because of the presumed emotional tie between the testator and this person, it is possible that the testator's own will was usurped by the person who had the testator's trust. Influencing a disposition is all right, but using undue influence is prohibited.

EXAMPLES:

1. David, who is succumbing to Alzheimer's, is placed in a nursing home. At the home, David becomes infatuated with his young nurse. The nurse, realizing the situation, convinces David to sign a will in her favor, intimating that if he doesn't sign it indicates he doesn't care for her, and she will have no reason to visit him. In this situation, David is considered to be under the undue influence of the nurse.
2. The lawyer who arranges Aida's sale of her spaghetti sauce recipe convinces Aida of the need for a will. He tells Aida that because of Loretta's uncertain situation and Evan's youth, in his legal opinion, it would be best if Aida created a testamentary trust naming him as trustee, giving the trustee total discretion to dispense the income and invade the corpus. Aida believes the lawyer has her best interests at heart, and because of his presumed expertise, she is convinced to execute a will according to his advice. This will will not stand. The lawyer used his position to influence Aida

to draw up a will that benefits him to the detriment of Aida's family.

Temporary Incapacity

There are times during which a person may be temporarily incapable of executing a will. For instance, he or she may be under the influence of alcohol or drugs (prescribed or otherwise) or may be under a temporary mental delusion. Under these circumstances the will might be invalid. However, many states permit a testator to acknowledge his signature to witnesses after the actual signing. If the testator is permitted such acknowledgment, and does so when the temporary disability no longer exists, the will is considered valid.

EXAMPLES:

1. Hyacinth is very nervous about signing her will, so, in order to gather strength and get some courage, she stops at a cocktail lounge before going to the lawyer's office. When Hyacinth signs the will, the legal assistant realizes that Hyacinth is slightly drunk, and suggests coffee and a little lunch. After sobering up, Hyacinth returns to acknowledge her signature in front of the witnesses. The will is considered valid.
2. Fern takes some prescribed medication for hypertension that has a slight temporary effect on her memory for a few hours after she takes the pills. Thirty minutes before signing her will, Fern takes her medication, and so when she signs the instrument her memory is affected. However, two hours later her memory is fine, and she acknowledges her signature in front of the witnesses. The instrument is valid. At the moment of acknowledgment Fern has testamentary capacity.

Will Provisions

Certain basic requirements are imposed by law with respect to the testamentary disposition of a person's assets. Before drafting a will, the client must be made aware of certain legal restrictions that are placed on his ability to execute a will.

Surviving Spouse

In most states a person is prohibited from disinheriting a surviving spouse. If the spouse is left out of the will or the testator attempts specifically to disinherit the spouse in a clause in the will, the spouse is still entitled to a statutory share (see Chapter 1). The client should be made aware of this so that there is no unpleasantness should the couple be having marital discord, and the spouse is left at least the statutory share in the will. Note that in some states, such as California where there is community property, a spouse may leave his or her portion of the property to persons other than the surviving spouse.

Antenuptial Agreements

A surviving spouse may voluntarily waive any right to a deceased spouse's property by means of a valid antenuptial agreement that delineates each person's property rights upon death. Provided that the agreement is valid, it will determine the surviving spouse's inheritance rights. This is also true for agreements regarding community property in those jurisdictions that recognize that type of property ownership.

EXAMPLE:

Prior to their marriage, Cornelia and Dr. Montague executed a valid antenuptial agreement in which each party agreed that, in the event of either person's death, and provided they had children, each one relinquished all property rights in favor of their issue. Because the agreement is valid, it controls each spouse's rights on the death of the other.

It is a good idea to refer to the antenuptial agreement specifically in the will to avoid problems of interpretation. This mention of outside legal documents in the will is known as **incorporation by reference**. Also, note that the antenuptial agreement simply determines minimum property rights—each spouse is still free to voluntarily give the other whatever he or she wants to in the will.

Omitted Children

Although a surviving spouse may not be disinherited, the law imposes no obligation on a person to leave property to his or her children or issue. However, the law does require that the testator mention the children in the will. Any child, or grandchild, not specifically named or mentioned in the will is considered omitted, or **pretermitted** and as such is entitled to an intestate portion of the decedent's estate. To avoid pretermission it is not necessary that the child be specifically disinherited by the parent. All that need be done is to mention the child in the will without leaving the child any property.

EXAMPLE:

In their wills, the Lears state that they have three daughters, Regina, Grace, and Cornelia, but when it comes to disposing their property, they do not leave anything to Regina, saying that they have sufficiently provided for her during their lives. Regina gets nothing, but is not pretermitted.

Advancements

An **advancement** is an inter vivos gift made to a child in anticipation of the child's inheritance. The advancement works to diminish the child's portion of the parent's estate. Any sizable gift made to a child may be considered an advancement, and it is necessary to document whether the property transfer is considered just a gift or an advancement against the child's inheritance.

EXAMPLE:

The Lears transfer the title to their home to Grace to make sure that she has a permanent place to live. They document this gift as an advancement. The house is valued at $350,000. When the Lears die, Grace's portion of their estates is reduced by $350,000, the value of the house she has already received in anticipation of her inheritance.

Charitable Gifts

Some statutes limit the amount of property that may be left to charities (see Chapter 9). Also, if the will is drawn up within a few months of the testator's death, the charitable gift may be considered void if the state has a **Mortmain Statute**. Mortmain, literally meaning "hand of death," limits charitable gifts made in immediate anticipation of death, under the principle that the testator may have been unduly influenced by being near death and is attempting to pave his or her way to heaven by making charitable donations. Not every jurisdiction has such provisions, so each state's statute must be individually scrutinized if the client wishes to make large charitable bequests.

Ademption

Ademption occurs when the property left in the will is no longer owned by the testator at death. This could happen because the testator lost or broke the property, sold it, or gave it away. Unless the will specifically provides for alternate gifts in case of ademption, the beneficiary may receive nothing. The client should be aware of this so alternate provisions can be made if the client so desires.

EXAMPLES:

1. Donna leaves her pearl ring to her daughter, Grace, in her will. Before she dies, Donna gives the ring to her granddaughter, Margaret. When Donna dies, Grace does not receive the ring because it no was no longer part of her property when Donna died. The gift has *adeemed.*
2. Donna leaves her pearl ring to her daughter, Grace, in her will. The will stipulates that should Donna not die possessed of the ring, Grace may select any item of jewelry of which Donna does die possessing. In this instance the gift has not adeemed—Grace gets a different piece of jewelry.

Lapsed Gifts

A **lapse** occurs if the testator outlives the beneficiary. At the testator's death there is no one to inherit the property. Under general law, if such a situation occurs, the lapsed gift becomes part of the testator's residuary estate (see below). Some states have an **anti-lapse statute** that provides that the gift goes to the heirs of the predeceased beneficiary. Also, the testator may make a specific provision in the will to deal with this problem, such as indicating alternate beneficiaries if the original beneficiary does not survive the testator.

Abatement

What happens if the cash in the estate is insufficient to pay the taxes and other estate debts? The estate still must pay these debts, which means that property is going to have to be sold to raise the necessary capital. The person who was to inherit the property will now only get the excess from the sale after the debts are paid. In these circumstances, the beneficiaries usually start arguing as to who should lose their inheritance because of these debts.

It is therefore a good idea to have the testator specify the order of **abatement** or sale of the property to meet the estate obligations or give the personal representative the discretion to determine the order. As a general rule, the order is usually cash gifts go first, then securities, personal property, and finally real estate. For an example of an abatement clause, see the following section. Most state statutes provide for an order of abatement if none is specified in the will.

Drafting a Will

Preparation

The following general principles should be considered before a will is drafted:

a) *Avoid using printed forms.* Many legal stationers and Internet Web sites provide printed will forms, but these forms are generally inadequate for the proper disposition of a person's estate. First of all, the printed form is mostly comprised of blank spaces that have to be filled in; it is simpler and far more professional to type the entire document, incorporating any of the standard clauses from the printed form that seem appropriate. Second, if the printed form is used, it may have trouble passing probate because of the combination of printing and / or handwriting or typing. The court scrutinizes a will for any irregularities (see Chapter 7), and this combination of writing may produce uncertainties. Third, even where a jurisdiction provides a statutory will, it may still need some individualization to be appropriate, even if the statutory will is excellently drafted, as in California. There is no such thing as a universal will that is perfect for every testator.

b) *Clearly describe all assets specifically given away in the will.* As discussed in Chapter 2, in order to provide an orderly disposition of a person's property, it is necessary to know what property the person possesses. Using Chapter 2 as a guideline, have all of the client's assets categorized as real property, tangible and intangible personal property, and cash. Make sure that every asset that is being specifically given in the will is properly described so as to avoid any confusion with respect to the property being discussed.

c) *Avoid all erasures.* Because the probate court analyzes wills for discrepancies, the court may become suspicious if a will contains erasures and corrections. After all, it is possible that the changes were made *after* the testator signed and without his or her knowledge. Nowadays, the universality of computers and word processors makes it quite simple to avoid having corrected documents.

d) *After the will is executed, make no changes on the will.* Once the will has been signed and witnessed, there can be no changes made on the face of the document. Should the client desire changes, a new will or codicil should be drawn up and executed.

e) *Use simple language.* Make sure that the language used is clear and precise, leaving no room for alternate interpretations. Always err on the side of precision, but do not become obsessed with overly technical terminology. Always use words of present tense, and avoid nondeclaratory statements.

f) *Number all pages and clauses and have each page signed.* At the top of every page after the first page indicate the number that page represents with respect to the entire will (e.g., "Page 5 of 8 Pages"). In this manner the testator (and the probate court) is guaranteed that no pages have been inserted or deleted. Also, make sure that the testator signs or initials the bottom of every page except the last page which he will completely sign on a line specifically provided for that purpose before the witnesses signatures. Although signing each page is not a legal requirement, it does provide evidence that the testator saw and approved each page, and makes it more difficult to insert clauses of which the testator is unaware.

g) *Always have a residuary clause.* As will be discussed below, one of the last clauses before the testator's signature should be a residuary clause in which the testator disposes of all property not otherwise disposed of in the will. This avoids problems that arise if the testator acquires substantial assets after the will has been executed.

h) *A marital deduction provision is strongly advised if the testator is married.* The marital deduction provides a major tax advantage for the surviving spouse, and the tax advantage is automatic even without a specific clause. (See Form 706 in Chapter 8.) However, it is still a good idea to insert such a clause in a will. Remember, it is only available for legally married couples.

i) *Never use angry words.* Despite the testator's true feelings about close family members, the will, once probated, is a public document, accessible to the entire world. There is no reason to permit a person's last statement to be vitriolic. It may even inspire the subject of the anger to challenge the document.

j) *Never use a video will.* Although popular for a while, no jurisdiction admits video wills to probate; only written documents are allowed. The testator who wishes to leave a video may do so, but must realize that it will not be used to dispose of his or her assets; for that he needs a written will.

k) *Provide a draft to the client before execution and discuss its provisions with him or her.* Before having the will signed and witnessed, give the client a draft of the will so he or she can make sure that it truly reflects his or her wishes. It is much easier to make changes on a draft than it is to re-execute a will.

l) *Do not make duplicate originals.* There should only be one executed will. Copies may be made for reference, and, if a computer or word processor is used, the disk will have a copy of the will. It is never a good idea to have several originals around. If the testator changes the will at a later date, all of the originals may not be destroyed, which could raise problems during probate administration (which is the true will?).

m) *Avoid joint and mutual wills.* Although somewhat popular, they have several problems. A **joint will** is a single will that is used for both the husband and wife, who sign the will together. When the first spouse dies, the will is probated, and it becomes an enforceable contract on the surviving spouse, meaning that the surviving spouse no longer has control over disposing of the family assets. **Mutual wills** are two identical wills, one for the husband and one for the wife, that are reciprocal or executed in consideration of some prearranged disposition of property. Each spouse is free to redo the will, however. Both these types of wills are used so that couples are "guaranteed" that the spouses will dispose of the property according to mutual wishes. After a long period of time, those wishes could change for either or both parties. It is a much better practice to do individual wills for each spouse; it avoids problems later on.

n) *Leave the will in a readily accessible place.* It is usually best to keep a will in a locked fireproof box in the testator's home and to inform the executor where the will can be found. If a will is kept in a safe deposit box, the box may be sealed on the testator's death, and if the will is filed with the probate court while the testator is alive (permitted in many jurisdictions), it may be difficult to retrieve the will if the testator wishes to cancel, destroy, or change it.

Bearing all of the foregoing in mind, as well as all of the information from the preceding chapters, it is now time to draft a will.

Clauses

The following clauses are provided as a sample for constructing and wording a last will and testament. Remember, it is only a guideline; individual situations may vary. However, if this checklist is followed, there will be no problem in drafting a simple will.

Heading. Always entitle the will at the top of the first page as "Last Will and Testament of" and insert the testator's name.

Exordium and Publication Clause. The opening clause of every will is known as the *exordium and publication clause.* This clause serves several purposes:

a) It identifies the testator.
b) It gives the testator's address and domicile.
c) It officially declares that the testator has testamentary capacity.
d) It acknowledges to the world that the testator intends this document to be his or her last will and testament.

I, ____________ now domiciled and residing in the State of ____________ at ____________, being over eighteen years of age and of sound and disposing mind and memory, and not acting under the duress,

> menace, fraud, or undue influence of any person or persons whomsoever, do hereby freely and voluntarily make, publish and declare this instrument to be my Last Will and Testament.

Family Status. It is generally a good idea to include a statement indicating the family status of the testator. Not only does this evidence testamentary capacity (knowing the natural bounty of his affections) but also avoids pretermission.

> [Loretta Jones:] I hereby declare that I have never been married, and have one child, my son, Evan Jones.
>
> [Hyacinth Bush:] I hereby declare that I am married, that my husband's name is Oscar Bush, and that we have one son, Byron Bush.

Appointment of a Personal Representative. Although many people make the appointment at the end of the will, because the executor is required to carry out the provision of this instrument it is logical to make the appointment at the beginning. Also, unless waived by the will, executors are required to post bond with the probate court to assure the faithful performance of their duties. If the testator wishes the executor to serve without bond, it should be so stated.

A testator may also indicate a successor and/or substitute executor in case the first person named cannot serve. If successors are named in the will, the court will try to go along with the testator's wishes. If no substitute is indicated, the court is free to appoint anyone it deems suitable.

Also, almost every jurisdiction requires the executor to be resident in the state, or if a nonresident, to post a bond or appoint a resident co-executor, and meet certain other criteria (Chapter 9). Therefore, make sure that the person appointed can qualify pursuant to the state statute.

> I hereby appoint, constitute, and designate ____________ and ____________, both residing in this State, to act as the Co-Executors of this, my Last Will and Testament. Should either of them, for any reason, fail or cease to act as my Executor(s), then I appoint as first substitute Executor ____________. Should any of the above-named persons, for any reason, fail or cease to act as my Executor(s), then I appoint as second substitute Executor ____________. I direct that none of my Executors shall be required to furnish bond or other security for the faithful performance of his duties, or, if any bond is required. I direct that no sureties be required thereon.

Appointment of Ancillary Executors. If the testator has property located in jurisdictions other than his or her domiciliary jurisdiction, an ancillary administration will have to be established in those states where the property is located. The testator can appoint residents of those states in the will to serve as ancillary executors. The clause is identical to the one above, except that it states that the persons are named as "ancillary Executors for property located in the State of ____________." Be sure the persons so named meet the requirements of the ancillary state's statute for personal representatives.

Appointment of Guardians. If the testator has minor or incapacitated dependents, a guardian for that person will need to be appointed. Remember, this person is legally responsible to the dependent, but has nothing to do with financial arrangement that may be made a separate clause in the will.

> I hereby appoint, constitute, and designate to act as the Guardian of __________. Should for any reason, fail or cease to act the Guardian of __________, then I hereby appoint __________ to act as the Guardian of __________. The Guardian shall be legally responsible for __________, acting as *loco parentis*. The Guardian shall not be required to furnish bond or other security for the faithful performance of his/her duties.

Additionally, it may be a good idea to appoint a guardian of the estate to protect the minor's interests if there is no guardian of his or her person immediately available because of death or failure to qualify. This guardian is responsible for guarding the assets of the estate for the minor until an appropriate guardian or trustee is appointed.

Right and Duties of the Personal Representative. The personal representative (and trustee if a trust is created in the will) only have such rights and duties as are designated in the will. The following represents three standard clauses that can be included to cover this area. Each paragraph may be numbered individually and consecutively.

> I hereby direct that whenever the terms "Executors" or "Trustees" are used in this Will they shall include, in both cases, only such persons as shall qualify, and their survivors and successors, whether originally named herein or appointed under the power herein conferred or by any Court. I authorize by Executors and/or Trustees, then acting by a majority or their number, in their discretion, to add to or decrease their number, or, subject to the above substitute appointments, to fill any vacancy in their number, or to appoint a successor Executor and/or Trustee in order to fill such vacancy when the same may occur, with the same rights and powers as if originally named as one of my Executors and/or Trustees. Such appointment and the acceptance thereof shall be duly acknowledged and filed in the office of the Clerk of the Court in which this Will shall have been probated. Any appointment of a successor Executor and/or Trustee in advance may be similarly revoked at any time before the occurrence of such vacancy. Such advance appointment need not be filed until the same becomes effective. I authorize those of my Executors and/or Trustees who have power or discretion in the matter in question to act by a majority of their number. None of my Executors and/or Trustees shall be required to furnish any bond even though not a resident of the State in which my Will shall have been probated. Each Executor and/or Trustees shall be chargeable only for his or her own willful default, and shall not be liable for any loss or damage to my estate unless caused by such willful default.
>
> My Executor(s) shall have full power and authority, without the necessity of order of Court, to sell, at either public or private sale, or to exchange, lease, pledge, or mortgage, in such manner and on such terms

> as my Executor(s) deem advisable, any or all property, real, personal, or mixed, belonging to my estate, and to execute all deeds, assignments, mortgages, leases, or other instruments necessary or proper for those purposes; to adjust, compromise, or otherwise settle claims of any nature in favor of or against my estate on such terms as my Executor(s) deems advisable; to make distributions wholly or partly in kind by allotting or transferring specific securities, other real or personal property, or undivided interests therein, at their then current values; to retain securities or other property owned by me at the time of my death, although the same may not, without this instruction, be considered a proper investment for Executors; and generally to perform any act and to execute and instrument with respect to such property as if my Executor(s) was the absolute owner thereof, but no power under this Will shall be exercised or enforceable if it would defeat qualification for any deduction otherwise available to my estate for estate tax purposes. Notwithstanding any other provisions of this Will, my Executor(s) shall, to the extent possible, not use any property otherwise excludable from my estate for estate tax purposes for payment of any obligations of my estate, including any obligations for taxes.
>
> I hereby vest my Executor(s) with full power to do anything (t)he(y) deem desirable in connection with any tax matter involving to any extent myself, my family, or my estate. My executor(s) shall have full power and discretion to make, or determine not to make, any and all elections available to me or my estate with respect to income, gift, estate, or generation skipping transfers, and my Executor(s) determination shall be final and binding on all parties. No compensating adjustments of any sort shall be required as a result of any election made or not made by my Executor(s) pursuant to this authority.

Funeral and Disposition of the Body. Many people insert clauses with respect to their wishes for funeral and burial or cremation. Unfortunately, by the time the will is probated, the testator is long since dead; however, by having the client insert this clause it causes him to think of what arrangements he wants and to see that they are provided for while he is alive.

Many people favor cremation, and indicate that they would like their ashes scattered. Most health laws prohibit scattering ashes, so any such disposition should be avoided.

> I hereby direct my Executor to see that I am buried according to the tenets of the ____________ faith. I wish my body to be buried in the ____________ Cemetery, and that no more than $____________ be spent on my funeral.

Also, if the testator served in the Armed Forces he is entitled to limited funeral and burial costs from the Veteran's Administration. The will should indicate this fact so that the executor can get some reimbursement from the government.

> I further direct my Executor to see that my estate receives as much reimbursement as possible for the cost of my funeral and burial from the Veteran's Administration because I am an honorably discharged veteran of the United States branch of service.

Minors Clause. A standard clause usually inserted into wills is a boilerplate provision dealing with gifts to minors. Regardless of who the heirs may be at the date of execution, they may be different by the date of death, and so the clause should be included. The purpose of this clause is to insure, to the best extent possible, that property left to a minor is kept intact until the minor reaches majority and is not squandered or dissipated by the minor or the guardian.

> Should any person entitled to any money or other property under this Will be then a minor, I authorize my Executor(s) and/or Trustee(s), in their discretion, to pay the same or any part thereof to either parent of said minor, or to his or her guardian, without bond, or to a custodian to be appointed by my Executor(s) and/or Trustee(s) pursuant to the Uniform Gift to Minors Act, or to retain the custody thereof and/or to apply the same to the use of said minor, granting to my Executor(s) and/or Trustee(s) a power in trust for such purposes, and the receipt by said parent, guardian, or custodian shall fully discharge said Executor(s) and/or trustee(s) in respect of such payments. All of the powers granted to my Executor(s) and/or Trustee(s) in this Will shall maintain in force and shall apply to such money or other property until such minor shall die or attain his or her majority.

Specific and General Testamentary Gifts. The next clauses, and the bulk of the will, concern the distribution of the testator's assets. The gifts should be divided according to the nature of the property given. Typically the order is: land, cash, personal property. Also, because of the tax deduction, the first gifts mentioned, regardless of the property given, are usually charitable gifts.

Gifts of real property are known as **devises** and the recipients are **devisees;** gifts of money are called **legacies** and the recipients, **legatees;** gifts of personal property, **bequests**, and the recipients, **beneficiaries**. Still, most recipients under a will are referred to as "beneficiaries" or "heirs." If the gift indicates a specific item of property, it is a **specific devise** (or legacy or bequest). If general property is stated, it is a **general devise** (or legacy or bequest). A **demonstrative legacy** is a gift of money to be paid from a particular source of funds.

When drafting the clauses, always indicate the relationship of the recipient to the testator and, if appropriate, where the recipient resides. This helps establish testamentary capacity and locate the beneficiary so he or she can receive the property.

Remember to describe the property carefully and to indicate whether the recipient is to receive other property should the particular asset have adeemed. Also, with real estate, indicate whether the devisee takes subject to, or free of, any mortgages on the property.

> I hereby give, devise, and bequeath to the American Cancer Society the sum of Five Hundred Dollars ($500). [specific legacy]
>
> I hereby give, devise, and bequeath my house located at ____________, and all the household effects therein to my daughter, free of all mortgages. [specific devise]

> I hereby give, devise, and bequeath all of the money located in account number ___________ at the ___________ Bank to my friend ___________. Should I die without having an account at said bank, this gift shall be considered adeemed. [demonstrative legacy]
>
> I hereby give, devise, and bequeath the cross I inherited from my Aunt Mae to my cousin ___________. Should I no longer die possessed of said cross at my death, then I hereby give to my cousin ___________ any item of personal property of which I die possessed of her choosing. Should my cousin ___________ predecease me, or not survive me by thirty days, this gift shall lapse and form a part of my residuary estate.

A special provision should be made for co-operative apartments.

> I hereby give, devise, and bequeath to ___________ all my right, title, and interest in and to my co-operative residence at ___________, of which I am the tenant-shareholder, together with the proprietary lease thereof and the stock owned by me at my death in the corporation owning the building in which said residence is located, subject to any charges thereon.

Likewise, a special clause may be used for community property.

> I hereby confirm to my spouse his/her one-half share of our community property. All the remainder of my one-half share of our community property I hereby give, devise, and bequeath to ___________.

Marital Deduction. Any property left to a surviving spouse should be specifically indicated as a marital deduction. The gift can take the form of a specific or general bequest, devise, or legacy, as indicated above, or may be in the form of a trust or residuary clause indicated below.

Trusts. Any trust created by will is known as a testamentary trust. As stated and explained in Chapter 4, the words used to create a trust are the same regardless of whether it is inter vivos or testamentary. However, two special types of trusts that refer to the marital deduction are exemplified here. The first is a Unified or A-B trust. Recall that in this type of situation the will must create two trusts.

> Should my spouse survive me, I give to my Trustees a sum equal to the largest amount that can pass free of federal estate tax by reason of the unified credit allowable to my estate, but no other credit, reduced by dispositions passing under Paragraph ___________ of this Will and property passing outside this Will which does not qualify for the marital or charitable deductions in computing the federal estate tax owed by my estate. For the purpose of establishing the sum disposed of by this Paragraph, the values finally fixed in the federal estate tax proceeding (or state estate tax proceeding in the event that no federal return is filed) relating to my estate shall be used.
>
> My Trustees shall hold said sum IN TRUST and invest and reinvest the same and pay the net income therefrom to my said spouse at least quarter-annually during his/her life, and at any time or from time to time

to pay him/her so much of the principal, whether the whole or a lesser amount, as my Trustees may in their sole, absolute, and uncontrolled discretion deem necessary, advisable, or expedient. In exercising their discretionary power, my Trustees may, but need not, consider the other resources of my spouse.

Upon my spouse's death, my Trustees shall pay all of the principal of the trust, as then constituted, to my issue surviving my said spouse, subject to the trust established in Paragraph __________ of this Will. Should none of my issue survive my said spouse, this principal shall form a part of my residuary estate.

The paragraph following this clause should create the B Trust, which, as indicated above, is meant for the benefit of the testator's issue.

The second special type of trust that should be considered is a trust that meets the requirements of a QTIP. As discussed in the earlier Chapters 1 and 4, the QTIP trust can be used in conjunction with a unified credit trust.

QTIP Trust

Should my said spouse survive me, I hereby give the sum of __________ to my Trustees, to hold the same in trust, to invest and reinvest the same and to pay the net income to my said spouse at least quarterly during his/her life. My Trustees may, at any time or from time to time, pay to my said spouse, or apply for his/her benefit, so much of the principal, whether the whole or a lesser amount, as my Trustees may in their sole, absolute, and uncontrolled discretion deem necessary, advisable, or expedient.

Upon my said spouse's death, my Trustees shall pay all or the principal of the trust, as then constituted, to my issue surviving my said spouse per stirpes. Should none of my issue survive my said spouse, the principal shall be given to my then living heirs-at-law per capita.

Simultaneous Death Clause. In order to avoid confusion, if persons die in a common disaster, most wills include a common disaster clause. Without provision for distribution of property when the testator and beneficiary die together, the estate may be taxed, in certain situations, as though each inherited property from the other. There are two methods to avoid this result: first, with each gift the testator can specify that the beneficiary must survive him or her by a certain number of days, and if the beneficiary does not survive that period, an alternate disposition is made of the property.

I hereby give, devise, and bequeath the sum of One Thousand Dollars ($1,000) to my cousin Rose. Should Rose predecease or not survive me by thirty days, I hereby give this One Thousand Dollars ($1,000) to my Aunt Fleur.

The second alternative is to insert a paragraph to cover all testamentary gifts.

Should any person named in this, my Last Will and Testament, predecease me, or die in a common disaster, or not survive me by thirty days, then the legacy, bequest, or devise given to him, her, or them shall form a part of my residuary estate.

Anti-Contest Clause. An anti-contest, or **in terrorem** clause, is used to discourage persons from contesting the will. However, several jurisdictions do not recognize these clauses (see Chapter 9), and for those states its insertion serves no purpose.

> Should any person named in this, my Last Will and Testament, contest this instrument, he or she shall forfeit the bequest, legacy, or devise given to him or her under this instrument.

This clause has the effect of divesting a beneficiary of the testamentary gift if he or she contests the will and loses; if the person wins, he or she receives an intestate share if the person is an intestate heir or a gift left to him or her under an earlier will (see below).

Family Omissions. This is a standard clause that may be inserted to dispel the thought that the testator has forgotten family members. This is a "nice" way of cutting persons out of the estate.

> I have specifically and intentionally omitted all of my other relations from this, my Last Will and Testament, and have done so after thorough examination and reflection of the past years.

Advancements. If any child received an advancement, it should be mentioned in the will to avoid family squabbles.

> I have not made any provision for my daughter Regina in this, my Last Will and Testament, because of all of the gifts and expenditures made on her behalf while I was alive which constitutes an advancement of any testamentary gift.

Provisions for Pets. Many people die leaving pets that must be cared for. Money and property cannot be left outright to animals, but property can be given to the person selected to care for the pet for the purpose of supporting the animal. This can be an outright gift, a conditional gift, or a trust can be established.

> I hereby give my cats to ___________ to keep or to find suitable homes for. None of my cats is to be declawed. If, in the best judgment of ___________ and Dr. ___________, my veterinarian, any of my cats is doing poorly and should be put to sleep, I hereby direct that said cat or cats be put to sleep without suffering. In order to maintain my cats, I hereby give ___________ the sum of ___________ to be used for their maintenance.

Residuary Clause. The residuary clause, or **residuum**, is used to dispose of property not otherwise distributed by the will. This clause can also be used as an alternative beneficiary for gifts in which the named recipient predeceases the testator, as well as for the disposition of after-acquired property. No will is ever complete without a residuum.

> I hereby give, devise, and bequeath all the rest, residue, and remainder of my estate—real, personal, and mixed—wherever the same may be located to __________.

Remember, the residuary taker may be a trust established during the life of the testator, a marital deduction, may itself be a trust created in its own clause, or multiple persons each receiving a specified percentage of the estate. Simply make sure that the wishes of the testator are carried out. It is not unusual for the bulk of a person's property to be disposed of by means of the residuum.

General Revocatory Clause. Although a later will, by operation of law, revokes earlier wills, it is usual to insert a general revocatory clause in the will.

> I hereby revoke, cancel, and terminate all other Wills, Testaments, and Codicils to Wills heretofore by me made.

Testimonium. The testimonium is the last clause in the will before the testator's signature. It is an indication that he is freely and voluntarily signing the will.

> IN WITNESS WHEREOF I have hereunto set my hand and seal this __________ day of __________, 20 ____.

Testator's Signature. Immediately after the testimonium, there should be a line for the testator to sign underwritten with the word "Testator."

Testators unable to sign their names may make a mark which will be acknowledged by the witnesses, or have their names signed by a third person. If someone signs on the testator's behalf, he must sign himself indicating that he is signing for the testator. This person should not be an attesting witness to the will.

Attestation Clause. The attestation clause is the statement signed by the witnesses. This clause, followed by the witnesses' signatures, is the only writing that may appear after the testator's signature.

> The foregoing instrument consisting of this and __________ other typewritten pages was, at the date hereof, subscribed, sealed, and published, and declared by __________ as and for his Last Will and Testament in our joint presence, and we, at the same time, at his request and in his presence and in the presence of each other, hereunto subscribed our names and residences as attesting witnesses the day and year last above written.

Witnesses' Signatures. Following the attestation clause there should be lines for the witnesses to sign. Most jurisdictions only require two witnesses, but a few require three. See Chapter 9 for the appropriate number for your jurisdiction, and for the requirements to be a witness.

One last word about the technical aspect of drafting a will. Always make sure that there is at least part of a clause preceding the testimonium that appears on the last page, and make sure that the testimonium, testator's signature, attestation, and witnesses' signatures all appear on the same page. This calls for some creative spacing, but it saves problems later on regarding questions of the integrity of the will.

Once the will is typed, staple it in a will cover prior to the execution of the document.

Executing a Will

Witnesses

Formal wills, in order to be valid and enforceable, must have the testator's signature witnessed. Every jurisdiction requires wills to be witnessed, generally by competent adults who are resident in the state in which the will is executed and who have never been convicted of a felony. For the requirements to be a witness for each jurisdiction, see Chapter 9.

Wills do not have to be notarized. Notarization is only required for written statements made under oath, such as affidavits. The will itself merely requires witnessing.

The witnesses are not involved with the contents of the will itself. Primarily, the purpose of the witnesses is to ascertain that the testator freely and voluntarily signed the instrument, that the testator knew the instrument was his or her will, and that the testator wished to have the signing witnessed. Additionally, witnesses may be called upon to testify as to the general capacity of the testator at the time of the signing—did he appear competent, did he appear to understand what he was doing, and so forth. Paralegals, law clerks, attorneys, and secretaries working in the office of the attorney who drafts the will are typically used as the witnesses to the will.

It is without question a bad idea to have any person who benefits from the will witness the testator's signature because of the obvious personal advantage to the witness/beneficiary. Several jurisdictions prohibit any beneficiary under a will to serve as a witness to that will because of the conflict of interest. If a problem does arise, most courts will permit the person to fulfill the function of the witness while divesting him or her of the gift under the will. The overriding consideration for the probate court is to uphold valid wills, and if a witness has to lose a bequest in order to find the will enforceable, the validity of the instrument prevails. If the witness happens to be an intestate heir of the decedent, he or she may still be entitled to an intestate portion of the estate even though he or she loses the testamentary gift. Note that this problem does not arise with respect to serving as the executor of the will. An executor may be the primary beneficiary under the will (and usually is), and the will, if all other requirements are met, will stand and the executor will receive the gift. The prohibition is only to insure the disinterest of the *witness*.

EXAMPLES:

1. In his will, Barney leaves a large bequest to his sister-in-law, Fleur. Fleur is one of the two witnesses to the will. In Barney's domicile, the law requires that a will have two witnesses. If Fleur is disqualified as a witness, Barney is intestate because the will does not meet the statutory requirements for execution; in order to avoid intestacy, Fleur will remain a witness but lose her bequest.
2. Barney's other witness is his wife, Fern, to whom he has left the bulk of his estate as a marital deduction. As above, Fern's status as a witness will prevail and she will lose her gift under the will. However, Fern is the primary intestate heir of Barney. As a spouse she cannot be disinherited, and so in this instance she loses her gift under the will but still is entitled to a statutory share of the estate. However, she may lose the tax benefit of the marital deduction.

Execution

The execution of a will is probably the most formal legal activity that exists, and the legal assistant generally plays a very important part in the process. The procedures follow a fairly typical pattern.

The lawyer calls the testator, the witnesses, and a notary into one room. All of the parties are introduced. The lawyer then has the testator read the exordium and testimonium of the will. The testator then counts the pages of the will and signs at the bottom of each page, then on the signature line appearing after the testimonium. The witnesses listen and see all of the preceding.

The lawyer reads the attestation clause to the witnesses, and asks the witnesses whether they understand what they are witnessing. If they do, each witness signs in the presence and sight of the testator and of each other. When all of the witnesses have signed, the will is considered **executed**—complete with respect to all legal requirements.

The specific requirements with respect to having the witnesses see the testator sign, or being permitted to have the testator acknowledge his or her signature previously made, and with respect to the witnesses seeing each other sign, varies from state to state. Chapter 8 provides a complete catalog of the state requirements. Note, however, that whatever the state requires must be met *exactly*; no variance is permitted, and the courts are extremely careful in making sure the formalities have been met.

EXAMPLE:

Tom goes to his lawyer to have his will executed. One of the witnesses called in by the attorney is almost nine months pregnant. Tom's state requires that the witnesses see each other sign. When it comes time to witness the will, the pregnant woman cannot sit at the table and reach the will, so she stands up, goes to a console, and with her back to the table signs her name as an attesting witness. This will is invalid. Even though it is most likely that the lady signed, the other witness did not actually "see" her sign — her back was to him.

If this result seems unduly severe, be aware that this example is based on a real case.

Once the formalities are met, the lawyer may ask the witnesses to sign an affidavit detailing what they have just witnessed. This affidavit is attached to the will and makes the will self-proving (see below). It is for the purpose of this affidavit that a notary was asked to join the group.

The will (and the affidavit) should be stapled into a will jacket before the execution takes place, and after execution the will may be placed in a will envelope. The client can then seal and sign the envelope flap, thereby keeping prying eyes from reading the contents of the will.

Take note that there are circumstances in which the self-proving affidavit may be insufficient. If there is a will contest, any contesting party has the right to examine the witnesses, as does the court.

The original will is given to the client. It is recommended that the will be kept at the client's home in a locked fireproof box, and that the client inform the person who is named as the executor in the will where the will is located. This way, when the client dies the will is readily available.

Never place a will in a safe deposit box! On death, all bank accounts and safe deposit boxes are sealed and can only be opened by court order. If the will is in the box, this creates additional problems in the administration of the estate. For a full discussion of estate administration and how to retrieve a will from a sealed safe deposit box, see Chapter 7.

The client may now die secure in the knowledge that he or she will die testate.

Self-Proving Wills

A **self-proving will** is a will to which has been affixed a notarized affidavit signed by the attesting witnesses, in which they affirm all of the information required by a probate court to admit the will to probate. The affidavit is notarized, not the will. Most jurisdictions permit self-proving wills, and the state statutes provide samples of the affidavit that can be used. Its import lies in the fact that if the will is self-proving, and if there is no will contest, the witnesses do not have to appear before the clerk of the probate court. If the will is not self-proving, the witnesses must testify under oath before an officer of the court as to all of the circumstances surrounding the execution of the will. If the will was executed 20 years prior to the testator's death, it would be quite complicated to locate the witnesses after that period of time and arrange for their appearance in court. A self-proving will does not prevent any person with standing to challenge the will from exercising his or her right to examine the witnesses personally.

A sample affidavit appears later in the chapter as part of the Sample Will. For a list of the jurisdictions that permit self-proving wills, see Chapter 9.

Miscellaneous Instruments

Almost without exception, today's paralegal will only be involved with the formal, written wills discussed above. However, some other types of instruments and dispositions must be covered here in order to provide a complete description of wills.

Nuncupative Wills

A **nuncupative will** is an oral will. Historically, oral wills were permitted for members of the Armed Services, mariners at sea, and persons *in extremis* due to accident or illness. On their deathbeds these persons told someone how they wanted their assets distributed. The only record of the disposition was the memory of the witness, and these types of wills are disfavored because of the lack of formality. Some jurisdictions still permit nuncupative wills, and have slightly expanded the category of testators who may make a nuncupative will, but generally the amount and type of property that can be disposed of in this fashion is limited. See Chapter 9. Most jurisdictions do not permit nuncupative wills, or if they do, limit their use. The modern trend is to delete the statutory provision for nuncupative wills when the statute is updated.

EXAMPLE:

Tom is in an airplane that is about to crash. As the plane descends, he tells the person in the next seat that, should he die, he wants his best friend to inherit all of his worldly goods. Tom does not survive, but his neighbor does. The neighbor might try to have this disposition enforced, but the state statute limits the amount of property that Tom can leave in this manner, and so the bulk of his estate passes by the laws of descent and distribution discussed in Chapter 3.

Holographic Wills

A **holographic will** is a will written in the testator's own handwriting, as opposed to being typed or printed. Once again, although historically possible, most jurisdictions no longer permit holographs, or when they do, they place stringent requirements on the instrument. Holographs may or may not be witnessed, depending upon the requirements of the particular state statute. For information regarding which states permit holographs and their requirements, see Chapter 9.

EXAMPLE:

Dr. Montague, feeling guilty about mismanaging his in-laws' trust fund, goes to a motel to kill himself. Before he pulls the trigger, he takes a piece of motel stationery with the motel letterhead on top and writes out a will, leaving half of his property to Cornelia and the other half to the trust fund.

Pursuant to his state statute, to be valid, a holograph must be *entirely* written in the testator's own hand. When the trust beneficiary tries to have the will enforced, it will be found invalid. Why? Because the stationery had the motel's name and address printed on it—the instrument was not *entirely* in the testator's own hand!

Note that although true in most jurisdictions, the above example might be found valid in some states that have different requirements for holographic wills. Be aware, though, that like nuncupative wills, holographs are generally disfavored (except in Louisiana—see Chapter 9).

Statutory Wills

A **statutory will** is a will form that is printed in the state statute for use by its domiciliaries. Testators who follow the provisions of the statutory will usually have the instruments pass probate without much trouble. Of course, as part of a general statute the statutory will may not take into consideration the particular needs of an individual testator.

Living Wills

A so-called **living will** is an instrument that indicates what type of life support treatment a person wants in the event he or she becomes incapable of speaking and whether he or she wants to donate organs. Almost every jurisdiction permits living wills, and the provisions usually appear in the state statute under its health care provisions. Most of the states provide samples that can be used. Where a living will is not permitted, the state usually permit **health care proxies**, who are people designated to make health care decisions for those no longer capable of making such decisions themselves.

Although it is a good idea to discuss living wills with clients, and to have one prepared for the client at the time of executing the formal will, some courts only accept the living will as a rebuttable indication of the person's wishes. A family member may be able to counteract the living will, and some medical institutions will not enforce them. For an example of a living will, see the Sample Will below.

Power of Attorney

A **power of attorney** is a document by which a person authorizes another person to act on the first person's behalf. Generally, a power of attorney takes effect when executed. Many people execute powers of attorney in favor of friends or relatives if they are going to be away from home for a while so that the friend or relative can take care of the home during the absence.

A **springing power of attorney** is a power of attorney that takes effect not upon execution, but at some time in the future, when the conditions specified in the power occur. Living wills are often incorporated into powers of attorney so that the power takes effect when the person granting the power becomes incapacitated. In many jurisdictions these powers of attorney are considered health care proxies, limiting action to health care decisions.

A **durable power of attorney**, by contrast, is a power of attorney that goes into effect upon execution of the document and remains in effect despite the future disability of the principal. When drafting a durable or springing power of attorney it is important to specify *exactly* how the person's incapacity is to be determined (e.g., by doctors, court, attorney, etc.). It is also necessary to specify exactly what authority is being granted to the attorney-in-fact. Always be as specific as possible to avoid the attorney's "jumping the gun" before the person is truly incapacitated.

EXAMPLE:

Loretta executes a springing power of attorney in Aida's favor, specifying that the power is to take effect only when two independent physicians affirm by affidavit that she, Loretta, is incapable of acting in her own behalf. At such time as the power of attorney becomes effective, Aida is given full authority to deal with Loretta's assets, just as if she were the owner of the property.

For an example of a springing power of attorney, see the Sample Will below.

Changing the Will

Simply because a will is properly drafted and executed does not mean that the client will not change his or her mind with respect to its provisions. A will only takes effect upon the testator's death, and the testator has the right and ability to **revoke** (or rescind) the will, or to make changes to an existing will. There are three major methods whereby a will may be changed: by amendment, by operation of law, and by revocation.

Amendment Through Codicils

A will may be amended by a separate instrument known as a **codicil**. The codicil must meet all of the formalities of a regular will. However, rather than reprinting the entire will, the codicil merely indicates changes to an existing will. The codicil still has the exordium and testimonium, along with the attestation clause and witnesses, and may also be self-proved. The other terms of the will are incorporated by reference into the codicil. A codicil is a dependent instrument, needing a main will to amend, whereas a will is an independent instrument.

Nowadays, because of computers and word processors, codicils rarely appear. Because the entire will is on a disk, it is just as easy, or easier, to make changes on the disk and reprint a brand new will incorporating the changes. Because all of the formalities of execution still have to be met, most firms use this method rather than codicils.

EXAMPLE:

Barney and Fleur have a falling out, and Barney wants to cut Fleur out of his will, giving her gift to his other sister-in-law, Hyacinth, instead. Barney can either have his attorney draw up a codicil, or have a new will printed up in which Fleur's name is deleted and substituted with Hyacinth's. In either instance, the instrument will have to be formally executed and witnessed.

Amendment Through Operation of Law

Changes in family status operate to modify a will. Any time a testator marries, divorces, or has a child, by operation of law his or her testamentary disposition may be changed. Remember, in most states a spouse may not be disinherited, a child or issue may not be pretermitted, and a divorced spouse is no longer a surviving spouse. Whenever a client undergoes a fundamental change in his or her family situation, his or her will should be reviewed and most probably changed.

EXAMPLE:

In Regina's first will she left the bulk of her property to her first husband as a marital deduction. When she divorced, this provision became inoperative, and she drew up a new will. When she remarried, her new husband was now legally entitled to a portion of her estate, even though he was not mentioned in this second will. Regina had a third will drafted, leaving property to her second husband as a marital deduction. As Regina and Leonard had children, new wills became necessary to avoid having the children pretermitted; had new wills not been executed, the daughters would be entitled to an intestate share of Regina's estate.

Note that in some jurisdictions these family changes (such as divorce) operate to revoke the existing will automatically, meaning that the person dies intestate; in other states these changes only modify the will with respect to the actual change: permitting after-born children and new spouses to inherit an intestate portion of the property, keeping all of the other will provisions intact. Always check the state statute to determine the effect of family changes on an existing will.

As a subset of this topic, some jurisdictions have enacted statutes, known as **Slayer Statutes,** under which a beneficiary or intestate heir loses his or her rights to the decedent's estate if the heir was criminally responsible for killing the decedent (even by manslaughter). A person is prohibited from benefiting from his own wrongdoing. See Chapter 3.

Also, any time a new will is executed, it revokes all prior wills and codicils. Note, however, that if a later will is found to be invalid, the probate court will look to see if an earlier will can be resurrected. The rationale is that the law presumes that a person would rather die testate than intestate, and the only reason the earlier will was revoked was because he or she believed the later will was valid. This legal theory is known as **dependent relative revocation**.

EXAMPLE:

When Barney dies, the probate court finds a technical problem in his last will and declares it invalid. This was the will in which he made a gift to Hyacinth. The original of Barney's earlier will still exists, and is then submitted to probate and found valid. Fleur now receives her bequest.

The doctrine of dependent relative revocation can only take effect if the earlier will is still in existence.

Revocation

In order to avoid the application of the doctrine of dependent relative revocation, or any confusion as to which of several is the testator's *last* will, the testator may physically destroy the instrument. A will may be physically revoked by the testator burning it, tearing it, writing "cancelled" on it, or by crossing out its provisions. However, it must be clear that the act of revocation was done by the testator (or at his direction) freely, voluntarily, and knowingly; otherwise the will will not be considered revoked.

EXAMPLES:

1. Learning about the doctrine of dependent relative revocation, Barney tears up his first will. Now if the second will is found invalid, Barney is intestate; the act of tearing up the will is an act of physical revocation.

2. Fleur hears about Barney's new will. She goes to Barney's house, finds the new will, and tears it up so that the only will that exists is the one in which she receives a bequest. In this instance the second will is not revoked — the testator did not revoke the will. No one else's action acts to revoke another person's will unless done at the testator's direction.

Will Contests

A **will contest** is a legal challenge to the validity of a document presented to a probate court as the last will and testament of the decedent. In order to initiate a will contest, the challenger must have standing (the legal right to initiate the lawsuit) to challenge the will. Any person who would benefit by having the document declared invalid has standing to institute a will contest. The persons who would benefit from a finding that the will is invalid fall into the following categories:

1. intestate heirs, if there is no other existing will
2. persons named in earlier wills who would benefit under the doctrine of dependent relative revocation
3. people named in a later will who claim the one presented is not the last will
4. creditors for heavily indebted estates

Only these persons have the right to challenge the will, and because of this, they are required to receive notice when a will is filed for probate.

EXAMPLE:

When Barney dies and his will is filed for probate, Fleur's boyfriend is furious because he had been told that Barney left Fleur a substantial inheritance. In the last will executed by Barney, Fleur's gift was given to Hyacinth. Fleur's boyfriend wants to contest the will. He cannot; he lacks standing. The boyfriend is neither an intestate heir nor a beneficiary under a previous will. On the other hand, if he could convince Fleur to fight the will, she would have standing because she would benefit if the filed will was found invalid and the earlier one was then admitted to probate.

There are seven grounds that can be used as the basis of a will contest.

1. *The will was not properly executed.* This challenge is to the formal requirements for executing a valid will, such as not having a sufficient number of witnesses, having the testator acknowledge

his or her signature when that is not allowed under the state statute, or, where allowed, the holograph was not entirely written in the testator's own hand, and so forth. This ground for will contests is totally dependent upon the requirements of the particular state statute with respect to execution.

2. *The testator's signature was forged.* A forgery comes about when the testator's "signature" is affixed to the will, but the testator neither signed the instrument nor directed anyone to sign on his or her behalf. This challenge requires proof by the testimony of witnesses who are familiar with the testator's signature, as well as that of handwriting experts.
3. *The will contains material mistakes, contradictions, and ambiguities.* This challenge is both technical and is concerned with the testamentary capacity of the testator. If the document intrinsically contains material mistakes and contradictions, it may appear that the testator did not truly know the nature and extent of his or her property and the natural bounty of his or her affections. Remember, the mistake must be material, not incidental.
4. *The will presented for probate was revoked.* As previously discussed, a will is revoked either by a new will, change in family status, or by the deliberate act of the testator. If any of these circumstances occur, the document presented to the court can be challenged. Remember, only the last validly executed will is the will of the decedent.
5. *The testator lacked testamentary capacity.* In order to prevail in a will contest based on a lack of testamentary capacity, the challenger has to prove that, at the time of executing the will, the decedent did not know the nature and extent of his or her property or the natural bounty of his or her affections. This is fairly hard to prove, especially if the document presented, on its face, bears no indication of lack of capacity. In these circumstances, the testimony of the witnesses to the will becomes extremely important, because they were present at the moment of execution. Whenever a will is challenged, the will is not considered self-proven, and the witnesses must appear in court.
6. *The will was induced by fraud.* Because a will must be entered into freely and intentionally, if the testator was defrauded into signing the document, it was not knowingly signed and is therefore invalid.
7. *The testator was induced to execute the will by undue influence. Undue influence* occurs when a person in a close position to the testator uses that position to convince the testator to execute his will in a particular fashion. The will does not have to benefit the person with the influence; it simply has to be shown that the person used the position of trust and confidence to influence the testamentary disposition. This ground for a will contest is the most prevalent and the one that receives the most notoriety.

EXAMPLES:

1. Dr. Montague executes a will but only has two witnesses. His state requires three witnesses to a will. The beneficiary of an earlier will can challenge this instrument on the grounds that it was improperly executed.
2. When Kingston dies, Regina submits a will to probate purporting to leave everything to Regina. Kingston's signature was forged by Regina's husband. Any of Kingston's blood relatives can challenge this instrument based on forgery.
3. In her will, Loretta declares that she has never been married, but leaves a bequest to her "husband, Jason Leroy," and further mentions that she has two children. These mistakes are material, indicating a lack of capacity, because Loretta does not appear to know her own family situation.
4. In his will, Tom leaves the shares in his "condominium" residence to his friends. There are no "shares" in a condominium; Tom owns a co-op. However, except for this error, the will is correct, indicating the address and description of the apartment. In this instance it would appear that the use of the word "condominium" was a typographical error, and the will will stand.
5. When Barney dies, Fleur submits the earlier will to probate, the will that left her a substantial bequest. Fern then submits the later will. If the later will is found valid, it revokes the earlier will.
6. In David's will he leaves the bulk of his assets to Hyacinth and Fern, with only a small bequest to Fleur. Fleur challenges the will, claiming that she was David's favorite daughter, and therefore, if he were competent when he executed the will, she would have received a larger bequest. Fleur must examine the witnesses as to their impression of David's state of mind when the will was signed.
7. Regina tells her parents that she will relinquish all claims to her house. She goes to her parents with papers to sign in which her rights are given up; however, in the pile of papers she has her parents sign is a will drawn in her favor. When Kingston dies, Regina attempts to probate this document. This document is obviously not Kingston's will. He thought he was signing an acknowledgment of Regina's release to rights to the house, not his last will and testament.
8. As David becomes more infirm, his daughters place him in a nursing home. In the home David becomes more and more dependent and close to his nurse, Barbara "Boom Boom" Latour. In his will, executed at the home, David leaves his entire estate

> to "his Boom Boom," who he says was the only one who truly cared for him at the end of his life. Hyacinth, Fern, and Fleur are in court in a heartbeat, challenging the will on the grounds of undue influence.

In order to avoid will contests, many people insert anticontest clauses in their wills. If the clause is valid in the particular jurisdiction (see Chapter 9), its insertion has a chilling effect on a potential challenger. The challenger who loses forfeits his or her gift under the will. Sometimes it is better to have the definite gift in the will rather then to risk losing it by instituting a will contest.

Sample Will and Accompanying Documents

The following is a sample will with accompanying documents for Hyacinth Bush. Note that some of the clauses are different from the ones mentioned above. This simply represents other clauses that may be inserted into a will.

Last Will and Testament of Hyacinth Bush

I, Hyacinth Bush, now domiciled and residing in the State of __________ at __________, being over eighteen years of age and of sound and disposing mind and memory, and not acting under the duress, menace, fraud, or undue influence of any person or persons whomsoever, do hereby freely and voluntarily make, publish, and declare this instrument to be my Last Will and Testament.

One

I hereby declare that I am married to Oscar Bush, and that I have one son, Byron.

Two

I hereby appoint, constitute, and designate my Husband, Oscar Bush, now residing in this State, to act as the Executor of this, my Last Will and Testament. Should my husband, Oscar Bush, not survive me by thirty (30) days, or for any reason, fail or cease to act as my Executor, then I appoint as substitute Executor my son Byron Bush of __________ to act as successor Executor of this, my Last Will and Testament. I direct that none of my Executors shall be required to furnish bond or other security for the faithful performance of his duties, or, if any such bond is required, I direct that no sureties be required thereon.

Three

I hereby direct that whenever the terms "Executors" or "Trustees" are used in this Will they shall include, in both cases, only such persons as shall qualify, and their survivors and successors, whether originally named herein or appointed under the powers herein conferred or conferred by any Court. I authorize my Executors and/or Trustees, then acting by a majority of their number, in their discretion, to add to or decrease their number, or, subject to the above substitute appointment, to fill any vacancy in their number, or to appoint a successor Executor and/or Trustee in order to fill such vacancy when the same may occur, with the same rights and powers as if originally named as one of my Executors and/or Trustees. Such appointment and the acceptance thereof shall be duly acknowledged in the office of the Clerk of the Court in which this Will shall have been probated. Any appointment of a successor Executor and/or Trustee in advance shall be similarly revoked at any time before the occurrence of such vacancy. Such advance appointment need not be filed until the same becomes effective. I authorize those of my Executors and/or Trustees who have power or discretion in the matter in question to act by a majority of their number. None of my Executors and/or Trustees shall be required to furnish bond even though not a resident of the State in which my Will shall have been probated. Each Executor and/or Trustee shall be chargeable only for his or her own willful default, and shall not be liable for any loss or damage to my estate unless caused by such willful default.

My Executor(s) shall have all of the powers granted to fiduciaries under _______________ of the State of __________, including but not limited to the following: my Executor(s) shall have full power and authority, without the necessity of order of Court, to sell, at either public or private sale, or to exchange, lease, pledge, or mortgage, in such manner and on such terms as my Executor(s) deems advisable, any or all property, real, personal, or mixed, belonging to my estate, and to execute all deeds, assignments, mortgages, leases, or other instruments necessary or proper for those purposes; to adjust, compromise, or otherwise settle claims of any nature in favor of or against my estate on such terms as my Executor(s) deems advisable; to make distributions wholly or partly in kind by allotting or transferring specific securities, other real or personal property, or undivided interests therein, at their then current values; to retain securities or other property owned by me at the time of my death, although the same may not, without this instruction, be considered a proper investment for Executors; and generally to perform any act and to execute any instrument with respect to such property as if my Executor(s) was the absolute owner thereof, but no power under this Will shall be exercised or enforceable if it would defeat qualifying for any deduction otherwise available to my estate for estate tax purposes. Notwithstanding any other provisions of this Will, my Executor(s) shall, to the extent possible, not use any property otherwise excludable from my estate for estate tax purposes for payment of any obligation of my estate, including any obligation for taxes.

I hereby vest my Executor(s) with full power to do anything (t)he(y) deems desirable in connection with any tax matter involving, to any extent, myself, my family, or my estate. My Executor(s) shall have full power and discretion to make, or determine not to make, any and all elections available to me or my estate with respect to income, gift, estate, or generation-skipping transfer taxes, and my Executor(s) determination shall be final and binding on all parties. No compensating adjustments of any sort shall be required as a result of any election made or not made by my Executor(s) pursuant to this authority.

Four

It is my wish and desire that, at my death, my body be cremated.

Five

Should any person entitled to any money or other property under this Will be then a minor, I authorize my Executor(s) and/or Trustees(s), in their discretion, to pay the same or any part thereof to either parent of said minor, or to his or her guardian, without bond, or to a custodian to be appointed by my Executor(s) and/or Trustee(s) pursuant to the Uniform Gifts to Minors Act, or to retain the custody thereof and/or to apply the same to the use of said minor, granting to my Executor(s) and/or Trustee(s) a power in trust for such purpose, and the receipt by said parent, guardian, or custodian shall fully discharge said Executor(s) and/or Trustee(s) in respect to such payments. All of the powers granted to my Executor(s) and/or Trustee(s) in this Will shall maintain in force and shall apply to such money or other property until such minor shall die or attain his or her majority.

Six

I hereby give and bequeath the sum of Ten Thousand Dollars ($10,000.00) to my sister, Fleur LaPlante. Should Fleur LaPlante predecease me or not survive me by thirty (30) days, this bequest shall become part of my residuary estate.

Seven

I hereby give and bequeath the sum of Ten Thousand Dollars ($10,000.00) to my sister, Fern Potts. Should Fern Potts predecease me or not survive me by thirty (30) days, this bequest shall become part of my residuary estate.

Eight

I hereby give and bequeath to my niece, Rose, my art deco bracelet. Should my niece, Rose, predecease me or not survive me by thirty (30) days, this bequest shall become part of my residuary estate.

Nine

Should any person named in this, my Last Will and Testament, contest this instrument, he, she, or they shall forfeit the legacy, bequest, or devise given to him, her, or them under this instrument.

Ten

I have specifically and intentionally omitted all of my other relations from this, my Last Will and Testament, and have done so after thorough examination and reflection of the past years.

Eleven

I hereby give, devise, and bequeath all the rest, residue, and remainder of my estate—real, personal, and mixed—wherever the same may be located to my husband, Oscar Bush, as a Marital Deduction. Should my husband, Oscar Bush, predecease me or not survive me by thirty (30) days, I hereby give and devise my residuary estate to my son, Byron Bush.

Twelve

I hereby revoke, cancel, and terminate all other Wills, Testaments, and Codicils to Wills heretofore by me made.

IN WITNESS WHEREOF I have hereunto set my hand and seal this __________ day of __________, 20____.

____
Testatrix

The foregoing instrument consisting of this and __________ other typewritten pages, was at the date hereof, subscribed, sealed, and published, and declared by __________ as and for her Last Will and Testament in our joint presence, and we, at the same time, at her request and in her presence and in the presence of each other, hereunto subscribed our names and residences as attesting witnesses the day and year last above written.

________________________ residing at ________________________

________________________ residing at ________________________

________________________ residing at ________________________

Affidavit of Subscribing Witnesses

State of ________________)
) ss:
County of ________________)

On __________, 20 ____, each of the undersigned, individually and severally, being duly sworn, deposes and says:

The within will was subscribed in our presence and sight at the end thereof by Hyacinth Bush, the Testator, on the ____ of ________, 20 ____.

Each of the undersigned thereupon signed his or her name as a witness at the end of said will at the request of said Testator and in her presence and sight and in the presence and sight of each other.

The Testator at the time of the execution of the said will was over the age of eighteen years and appeared to the undersigned to be of sound mind and memory and was in all respects competent to make a will and was not under any restraint.

The within will was shown to the undersigned at the time the affidavit was made, and was examined by each of them as to the signature of said testator and of the undersigned.

The foregoing instrument was executed by the Testator and witnessed by each of the undersigned affiants under the supervision of __________, attorney for the Testator at ________.

____
Affiant

____
Affiant

Severally subscribed and
sworn to before me on:

____
Notary Public

Living Will

To my family, my physician, lawyer, clergyman, any medical facility in whose care I happen to be, and any individual who may become responsible for my health, welfare, or affairs:

If the time comes when I can no longer take part in decisions concerning my life, I wish and direct the following:

If a situation should arise in which there is no reasonable expectation for my recovery from extreme physical or mental disability, I direct that I be allowed to die and not be kept alive by medications, artificial means, life support equipment, or heroic measures. However, I do request that medication be administered to me to alleviate suffering even though this may shorten my remaining life.

This statement is made after careful consideration and is in accordance with my convictions and beliefs.

If any of my tissues or organs are sound and would be of value as transplants to other people, I freely give my permission for such donation.

In witness whereof, I state that I have read this, my living will, know and understand its contents, and sign my name below.

Dated: ______________________________

Hyacinth Bush

Witness:

Witness:

Springing Power of Attorney

KNOW ALL MEN BY THESE PRESENTS THAT I, HYACINTH BUSH of __________, in the County of __________, State of __________, do hereby constitute and appoint John Starr of __________ to be my true and lawful attorney-in-fact with full power to act in my name and stead and on my behalf to do in my name, place, and stead in any way in which I myself could do, if I were personally present, with respect to the following matters, to the extent that I am permitted by law to act through an agent:

Real estate transactions;
Chattel and goods transactions;
Bond, share, and commodity transactions;
Banking transactions;
Business operating transactions;
Insurance transactions;
Estate transactions;
Claims of any type or nature;
Records, reports, and statements;
Access to safe deposit boxes;
Ability to sign tax returns;
The power to settle, prepare, or in any other way arrange tax matters;
The power to deal with retirement plans;
The power to fund inter vivos trusts;
The power to borrow funds;
The power to enter buy/sell agreements;
The power to forgive and collect debts;
The power to complete charitable pledges;
The power to make statutory elections and disclaimers;
The power to pay salaries and fees;
The power to settle, pursue, or appeal litigation;

Full and unqualified authority to my attorney-in-fact to delegate any or all of the foregoing powers to any person or persons whom my attorney-in-fact shall select;

The power to take any steps and do any acts that my attorney-in-fact may deem necessary or convenient in connection with the exercise of any of the foregoing powers.

This power of attorney shall be binding on me and my heirs, executors and administrators, and shall remain in force up to the time of the receipt by my attorney-in-fact of a written revocation signed by me.

I hereby agree that any third party receiving a duly executed copy or facsimile of this instrument may act hereunder, and that revocation or termination hereof shall be ineffective as to such third party unless and until actual notice or knowledge of such revocation or termination shall have been received by such third party, and I, for myself and for my heirs, executors, legal representatives and assigns, hereby agree to indemnify and hold harmless any such third party by reason of such third party having relied on the provisions of this instrument.

This power of attorney shall not be affected by my disability or incompetence, and shall only become effective upon my disability or incapacity. I shall be deemed disabled or incapacitated upon written certification of two independent physicians who have examined me and who believe that I am incapacitated, mentally or physically, and am therefore incapable of attending to my personal business and affairs.

IN WITNESS WHEREOF I have hereunto set my hand and seal this __________ day of __________, 20 _____.

____

Hyacinth Bush, Principal

State of ________________)
) ss:
County of ______________)

On the __________ day of ____, 20 ____, before me personally came Hyacinth Bush to me known, and known to me to be the individual described in, and who executed the foregoing instrument, and she acknowledged to me thats she executed the same.

____

Notary Public

The following represents the signature of my attorney-in-fact:

____

Attorney-in-fact

State of ________________)
) ss:
County of ______________)

On the __________ day of ____, 20 ____, before me personally came __________, to me known, and known to me to be the individual described in the foregoing instrument as the attorney-in-fact, and who signed the foregoing instrument, and she acknowledged to me that she signed the same.

____
Notary Public

SITUATIONAL ANALYSIS

Loretta Jones

Loretta needs a will in which she provides for the guardianship of Evan should she die while Evan is still a minor, and to make sure that her estate goes to the trust she has previously established at her bank (along with the proceeds of her life insurance policy). The will should be self-proving, and Loretta should have a durable power of attorney to provide for circumstances when she may be too incapacitated to care for Evan. Temporary guardianship for Evan should also be made part of her durable power of attorney.

Kingston and Donna Lear

The Lears should have very simple self-proving wills. Because of their problems with Regina, most of their property should be transferred while alive, either into inter vivos trusts or into joint tenancies. Consequently, when they die, there will be little property that is actually transferred by testamentary disposition.

In their durable powers of attorney, each could appoint the other to act as the attorney-in-fact for those situations in which one is incapacitated and provide for substitute attorneys if both are incapacitated.

The Lears should have separate wills, not a joint will.

The Bush Family

Oscar and Hyacinth have a fairly straightforward situation. They should make sure that the bulk of their estates pass to each other as marital deductions. Depending upon the size of the estate, they may want to create an A-B trust, but in any event a QTIP trust may be advisable to keep the assets intact for Byron. Also, Hyacinth has indicated a desire to leave small bequests to her father, sisters, and nieces.

As with all of the families, durable powers of attorney and living wills are advisable, but are dependent upon the wishes of the individuals.

Tom Poole

Tom's estate is also fairly simple. Basically, he can divide his assets among his family and friends and designate one of them as his executor. His will can be drafted from the sample clauses indicated in this chapter.

CHAPTER SUMMARY

Writing and executing a will comprises some of the most formal proceedings that exist in the law. Because the testator is no longer able to speak for himself or herself, the court requires a great deal of formality to assure that the actual wishes of the decedent are carried out. In furtherance of these concepts, the legal assistant plays an extremely important role.

The paralegal may be called upon to testify as to the demeanor and capacity of the decedent; because the paralegal is involved in the drafting and execution of the will, he or she is in an excellent position to observe the testator. Also, because the paralegal generally will draft the initial version of the will, he or she is closely associated with the testator in the preparation of the will, which can give a good indication as to the testator's testamentary capacity.

The legal assistant will draft the will, as well as all of the accompanying documents, such as the affidavit of the subscribing witnesses in order to make the will self-proving, a living will, and a durable power of attorney. The paralegal generally assists the attorney in the execution of these documents, either as a witness or as a notary.

If an interested party with standing institutes a will contest, the paralegal will assist the attorney in either defending the will on behalf of the personal representative, or in attacking the will on behalf of one of the decedent's heirs.

Most importantly, the paralegal will help the client understand the nature of all of the documents and the execution procedures. Additionally, the paralegal may be responsible for updating the client's folder to make sure that there have been no material changes in the client's family or financial situation that would require the preparation of a new will.

Very few areas of law provide the legal assistant with the direct client contact and responsibility that are afforded by the estate field.

Key Terms

Abatement: Process of selling estate property to pay debts.
Ademption: Loss of a testamentary gift because the testator no longer owns the property at his or her death.
Advancement: Inter vivos gift to children in anticipation of their share of the parent's estate.
Anti-lapse statute: State law providing that gifts to deceased heirs go to those person's heirs.
Attestation: Clause signed by witnesses to a will.
Beneficiary: Recipient of personal property under a will.
Bequest: Testamentary gift of personal property.
Codicil: Formal document used to amend a will.
Demonstrative legacy: Testamentary gift of money from a particular source.

Dependent relative revocation: Court doctrine holding that if a later will is found invalid, an earlier valid will shall be probated.
Devise: Testamentary gift of real property.
Devisee: Recipient of testamentary gift of realty.
Durable power of attorney: Power of attorney that takes effect upon execution and lasts despite the incapacity of the principal.
Execution of a will: Formal signing and witnessing of a will.
Exordium: Introductory paragraph of a will.
Fraud: Misrepresentation to induce a person to sign a will.
General revocatory clause: Will provision revoking earlier wills and codicils.
Health care proxy: Document appointing another to make health care decisions for the principal.
Holographic will: Will written in the testator's own hand.
In terrorem clause: Anti-contest clause.
Incorporation by reference: Including terms of an independent document by making specific allusion to in another document.
Joint will: One will used for two persons.
Legacy: Testamentary gift of money.
Legatee: Recipient of money under a will.
Lapse: Provision in a will indicating that if a recipient of a gift under the will predeceases the testator, the gift forms a part of the testator's residuum.
Living will: Instrument indicating a person's wishes with respect to life termination should he be unable to speak for himself.
Marital deduction: Tax provision permitting property that goes to a surviving spouse to go tax free.
Menace: Threats use to induce a person to sign a will.
Mortmain Statute: Law limiting charitable gifts under a will.
Mutual will: Identical wills executed by two persons.
Nuncupative will: Oral will permitted in limited situations.
Power of attorney: Authorization for one person to act on another's behalf.
Pretermission: Omitting mention of a child or issue in a will; the omitted child or issue is entitled to an intestate share of the estate.
QTIP trust: Special trust that qualifies for a marital deduction.
Residuum: The residuary estate.
Self-proving will: Will with affidavit of attesting witnesses attached.
Simultaneous death clause: Provision indicating how property is to be distributed if the testator and the heir die in a common disaster.
Slayer Statute: Law prohibiting a murderer from inheriting from his victim.
Springing power of attorney: Power of attorney that takes effect at some point in the future.
Statutory will: Form will appearing in the state statutes.
Testamentary capacity: Knowing the nature and extent of one's property and the natural bounty of one's affections.
Testimonium: Last clause in a will.

Undue influence: Ability of a person in a close relationship to the testator to use that position to cause the testator to make a particular testamentary disposition.

Will contest: Legal challenge to the validity of an instrument filed for probate.

Case Studies

1. Can an attorney be held liable if she drafts a will for a client without first ascertaining the client's testamentary capacity?

An elderly woman was in the hospital suffering with cancer. After surgery the woman experienced confusion, disorientation, and may have been subject to hallucinations. A friend of the woman's called an attorney and told the attorney that the woman wanted to make a new will. The attorney did not know either person. The attorney met with the woman in the hospital for 45 minutes and drafted and executed a will in favor of the friend who had made the telephone call. The testatrix died shortly thereafter, and the niece, the only heir, sued the attorney. The court held that a lawyer who fails to investigate the testamentary capacity of his or her client is not liable in tort or contract to a beneficiary disinherited by the will drafted by the attorney. *Gorsalon v. Superior Court of Alameda County*, 19 Cal. App. 4th 136 (1993). What is your opinion of the law absolving a lawyer from liability under these circumstances?

2. The brother of the decedent contested a will submitted to probate based on the undue influence of the executor. The will in question, executed by the 90-year-old decedent, left his estate equally to his three surviving children and the grandchildren of his deceased son, per stirpes. The decedent's brother had filed with the court to be appointed the administrator of his brother's intestate estate, but the petition was blocked by the submission of the will for probate. The decedent was under the care of the named executor during his last year.

In this instance the person who was alleged to have exerted the undue influence was not named a beneficiary under the will. Why, then, did the decedent's brother question the will? Although not stated in the case, it appears the brother was hoping to receive a fee as the personal representative. Regardless of whether the decedent died testate or intestate, the disposition of his estate would have been exactly the same; the only difference being in who received the administration fee. Although the case rightly went against the challenger, it is important to point out that not all benefits from an estate come by being given a direct gift under the will. Fees for administering the estate and/or any trusts established by the will can be quite lucrative and may be the subtle benefit actually being questioned. *Estate of Jernigan*, 793 S.W.2d 88 (Tex. Ct. App. 1990).

3. A full-blooded Native American was adopted at age 12 by a family outside of the reservation with whom he lived for over 15 years. At the death of his adopted father the man returned to his natural family, and then entered the army. He was subsequently medically discharged with

paranoid schizophrenia. For the next two decades he was periodically placed in various hospitals for chronic conditions. At one point he requested to be taken to the reservation so that he could execute his will. Under this will he left all of his property to his natural sister and nothing to his adoptive family. He subsequently died of acute alcohol poisoning. The man's adoptive family challenged the will base on the deceased's testamentary capacity. Even though the man was mentally ill the court concluded that at the moment he made the will, according to the officer of the Bureau of Indian Affairs who wrote up the will for the man, he knew the nature of his property and the natural bounty of his affections, thereby having sufficient ability to execute a will. *Estate of Loupe*, 878 P.2d 1168 (Utah App. 1994).

4. In *Matter of the Estate of Itta*, 225 A.D. 2d 548 (1996), the appeal concerned a will contest involving a brother and a sister over their father's will that disinherited the sister. One week after the 94-year-old father was admitted to a nursing home, the brother, without the knowledge of the sister and against doctors' advice, took the father to a lawyer's office where the father executed a will leaving his entire estate to the brother. Other evidence indicated that when the father was in a weakened state the brother had misappropriated funds from the father's accounts. Under these circumstances, the will contained unexplained departures from a previously executed will and the fact that the will was prepared in secrecy indicates that it may have been executed contrary to the father's wishes. The court sent the matter back to the lower court for a full hearing. Apparently, family affection is irrelevant when money is involved!

5. May a written will be revoked by an oral declaration?

As discussed earlier, a will may only be revoked by a new will, a change in family status, or by the physical act of the testator. In a case decided in Minnesota, one of the challenges to the validity of a will submitted to probate was the allegation that the testatrix revoked her will orally, saying to various persons that she wanted to change her will. The court held that mere oral statements by the testatrix only indicate an inchoate intent to revoke, but do not in and of themselves revoke a valid will. Revocation can only be accomplished by adhering to the formalities of the state statute with respect to revocation. *In re Estate of Schroeder*, 441 N.W.2d 522 (Minn. Ct. App. 1989).

EXERCISES

1. Analyze the sample will and accompanying documents for Hyainth Bush appearing in the chapter. Why are some of the clauses different from those given earlier in the chapter? Why doesn't his will contain *all* of the provisions indicated for drafting a will?
2. Draft a will for Kingston Lear. Assume that Kingston and Donna live in your jurisdiction. Their house is valued at $658,000 and is

held by them as tenants by the entirety. The house that Regina is living in is valued at $426,000 and is held by Donna and Kingston as joint tenants.

The Lears have stocks and bonds, not previously placed in trust, valued at $228,000, cash of $62,000, and their household effects are valued at $1,720,000. Kingston's personal effects (clothing, jewelry, car, etc.) are valued at $18,000. Additionally, Kingston has an annuity that will pay Donna, as his survivor, $30,000 per year for life. Kingston also has stock in his medical practice, a professional corporation, but its value is presently undetermined.

Donna holds a $2,000,000 life insurance policy on Kingston's life.

Kingston wants to provide an income to Donna for her life, and then wants his property to go to his children and grandchildren (except for Regina), but does not know the appropriate proportion to give to each person.

When drafting the will, use any other information regarding Kingston appearing in the text up to this point, and try to minimize his taxes and see that his wishes are fulfilled.

3. Draft your own will.
4. Draw up a durable power of attorney for yourself. What powers do you want your attorney-in-fact to have? Why? How would you determine incompetence?
5. Discuss the type of evidence you would need to propose or defend a will contest based on undue influence or lack of testamentary capacity.

ANALYTICAL PROBLEM

In his will a man gives his son a testamentary power of appointment. The will specifies that the son shall appoint by his will by specifically referring to the power created by the father's will. In the son's will, he leaves his entire residual estate, including all property over which he held a power of appointment, to a college. The father's other heirs challenge the exercise of the power. Decide the case.

6 Estate Planning for the Elderly

CHAPTER OVERVIEW

The purpose of this chapter is to discuss various strategies to assist both the elderly and their adult childern and caretakers in maintaining a dignified and meaningful old age. Because of the aging of the Amercian population, more and more emphasis has been directed to procedures that can insure that the elderly retain their assets and property and still be afforded necessary health care and living assistance.

Americans are living longer than they ever have in history and, according to government statistics, the fastest growing percentage of the population in the last decade of the twentieth century were those persons between the ages of 90 and 95. One of the main concerns of people as they age is that they be able to maintain an independent lifestyle. To achieve this objective, certain estate planning strategies have been specifically developed beyond the general estate planning devices otherwise examined in this text.

This chapter is not concerned with the different types of plans and documents that have been discussed in the other chapters; rather it is designed to incorporate an analysis of other laws and documents that are primarily applicable to older individuals. With the ever-increasing costs of medical care, and the longer life expectancies of most Americans, the need to plan for long-term care has reached gargantuan proportions, especially as more and more middle-aged adults find themselves in the situation of having to care for aging and deteriorating parents.

This chapter will discuss health care issues facing the elderly, guardianship procedures, income maintenance, and some ethical concerns involved in dealing with an elderly client.

Health Care and the Elderly

The United States does not have a universal health care system. Although some medical aid is provided by the goverment in the form of Medicare and Medicaid, it is still the responsibility of every citizen to insure that he or she can cover the costs of health needs that are not part of the govermental program.

Medicare

In order to qualify for **Medicare,** the federally funded health insurance program, an individual must be entitled to receive Social Security benefits because he or she is either 65 years of age or has been disabled for a period of not less than 24 months. Medicare coverage is not based on a person's income or assets, but simply on a person meeting the qualifying standards. (See section on Social Security on pg. 165.)

EXAMPLE:

David, Hyacinth's father, is in his 80s and receives Social Security benefits based on his past work as a florist. Because he receives Social Security, he is automatically entitled to Medicare.

EXAMPLE:

Aida Jones is involved in a car accident and loses her ability to walk. If this disability continues for 24 months, she will qualify to receive Medicare to assist her in meeting her medical bills, even though she is not old enough to receive Social Security retirement benefits.

Medicare coverage is divided into two sections, Part A and Part B. Part A coverage is automatic when a person applies for Social Security benefits, whereas Part B is optional and requires a minimal premium payment from the enrollee. A person can apply for Medicare during the **initial enrollment period,** defined as the three months preceding or following the date on which the person can apply for Social Security, typically the person's 65th birthday. If the individual does not enroll during this time period, he or she may still enroll during the first three months of each year, referred to as the **general enrollment period.**

EXAMPLE:

Kingston was still working when he turned 65, and so did not bother to enroll for Medicare. Now, as part of his estate planning strategy, to make sure that his medical care will be covered, he decides to enroll for Medicare in March during the general enrollment period.

EXAMPLE:

David Laplante enrolled for Medicare two weeks after he turned 65 during his initial enrollment period.

If a person continues to work after his or her 65th birthday and is covered by an employee health insurance plan, he or she may enroll for Medicare on the first day of the first month after his or her employee group health insurance terminates. This ability to enroll continues for seven months after the group health insurance terminates, and is called the **special enrollment period.** Should the individual fail to enroll within this time frame, he or she may still enroll during the general enrollment period.

EXAMPLE:

Tom Poole is covered by a group health insurance policy provided by his employer. Tom expects to keep working until he is 70 years old, and so will be covered by this insurance during his entire work life. When he retires, he may enroll for Medicare starting on the first day of the first month following his retirement (when the coverage stops), or may enroll during any January, February, or March during the general enrollment period.

Part A Medicare covers inpatient hospital care and is funded directly by tax dollars. Part B is funded by the monthly premiums paid by the enrollee and covers some medical services, outpatient and home care, and certain medical equipment.

Part A's hospital care covers 100 percent of the first 60 days, less a deductible (an amount the recipient must pay before coverage begins), 75 percent of the next 30 days, and will cover an additional 60 lifetime days if the hospital care exceeds 90 days total. The 60 lifetime days also requires the patient to pay a portion of the costs.

Part A will also pay for inpatient rehabilitation services and skilled nursing care if the patient has been in the hospital for three consecutive days. Medicare pays for the first 20 days of the skilled nursing care, then will pay a portion of such care for the next 80 days. To be eligible for the skilled nursing care benefits, the care must be certified as necessary by a physician.

EXAMPLE:

Aida, who now qualifies for Medicare because of her disability, is put in the hospital for an unrelated respiratory problem. She stays in the hospital for one week, and upon discharge is sent to a skilled nursing facility for rehabilitation. In this instance, it is most likely that Medicare will pick up cost of the nursing facility.

Medicare Part A will also cover home health care provided that a physican signs a specified plan of care for the patient, the patient is confined to home, and the patient needs nursing care on a periodic basis, such care being provided by a certified Medicare provider. Hospice care is provided by Medicare only for persons who are terminally ill, and the recipient must opt out of all other Medicare programs. This requirement is based on the fact that the patient is not expected to survive.

Part B coverage is optional, and pays 80 percent of approved charges for various medical services that would not be covered by Part B. For persons who receive Social Security benefits and who elect Part B coverage, the premiums are automatically deducted from their Social Security checks.

As can be seen, persons who are covered by Medicare Parts A and B still remain liable for a percentage of their health care, especially if they require extensive and lengthy medical treatments. Because of this limited coverage, as part of the medical component of an estate plan for the elderly, individuals who can afford to should obtain private insurance coverage to meet the portion of their health care costs not covered by Medicare.

Generally, the private health insurance that an elderly individual might consider falls into three categories: policies that provide coverage for specified health care; **supplemental insurance** that pays for health care not covered by other policies; and disability and accident insurance that covers injuries that result in short- or long-term disability. For estate planning concerns, probably the most important to consider would be the supplemental insurance policy.

Supplemental insurance policies fall into two broad categories: Medicare supplemental insurance, called **Medi-gap,** and long-term care insurance. Medi-gap insurance is designed to cover all costs not covered by Medicare Parts A and B. Every state mandates an open enrollment period for such coverage. The state is involved because Medicare is operated by both the state and federal government. Long-term care insurance is designed to pay for nursing home stays and other extended hospital treatment beyond the period covered by Medicare and other insurance policies. Both of these types of policies are appropriate for persons who feel they may be facing such long-term needs and who do not have unlimited private resources to cover such expenses.

EXAMPLE:

In order not to be a burden on Byron, Hyacinth and Oscar take out a long-term care insurance policy. Even though the premiums are quite high, the insurance will enable them to keep their assets intact to pass on to Byron. The cost of the long-term care for Oscar's parents wiped out their life savings, and he does not want to see this happen to him.

Medicaid

For low-income individuals, those persons whose income and assets do not exceed certain prescribed levels (the amounts change periodically and must be checked as the need arises), the government provides health insurance in the form of **Medicaid.** Medicaid is designed only for low-income individuals. To qualify the applicant must prove that he or she falls within the government guidelines. Because the extent of Medicaid coverage is more far-reaching than Medicare, many individuals who are faced with the need of long-term care and who do not have private policies to cover the costs attempt to qualify for Medicaid by divesting themselves of their assets to meet the Medicaid guidelines.

In order to avoid fraudulent transfers of assets simply to meet Medicaid guidelines, certain restrictions have been placed on such divestitures. Penalties are imposed for transferring income and/or assets less than 36 months prior to applying for Medicaid (the period is 60 months if the transfer is made to a trust). These **look-back** rules apply for all applications for Medicaid made after August 10, 1993 (different rules applied for applications for Medicaid made prior to this period). Certain transfers are exempt from this look-back period, such as inter-spousal transfers, transfers to a blind or disabled child, transfers for market value, and transfers for a purpose other than seeking Medicaid. For estate planning purposes, if a person believes that long-term care will be a reality, and he or she lacks the resources to meet such costs, either directly or indirectly by means of insurance, it might be worthwhile to create a trust to which assets may be transferred so that the transfer will have taken place more than 60 months prior to applying for Medicaid.

If a person would otherwise qualify for Medicaid except for the amount of his or her income, the person will still qualify for Medicaid in any month that his or her medical costs exceed his or her income, under a provision called the **surplus income** or **spend-down program.**

EXAMPLE:

In planning for their future, Tom Poole's parents start to transfer their assets to Tom and his brother, and have created a trust for other assets so that, should the need arise, they may be able to qualify for Medicaid.

EXAMPLE:

Two years after Tom's father created a trust for his assets, he becomes seriously ill and requires 24-hour-a-day care. When his family applies for Medicaid, he does not qualify because the transfer was made only 24 months prior to the application. Tom's father may receive Medicaid after another 36 months.

Probably one of the most pressing concerns in estate planning for the elderly is to provide some mechanism whereby extensive health care needs may be met.

Related Health Care Documents

In order to insure that a person's wishes with respect to his or her health care will be carried out under circumstances in which the person cannot speak for him or her self, documents have been created, collectively referred to as **advance directives.** These documents, which fall into three broad categories, give the ultimate health care decision-making power to someone other than the patient. The three types of such directives are:

Health Care Proxies. This document is a legal instrument by which an individual nominates another person to make health care decisions for the individual should he or she become incapable of speaking for him or her self.

EXAMPLE:

Fern has to go into the hospital for surgery. Several weeks prior to her admission she executes a health care proxy in which she nominates Hyacinth, her eldest sister, to make any decisions regarding her treatment should she not be able to make those decisions for herself due to medication or complications with the surgery.

Living Wills. This is an instrument that indicates the person's wishes with respect to life support systems and organ donations should the person become unable to speak for him or her self. These documents are used by the courts to determine a person's wishes so that appropriate medical treatment may be given or withheld.

EXAMPLE:

Oscar has executed a living will in which he indicates that he does not wish to be placed on a life support system if it is medically determined that he does not have a chance to recover a normal life.

Do-Not-Resuscitate (DNR) directive. This is a document by which the signatory states that he or she does not wish to be resuscitated or maintained on life support systems should he or she become incompetent. Unlike a health care proxy, neither a living will nor a DNR directive authorizes someone other than the signatory to make any health care decisions on behalf of the signatory.

EXAMPLE:

David executed a DNR directive several years ago. He is now in the hospital where his life is being maintained by a life-support system, and he suffers a massive heart attack. Even though his daughters want him to be resuscitated, the hospital may honor his DNR directive.

Be aware that the directives discussed above are in addition to the powers of attorney analyzed in previous chapters of this text. In many jurisdictions (but not all), a power of attorney may be used to the same effect as a health care proxy, but each state's statutes must be individually examined.

Guardianship

Guardianship is the appointment of a person to take legal responsibility for the care and management of another who is unable to care for him or her self. Although at one time the concept of guardianship was associated with the concept of incompetence, current guardianship is limited to a factual determination as to whether a person is physically, mentally, or emotionally capable of taking care of his or her personal, financial, or health care needs. To this end, the courts make a determination as to whether the individual is capable of acting on his or her own; if not, the court will authorize someone to act on that person's behalf in the least intrusive way possible. The modern concept of guardianship is to allow the **incapacitated person,** formerly referred to as a **ward,** as much independence as possible.

To protect incapacitated persons from being taken advantage of by unscrupulous relatives and strangers, it is the duty of the state to determine whether a person is in need of assistance in caring for him or her self and, if so, to see that an appropriate person is appointed to assist the incapacitated individual. The state makes these determinations by means of a judicial process, and the court is empowered to oversee any guardianship that it authorizes.

EXAMPLE:

Leonard Dodge goes to court to have Donna and Kingston declared in need of guardianship and to have his wife appointed as their guardian. Simply because the Lears are elderly does not mean that they are incapable of taking care of themselves, and the court will investigate Leonard's assertions before it will authorize anyone to act on the Lears' behalf.

In making its determination as to whether an individual is in need of guardianship, the court looks at the individual's level of activity and his or her demonstrable capacity to manage his or her own affairs. In any instance, the court will always look to the least restrictive alternative as possible in order to permit the individual to remain as independent as possible.

EXAMPLE:

In assessing Leonard's claim that the Lears are incapable of managing their own affairs, the court will look at the couple's daily lifestyle, the degree of independence they demonstrate, and their ability to cope with their financial and medical needs.

Guardianship law is basically one of state prerogative, and the only federal legislation dealing with the subject comes under the Social Security Act, which requires that each state provide protective services to guard the needs of all persons who receive Social Security benefits. To determine the guardianship procedures in a given jurisdiction, that state's law must be analyzed.

Generally, before a court appoints a guardian, it must first determine that the alleged incapacitated person cannot manage his or her own affairs. To assist in making this determination, the court typically appoints an independent person to make an evaluation of the alleged incapacitated person, concentrating on the individual's functional abilities. Usually, the court will have a hearing to evaluate this independent report, and the alleged incapacitated person has the right to be represented at the hearing and to present evidence on his or her own behalf. If the court finds that the individual is in need of assistance, it will appoint a guardian.

The powers and duties of a guardian are determined by the court that authorizes the appointment. Generally, guardians fall into four main categories:

1. Guardian of the estate: appointed by the court to manage the finances of the incapacitated person.

EXAMPLE:

Loretta Jones finds that her mother is no longer able to manage her finances, although in every other respect she can take care of herself. If the court agrees, Loretta may be appointed Aida's guardian of her estate, a position formerly referred to as a *conservator.*

2. Guardian of the Person: appointed by the court to deal with the physical and legal needs of the incapacitated person, but who has no control over the person's finances.

EXAMPLE:

David, because of several physical problems, is now required to take multiple pills, and he gets confused as to the timing and order of taking the medication. In this instance the court might appoint Fern to act as David's guardian of the person to see that he has appropriate medical care.

3. Plenary guardian: appointed by the court to act as the guardian of both the person and the property of the incapacitated person.

EXAMPLE:

David's condition deteriorates, and so the court may decide that he can no longer act in his own best interest and appoints Fern as his plenary guardian to take care of his person and property.

4. Limited guardian: appointed by the court to act in a particular matter only.

EXAMPLE:

Kingston becomes physically incapacitated and can no longer conduct certain financial transactions that require travel, and so the court appoints Donna to act as his limited guardian only with respect to those financial transactions that require travel.

Once a guardian has been appointed, the court maintains control and supervision over the guardian's activities to insure that the guardian is acting in the best interest of the incapacitated person.

Alternatives to guardianship: Generally, before a guardian is appointed by the court, it must be demonstrated that less intrusive alternatives would not be appropriate. Such alternatives include:

a) **Power of attorney,** discussed in Chapter 5, who will be able to act for an individual who is mentally competent when the power is executed and is authorized only to the extent specified in the enabling document.
b) **Representative payee,** permitted under the Social Security Act, who is authorized to receive Social Security benefits on behalf of the recipient once the Social Security Administration has determined that the recipient cannot manage his or her own affairs.
c) **Joint ownership,** discussed in Chapter 2, whereby two or more persons have control over the subject property.
d) **Revocable trust,** discussed in Chapter 4, whereby a person's property is managed by a trustee for his or her benefit, and which is capable of being terminated by the beneficiary.
e) **Civil commitment,** which is the most drastic of all solutions to this problem, whereby the person is placed in a mental facility because he or she may do physical harm to him or her self

As the American population ages, more and more individuals are faced with the situation in which it may become necessary to seek guardianship because of physical or mental deterioration associated with the aging process.

Income Maintenance

Many older American are unable to work and one of their main concerns is the ability to maintain an adequate level of income to support their lifestyles. This section of the chapter will discuss some methods, outside private savings and investment, that exist to assist the elderly with retirement income.

Social Security

The first major legislation directed to assuring older individuals that they would not spend their last years in penury was the **Social Security Act of 1933.** The purpose behind Social Security was to provide working Americans with a government-backed pension plan to guarantee them an income upon retirement. However, in recent years the government has indicated that the current Social Security program is not going to be able to keep up with the demands of an ever-aging society, and certain reforms will be necessary in order to insure the continuation of Social Security, which is the financial mainstay of a majority of Americans.

Pursuant to the provisions of the Social Security Act, a federal tax is levied on the wages of employees. This tax is imposed both on the worker and on the employer who is required to contribute to the program, which is administered by the **Social Security Administration.** The funds so collected are used to provide retirement and disability benefits, as well as health care benefits in the form of Medicare and Medicaid, as was discussed above.

To qualify for Social Security retirement benefits, the employee must meet the following requirements:

1. The employee must be **fully insured,** meaning that he or she has worked and contributed to the find for a minimum of 40 quarters (basically 10 years) and,

EXAMPLE:

Tom has worked at his job for over 15 years. At this point he is deemed fully insured, entitling him to Social Security benefits on his retirement. The amount of such benefits will depend upon how many years he works and how much he eventually earns and contributes to the system. Being fully insured only guarantees that the person is entitled to Social Security benefits, not the amount of such benefits.

2. The employee must be at least 62 years of age.

EXAMPLE:

Even though Tom is now fully insured, he must wait until he reaches the age of 62 before he can collect those benefits.

Social Security benefits are also available to the surviving spouses of workers who were entitled to benefits, as well as to the dependent children of such workers. Surviving spouses are entitled to receive benefits once they attain the age of 60 or, if they are disabled, the age of 50. Unmarried dependent children may receive survivor benefits until they reach the age of 18, or 19 if they are students. Disabled dependent children may receive survivor benefits until they are 21, at which point they are able to receive benefits in their own right.

Self-employed individuals may also receive Social Security benefits provided that they work the requisite number of quarters and contribute to the plan at the rate established for self-employed persons.

Supplemental Security Income

Since July 1, 1974, the government has provided **Supplemental Security Income (SSI)** benefits to very low-income individuals and families who meet specified financial criteria. These benefits are made by both the federal and state governments.

To qualify for SSI benefits, the individual must be:

1. A United States citizen or lawful permanent resident or qualified alien
2. 65 years of age or older or blind or disabled

EXAMPLE:

Aida has become disabled and no longer has any source of income. She may qualify for SSI benefits, even though she is not yet 65 years old.

In order to receive SSI benefits, the individual must meet certain income and asset tests or be living in a public institution. The exact calculations used to determine the eligibility of an individual is beyond the scope of this book. However, the amount of benefits received is adjusted annually to reflect the cost of living increases. SSI was developed to provide a minimum income to the poverty-stricken elderly and disabled, calculated at a lower rate than Social Security benefits.

Veterans' Benefits

At the present time more than 70 million Americans qualify to receive veterans' benefits, either in their own right or as dependents of qualifying veterans. Veterans' benefits are administered by the **Department of Veterans' Affairs.**

To qualify for benefits, the person must either be a veteran, the spouse or surviving spouse or a veteran, the child or surviving child of a veteran, or the dependent parent of a veteran. To be deemed a "veteran," the individual must have served in active military duty and have received an honorable or general discharge.

If the veteran served prior to September 8, 1980, any length of service is permitted; after that date the person must have served at least 24 months or for the full period for which he or she was called. This 24-month period does not apply to persons who were discharged because of injury or disability.

Veterans' benefits provide income for persons who were injured during service. If the veteran served during wartime, he or she may qualify for **non-service connected disability benefits**. These benefits payments for are disabling injuries that occur outside of military service, unless the injury was caused by the person's own willful conduct.

In addition to income benefits for disabled veterans, all veterans are entitled to the following benefits:

1. Burial in a VA cemetery, along with the spouse and minor child
2. A burial allowance of $1500 if the death is service-connected or $300 if it is not service-connected
3. A headstone if the veteran is buried in a VA cemetery
4. A burial plot allowance of $150 if the veteran died of a non-service connected cause and was receiving veterans' benefits at the time of death or died in a VA hospital

Private Pension Plans

Because of the problems with the Social Security system, many Americans maintain private pension plans to provide themselves with a retirement income. These private pension plans fall into three broad categories:

1. Plans funded by the individual alone
2. Plans funded by the individual's employer
3. Plans funded by both the individual and the employer

Plans Funded by the Individual

Three types of plans may be funded by the recipient alone:

1. Individual Retirement Accounts (IRAs). Under federal tax law, a person may contribute up to $2,000 each year into such accounts as a deduction from his or her taxable income. The interest or dividends that accrue on these accounts are not taxed until the individual begins to draw on the account at retirement. Should the person withdraw some or all of these funds prior to attaining the age of 59½, a tax penalty is imposed on the withdrawal.

2. IRA-Plus (Roth) Accounts. As of August 5, 1997, persons may contribute to these accounts, which do not provide for the IRA tax deduction, but whose income is tax-free after five years. The benefit of this type of account is that the depositor can withdraw the funds at any time without a tax penalty, and he or she does not have to start withdrawing funds at age 70½, which is required with the regular IRA account.

Plans Funded by the Individual's Employer

These accounts are subject to the provisions of the **Employee Retirement Income Security Act (ERISA) of 1974,** which was enacted to protect employee pension plans from being mismanaged by the employers. Under the provisions of ERISA, there are two types of employer benefit plans: a **pension benefit plan** that provides income during retirement to the employee, and a **welfare benefit plan** that is designed to provide medical and non-pension benefits to the employee.

Pension benefit plans are subdivided into **defined benefit plans** that provide income based on a fixed calculation determined by the employee's length of service, and **defined contribution plans,** also called **individual account plans**, in which the employer, and sometimes the employee, contribute annual sums to the account, and the eventual pension is determined by the amount in such fund upon retirement.

ERISA protects the employee by imposing strict fiduciary duties on the employer, thereby guaranteeing that the retired worker will receive the pension to which he or she is entitled. However, ERISA does not mandate survivor benefits; each plan must be analyzed to determine whether the employee's survivor may receive any income.

Ethical Concerns

One of the primary ethical considerations facing anyone dealing with the elderly is the elderly person's mental competence. Legally, **competency** refers to a person's ability to make decisions for him or her self. One must be aware of the distinction between being legally incompetent and merely being eccentric, and when dealing with an elderly client the professional must make an individual determination as to whether the client is capable to make his or her own decisions.

In many instances elderly persons are accompanied by family members or friends when professional advice is sought, and the professional must ascertain exactly who is the client. If the elderly person has been placed under guardianship, the court has already determined that he or she is not competent to act on his or her own behalf. However, if the individual is merely accompanied by another person, the elderly individual is the client and the professional cannot be directed by the accompanying family member. It is of prime importance that the ability of the elderly individual to conduct his or her own affairs is appropriately evaluated by the professional.

Further, as discussed in earlier chapters, the professional must determine whether the elderly client is acting under the undue influence of a family member or friend. If such is the case, it is most probable that the work performed will be undone.

EXAMPLE:

Hyacinth takes her father to a lawyer to have the lawyer draft David's will. Hyacinth is a very domineering sort of person, and the attorney must determine that David is acting under his own wishes, especially if Hyacinth indicates David wishes to leave everything to her in the will and David merely nods agreement to this statement.

SITUATIONAL ANALYSIS

Loretta Jones

Loretta may soon be faced with the problem of caring for Aida should Aida's physical condition deteriorate. Because of Aida's age, Loretta should make sure that Aida has elected Part B Medicare coverage and, if Loretta believes Aida may eventually need 24-hour-a-day care, she may start the process of spending down Aida's assets.

Further, Aida should probably execute a health care proxy for Loretta and, if she has any distinct wishes with respect to life support, a living will and DNR directive may be appropriate.

The Bush Family

Because of his government employment, Oscar's insurance and pension may be sufficient to provide for his and Hyacinth's needs as they age. However, even persons whose insurance and retirement income may seem sufficient still should plan for future catastrophes. The Bushes may wish to consider starting to spend down their assets by making annual gifts to their son so that, if the need arises, they may qualify for Medicaid. Also, they may considered acquiring Medi-Gap insurance to cover those costs not covered by Medicare.

The Lear Family

Even though the Lears are well-off, long-term care may have a devastating effect on their assets, resources, and lifestyle of the survivor. For this reason, the Lears should consider creating a living trust in which they can place their assets. That was if they do need extensive 24-hour-a-day care, they may be able to qualify for Medicaid, provided the transfer to the trust is made at least 60 months prior to their applying for such a program. Also, because they do have a significant income, they may want to consider private long-term care health and disability insurance.

Tom Poole

Despite the fact that Tom is relatively young, it is not too early for him to make certain decisions with respect to nominating a health care proxy and indicating his wishes with respect to life support by means of a living will and Do-Not-Resuscitate directive. Even the relatively young may be struck down and become incapable of speaking for themselves, and so it is a wise practice to have health care wishes written down so that they may be given effect when a person can no longer specify his or her wishes.

CHAPTER SUMMARY

As Americans continue to live longer and more productive lives, it becomes increasingly important that they create estate plans to cover life problems of the elderly. The three most important areas of such estate planning for the elderly concern their health care, their mental and physical competence, and their income maintenance.

The government provides some form of health insurance for the elderly (and disabled) by means of Medicare and Medicaid. Medicare is available for all persons entitled to receive Social Security benefits, and covers basic health care bills. For persons receiving Medicare, this basic insurance can be federally supplemented by electing to contribute to Medicare's Part B coverage that takes care of medical expenses not covered by basic Medicare. Also, a person might consider private supplemental Medi-Gap insurance. Medicaid recipients, those persons with extremely low incomes, are granted greater health coverage; however, in order to meet Medicaid's income and asset requirements, many people have to spend down their assets. Medicaid looks at all asset transfers of applicants, and to qualify such transfers must have been made at least 36 months prior to applying to the program (60 months for transfers to trusts).

As people age, their mental and physical abilities may deteriorate. If and when such deterioration devolves to the point at which a person is no longer capable of caring for him or her self, the court may authorize a guardian to see that the elderly person, once deemed incapacitated, can receive the care and attention he or she needs. Under modern guardianship law, the guardian is only authorized to act in the least intrusive way possible so as to afford the incapacitated person as much independence as he or she is capable of handling.

For most working Americans, one of the primary sources of retirement income comes in the form of Social Security benefits. Social Security was initially created to provide a safety net for working Americans so that they would not retire in poverty. However, because of the increasing longevity of Americans and the decline in the birthrate, Social Security benefits may no longer be sufficient to insure that a recipient can maintain a decent lifestyle. For this reason, many people, as part of their estate plan, contribute to private pension plans to provide additional retirement income. Many of these plans, if part of an employee benefit program, are regulated by ERISA to impose strict fiduciary duties on the fund managers to assure the workers that these plans will not be mismanaged.

Key Terms

Advance directives: Document that expresses the health care wishes of the signatory.

Civil commitment: Confinement of a person to a mental health facility.

Competency: The legal ability to make decisions for oneself.

Defined benefit plan: Pension plan in which the amount of the pension is specifically determined by the employee's length of service and salary.

Defined contribution plan: Pension plan in which the pension is determined by the amount of the contributions made to the plan during the pensioner's period of employment.

Department of Veterans' Affairs: Federal agency that administers veterans' benefits.

Do-Not-Resuscitate Directive: Document indicating that the signatory does not wish to be resuscitated or kept on a life support system.

Employee Retirement Income Security Act (ERISA): Federal statute that imposes fiduciary duties on managers of private pension plans.

Fully insured: Having worked at least 40 quarters to be qualified to receive Social Security benefits.

General enrollment period: Yearly period during which persons may enroll in Medicare Part B.

Guardian of the estate: Guardian to manage the property of an incapacitated person.

Guardian of the person: Person legally authorized to manage the personal, non-financial, affairs of an incapacitated person.

Health care proxy: Legal document authorizing someone other than the principal to make health care decisions for the principal should the principal be unable to speak for him or her self.

Incapacitated person: Current term for a ward.

Individual account plan: Defined contribution plan.

Individual retirement account (IRA): Private pension plan given favorable tax treatment.

Individual retirement account-plus (Roth): Form of IRA that permits withdrawal without tax penalties.

Initial enrollment period: Period during which an eligible person can enroll for Medicare.

Joint ownership: Two or more person holding title to property with rights of survivorship.

Limited guardianship: Guardianship for a limited purpose.

Living will: Document indicating the signatory's wishes with respect to life support should the signatory become incapacitated.

Look-back period: Period of time the government will review to determine whether an applicant for Medicaid has improperly divested him or her self of his or her assets.

Medicaid: Federally funded program providing medical care to low-income persons.

Medicare: Federally funded health insurance for persons who receive Social Security.

Medi-gap insurance: Supplemental insurance designed to provide payment for items not covered by Medicare.

Non-service related disability: Disability resulting from an occurrence that did not take place during military service.

Pension benefit plan: Pension plan that provides for retirement income.

Plenary guardian: Guardian of both the person and the property of an incapacitated person.

Power of attorney: Legal document authorizing someone to act on the behalf of the signatory.

Representative payee: Person authorized by the Social Security Administration to receive benefits on behalf of the recipient of Social Security benefits.

Revocable trust: Trust that may be terminated by the creator.

Social Security Act of 1933: Federal statute that provides for retirement income for qualified workers.

Social Security Administration: Federal agency that administers Social Security benefits.

Special enrollment period: Time period in which the working elderly can enroll in Medicare.

Spend-down program: Method whereby a person divests him or her self of assets in order to qualify for Medicaid.

Supplemental insurance: Health care coverage designed to provide benefits for care not covered by Medicare or other insurance programs.

Supplemental Security Income (SSI): Government transfer payments to very low-income persons.

Surplus income: Income above the limit to qualify for Medicaid.

Ward: Former term for an incapacitated person.

Welfare benefit plan: Employee benefit plan that provides for medical care and benefits other than retirement income.

Case Studies

1. What factor should a court look at to determine the wishes of an elderly patient with respect to maintaining her life on life support systems?

An elderly woman was declared mentally incompetent as the result of suffering multiple strokes. She was unable to obtain food or drink without medical assistance, and the question arose as to whether she should be kept alive by medical intervention. To determine her wishes, the court looked at statements she had made prior to becoming incompetent. The patient had previously indicated that she was opposed to life-sustaining treatments. However, the court noted that all of these statements were made in the context of persons dying of cancer. The instant patient was not dying, but required assistance in eating because of a decline in her gag reflex. The appellate court eventually concluded that the patient did not express any specific statement with respect to life support treatment under her conditions, and so the hospital was ordered to insert a feeding tube. *In re Westchester County Medical Center*, 72 N.Y. 2d 517, 534 N.Y.S. 2d 886 (1988).

2. A dental bill was denied coverage by an insurance company pursuant to an employee benefit plan. The employee sued, alleging that the plan has been misrepresented. The legal basis of the suit lied in the Employee Retirement Income Security Act. The federal court eventually dismissed the suit because the employer only conducted business in the state of Texas. In order to come within the provisions of ERISA, the employer must be involved in interstate commerce. *Sheffield v. Allstate Life Insurance Co.*, 756 F. Supp. 309 (S.D. Texas 1991).

3. What should be the standard of care imposed on a guardian of property?

A conservator moved to resign his position, and the attorney for the incapacitated person objected, stating that the guardian failed to perform his duties in an appropriate manner. The lower court held for the guardian, stating that he "exercised such care as a prudent person would exercise in dealing with his own property." The appellate court eventually reversed, stating that a guardian must be held to an even higher standard that includes avoiding risks that he might take with his own property and can take no risk that would endanger the integrity of the property. This is a higher standard than that imposed on most trustees and fiduciaries. *In re Conservatorship of Estate of Martin*, 228 Neb. 103, 421 N.W. 2d 463 (1988).

4. May an elderly person who is terminally ill decide to take his own life and seek medical assistance in so doing without violating criminal suicide statutes?

The state of Washington prosecuted several doctors who assisted elderly, terminally ill patients commit suicide. All of the patients were mentally competent. The United States Supreme Court held that such statutes that make it a crime to assist a person in committing suicide are not unconstitutional as violative of the due process clause even when applied to competent, terminally ill adults who wish to hasten their deaths by obtaining medication prescribed by doctors. *Washington v. Glucksberg*, 521 U.S. 702 (1997).

EXERCISES

1. List various factors that might be used to determine a person's competency.
2. Obtain a copy of a long-term health care insurance policy and analyze its provisions.
3. Social Security was created to provide older Americans with retirement income, but in many instances the amount received is insufficient to provide the recipient with a decent standard of living. If the recipient continues to earn money, a portion of the Social Security payment may be taxed. What is your opinion of this? How do you think Social Security should be reformed?
4. Check your state's statute for the requirement to be appointed a guardian.
5. Discuss the potential abuses that might occur with guardianship.

ANALYTICAL PROBLEM

Recently much attention has been focused on a person's right to die and/or be maintained on life support systems. What factors and proof should be taken into consideration by a court in its determination as to whether a given individual has expressed a wish one way or the other?

Social Security Form

SOCIAL SECURITY ADMINISTRATION TOE 250 Form Approved OMB No. 0960-0014

	FOR SSA USE ONLY								FOR SSA USE ONLY
	Name or Bene. Sym.	Program	Date of Birth	Type	Gdn.	Cus.	Inst.	Nam.	
REQUEST TO BE SELECTED AS PAYEE									
									DISTRICT OFFICE CODE
PRINT IN INK:									STATE AND COUNTY CODE:

The name of the NUMBER HOLDER	SOCIAL SECURITY NUMBER
The name of the PERSON(S) (if different from above) for whom you are filing (the "claimant(s)")	SOCIAL SECURITY NUMBER(S)

Answer item 1 ONLY if you are the claimant and want your benefits paid directly to you.

1. I request that I be paid directly.

   CHECK HERE ☐ and answer only items 3, 5, 6, and 8 before signing the form on page 4.

I REQUEST THAT THE SOCIAL SECURITY, SUPPLEMENTAL SECURITY INCOME, BLACK LUNG OR SPECIAL VETERANS BENEFITS FOR THE CLAIMANT(S) NAMED ABOVE BE PAID TO ME AS REPRESENTATIVE PAYEE.

2. Explain why you think the claimant is not able to handle his/her own benefits.
   (In your answer, describe how he/she manages any money he/she receives now.)

   ☐ Claimant is a minor child.

3. Explain why you would be the best representative payee. (Use Remarks if you need more space.)

4. If you are appointed payee, how will you know about the claimant's needs?
   - ☐ Live with me or in the institution I represent.
   - ☐ Daily visits.
   - ☐ Visits at least once a week.
   - ☐ By other means. Explain:

5. Does the claimant have a court-appointed legal guardian? ☐ YES ☐ NO

   IF YES, enter the legal guardian's:

   NAME ______________________

   ADDRESS ______________________

   PHONE NUMBER ______________________

   TITLE ______________________

   DATE OF APPOINTMENT ______________________

   Explain the circumstances of the appointment. (Use remarks if you need more space.)

Social Security Form (Continued)

6. (a) Where does the claimant live?

☐ Alone
☐ In my home (Go to (b).)
☐ With a relative (Go to (b).)
☐ With someone else (Go to (b).)
☐ In a board and care facility (Go to (b).)
☐ In a public institution (Go to (c).)
☐ In a private institution (Go to (c).)
☐ In a nursing home (Go to (c).)
☐ In the institution I represent (Go to (c).)

(b) Enter the names and relationships of any other people who live with the claimant.

NAME	RELATIONSHIP

(c) Enter the claimant's residence and mailing addresses (if different from yours).
Residence: **Mailing:** **Telephone Number:**

(d) Do you expect the claimant's living arrangements to change in the next year?
☐ YES ☐ NO If YES, explain what changes are expected and when they will occur. (Use Remarks if you need more space.)

7. If you are applying on behalf of minor child(ren) and you are not the parent,

Does the child(ren) have a living natural or adoptive parent? ☐ YES ☐ NO

If YES, enter: (a) Name of parent ______

(b) Address of parent ______

(c) Telephone number ______

(d) Does the parent show interest in the child? ☐ YES ☐ NO

Please explain. ______

8. List the names and relationship of any (other) relatives or close friends who have provided support and/or show active interest with the claimant. Describe the type and amount of support and/or how interest is displayed.

NAME	ADDRESS/PHONE NO.	RELATIONSHIP	DESCRIBE SUPPORT/INTEREST

9. Check the block that describes your relationship to the claimant.

(a) ☐ Official of bank, agency or institution with responsibility for the person. Enter below which you represent:

☐ Bank
☐ Social Agency
☐ Public Official
☐ Institution:
☐ Federal
☐ State/Local
☐ Private non-profit
☐ Private proprietary institution. Is the institution licensed under State law? ☐ YES ☐ NO

IF (a) ABOVE CHECKED, COMPLETE ONLY QUESTIONS 10 AND 11 AND SIGN THE FORM ON PAGE 4.

(b) ☐ Parent
(c) ☐ Spouse
(d) ☐ Other Relative - Specify ______
(e) ☐ Legal Representative
(f) ☐ Board and Care Home Operator
(g) ☐ Other Individual - Specify ______

IF (b), (c), (d), or (e) ABOVE CHECKED, GO ON TO QUESTION 12

Form **SSA-11-BK** (5-2003) EF (5-2003) Page 2

Social Security Form (Continued)

INFORMATION ABOUT INSTITUTIONS, AGENCIES AND BANKS APPLYING TO BE REPRESENTATIVE PAYEE

10. (a) Enter the name of the institution ______

(b) Enter the EIN of the institution ______

11. Is the claimant indebted to your institution for past care and maintenance? ☐ YES ☐ NO
If YES, give the amount of the debt, the date(s) the debt was incurred and the description of the debt.

INFORMATION ABOUT INDIVIDUALS APPLYING TO BE REPRESENTATIVE PAYEE

12. Enter: YOUR NAME ______

DATE OF BIRTH ______

SOCIAL SECURITY NUMBER ______

ANY OTHER NAME YOU HAVE USED ______

OTHER SSN'S YOU HAVE USED ______

13. How long have you known the claimant? ______

14. Does the claimant owe you any money now or will he/she owe you money in the future? ☐ YES ☐ NO
If YES, enter the amount he/she owes you, the date(s) the debt was/will be incurred and describe why the debt was/will be incurred.

15. If the claimant lives with you, who takes care of the claimant when work or other activity takes you away from home? What is his/her relationship to the claimant?

16. (a) Main source of your income

☐ Employed (answer (b) below)
☐ Self-employed (Type of Business ______)
☐ Social Security or Black Lung benefits (Claim Number ______)
☐ Pension (describe ______)
☐ Supplemental Security Income payments (Claim Number ______)
☐ AFDC (County & State ______)
☐ Other Welfare (describe ______)
☐ Other (describe ______)

(b) Enter your employer's name and address:

How long have you been employed by this employer? ______

(If less than 1 year, enter name and address of previous employer in Remarks.)

17. Have you ever been convicted of a felony? ☐ YES ☐ NO

If YES: What was the crime? ______

On what date were you convicted? ______

What was your sentence? ______

If imprisoned, when were you released? ______

If probation ordered, when did/will your probation end? ______

Social Security Form (Continued)

18. How long have you lived at your current address? **(Give Date MM/YY)**
(If less than 1 year, enter previous address in Remarks.) ____________________

REMARKS: *(This space may be used for explaining any answers to the questions. If you need more space, attach a separate sheet.)*

PLEASE READ THE FOLLOWING INFORMATION CAREFULLY BEFORE SIGNING THIS FORM

I/my organization:

- Must use all payments made to me/my organization as the representative payee for the claimant's current needs or (if not currently needed) save them for his/her future needs.
- May be held liable for repayment if I/my organization misuse the payments or if I/my organization am/is at fault for any overpayment of benefits.
- May be punished under Federal law by fine, imprisonment or both if I/my organization am/is found guilty of misuse of Social Security or SSI benefits.

I/my organization will:

- Use the payments for the claimant's current needs and save any currently unneeded benefits for future use.
- File an accounting report on how the payments were used, and make all supporting records available for review if requested by the Social Security Administration.
- Reimburse the amount of any loss suffered by any claimant due to misuse of Social Security or SSI funds by me/my organization.
- Notify the Social Security Administration when the claimant dies, leaves my/my organization's custody or otherwise changes his/her living arrangements or he/she is no longer my/my organization's responsibility.
- Comply with the conditions for reporting certain events (listed on the attached sheets(s) which I/my organization will keep for my/my organization's records) and for returning checks the claimant is not due.
- File an annual report of earnings if required.
- Notify the Social Security Administration as soon as I/my organization can no longer act as representative payee or the claimant no longer needs a payee.

I declare under penalty of perjury that I have examined all the information on this form, and on any accompanying statements or forms, and it is true and correct to the best of my knowledge.

SIGNATURE OF APPLICANT	DATE *(Month, day, year)*
Signature *(First name, middle initial, last name) (Write in ink)* **SIGN HERE ▶**	Telephone number(s) at Which You May Be Contacted During the Day

Print Your Name & Title *(if a representative or employee of an institution/organization)*

Mailing Address *(Number and street, Apt. No., P.O. Box, or Rural Route)*

City and State	Zip Code	Name of County

Residence Address *(Number and street, Apt. No., P.O. Box, or Rural Route)*

City and State	Zip Code	Name of County

Witnesses are only required if this application has been signed by mark (X) above. If signed by mark (X), two witnesses to the signing who know the applicant making the request must sign below, giving their full addresses.

1. SIGNATURE OF WITNESS	2. SIGNATURE OF WITNESS
ADDRESS *(Number and street, City, State and ZIP Code)*	ADDRESS *(Number and street, City, State and ZIP Code)*

Form **SSA-11-BK** (5-2003) EF (5-2003) Page 4

Social Security Form (Continued)

SOCIAL SECURITY

Information for Representative Payees Who Receive Social Security Benefits

YOU MUST NOTIFY THE SOCIAL SECURITY ADMINISTRATION PROMPTLY IF ANY OF THE FOLLOWING EVENTS OCCUR AND PROMPTLY RETURN ANY PAYMENT TO WHICH THE CLAIMANT IS NOT ENTITLED:

- the claimant DIES (Social Security entitlement ends the month before the month the claimant dies);
- the claimant MARRIES, if the claimant is entitled to child's, widow's, mother's, father's, widower's or parent's benefits, or to wife's or husband's benefits as a divorced wife/husband, or to special age 72 payments;
- the claimant's marriage ends in DIVORCE or ANNULMENT, if the claimant is entitled to wife's, husband's or special age 72 payments;
- the claimant's SCHOOL ATTENDANCE CHANGES if the claimant is age 18 or over and entitled to child's benefits as a full time student;
- the claimant is entitled as a stepchild and the parents DIVORCE (benefits terminate the month after the month the divorce becomes final);
- the claimant is under FULL RETIREMENT AGE (FRA) and WORKS for more than the annual limit (as determined each year) or more than the allowable time (for work outside the United States);
- the claimant receives a GOVERNMENT PENSION or ANNUITY or the amount of the annuity changes, if the claimant is entitled to husband's, widower's, or divorced spouse's benefits;
- the claimant leaves your custody or care or otherwise CHANGES ADDRESS;
- the claimant NO LONGER HAS A CHILD IN CARE, if he/she is entitled to benefits because of caring for a child under age 16 or who is disabled;
- the claimant is confined to jail, prison, penal institution or correctional facility for CONVICTION OF A CRIME;
- the claimant is confined to a public institution by court order in connection WITH A CRIME.

IF THE CLAIMANT IS RECEIVING DISABILITY BENEFITS, YOU MUST ALSO REPORT IF:

- the claimant's MEDICAL CONDITION IMPROVES;
- the claimant STARTS WORKING;
- the claimant applies for or receives WORKER'S COMPENSATION BENEFITS, Black Lung Benefits from the Department of Labor, or a public disability benefit;
- the claimant is DISCHARGED FROM THE HOSPITAL (if now hospitalized).

IF THE CLAIMANT IS RECEIVING SPECIAL AGE 72 PAYMENTS, YOU MUST ALSO REPORT IF:

- the claimant or spouse becomes ELIGIBLE FOR PERIODIC GOVERNMENTAL PAYMENTS, whether from the U.S. Federal government or from any State or local government;
- the claimant or spouse receives SUPPLEMENTAL SECURITY INCOME or PUBLIC ASSISTANCE CASH BENEFITS;
- the claimant or spouse MOVES outside the United States (the 50 States, the District of Columbia and the Northern Mariana Islands).

In addition to these events about the claimant, you must also notify us if:

- YOU change your address;
- YOU are convicted of a felony.

BENEFITS MAY STOP IF ANY OF THE ABOVE EVENTS OCCUR. You should read the informational booklet we will send you to see how these events affect benefits. You may make your reports by telephone, mail or in person.

REMEMBER:

- payments must be used for the claimant's current needs or saved if not currently needed;
- you may be held liable for repayment of any payments not used for the claimant's needs or of any over payment that occurred due to your fault;
- you must account for benefits when so asked by the Social Security Administration. You will keep records of how benefits were spent so you can provide us with a correct accounting;
- to tell us as soon as you know you will no longer be able to act as representative payee or the claimant no longer needs a payee.

Keep in mind that benefits may be deposited directly into an account set up for the claimant with you as payee. As soon as you set up such an account, contact us for more information about receiving the claimant's payments using direct deposit.

Form **SSA-11-BK** (5-2003) EF (5-2003) Page 5

Social Security Form (Continued)

A REMINDER TO PAYEE APPLICANTS

TELEPHONE NUMBER(S) TO CALL IF YOU HAVE A QUESTION OR SOMETHING TO REPORT		SSA OFFICE	DATE REQUEST RECEIVED
	BEFORE YOU RECEIVE A DECISION NOTICE		
	AFTER YOU RECEIVE A DECISION NOTICE		

RECEIPT FOR YOUR REQUEST

Your request for Social Security benefits on behalf of the individual(s) named below has been received and will be processed as quickly as possible.

You should hear from us within ____ days after you have given us all the information we requested. Some claims may take longer if additional information is needed.

In the meantime, if you change your address, or if there is some other change that may affect the benefits payable, you — or someone for you — should report the change. The changes to be reported are listed on the reverse.

Always give us the claim number of the beneficiary when writing or telephoning about the claim.

If you have any questions about this application, we will be glad to help you.

BENEFICIARY	SOCIAL SECURITY CLAIM NUMBER

THE PRIVACY ACT
We are required by section 205(j) and 205(a) of the Social Security Act to ask you to give us the information on this form. This information is needed to determine if you are qualified to serve as representative payee. Although responses to these questions are voluntary, you will not be named representative payee unless you give us the answers to these questions.

Sometimes the law requires us to give out the facts on this form without your consent. We must release this information to another person or government agency if Federal law requires that we do so or to do the research and audits needed to administer or improve our representative payee program.

We may also use the information you give us when we match records by computer. Matching programs compare our records with those of other Federal, state or local government agencies. Many agencies may use matching programs to find or prove that a person qualifies for benefits paid by the Federal government. The law allows us to do this even if you do not agree to it.

Explanation about these and other reasons why information you provide us may be used or given out are available in Social Security offices. If you want to learn more about this, contact any Social Security office.

PAPERWORK REDUCTION ACT STATEMENT
This information collection meets the requirements of 44 U.S.C. § 3507, as amended by Section 2 of the Paperwork Reduction Act of 1995. You do not need to answer these questions unless we display a valid Office of Management and Budget control number. We estimate that it will take about 10.5 minutes to read the instructions, gather the facts, and answer the questions. **SEND THE COMPLETED FORM TO YOUR LOCAL SOCIAL SECURITY OFFICE. The office is listed under U. S. Government agencies in your telephone directory or you may call Social Security at 1-800-772-1213.** *You may send comments on our time estimate above to: SSA, 1338 Annex Building, Baltimore, MD 21235-6401.* ***Send only comments relating to our time estimate to this address, not the completed form.***

Social Security Form (Continued)

SUPPLEMENTAL SECURITY INCOME
Information for Representative Payees Who Receive Social Security Benefits

YOU MUST NOTIFY THE SOCIAL SECURITY ADMINISTRATION PROMPTLY IF ANY OF THE FOLLOWING EVENTS OCCUR AND PROMPTLY RETURN ANY PAYMENT TO WHICH THE CLAIMANT IS NOT ENTITLED:

- the claimant or any member of the claimant's household DIES (SSI eligibility ends with the month in which the claimant dies);
- the claimant's HOUSEHOLD CHANGES (someone moves in/out of the place where the claimant lives);
- the claimant LEAVES THE U.S. (the 50 states, the District of Columbia, and the Northern Mariana Islands) for 30 consecutive days or more;
- the claimant MOVES or otherwise changes the place where he/she actually lives (including adoption, and whereabouts unknown);
- the claimant is ADMITTED TO A HOSPITAL, skilled nursing facility, nursing home, intermediate care facility, or other institution;
- the INCOME of the claimant or anyone in the claimant's household CHANGES (this includes income paid by organization as employer);
- the RESOURCES of the claimant or anyone in the claimant's household CHANGES (this includes when conserved funds reach over $2,000);
- the claimant or anyone in the claimant's household MARRIES;
- the marriage of the claimant or anyone in the claimant's household ends in DIVORCE or ANNULMENT;
- the claimant SEPARATES from his/her spouse;
- the claimant is confined to jail, prison, penal institution or correctional facility for CONVICTION OF A CRIME;
- the claimant is confined to a public institution by court order in connection WITH A CRIME;
- the claimant LEFT A JURISDICTION WITHIN THE U.S. to avoid prosecution or custody or confinement after CONVICTION FOR A CRIME that is a felony, or in New Jersey, a high misdemeanor;
- the claimant is in VIOLATION of a condition of probation or parole.

IF THE CLAIMANT IS RECEIVING PAYMENTS DUE TO DISABILITY OR BLINDNESS, YOU MUST ALSO REPORT IF:

- the claimant's MEDICAL CONDITION IMPROVES;
- the claimant GOES TO WORK;
- the claimant's VISION IMPROVES, if the claimant is entitled due to blindness;

In addition to these events about the claimant, you must also notify us if:

- YOU change your address;
- YOU are convicted of a felony.

PAYMENT MAY STOP IF ANY OF THE ABOVE EVENTS OCCUR. You should read the informational booklet we will send you to see how these events affect benefits. You may make your reports by telephone, mail or in person.

REMEMBER:

- payments must be used for the claimant's current needs or saved if not currently needed. (Savings are considered resources and may affect the claimant's eligibility to payment.);
- you may be held liable for repayment of any payments not used for the claimant's needs or of any overpayment that occurred due to your fault;
- you must account for benefits when so asked by the Social Security Administration. You will keep records of how benefits were spent so you can provide us with a correct accounting;
- to let us know as soon as you know you are unable to continue as representative payee or the claimant no longer needs a payee;
- you will be asked to help in periodically redetermining the claimant's continued eligibility or payment. You will need to keep evidence to help us with the redetermination (e.g., evidence of income and living arrangements).
- you may be required to obtain medical treatment for the claimant's disabling condition if he/she is eligible under the childhood disability provision.

Keep in mind that payments may be deposited directly into an account set up for the claimant with you as payee. As soon as you set up such an account, contact us for more information about receiving the claimant's payments using direct deposit.

Social Security Form (Continued)

A REMINDER TO PAYEE APPLICANTS

TELEPHONE NUMBER(S) TO CALL IF YOU HAVE A QUESTION OR SOMETHING TO REPORT	BEFORE YOU RECEIVE A DECISION NOTICE	SSA OFFICE	DATE REQUEST RECEIVED
	AFTER YOU RECEIVE A DECISION NOTICE		

RECEIPT FOR YOUR REQUEST

Your request for SSI payments on behalf of the individual(s) named below has been received and will be processed as quickly as possible.

You should hear from us within_____ days after you have given us all the information we requested. Some claims may take longer if additional information is needed.

In the meantime, if you change your address, or if there is some other change that may affect the benefits payable, you — or someone for you — should report the change. The changes to be reported are listed on the reverse.

Always give us the claim number of the beneficiary when writing or telephoning about the claim.

If you have any questions about this application, we will be glad to help you.

BENEFICIARY	SOCIAL SECURITY CLAIM NUMBER

THE PRIVACY ACT

We are required by section 205(j) and 205(a) of the Social Security Act to ask you to give us the information on this form. This information is needed to determine if you are qualified to serve as representative payee. Although responses to these questions are voluntary, you will not be named representative payee unless you give us the answers to these questions.

Sometimes the law requires us to give out the facts on this form without your consent. We must release this information to another person or government agency if Federal law requires that we do so or to do the research and audits needed to administer or improve our representative payee program.

We may also use the information you give us when we match records by computer. Matching programs compare our records with those of other Federal, state or local government agencies. Many agencies may use matching programs to find or prove that a person qualifies for benefits paid by the Federal government. The law allows us to do this even if you do not agree to it.

Explanation about these and other reasons why information you provide us may be used or given out are available in Social Security offices. If you want to learn more about this, contact any Social Security office.

PAPERWORK REDUCTION ACT STATEMENT

This information collection meets the requirements of 44 U.S.C. § 3507, as amended by Section 2 of the Paperwork Reduction Act of 1995. You do not need to answer these questions unless we display a valid Office of Management and Budget control number. We estimate that it will take about 10.5 minutes to read the instructions, gather the facts, and answer the questions. **SEND THE COMPLETED FORM TO YOUR LOCAL SOCIAL SECURITY OFFICE. The office is listed under U. S. Government agencies in your telephone directory or you may call Social Security at 1-800-772-1213.** *You may send comments on our time estimate above to: SSA, 1338 Annex Building, Baltimore, MD 21235-0001.* ***Send only comments relating to our time estimate to this address, not the completed form.***

Form **SSA-11-BK** (5-2003) EF (5-2003) Page 8

Social Security Form (Continued)

BLACK LUNG BENEFITS

Information for Representative Payees Who Receive Black Lung Benefits

YOU MUST NOTIFY THE SOCIAL SECURITY ADMINISTRATION PROMPTLY IF ANY OF THE FOLLOWING EVENTS OCCUR AND PROMPTLY RETURN ANY PAYMENT TO WHICH THE CLAIMANT IS NOT ENTITLED:

- the claimant DIES;
- the claimant receives STATE WORKER'S COMPENSATION based on the miner's disability, or the amount of such compensation changes;
- the miner receives UNEMPLOYMENT INSURANCE;
- the claimant IS WORKING or RETURNS TO WORK;
- the claimant MARRIES or REMARRIES, if the claimant is entitled to child's, widow's, brother's or sister's benefits;
- the claimant begins to RECEIVE SUPPORT PAYMENTS from his/her spouse, if the claimant is entitled to brother's or sister's benefits;
- the claimant is ADOPTED, if the claimant is entitled to child's benefits;
- the claimant's MEDICAL CONDITION IMPROVES, if the claimant is entitled to disabled child's brother's or sister's benefits;
- the claimant is age 18 to 23 and STOPS ATTENDING SCHOOL, if the claimant is entitled to child's, sister's or brother's benefits.

In addition to these events about the claimant, you must also notify us if:

- YOU change your address;
- YOU are convicted of a felony.

BENEFITS MAY STOP IF ANY OF THE ABOVE EVENTS OCCUR. You should read the informational booklet we will send you to see how these events affect benefits. You may make your reports by telephone, mail or in person.

REMEMBER:

- payments must be used for the claimant's current needs or saved if not currently needed;
- you may be held liable for repayment of any payments not used for the claimant's needs or of any overpayment that occurred due to your fault;
- you must account for benefits when so asked by the Social Security Administration. You will keep records of how benefits were spent so you can provide us with a correct accounting;
- to let us know as soon as you know you are unable to continue as representative payee or the claimant no longer needs a payee.

Keep in mind that benefits may be deposited directly into an account set up for the claimant with you as payee. As soon as you set up such an account, contact us for more information about receiving the claimant's payments using direct deposit.

Social Security Form (Continued)

A REMINDER TO PAYEE APPLICANTS

TELEPHONE NUMBER(S) TO CALL IF YOU HAVE A QUESTION OR SOMETHING TO REPORT	BEFORE YOU RECEIVE A DECISION NOTICE	SSA OFFICE	DATE REQUEST RECEIVED
	AFTER YOU RECEIVE A DECISION NOTICE		

RECEIPT FOR YOUR REQUEST

Your request for Black Lung benefits on behalf of the individual(s) named below has been received and will be processed as quickly as possible.

You should hear from us within _____ days after you have given us all the information we requested. Some claims may take longer if additional information is needed.

In the meantime, if you change your address, or if there is some other change that may affect the benefits payable, you — or someone for you — should report the change. The changes to be reported are listed on the reverse.

Always give us the claim number of the beneficiary when writing or telephoning about the claim.

If you have any questions about this application, we will be glad to help you.

BENEFICIARY	SOCIAL SECURITY CLAIM NUMBER

THE PRIVACY ACT

We are required by section 205(j) and 205(a) of the Social Security Act to ask you to give us the information on this form. This information is needed to determine if you are qualified to serve as representative payee. Although responses to these questions are voluntary, you will not be named representative payee unless you give us the answers to these questions.

Sometimes the law requires us to give out the facts on this form without your consent. We must release this information to another person or government agency if Federal law requires that we do so or to do the research and audits needed to administer or improve our representative payee program.

We may also use the information you give us when we match records by computer. Matching programs compare our records with those of other Federal, state or local government agencies. Many agencies may use matching programs to find or prove that a person qualifies for benefits paid by the Federal government. The law allows us to do this even if you do not agree to it.

Explanation about these and other reasons why information you provide us may be used or given out are available in Social Security offices. If you want to learn more about this, contact any Social Security office.

PAPERWORK REDUCTION ACT STATEMENT

This information collection meets the requirements of 44 U.S.C. § 3507, as amended by Section 2 of the Paperwork Reduction Act of 1995. You do not need to answer these questions unless we display a valid Office of Management and Budget control number. We estimate that it will take about 10.5 minutes to read the instructions, gather the facts, and answer the questions. **SEND THE COMPLETED FORM TO YOUR LOCAL SOCIAL SECURITY OFFICE. The office is listed under U. S. Government agencies in your telephone directory or you may call Social Security at 1-800-772-1213.** *You may send comments on our time estimate above to: SSA, 1338 Annex Building, Baltimore, MD 21235-0001.*
Send only comments relating to our time estimate to this address, not the completed form.

Form **SSA-11-BK** (5-2003) EF (5-2003) Page 10

Social Security Form (Continued)

SPECIAL BENEFITS FOR WORLD WAR II VETERANS

Information for Representative Payees Who Receive Special Benefits for WW II Veterans

YOU MUST NOTIFY THE SOCIAL SECURITY ADMINISTRATION PROMPTLY IF ANY OF THE FOLLOWING EVENTS OCCUR AND PROMPTLY RETURN ANY PAYMENT TO WHICH THE CLAIMANT IS NOT ENTITLED:

- the claimant DIES (special veterans entitlement ends the month after the claimant dies);
- the claimant returns to the United States for a calendar month or longer;
- the claimant moves or changes the place where he/she actually lives;
- the claimant receives a pension, annuity or other recurring payment (includes workers' compensation, veterans benefits or disability benefits), or the amount of the annuity changes;
- the claimant is or has been deported or removed from U.S.;
- the claimant left a jurisdiction within the U.S. to avoid prosecution or custody or confinement after conviction for a crime that is a felony, or in New Jersey, a high misdemeanor;
- the claimant is in violation of a condition of probation or parole.

In addition to these events about the claimant, you must also notify us if:
- YOU change your address;
- YOU are convicted of a felony.

BENEFITS MAY STOP IF ANY OF THE ABOVE EVENTS OCCUR. You can make your reports by telephone, mail or in person. You can contact any U.S. Embassy, Consulate, Veterans Affairs Regional Office in the Philippines or any U.S. Social Security Office.

REMEMBER:
- payments must be used for the claimant's current needs or saved if not currently needed;
- you may be held liable for repayment of any payments not used for the claimant's needs or of any overpayment that occurred due to your fault;
- you must account for benefits when so asked by the Social Security Administration. You will keep records of how benefits were spent so you can provide us with a correct accounting;
- to let us know, as soon as you know you are unable to continue as representative payee or the claimant no longer needs a payee.

Social Security Form (Continued)

A REMINDER TO PAYEE APPLICANTS

TELEPHONE NUMBER(S) TO CALL IF YOU HAVE A QUESTION OR SOMETHING TO REPORT	BEFORE YOU RECEIVE A DECISION NOTICE	SSA OFFICE	DATE REQUEST RECEIVED
	AFTER YOU RECEIVE A DECISION NOTICE		

RECEIPT FOR YOUR REQUEST

Your request for Special benefits for WW II Veterans on behalf of the individual(s) named below has been received and will be processed as quickly as possible.

You should hear from us within _____ days after you have given us all the information we requested. Some claims may take longer if additional information is needed.

In the meantime, if you change your address, or if there is some other change that may affect the benefits payable, you — or someone for you — should report the change. The changes to be reported are listed on the reverse.

Always give us the claim number of the beneficiary when writing or telephoning about the claim.

If you have any questions about this application, we will be glad to help you.

BENEFICIARY	SOCIAL SECURITY CLAIM NUMBER

THE PRIVACY ACT

We are required by section 205(j) and 205(a) of the Social Security Act to ask you to give us the information on this form. This information is needed to determine if you are qualified to serve as representative payee. Although responses to these questions are voluntary, you will not be named representative payee unless you give us the answers to these questions.

Sometimes the law requires us to give out the facts on this form without your consent. We must release this information to another person or government agency if Federal law requires that we do so or to do the research and audits needed to administer or improve our representative payee program.

We may also use the information you give us when we match records by computer. Matching programs compare our records with those of other Federal, state or local government agencies. Many agencies may use matching programs to find or prove that a person qualifies for benefits paid by the Federal government. The law allows us to do this even if you do not agree to it.

Explanation about these and other reasons why information you provide us may be used or given out are available in Social Security offices. If you want to learn more about this, contact any Social Security office.

PAPERWORK REDUCTION ACT STATEMENT

This information collection meets the requirements of 44 U.S.C. § 3507, as amended by Section 2 of the Paperwork Reduction Act of 1995. You do not need to answer these questions unless we display a valid Office of Management and Budget control number. We estimate that it will take about 10.5 minutes to read the instructions, gather the facts, and answer the questions. **SEND THE COMPLETED FORM TO YOUR LOCAL SOCIAL SECURITY OFFICE. The office is listed under U. S. Government agencies in your telephone directory or you may call Social Security at 1-800-772-1213.** *You may send comments on our time estimate above to: SSA, 1338 Annex Building, Baltimore, MD 21235-0001.*
Send only comments relating to our time estimate to this address, not the completed form.

Form **SSA-11-BK** (5-2003) EF (5-2003) Page 12

7 Estate Administration

CHAPTER OVERVIEW

When a person dies, it is the obligation of his or her personal representative or next of kin to see that the estate is administered according to the estate laws of the state in which the decedent owned property. Typically, the personal representative or next of kin will consult with an attorney in order to facilitate the administrative process, and the attorney will rely almost completely on the legal assistant. In no other area of law is the legal assistant given the amount of responsibility and detail as he or she is in the area of estate administration.

The process of administering an estate can be divided into three broad categories: preprobate obligations; the actual probate process; and the distribution and winding up of the estate. In each of these three areas the paralegal is the primary person with whom the personal representative and the probate court deals.

The preprobate concerns of the legal assistant are to locate all wills executed by the decedent, arrange for a family conference (if such is necessary), to explain the administrative process to the relatives, and to assist the attorney in providing for the operation of any business for which the decedent was responsible.

The probate administration of the estate involves petitioning the court for Letters authorizing the personal representative to act on behalf of the estate, regardless of whether the decedent died testate or intestate. The paralegal is responsible for notifying all parties who have an interest in the estate that a petition for administering the estate has been filed with the probate court, and, if any will contest is noted, to assist the attorney in the preparation of the defense of the estate. Finally, the paralegal will be the person who physically obtains the Letters from the court.

The last, and largest, phase of estate administration concerns gathering all of the decedent's assets, determining all liabilities, and seeing that all taxes and debts are paid. The legal assistant will be responsible for organizing and categorizing all assets and liabilities, preparing checks or title transfer documents for the heirs, obtaining receipts and releases for all distributions made, and assisting the estate accountant in the preparation of all tax returns. Finally, once the estate has been distributed, the paralegal will prepare the final estate accounting for the court.

The legal assistant is given a great deal of autonomy with respect to administering the estate; the lawyer and accountant only get involved in formal phases of the work if there is some particularly unusual or difficult aspect to the estate, such as a will contest or a bankrupt estate. For the paralegal who enjoys responsibility and independence the estate field provides the perfect opportunity for his or her talents.

Note that the procedures and forms that follow are given as general examples. Procedures and forms may vary not only from jurisdiction to jurisdiction, but from county to county as well.

The Preprobate Process

When a person dies, automatically all of his or her bank accounts, brokerage accounts, and other property are sealed pending orders from the appropriate court authorizing a personal representative to deal with the decedent's assets. The accounts and property are frozen in order to protect the government and creditors of the estate. However, many times these assets are either jointly held or are used to support a family, and prior to Letters being issued by the court some access to this property may be necessary. It is the responsibility of the attorney and paralegal to see that interim authorization is granted by the court. In order to obtain the authorization, several documents must be obtained and prepared. Most of these forms are available from the probate court or can be found in form books for each state code. Examples of the forms discussed appear where appropriate in the text, and further examples are provided in the Appendix.

Death Certificate

Death certificates are official documents issued by the state Department of Health or local health authority as proof of the death of its citizens. They are usually issued shortly after the death, unless an autopsy is required. Autopsies are required if the decedent dies under violent circumstances, by misadventure, or under circumstances that are not readily ascertainable (such as a person who is ill with several medical problems and the exact cause of death could be any of the diseases). Obtaining copies of the death certificate is important because it is necessary as proof of death for the court.

EXAMPLE:

David suffers from diabetes, heart ailments, and colitis. When Fern and Barney return home, they find David dead on the front door steps to the house. Because it cannot be determined if he died from any of his illnesses, or tripped and died when his head hit the stairs, an autopsy would be required.

Exhibit 1: Death Certificate

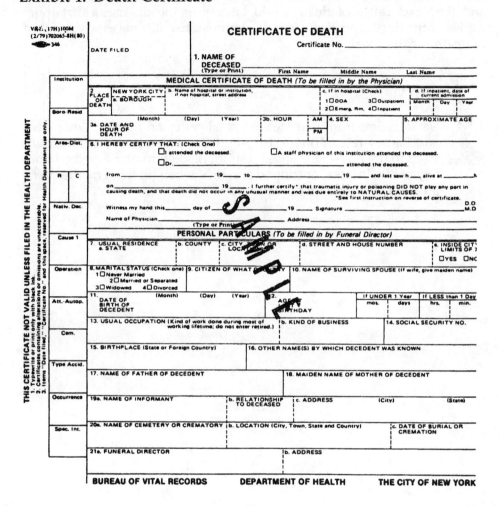

VR-? (17H)100M
(2/79)702065-8H(80)
346

DATE FILED

CERTIFICATE OF DEATH

Certificate No. ______________

1. NAME OF DECEASED (Type or Print) ______________
First Name Middle Name Last Name

MEDICAL CERTIFICATE OF DEATH *(To be filled in by the Physician)*

2 PLACE OF DEATH | NEW YORK CITY a. BOROUGH | b. Name of hospital or institution, if not hospital, street address | c. If in hospital (Check) 1☐ DOA 3☐ Outpatient 2☐ Emerg. Rm. 4☐ Inpatient | d. If inpatient, date of current admission Month Day Year

3a. DATE AND HOUR OF DEATH (Month) (Day) (Year) | 3b. HOUR AM PM | 4. SEX | 5. APPROXIMATE AGE

6. I HEREBY CERTIFY THAT: (Check One)
☐ I attended the deceased. ☐ A staff physician of this institution attended the deceased.
☐ Dr. ______________ attended the deceased.

from ______________ 19____ to ______________ 19____ and last saw h____ alive at ________M

on ______________ 19____. I further certify* that traumatic injury or poisoning DID NOT play any part in causing death, and that death did not occur in any unusual manner and was due entirely to NATURAL CAUSES.
*See first instruction on reverse of certificate.

Witness my hand this ______ day of ______________ 19____ Signature ______________ D.O. M.D.

Name of Physician ______________ (Type or Print) Address ______________

PERSONAL PARTICULARS *(To be filled in by Funeral Director)*

7. USUAL RESIDENCE a. STATE | b. COUNTY | c. CITY, TOWN OR LOCATION | d. STREET AND HOUSE NUMBER | e. INSIDE CITY LIMITS OF ? ☐ YES ☐ NO

8. MARITAL STATUS (Check one) 1☐ Never Married 2☐ Married or Separated 3☐ Widowed 4☐ Divorced | 9. CITIZEN OF WHAT COUNTRY | 10. NAME OF SURVIVING SPOUSE (If wife, give maiden name)

11. DATE OF BIRTH OF DECEDENT (Month) (Day) (Year) | 12. AGE AT LAST BIRTHDAY | If UNDER 1 Year mos. days | If LESS than 1 Day hrs. min.

13. USUAL OCCUPATION (Kind of work done during most of working lifetime; do not enter retired.) | b. KIND OF BUSINESS | 14. SOCIAL SECURITY NO.

15. BIRTHPLACE (State or Foreign Country) | 16. OTHER NAME(S) BY WHICH DECEDENT WAS KNOWN

17. NAME OF FATHER OF DECEDENT | 18. MAIDEN NAME OF MOTHER OF DECEDENT

19a. NAME OF INFORMANT | b. RELATIONSHIP TO DECEASED | c. ADDRESS (City) (State)

20a. NAME OF CEMETERY OR CREMATORY | b. LOCATION (City, Town, State and Country) | c. DATE OF BURIAL OR CREMATION

21a. FUNERAL DIRECTOR | b. ADDRESS

BUREAU OF VITAL RECORDS DEPARTMENT OF HEALTH THE CITY OF NEW YORK

Institution | Boro-Resid | Area-Dist. | R | C | Nativ. Dec. | Cause 1 | Operation | Att.-Autop. | Cem. | Type Accid. | Occurrence | Spec. Int.

THIS CERTIFICATE NOT VALID UNLESS FILED IN THE HEALTH DEPARTMENT
1. Typewrite or print only with black ink.
2. Certificates containing alterations or omissions are unacceptable.
3. Items "Date filed," "Certificate No." and this space, reserved for Health Department use only.

SAMPLE

Petition to Open Safe Deposit Box

There are two circumstances in which the court will be asked to permit the opening of a safe deposit box prior to granting permanent Letters. The first is if the will of the decedent cannot be found and it is suspected that it was left in the safe deposit box. The other circumstance is if it can be shown that the decedent shared the box with some other person, and that person needs something from it. (Money and jewelry are not considered sufficiently important to warrant opening the box.) If the court grants the request, the box must be opened in front of representatives from the bank and the state taxing authority, and the only item that may be removed from the box is the will or property specified in the court order. The paralegal will have to prepare the order for the court to sign (the court generally does not prepare documents itself, but will sign orders presented to it if the order is in accordance with its ruling). The specific procedures may vary from jurisdiction to jurisdiction.

EXAMPLE:

Hyacinth, as David's eldest daughter, petitions the court to open David's safe deposit box to locate his will. When the box is opened, the will is found inside. Hyacinth, who has shared the box with her father, wants to remove an onyx brooch to wear during the period of mourning. Only the will may be removed; the brooch must stay in the box until its ownership is determined.

Exhibit 2: Petition to Open Safe Deposit Box

Surrogate's Court
County of New York

In the Matter of the Application for a Search of a Safe Deposit Box for the Will of

Deceased

Petition to Open Safe Deposit Box

To The Surrogate's Court of the County of New York:

The petition of respectfully alleges:

The petitioner resides at

and is the of who died

in the County of

on the day of 19, , and at the time of h death resided at

in the County of New York.

The name of each person who at the date of the deceased's death was a distributee of the deceased by reason of being related to the deceased as spouse, child, issue of a deceased child, adopted child, issue of a deceased adopted child, father, mother, brother or sister of the whole blood or of the half blood or issue of a deceased brother or sister and the names of all other distributees of the deceased are as follows:

Name	*Relationship*

The said deceased had a private safe in the vault of the

, a corporation

doing business in the City of New York, whose address is

. The petitioner believes that deceased may have left in said private safe a will and insurance policies on the life of deceased payable to named beneficiaries and a cemetery deed or instructions respecting burial and petitioner requests that an order be made directing the officer or other authorized employee or agent of the said corporation, in the presence of a representative of the State Tax Commission, to examine the said safe for the purpose of ascertaining if a will or wills or insurance policies on the life of deceased payable to named beneficiaries or a cemetery deed or instructions respecting burial of said deceased be deposited therein, and if any will be found, that the same be deposited in this court, and insurance policies on the life of deceased be delivered to the named beneficiaries and the cemetery deed or instructions respecting burial be delivered to petitioner.

No probate or administration proceeding is pending nor is there any will of deceased on file in this court.

No prior application has been made for the relief herein requested.

Petetioner designates to attend and participate with or in place of at the opening of the above safe deposit box.

Dated: , 19

Petitioner

Use BLACK ink only, as this sheet will be photograph

Petition to Search

If the will is not found in the safe deposit box, it may be necessary to search other property of the decedent, such as an office or apartment. If the next of kin does not have access to the property by law, as a cotenant or joint owner, it is necessary to petition the court to search the premises to locate the will and, perhaps, insurance policies. Once again, the paralegal must prepare the petition and the order for the court.

EXAMPLE:

Dr. Montague dies, and Cornelia cannot locate his will. She believes it may be in the office he kept to manage his real estate investments, but the landlord has sealed the premises. Cornelia can go to the court to get an order permitting her to search the office for the will.

Exhibit 3: Petition to Search

Form B 1

Surrogate's Court
County of New York

In the Matter of the Application for a Search of

for the Will of

Deceased

Petition to Search

To The Surrogate's Court of the County of New York:

The petition of respectfully alleges:

The petitioner resides at

and is the of who died

in the County of

on the day of 19 , and at the time of h death resided at

in the County of New York.

The name of each person who at the date of the deceased's death was a distributee of the deceased by reason of being related to the deceased as spouse, child, issue of a deceased child, adopted child, issue of a deceased adopted child, father, mother, brother or sister of the whole blood or of the half blood or issue of a deceased brother or sister and the names of all other distributees of the deceased are as follows:

Name	*Relationship*

The said deceased had a at

New York, N. Y. The petitioner believes that deceased may have left in said a will and insurance policies on the life of deceased payable to named beneficiaries and a cemetery deed or instructions respecting burial and petitioner requests that an order be made directing the person in charge of said premises, in the presence of a representative of the State Tax Commission and a representative of the Surrogate's Court, to examine the said for the purpose of ascertaining if a will or wills or insurance policies on the life of deceased payable to named beneficiaries or a cemetery deed or instructions respecting burial of said deceased be deposited therein, and if any will be found, that the same be deposited in this court, and insurance policies on the life of deceased be delivered to the named beneficiaries and the cemetery deed or instructions respecting burial be delivered to petitioner.

No probate or administration proceeding is pending nor is there any will of deceased on file in this court.

No prior application has been made for the relief herein requested.

Dated

Petitioner

Use BLACK ink only, as this sheet will be photographed.

Petition for Guardian ad Litem

A **guardian ad litem** is a person appointed by the court to represent a minor or incompetent person during the court process. If the decedent left minor children or dependents and did not provide for guardianship by the terms of the will, a competent adult must petition the court for guardianship.

EXAMPLE:

When Loretta dies, Aida petitions the court for guardianship of Evan until Loretta's estate is administered. As a close relative (grandmother) the court may grant her petition, even if Evan's father, Jason Leroy, is attempting to gain permanent guardianship. The guardian ad litem's responsibilities are only for the term of the litigation and are not permanent. Permanent guardianship will be determined by the court during the judicial process.

Petition for Family Allowance

If the family's money was all in accounts held by the decedent, on his or her death these assets may be frozen until the estate administration is completed. If the family is dependent upon these funds for maintenance, the court may be petitioned to permit the family to draw an allowance from the decedent's funds. The necessary allowance must be proved to the court, and the creditors of the decedent may have the right to object. If granted, the family may only draw an allowance up to the limit established by the court order.

EXAMPLE:

Oscar dies unexpectedly. All of the family funds were in his name, and Hyacinth needs some money for her support and Byron's tuition. In these circumstances she may petition the court for a family allowance pending the administration of the estate.

Petition for Interim (Preliminary, Temporary) Letters

If the decedent was operating a business, in order to continue the operation until the estate is settled it may be necessary to petition the court for interim Letters for the specific purpose of operating the business entity. Once again, creditors may have the right to object to the appointment and may themselves petition the court for the right to carry on the business pending formal administration.

EXAMPLE:

When Dr. Montague dies, Cornelia petitions the court for interim Letters in order to continue her husband's real estate business that he operated as a sole proprietor. Until formal administration of the estate is established it is still necessary that the business be maintained for the benefit of the tenants, creditors, and heirs.

In addition to the filing of the aforementioned forms, the paralegal may also be called upon to assist the attorney at a family conference and will help explain the entire estate administration process to the family members and obtain signatures for petitions and/or waivers whenever such may be necessary.

Probate Administration

The official administration of an estate begins with the filing of a petition for probate with the appropriate court (see Chapter 8). The petitioner is the person who is requesting to be appointed the personal representative of the decedent. Three types of probate may be permitted. The most common form is the formal probate proceeding in which all of the forms and documents discussed in the text are prepared. The second form of probate is known as a **summary proceeding**, which is permitted, in certain jurisdictions, when there is only one will filed, no will contest, and a relatively small estate is involved. In these proceedings the estate can be closed by affidavit of the personal representative. **Informal proceedings** are also sometimes permitted for small estates (the amount qualifying as "small" depends upon the jurisdiction). In informal proceedings no notice is required to be given to interested parties (see below). In the jurisdictions in which summary and informal proceedings are permitted the process is streamlined, and the forms vary from the forms used for a formal probate. Once again, these forms are available from the court and appear in state formbooks and on the Internet.

Exhibit 4: Informal Proceeding Forms

OFFICE OF BEVERLY B. KAUFMAN, COUNTY CLERK, HARRIS COUNTY, TEXAS
PROBATE COURTS DEPARTMENT

AFFIDAVIT OF DISTRIBUTEES • SMALL ESTATE • WITH JUDGE'S ORDER OR APPROVAL
§ 137, TEXAS PROBATE CODE

In Matters of Probate	§	Docket No. ______________________
Probate Court No. ____	§	Style of
Harris County, Texas	§	Estate: ______________________ Deceased

To the Honorable Judge of said Court:

This, the affidavit of all of the distributees of the estate of ______________________

______________________, deceased, is respectfully submitted and shows:

1. That ______________________ died on or about

______________________, at ______________________.
(City and State)

2. That the domicile of the decedent, at the time of death was ______________________, County, Texas.

*

3. That no petition for the appointment of a personal representative of the decedent's estate is pending or has been granted.

4. That more than thirty days have elapsed since the death of the decedent.

5. That the value of the entire assets of the estate, not including homestead and exempt property, does not exceed fifty thousand dollars ($50,000.00).

6. That the assets of the decedent, excluding homestead and exempt property, are as follows:

7. That all the known liabilities of the decedent's estate are as follows:

8. That the names, addresses, and telephone numbers of all distributees, and their right to receive money or property or to have such evidences of money, property or other rights, to the extent that the assets, exclusive of homestead. and exempt property, exceed the known liabilities of the estate are as follows:

Names, Addresses, and Phone Numbers of Distributees	Capacity in which claim is made	Portion of Estate to which entitled
Example: John Doe • 1000 Main St. • Houston, Texas 77000 (713) 755-6425	*Son*	½

* Other facts showing venue if necessary

Exhibit 4: *(Continued)*

Names, Addresses and Phone Numbers of Distributees	Capacity in which claim is made	Portion of Estate to which entitled

9. **Legal Description of real property belonging to the estate of the decedent including homestead and exempt property.**

10. **§ 137 of the Texas Probate Code does not affect the disposition of property under the terms of a Will or other testamentary document, nor does it transfer title to real property other than the Decedent's homestead.**

Wherefore the distributees of the estate pray that the court enter an order and approve the distribution of that part of the estate to which each distributee is entitled without awaiting the appointment of a personal representative.

Signature of Distributees	

Before me, the undersigned authority, on this day personally appeared:	

who being by me duly sworn upon oath states that the foregoing affidavit is true and correct in every respect. Sworn and subscribed to by the named distributees on: ________________________.

____

____

Notary Public in and for the State of Texas

Exhibit 4: *(Continued)*

HEIRSHIP AFFIDAVIT
(To be filled out and signed by two Disinterested Witnesses)

Before me, the undersigned authority, on this day personally appeared ______________________________

and ______________________________, who being first by me duly sworn on oath state:

I.

I, ______________________________, reside at ______________________________,

______________________________ County, ______________________________. I am

personally acquainted with the family history and facts of heirship of ______________________________,

deceased, hereinafter called "Decedent" who was my ______________________________.

I knew Decedent for __________ years.

I, ______________________________, reside at ______________________________,

______________________________ County, ______________________________. I am

personally acquainted with the family history and facts of heirship of ______________________________,

deceased, hereinafter called "Decedent" who was my ______________________________.

I knew Decedent for __________ years.

II.

Decedent was married to ______________________________ on

______________________________, and remained married until his/her death and was never divorced.

OR

Decedent was never married.

OR

Decedent was not married at the time of death but was married to ______________________________

on______________________________, and was widowed/divorced on ______________________________

III.

Decedent died on ______________________________, in ______________________________,

______________________________ County, ______________________________, without leaving a Will. There was no administration nor was any necessary, there being no debts at this time.

Form No. CC-D-02-03-40 (Rev. 03/94)

Exhibit 4: *(Continued)*

IV.

1. Decedent had no children.

OR

1. Decedent had the following children by birth or adoption: (List all children, living or deceased, if deceased indicate).

Name	Address	Age	Alive or Deceased

Decedent never adopted any children nor cared for any children in the home other than the above named children.

2. If any child of Decedent is deceased, list all children of the deceased child or children.

Deceased child: ____________________

Children of deceased child

Name	Address	Age	Alive or Deceased

Deceased child: ____________________

Children of deceased child

Name	Address	Age	Alive or Deceased

Exhibit 4: *(Continued)*

3. (If decedent was not survived by children or grandchildren, then, complete.) Decedent was survived by his/her parent or parents:

Name	Address

AND/OR

3. (If Decedent was not survived by his/her parents or only one parent, the complete.) Decedent was survived by the following brother(s) and/or sister(s):

Name	Address	Age	Alive or Deceased

AND/OR

3. If any brother(s) or sister(s) have predeceased Decedent complete.

Name of deceased brother/sister: ______________________________

Children of deceased brother/sister

Name	Address	Age	Alive or Deceased

Exhibit 4: *(Continued)*

The above Statements are true and correct.

Executed on ____.

____
Disinterested Witness

____
Disinterested Witness

Subscribed and sworn to before me, by ______________________________ on

______________________, to certify which witness my hand and seal of office.

____
Notary Public in and for the State of Texas

STATE OF TEXAS §

COUNTY OF HARRIS §

Before me, the undersigned authority, on this day personally appeared ______________________ known to me to be the person whose name is subscribed to the foregoing instrument, and acknowledged to me that he executed same for the purposes and considerations therein expressed.

____
Notary Public in and for the State of Texas

Subscribed and sworn to before me, by ______________________________ on

______________________, to certify which witness my hand and seal of office.

____
Notary Public in and for the State of Texas

STATE OF TEXAS §

COUNTY OF HARRIS §

Before me, the undersigned authority, on this day personally appeared ______________________ known to me to be the person whose name is subscribed to the foregoing instrument, and acknowledged to me that he executed same for the purposes and considerations therein expressed.

____
Notary Public in and for the State of Texas

Note: If blanks are not sufficient for information, a separate sheet may be attached.

Exhibit 4: *(Continued)*

OFFICE OF BEVERLY B. KAUFMAN, COUNTY CLERK, HARRIS COUNTY, TEXAS
PROBATE COURTS DEPARTMENT

IN MATTERS OF PROBATE	§	DOCKET NO. ____________
	§	
PROBATE COURT NO. _______	§	
	§	STYLE OF DOCKET: ____________________
HARRIS COUNTY, TEXAS	§	DECEASED

ORDER AND APPROVAL OF JUDGE FOR AFFIDAVIT OF DISTRIBUTEES - SMALL ESTATES

(§137, TEXAS PROBATE CODE)

The foregoing affidavit of the distributees of the estate of ____________________

____________________, deceased, has been examined, considered, and approved by the Court on ____________________,
and it is therefore ordered, adjudged and decreed that the distributees of the estate, hereinabove named, are entitled to the part of the estate as set out in the affidavit without awaiting the appointment of a personal representative.

____
Judge of Probate Court No. _________

CERTIFICATE OF RECORD

I, the Clerk of the Probate Court No. ________ of Harris County, Texas, do hereby certify that the foregoing instrument, Film Code No. ____________________ through Film Code No. ____________________,
is a true and correct record of said instrument as filed and recorded in the Probate Records of Harris County, as approved by the Judge of said Court for recording in the "Small Estate" Records of Harris County, Texas.

BEVERLY B. KAUFMAN
County Clerk, Harris County, Texas

____
DEPARTMENT HEAD

FORM NO. CC-D-02-03-40-A (Rev. 03/94)

Petition for Letters of Administration

If the decedent dies without a valid will, he or she is deemed to have died intestate. The court is then petitioned to grant **Letters of Administration.** As previously discussed, Letters of Administration are court orders authorizing the personal representative of an intestate to administer the estate. The petition asks for the decedent's name and address, the date and place of the decedent's death, the name, address, and relationship of the petitioner to the decedent. It also requires the petitioner to state affirmatively that a diligent search had been made for a will without success. All of the intestate heirs must be indicated, specifying any who are under a disability (age, mental, or physical problems). Finally, the petitioner is required to indicate the value of the decedent's estate. This last is for the purpose of establishing a court fee, which is usually calculated on a sliding scale dependent upon the size of the estate. The petition must be signed and **verified**—a statement under oath that the statements made in the petition are true. The petition must also have a copy of the death certificate attached and, for convenience, the petitioner typically signs an oath of office at the same time so that if the petition is granted the oath is already on file. Once granted, the petitioner, now the Administrator may have to post a bond with the court. Every jurisdiction has statutory requirements to be appointed a personal representative. For each state's requirements, see Chapter 9.

EXAMPLE:

Aida dies without a will. Loretta, as Aida's next of kin, petitions the probate court to be appointed the Administratrix of Aida's estate. Because there is no will waiving bond, Loretta may be required to post a bond with the court depending upon the law of her jurisdiction, even though she is Aida's only child.

Exhibit 5: Petition for Letters of Administration

PETITION FOR LETTERS OF ADMINISTRATION (Rev. 5-90) CCP-302

CLERK OF THE CIRCUIT COURT OF COOK COUNTY, ILLINOIS

Estate of

Deceased

No.

Docket

Page

Hearing on petition set for
__________, 19 ___
_____ M., Room _____
Richard J. Daley Center
Chicago, Illinois 60602

PETITION FOR LETTERS OF ADMINISTRATION

______________________________________, states under the penalties of perjury:

1. ______________________________, whose place of residence at the time of death was

____,
(address) (city) (county) (state)

died ____________________, 19___, at ______________________________ leaving no will.
(city) (state)

2. The approximate value of the estate in this state is:

Personal	Real	Annual Income From Real Estate
\$................	\$...............	\$.................

3. The names and post-office addresses of decedent's heirs are set forth on Exhibit A and made a part of this petition. (Indicate the relationship and whether an heir is a minor or disabled person.)

4. The names and post-office addresses of persons who are entitled to nominate an administrator in preference to (P) or equally with (E) petitioner are set forth on Exhibit A made a part of this petition. If none, so state: ________________.

5. Petitioner is a ______________________________ of decedent and is legally qualified to act, or to nominate a resident of Illinois to act, as administrator.

*6. The name and post-office address of the personal fiduciary designated to act during independent administration for each heir who is a minor or disabled person are shown on Exhibit A made a part of this petition.

Petitioner asks that Letters of Administration issue to the following, qualified and willing to act:

Name Post-Office Address

Atty Name
Firm Name
Attorney for Petitioner
Address
City & Zip
Telephone
Atty No.

____
Petitioner

Address ______________________________

____

____
Attorney Certification

If a consul or consular agent is to be notified, name country: ______________________________

*If supervised administration is requested, so state and strike Paragraph 6.

AURELIA PUCINSKI, CLERK OF THE CIRCUIT COURT OF COOK COUNTY

Petition for Letters Testamentary

If the decedent died with a valid will, the petition requests **Letters Testamentary**—court authorization for the personal representative of a testate to administer the estate. The petition is generally very similar to the Petition for Letters of Administration, except that in this instance it also indicates the date of execution of the will and codicils being presented for probate, and names all of the persons who will inherit property under the will. The Petition for Letters Testamentary must be accompanied by the death certificate and the *original* of the will and all codicils, including any self-proving affidavits. Copies cannot be submitted to the court. This petition is also verified and may contain the oath of office. Once approved, the petitioner becomes the **Executor** of the estate.

EXAMPLE:

Barney is named Executor in Rose's will. When Rose dies, Barney petitions the court for Letters Testamentary. In her will Rose waived bond, so in this instance Barney does not have to post a bond with the court.

Exhibit 6: Petition for Letters Testamentary

ATTORNEY OR PARTY WITHOUT ATTORNEY *(Name and Address)*: TELEPHONE NO.: ATTORNEY FOR *(Name)*:	FOR COURT USE ONLY
SUPERIOR COURT OF CALIFORNIA, COUNTY OF STREET ADDRESS MAILING ADDRESS CITY AND ZIP CODE: BRANCH NAME:	
ESTATE OF (NAME): DECEDENT	
PETITION FOR ☐ **Probate of Will and for Letters Testamentary** ☐ **Probate of Will and for Letters of Administration with Will Annexed** ☐ **Letters of Administration** ☐ **Letters of Special Administration** ☐ **Authorization to Administer Under the Independent Administration of Estates Act** ☐ **with limited authority** **(For deaths after December 31, 1984)**	CASE NUMBER: HEARING DATE: DEPT.: TIME:

1. Publication will be in *(specify name of newspaper)*:
   a. ☐ Publication requested.
   b. ☐ Publication to be arranged.

(Signature of attorney or party without attorney)

2. **Petitioner** *(name of each)*:
   requests
   a. ☐ decedent's will and codicils, if any, be admitted to probate.
   b. ☐ *(name)*:
   be appointed (1) ☐ executor (3) ☐ administrator
   (2) ☐ administrator with will annexed (4) ☐ special administrator
   and Letters issue upon qualification.
   c. ☐ that ☐ full ☐ limited authority be granted to administer under the Independent Administration of Estates Act.
   d. ☐ bond not be required for the reasons stated in item 3d.
   ☐ $ bond be fixed. It will be furnished by an admitted surety insurer or as otherwise provided by law. *(Specify reasons in Attachment 2d if the amount is different from the maximum required by Probate Code, § 8482.)*
   ☐ $ in deposits in a blocked account be allowed. Receipts will be filed. *(Specify institution and location)*:

3. a. Decedent died on *(date)*: at *(place)*:
   ☐ a resident of the county named above.
   ☐ a nonresident of California and left an estate in the county named above located at *(specify location permitting publication in the newspaper named in item 1)*:
   b. Street address, city, and county of decedent's residence at time of death:
   c. Character and estimated value of the property of the estate
   (1) Personal property . . . . $
   (2) Annual gross income from
   (i) ☐ real property . . . . $
   (ii) ☐ personal property . . . . . . $
   Total . . . . . . $
   (3) Real property: $ *(If full authority under the Independent Administration of Estates Act is requested, state the fair market value of the real property less encumbrances.)*
   d. ☐ Will waives bond. ☐ Special administrator is the named executor and the will waives bond.
   ☐ All beneficiaries are adults and have waived bond, and the will does not require a bond. *(Affix waiver as Attachment 3d.)*
   ☐ All heirs at law are adults and have waived bond. *(Affix waiver as Attachment 3d.)*
   ☐ Sole personal representative is a corporate fiduciary.

(Continued on reverse)

Exhibit 6: *(Continued)*

ESTATE OF (NAME): DECEDENT	CASE NUMBER:

3. e. ☐ Decedent died intestate.
☐ Copy of decedent's will dated: ☐ codicils dated: are affixed as Attachment 3e.
☐ The will and all codicils are self-proving *(Probate Code, § 8220).*

Attach a typed copy of a holographic will and a translation of a foreign language will.

Appointment of personal representative *(check all applicable boxes)*
(1) Appointment of executor or administrator with will annexed
☐ Proposed executor is named as executor in the will and consents to act.
☐ No executor is named in the will.
☐ Proposed personal representative is a nominee of a person entitled to Letters. *(Affix nomination as Attachment 3f(1).)*
☐ Other named executors will not act because of ☐ death ☐ declination ☐ other reasons *(specify in Attachment 3f(1)).*
(2) Appointment of administrator
☐ Petitioner is a person entitled to Letters. *(If necessary, explain priority in Attachment 3f(2).)*
☐ Petitioner is a nominee of a person entitled to Letters. *(Affix nomination as Attachment 3f(2).)*
☐ Petitioner is related to the decedent as *(specify)*:
(3) ☐ Appointment of special administrator requested. *(Specify grounds and requested powers in Attachment 3f(3).)*
g. Proposed personal representative is a ☐ resident of California ☐ nonresident of California *(affix statement of permanent address as Attachment 3g)* ☐ resident of the United States ☐ nonresident of the United States.

4. ☐ Decedent's will does not preclude administration of this estate under the Independent Administration of Estates Act.

5. a. The decedent is survived by
(1) ☐ spouse ☐ no spouse as follows: ☐ divorced or never married ☐ spouse deceased
(2) ☐ child as follows: ☐ natural or adopted ☐ natural adopted by a third party ☐ step ☐ foster
☐ no child
(3) ☐ issue of a predeceased child ☐ no issue of a predeceased child
b. Petitioner ☐ has no actual knowledge of facts ☐ has actual knowledge of facts reasonably giving rise to a parent-child relationship under Probate Code section 6408(b).
c. ☐ All surviving children and issue of predeceased children have been listed in item 8.

6. *(Complete if decedent was survived by (1) a spouse but no issue (only a or b apply); or (2) no spouse or issue. Check the* ***first*** *box that applies)*:
a. ☐ The decedent is survived by a parent or parents who are listed in item 8.
b. ☐ The decedent is survived by issue of deceased parents, all of whom are listed in item 8.
c. ☐ The decedent is survived by a grandparent or grandparents who are listed in item 8.
d. ☐ The decedent is survived by issue of grandparents, all of whom are listed in item 8.
e. ☐ The decedent is survived by issue of a predeceased spouse, all of whom are listed in item 8.
f. ☐ The decedent is survived by next of kin, all of whom are listed in item 8.
g. ☐ The decedent is survived by parents of a predeceased spouse or issue of those parents, if both are predeceased, all of whom are listed in item 8.

7. *(Complete only if no spouse or issue survived the decedent)* Decedent ☐ had no predeceased spouse ☐ had a predeceased spouse who (1) ☐ died not more than 15 years before decedent owning an interest in **real property** that passed to decedent,
(2) ☐ died not more than five years before decedent owning **personal property** valued at $10,000 or more that passed to decedent,
(3) ☐ neither (1) nor (2) apply. *(If you checked (1) or (2), check only the* ***first*** *box that applies)*:
a. ☐ The decedent is survived by issue of a predeceased spouse, all of whom are listed in item 8.
b. ☐ The decedent is survived by a parent or parents of the predeceased spouse who are listed in item 8.
c. ☐ The decedent is survived by issue of a parent of the predeceased spouse, all of whom are listed in item 8.
d. ☐ The decedent is survived by next of kin of the decedent, all of whom are listed in item 8.
e. ☐ The decedent is survived by next of kin of the predeceased spouse, all of whom are listed in item 8.

8. **Listed in Attachment 8** are the names, relationships, ages, and addresses of all persons named in decedent's will and codicils, whether living or deceased, and all persons checked in items 5, 6, and 7, so far as known to or reasonably ascertainable by petitioner, **including** stepchild and foster child heirs and devisees to whom notice is to be given under Probate Code section 1207.

9. ☐ Number of pages attached:

Date:

▶ ______________________ (SIGNATURE OF PETITIONER*)   ▶ ______________________ (SIGNATURE OF PETITIONER*)

I declare under penalty of perjury under the laws of the State of California that the foregoing is true and correct.
Date:

.... (TYPE OR PRINT NAME)   ▶ ______________________ (SIGNATURE OF PETITIONER*)

* All petitioners must sign the petition. Only one need sign the declaration.

DE-111 [Rev. July 1, 1989] **PETITION FOR PROBATE** Page two

Notice and Waivers of Notice

All persons who have an interest in the estate must be notified that a petition to administer the estate has been filed with the probate court. In some jurisdictions this notice is called a **citation**. The persons who are considered "interested parties" are:

1. all intestate heirs
2. all persons named in the will and codicils, if a will exists
3. all creditors, if the estate is heavily in debt
4. all persons who were named in earlier wills and codicils

These persons are entitled to receive notice because they have standing to challenge the petition (see Chapter 5). When a petition is filed with the court, the court sets a hearing date at which time any person who wishes to challenge the petition must make an appearance. The process can be speeded up if, when the petition is filed, the court is given waivers of notice signed by all of the interested parties. These waivers can usually be obtained from the immediate family. However, if it appears that there may be a problem, it may be best not to ask for waivers. Some people think that they are being defrauded if a waiver is requested, and may institute a contest just because they think they are being cheated, whereas if they simply receive a notice they will not challenge the petition. It is a psychological factor that must be weighed by the attorney.

If waivers are not obtained, the paralegal must submit proof of service of the notice to the court, usually with an affidavit of service and receipts for certified return receipt mail. The paralegal is responsible for seeing that notice is properly served.

EXAMPLE:

Regina unexpectedly dies. When Leonard submits her will to probate, Kingston and Donna must be notified, not as intestate heirs (because Regina's husband and children destroy their claims) but as potential creditors of the estate. They are involved in litigation with Regina over title to the house, so they are potential challengers to the estate.

Exhibit 7: Notices and Waivers

ATTORNEY OR PARTY WITHOUT ATTORNEY *(Name and Address)*: TELEPHONE NO.: ATTORNEY FOR *(Name)*:	FOR COURT USE ONLY
SUPERIOR COURT OF CALIFORNIA, COUNTY OF STREET ADDRESS: MAILING ADDRESS: CITY AND ZIP CODE: BRANCH NAME:	
ESTATE OF (NAME): DECEDENT	
NOTICE OF PETITION TO ADMINISTER ESTATE **OF *(name)*:**	CASE NUMBER:

1. To all heirs, beneficiaries, creditors, contingent creditors, and persons who may otherwise be interested in the will or estate, or both, of *(specify all names by which decedent was known)*:

2. A PETITION has been filed by *(name of petitioner)*:
in the Superior Court of California, County of *(specify)*:
3. THE PETITION requests that *(name)*:
be appointed as personal representative to administer the estate of the decedent.
4. ☐ THE PETITION requests the decedent's WILL and codicils, if any, be admitted to probate. The will and any codicils are available for examination in the file kept by the court.
5. ☐ THE PETITION requests authority to administer the estate under the Independent Administration of Estates Act. (This authority will allow the personal representative to take many actions without obtaining court approval. Before taking certain very important actions, however, the personal representative will be required to give notice to interested persons unless they have waived notice or consented to the proposed action.) The independent administration authority will be granted unless an interested person files an objection to the petition and shows good cause why the court should not grant the authority.
6. ☐ A PETITION for determination of or confirmation of property passing to or belonging to a surviving spouse under California Probate Code section 13650 IS JOINED with the petition to administer the estate.
7. A HEARING on the petition will be held

on *(date)*:	at *(time)*:	in Dept.:	Room:

located at *(address of court)*:

8. IF YOU OBJECT to the granting of the petition, you should appear at the hearing and state your objections or file written objections with the court before the hearing. Your appearance may be in person or by your attorney.
9. IF YOU ARE A CREDITOR or a contingent creditor of the deceased, you must file your claim with the court and mail a copy to the personal representative appointed by the court within four months from the date of first issuance of letters as provided in section 9100 of the California Probate Code. The time for filing claims will not expire before four months from the hearing date noticed above.
10. YOU MAY EXAMINE the file kept by the court. If you are a person interested in the estate, you may file with the court a formal Request for Special Notice of the filing of an inventory and appraisal of estate assets or of any petition or account as provided in section 1250 of the California Probate Code. A Request for Special Notice form is available from the court clerk.
11. ☐ Petitioner ☐ Attorney for petitioner *(name)*:

(address):

▶
(SIGNATURE OF ☐ PETITIONER ☐ ATTORNEY FOR PETITIONER)

12. This notice was mailed on *(date)*: at *(place)*: California.

(Continued on reverse)

NOTE: If this notice is published, print the caption, beginning with the words NOTICE OF PETITION, and do not print the information from the form above the caption. The caption and decedent's name must be printed in at least 8-point type and the text in at least 7-point type. Print the case number as part of the caption. Print items preceded by a box only if the box is checked. Do not print the *italicized* instructions in parentheses, the paragraph numbers, the mailing information, or the material on the reverse.

Form Approved by the Judicial Council of California DE-121 [Rev. July 1, 1989]   **336**   **NOTICE OF PETITION TO ADMINISTER ESTATE** (Probate)   Probate Code, § 8100   76N585B(RP054) - 7/89

Exhibit 7: *(Continued)*

ESTATE OF (NAME): DECEDENT	CASE NUMBER:

PROOF OF SERVICE BY MAIL

1. I am over the age of 18 and not a party to this cause. I am a resident of or employed in the county where the mailing occurred.
2. My residence or business address is *(specify)*:

3. I served the foregoing **Notice of Petition to Administer Estate** on each person named below by enclosing a copy in an envelope addressed as shown below AND
   a. ☐ **depositing** the sealed envelope with the United States Postal Service with the postage fully prepaid.
   b. ☐ **placing** the envelope for collection and mailing on the date and at the place shown in item 4 following our ordinary business practices. I am readily familiar with this business' practice for collecting and processing correspondence for mailing. On the same day that correspondence is placed for collection and mailing, it is deposited in the ordinary course of business with the United States Postal Service in a sealed envelope with postage fully prepaid.

4. a. Date of deposit: b. Place of deposit *(city and state)*:

5. ☐ I served with the Notice of Petition to Administer Estate a copy of the petition and other documents referred to in the notice.

I declare under penalty of perjury under the laws of the State of California that the foregoing is true and correct.
Date:

(TYPE OR PRINT NAME) ▶ (SIGNATURE OF DECLARANT)

NAME AND ADDRESS OF EACH PERSON TO WHOM NOTICE WAS MAILED

Exhibit 7: *(Continued)*

Note.—If affidavit of service be made outside the State of New York, it must be authenticated in the manner prescribed by CPLR 2309 (c).

AFFIDAVIT OF SERVICE OF CITATION

State of New York } **ss.:**
County of

....

of.., being duly sworn, says that he is over the age of eighteen years; that he made personal service of the within citation on the persons named below, whom deponent knew to be the persons mentioned and described in said citation, by delivering to and leaving with each of them personally a true copy of said citation, as follows:

Specify clearly time and place of service of each party served.

On the..................day of.., 19 , at..............................
....

On the..................day of.., 19 , at..............................
....

On the..................day of.., 19 , at..............................
....

On the..................day of.., 19 , at..............................
....

On the..................day of.., 19 , at..............................
....

....

Sworn to before me on the

day of , 19

....
Notary Public, State of New York

N.B.—When citation is served personally, it will promote convenience of the parties if the attorney for petitioner will place his name and address upon the citation.

Exhibit 7: *(Continued)*

UF Form 248

File No. ______________________, 19____.

CITATION

The People of the State of New York
By the Grace of God Free and Independent,

TO

A petition having been duly filed by

who is domiciled at

YOU ARE HEREBY CITED TO SHOW CAUSE before the Surrogate's Court, New York County, at Room 50 the Courthouse, in the County of New York, New York, on 19 , at 10 A.M., why LETTERS OF ADMINISTRATION of the goods, chattels and credits which were of , deceased, who at the time of h death was domiciled at , in the County of New York, New York, should not be granted to

Dated, Attested and Sealed, , 19

HON.

(L. S.) Surrogate, New York County

Clerk.

Name of Attorney...Tel. No.....................

Address of Attorney...

This citation is served upon you as required by law. You are not obliged to appear in person. If you fail to appear it will be assumed that you do not object to the relief requested. You have a right to have an attorney-at-law appear for you.

Exhibit 7: *(Continued)*

Waiver of Notice **(Rev. 1-92) CCP-303**

IN THE CIRCUIT COURT OF COOK COUNTY, ILLINOIS

Estate of } **No.**

} **Docket**

Deceased } **Page**

WAIVER OF NOTICE

The undersigned heirs of the decedent, *or legatees under decedent's will dated____________________

____________________, 19______,____________________, having been advised that a petition has been filed by

(and codicil dated ______________, 19__________)

____

*(a) for the admission to probate of that will, and
(b) for the appointment of____as

____of the estate,

(representative) (independent representative)

consent to that appointment and waive:

(a) notice of the hearing on the petition.
*(b) notice of rights to require formal proof of the will and to contest the admission or denial of admission of the will to probate.
**(c) notice of rights in independent administration.

____

____

____

____

____

* Strike if no will.
** Strike if supervised administration

☛ *SEE REVERSE SIDE*

Exhibit 7: *(Continued)*

RIGHT OF HEIRS OR LEGATEES (APPLICABLE WHERE DECEDENT LEFT A WILL)

Within 42 days after the effective date of the original order of admission, any heir or legatee may file a petition with the court to require proof of the will by testimony of the witnesses to the will in open court or other evidence, as provided in section 6-21 of the Probate Act of 1975 (Ill. Rev. Stat. Ch. 110 1/2, Par. 6-21).

Each heir or legatee also has the right under section 8-1 or 8-2 of the Illinois Probate Act of 1975 (Ill. Rev. Stat. Ch. 110 1/2, Par. 8-1, 8-2) to contest the validity of the will or the denial of admission by filing a petition with the court within six months after entry of the order admitting or denying the will.

RIGHTS OF INTERESTED PERSONS DURING INDEPENDENT ADMINISTRATION (APPLICABLE WHERE AN INDEPENDENT REPRESENTATIVE IS APPOINTED).

Independent administration means that the executor or administrator will not have to obtain court orders or file estate papers in court during probate. The estate will be administered without court supervision, unless an interested person asks the court to become involved.

Under section 28-4 of the Probate Act of 1975 (Ill. Rev. Stat. Ch.110 1/2, Par. 28-4) any interested person may terminate independent administration at any time by mailing or delivering a petition to terminate to the clerk of the court. However, if there is a will which directs independent administration, independent administration will be terminated only if the court finds there is good cause to require supervised administration; and if the petitioner is a creditor or nonresiduary legatee, independent administration will be terminated only if the court finds that termination is necessary to protect the petitioner's interest.

In addition to the right to terminate independent administration any interested person may petition the court to hold a hearing and resolve any particular question that may arise during independent administration, even though supervised administration has not been requested. (Ill. Rev. Stat. Ch. 110 1/2, Par. 28-5) The independent representative must mail or deliver a copy of the estate inventory and accounting to each interested person, and must send notice to or obtain the approval of each interested person before the estate can be closed. (Ill. Rev. Stat. Ch. 110 1/2, Pars. 28-6, 28-11) Any interested person has the right to question or object to any item included in or omitted from any inventory or account or to insist on a full court accounting of all receipts and disbursements with prior notice, as required in supervised administration. (Ill. Rev. Stat. Ch. 110 1/2, Par. 28-11)

ATTY NAME
FIRM NAME
ATTORNEY FOR
ADDRESS
CITY & ZIP
TELEPHONE
ATTORNEY NO.

AURELIA PUCINSKI, CLERK OF THE CIRCUIT COURT OF COOK COUNTY, ILLINOIS

Probate Hearing

At the date established for the hearing, any person with standing who has not waived his or her right may note a challenge to the petition. The purpose of the hearing is to prove the validity of the will or the fact that no will exists. If someone does challenge the petition, a court date will be set for a complete hearing on the matter. A probate hearing has all of the formalities of a trial, and the paralegal must assist the attorney in all of the litigation preparation. If no challenge is noted, the court will sign the orders (previously prepared by the paralegal) granting the petition and authorizing the Letters.

Prior to the hearing date, if the will was not self-proving, the paralegal must arrange with the witnesses to the will and codicils to appear in court to be examined by the clerk of the court. If there is a will contest, the witnesses will usually have to appear at the hearing—the self-proving affidavit will no longer have any effect.

Also, during this period, if the attorney has determined that the surviving spouse should waive or select a **right of election,** the paralegal should prepare all the appropriate documents indicating that the spouse will take under the will or under the statute. Remember, a surviving spouse cannot be disinherited in most jurisdictions. If the couple had any prenuptial agreement, that agreement must also be scrutinized to determine the survivor's property rights with respect to the estate.

EXAMPLE:

When David's last will is presented for probate, Fleur, as an intestate heir, is notified. Fleur challenges the validity of the will, maintaining that it is invalid and that an earlier will executed by David should be the one to be probated. The court will set a hearing date to determine the validity of Fleur's claims.

Letters

Once the court grants the petition, or decides the challenge, it will order letters to be issued to the person it has decided is the decedent's personal representative. The paralegal must obtain the letters from the court and see that any bond, if necessary, is posted on behalf of the personal representative. It is always a good idea to obtain several copies of the letters (there is a small fee for each copy) because many of the persons with control over the decedent's assets will require the letters before they release the property. Once the letters have been issued, the actual process of estate administration can begin.

EXAMPLE:

Before the bank will agree to let Hyacinth open Oscar's safe deposit box she must give them proof of her authority. The bank will require Hyacinth to give them her Letters Testamentary, which it will keep to protect its own liability.

Exhibit 8: Order and Letters

ORDER ADMITTING WILL TO PROBATE AND APPOINTING REPRESENTATIVE (Rev. 6-89) CCP-319

IN THE CIRCUIT COURT OF COOK COUNTY, ILLINOIS
COUNTY DEPARTMENT, PROBATE DIVISION

Estate of] No.
] Docket
Deceased] Page

ORDER ADMITTING WILL TO PROBATE AND APPOINTING REPRESENTATIVE

On petition for admission to probate of the will of the decedent and for issuance of letters of office, the will having been proved as provided by law;

IT IS ORDERED THAT:

1. The will of ______________________________ dated ______________, 19___, ______________ be admitted to probate;
(and codicil dated __________, 19___)

2. Letters of office as ______________________________
(executor) (independent executor) (administrator with will annexed) (independent administrator with will annexed)

issue to ______________________________.

*3. The representative file an inventory within 60 days.

ENTER:

____
Judge Judge's No.

Atty Name
Firm Name
Attorney for Petitioner
Address
City & Zip
Telephone
Atty No.

*Strike if independent administration.

AURELIA PUCINSKI, CLERK OF THE CIRCUIT COURT OF COOK COUNTY

Exhibit 8: *(Continued)*

ATTORNEY OR PARTY WITHOUT ATTORNEY *(Name and Address)*: TELEPHONE NO.:	FOR COURT USE ONLY
ATTORNEY FOR *(Name)*:	
SUPERIOR COURT OF CALIFORNIA, COUNTY OF STREET ADDRESS: MAILING ADDRESS: CITY AND ZIP CODE: BRANCH NAME:	
ESTATE OF (NAME): DECEDENT	
LETTERS ☐ **TESTAMENTARY** ☐ **OF ADMINISTRATION** ☐ **OF ADMINISTRATION WITH WILL ANNEXED** ☐ **SPECIAL ADMINISTRATION**	CASE NUMBER:

LETTERS

1. ☐ The last will of the decedent named above having been proved, the court appoints *(name)*:

   a. ☐ Executor
   b. ☐ Administrator with will annexed

2. ☐ The court appoints *(name)*:

   a. ☐ Administrator of the decedent's estate
   b. ☐ Special administrator of decedent's estate
      (1) ☐ with the special powers specified in the Order for Probate
      (2) ☐ with the powers of a general administrator

3. ☐ The personal representative is authorized to administer the estate under the Independent Administration of Estates Act ☐ **with full authority** ☐ **with limited authority** (no authority, without court supervision, to (1) sell or exchange real property or (2) grant an option to purchase real property or (3) borrow money with the loan secured by an encumbrance upon real property).

WITNESS, clerk of the court, with seal of the court affixed.

Date:

Clerk, by ______________________________, Deputy

(SEAL)

AFFIRMATION

1. ☐ PUBLIC ADMINISTRATOR: No affirmation required (Prob. Code, § 1140(b)).

2. ☐ INDIVIDUAL: **I solemnly affirm** that I will perform the duties of personal representative according to law.

3. ☐ INSTITUTIONAL FIDUCIARY *(name)*:

   I solemnly affirm that the institution will perform the duties of personal representative according to law.
   I make this affirmation for myself as an individual and on behalf of the institution as an officer.
   (Name and title):

4. Executed on *(date)*:
   at *(place)*: , California.

▶ ______________________________
(SIGNATURE)

CERTIFICATION

I certify that this document is a correct copy of the original on file in my office and the letters issued the personal representative appointed above have not been revoked, annulled, or set aside, and are still in full force and effect.

(SEAL)

Date:
Clerk, by

____
(DEPUTY)

Form Approved by the Judicial Council of California DE-150 [Rev. July 1, 1988] **201** **LETTERS (Probate)** Probate Code, §§ 463, 465, 501, 502, 540 Code of Civil Procedure, § 2015.6

76L192E - RP009

Estate Administration

If the decedent left property located in jurisdictions other than that of his domicile, one of the first tasks of the personal representative is to see that an ancillary administration is established in those other states (see Chapter 1). The same procedures and forms discussed above will have to be filed in the probate court of the ancillary state in which the decedent left property.

If the will created any trusts or guardianships, the personal representative must see that these people are legally appointed by the court. Only after the court has approved the appointment may the personal representative turn over property to these fiduciaries. Also, if any temporary letters had been issued by the court, the personal representative must see that the authority is revoked so that there will be no confusion in administering the estate. In all of these matters most of the responsibility for completing and filing the forms is generally left up to the paralegal.

The administrative process of handling an estate follows a fairly typical format:

a) *Open any safe deposit boxes left by the decedent.* As discussed above, whenever a decedent's safe deposit box is opened, a representative from the bank and the state taxing authority must be present to inventory the contents. The paralegal must arrange with all of these persons a mutually convenient time for accomplishing the task.
b) *Establish an estate checking account.* In order to collect income and make distributions, it is necessary that an estate checking account be established. This will also help in maintaining records for the estate and for any fiduciary taxes that might become due (see Chapter 8).
c) *Obtain an estate tax identification number.* Every estate and trust must obtain a tax ID number from the IRS by filing Form SS-4. The paralegal will see that the form is completed and mailed.
d) *Prepare an inventory of all of the estate's assets.* All of the estate property must be collected and categorized prior to distribution. This process of collecting and categorizing the decedent's property is known as **marshalling the assets**. It is the responsibility of the legal assistant to help see that all property is accounted for and appropriately valued, including obtaining appraisals if necessary. For a simple method of categorization, see Chapter 8.
e) *Publish a notice of administration to notify creditors.* Many jurisdictions require that the personal representative publish a notice of administration in a newspaper of general circulation in order to alert creditors of the decedent that the decedent's estate is being administered. Some states also require or permit personal notice to creditors. By statute, creditors must present their claims within a set period of time from the date of the notice or lose

all rights (see Chapter 9). As claims are presented, the paralegal must help determine whether the claims are justified and, if so, see that the claims are paid.

f) *Obtain receipts and releases for estate distributions.* As the assets of the estate are disbursed, either by paying taxes, creditors, or heirs, the paralegal must see that receipts and releases are obtained from the persons receiving estate funds. In this manner no claim can be made later that a person did not receive property to which he or she was entitled. Some states require releases from each beneficiary, which must be filed with the court in order to release any administration bond and terminate the administration.

   If the estate funds are insufficient to meet its expenses and debts, the personal representative is responsible for abating the property in order to pay off creditors. This process was discussed in the previous chapter.

g) *Prepare all appropriate tax returns.* Before an estate can be closed, all taxes on the estate must be paid, and the paralegal generally helps in the preparation of all of the necessary tax returns. For a complete discussion of estate taxation, see the following chapter.

h) *Close all ancillary administrations.* Before the domiciliary administration can be closed, the personal representative must see that all secondary administrations have been wound up and the ancillary personal representatives discharged.

i) *Prepare and file an accounting with the court.* Most jurisdictions require that an accounting be filed by the personal representative once the estate has been distributed. The purpose of the accounting is to assure the court that the estate has not been mishandled. Once again, all persons who had a financial interest in the estate must be notified so that they may contest any irregularities in the accounts. Only when the accounting has been accepted by the court and the order signed may the personal representative be dismissed and have his or her bond returned.

EXAMPLES:

1. Once the administration of Oscar's estate has been established, Hyacinth opens up a checking account in the same bank in which Oscar's safe deposit box was located. Hyacinth uses this estate checking account to distribute the estate funds.

2. When Tom dies, his personal representative must itemize all of Tom's property to determine its value. Tom dies owning a cooperative apartment, corporate stocks and bonds, government bonds, and jewelry. Each item must be categorized and quantified.

3. When Loretta receives her Letters of Administration for her mother's estate, she immediately publishes a notice in her local newspaper. In her state creditors have four months from the date of publication in which to present claims, and Loretta wants to close the estate as soon as possible.
4. The lawyer who represented Aida in the sale of her spaghetti sauce sees the notice of administration in the newspaper and presents a bill for his fee, which he claims Aida did not pay. If Loretta finds the claim justified, when she pays the lawyer she has him sign a receipt that states he has received payment, and a release that releases Aida's estate and her heirs from any further liability with respect to his legal fees.
5. In going through Tom's papers, his brother discovers that Tom owned a timeshare in a different state. An ancillary administration must be established, and the property disposed of, before Tom's estate can be finally settled.
6. Even though Loretta is Aida's only intestate heir, Loretta must still file an accounting with the court. An accounting is mandatory in her state, and because she had to post bond, in order to get her bond returned the court must approve her estate accounts.

Exhibit 9: Final Accounting

ATTORNEY OR PARTY WITHOUT ATTORNEY *(Name and Address)*: TELEPHONE NO.: | *FOR COURT USE ONLY*

ATTORNEY FOR *(Name)*:

SUPERIOR COURT OF CALIFORNIA, COUNTY OF

STREET ADDRESS:
MAILING ADDRESS:
CITY AND ZIP CODE:
BRANCH NAME:

ESTATE OF (NAME):

☐ DECEDENT ☐ CONSERVATEE ☐ MINOR

INVENTORY AND APPRAISEMENT

☐ **Complete** ☐ **Final**
☐ **Partial No.:** ☐ **Supplemental**
☐ **Reappraisal for Sale**

CASE NUMBER:

Date of Death of Decedent or of Appointment of Guardian or Conservator:

APPRAISALS

1. Total appraisal by representative (attachment 1) $
2. Total appraisal by referee (attachment 2) $

TOTAL: $

DECLARATION OF REPRESENTATIVE

3. Attachments 1 and 2 together with all prior inventories filed contain a true statement of ☐ all ☐ a portion of the estate that has come to my knowledge or possession, including particularly all money and all just claims the estate has against me. I have truly, honestly, and impartially appraised to the best of my ability each item set forth in attachment 1.
4. ☐ No probate referee is required ☐ by order of the court dated *(specify)*:

I declare under penalty of perjury under the laws of the State of California that the foregoing is true and correct.

Date:

(TYPE OR PRINT NAME) (Include title if corporate officer) (SIGNATURE OF PERSONAL REPRESENTATIVE)

STATEMENT REGARDING BOND

(Complete if required by local court rule)

5 ☐ Bond is waived.
6. ☐ Sole personal representative is a corporate fiduciary.
7. ☐ Bond filed in the amount of: $ ☐ Sufficient ☐ Insufficient
8. ☐ Receipts for: $ have been filed with the court for deposits in a blocked account at *(specify institution and location)*:

Date:

(SIGNATURE OF ATTORNEY OR PARTY WITHOUT ATTORNEY)

DECLARATION OF PROBATE REFEREE

9. I have truly, honestly, and impartially appraised to the best of my ability each item set forth in attachment 2.
10. A true account of my commission and expenses actually and necessarily incurred pursuant to my appointment is

Statutory commission: $
Expenses *(specify)*: $
TOTAL: $

I declare under penalty of perjury under the laws of the State of California that the foregoing is true and correct.

Date:

(TYPE OR PRINT NAME) (SIGNATURE OF REFEREE)

(Instructions on reverse)

200 Form Approved by the Judicial Council of California DE-160, GC-040 [Rev. January 1, 1985]

INVENTORY AND APPRAISEMENT (Probate)

761552H RP007 — 1-85 Prob C 600-611, 2610-2616

Exhibit 9: *(Continued)*

INSTRUCTIONS

See Probate Code, §§ 604, 608, 609, 611, 2610-2616 for additional instructions.

If required in a decedent's estate proceeding by local court rule, furnish an extra copy for the clerk to transmit to the assessor (Probate Code, § 600).

See Probate Code, §§ 600-602 for items to be included.

If the minor or conservatee is or has been during the guardianship or conservatorship confined in a state hospital under the jurisdiction of the State Department of Mental Health or the State Department of Developmental Services, mail a copy to the director of the appropriate department in Sacramento (Probate Code, § 2611).

The representative shall list on attachment 1 and appraise as of the date of death of the decedent or date of appointment of the guardian or conservator at fair market value moneys, currency, cash items, bank accounts and amounts on deposit with any financial institution (as defined in Probate Code, § 605), and the proceeds of life and accident insurance policies and retirement plans payable upon death in lump sum amounts to the estate, except items whose fair market value is, in the opinion of the representative, an amount different from the ostensible value or specified amount.

The representative shall list on attachment 2 all other assets of the estate which shall be appraised by the referee.

If joint tenancy and other assets are listed for appraisal purposes only and not as part of the probate estate, they must be separately listed on additional attachments and their value excluded from the total valuation of attachments 1 and 2.

Each attachment should conform to the format approved by the Judicial Council (see form Inventory and Appraisement (Attachment) (DE-161, GC-041) and Cal. Rules of Court, rule 201).

Exhibit 9: *(Continued)*

ESTATE OF:

CASE NUMBER:

ATTACHMENT NO:

(IN DECEDENTS' ESTATES, ATTACHMENTS MUST CONFORM TO PROBATE CODE 601 REGARDING COMMUNITY AND SEPARATE PROPERTY)

PAGE . . . . . OF . . . . . TOTAL PAGES
(ADD PAGES AS REQUIRED)

Item No.	Description	Appraised value
1.		$

200A Form Approved by the Judicial Council of California Effective January 1, 1976

INVENTORY AND APPRAISEMENT (ATTACHMENT)

761350C/10-87
Prob C 481, 600–605, 784, 1550, 1901

Once all creditors have been paid, taxes filed, property distributed, and an accounting filed, the estate is considered closed and the paralegal's job is done.

CHAPTER SUMMARY

In no other area of law is the paralegal given the degree of independence and responsibility that he or she receives in the field of estate administration. All of the court filings and all of the estate record-keeping are the responsibility of the legal assistant, and in fulfilling these functions the paralegal works in close association with the personal representative, the heirs and creditors of the decedent, and the estate accountant. Unless a challenge to the petition is filed with the probate court, the attorney, for the most part, leaves the administrative process in the hands of the legal assistant.

Most probate courts make available, at no or minimal charges, all of the forms necessary to get an estate through probate, and many of these packets even include a tickler, or checklist, of all of the forms in the order in which they must be prepared. Additionally, the clerks of the probate court are usually very helpful in explaining each of the requisite forms and in assisting in their preparation. Anyone who plans to go into the estate area should become familiar with the probate court and its personnel in his or her county.

The general steps necessary to probate an estate typically follow in this order:

1. obtain death certificate
2. obtain original will or codicil (if any); if necessary, obtain Order to Search or Open Safe Deposit Box
3. obtain Temporary Letters, if necessary
4. prepare and file appropriate petition
5. pay filing fees
6. send notice to interested parties or obtain waivers
7. set hearing date
8. obtain Letters and arrange for bond
9. notify creditors (privately or by publication)
10. obtain tax ID number for the estate
11. establish estate checking account
12. marshal assets (open safe deposit box)
13. pay debts
14. prepare tax returns
15. distribute estate and obtain receipts and releases
16. prepare final accounting
17. send notice of final accounting

18. have accounting hearing and get release from court
19. get back bond

Key Terms

Administrator: Personal representative of an intestate.
Citation: Notice sent to parties with standing to contest the probate petition.
Death certificate: Official government document proving a person's death.
Executor: Personal representative of a testate.
Guardian ad litem: Competent adult appointed by a court to represent persons under an incapacity during litigation.
Informal probate proceedings: Probate permitted in certain jurisdictions for small estate in which no notice is required.
Letters of Administration: Court authorization to act granted to an administrator.
Letters testamentary: Court authorization to act granted to an executor.
Marshalling assets: Collecting and categorizing the estate of a decedent.
Petition for a family allowance: Request to the court to permit the family to use estate funds pending probate.
Petition for interim letters: Request to the court to authorize a person to act on behalf of the decedent until final Letters are granted.
Petition for letters of administration: Request to the court to appoint a personal representative for an intestate.
Petition for letters testamentary: Request to the court to appoint a personal representative for a person who died with a will.
Petition for preliminary letters: Petition for Interim Letters.
Petition for temporary letters: Petition for Interim Letters.
Petition to open safe deposit box: Request to the court to allow safe deposit box to be opened to locate a will.
Petition to search: Request to the court to allow property to be searched to locate a will.
Probate hearing: Court procedure to prove the validity of a will or appointment of an administrator.
Right of election: Right of surviving spouse to elect to take by the will or by statutory share.
Summary proceedings: Shortened probate proceedings permitted in certain jurisdiction for small estates.
Supervised administration: Court scrutinizing every aspect of the estate administration.
Tickler: Checklist.
Unsupervised administration: Administration in which the court does not get involved in every aspect of the process.
Verification: Statement under oath that the statements in the petition to the court are true and accurate.

Case Studies

1. A man died leaving a will in which he left his entire estate to his surviving spouse and disinherited his three brothers, who were his heirs-at-law. In filing her petition for probate, the widow omitted the names and addresses of her brothers-in-law and did not send them notice of the petition. The widow did publish notice of the petition in the newspaper. After the will was admitted, the brothers sued to have the estate reopened so that they could contest the will, stating as their grounds that the widow failed to meet the statutory notice requirements with respect to the heirs-at-law. In denying their claim, the court held that because the will was valid and notice was published, the estate would not be reopened. The brothers were in no way injured by the widow's actions. Therefore, the notice requirement may be met in several different ways. *D'Ambra v. Cole*, 572 A.2d 268 (R.I. 1990).

2. Who has the right to be appointed the personal representative of a decedent?

A young man was killed in an automobile accident and was survived by his mother and his natural minor child and the child's 17-year-old mother. His entire estate consisted of $400 and the wrongful death action. The mother petitioned the court and was appointed the administrator of the estate. When the minor child's mother reached her 18th birthday, she filed a petition with the court to be appointed the administrator in place of the mother, claiming her preference right as the natural guardian of the deceased's minor child. The court refused to reverse the appointment, stating that at the time the appointment was made the girl was too young to be appointed, and that letters once granted cannot be revoked unless the person seeking such relief had been entitled to a preference at the time the appointment was made, which the girl was not because of her age. *Estate of Fisher v. Ragans*, 503 So. 2d 926 (Fla. App. 1987).

3. Does a self-proving will negate the necessity of examining the witnesses personally?

A New York resident died in South Carolina. His will was executed in South Carolina with South Carolinian witnesses. When the will was filed for probate in New York, the decedent's brother, his only distributee, filed a will contest and demanded to examine the witnesses to the will. The proponent of the will submitted affidavits of the attesting witnesses, claiming that the will was self-proving and that examination of the out-of-state witnesses was unnecessary. The court disagreed.

The court stated that the Surrogate Court must assure itself that all of the requirements for a properly executed will have been met before it admits a will to probate. When an objection is filed against the will, the objector has every right to examine the witnesses to make sure that the testamentary requirements have been met. The witnesses may be examined out of state by special commission, deposition, or interrogatories, and the estate is responsible for bearing the costs of the examination for any witness called by the proponent to prove the validity of the will. The opponent would have to bear the costs of his own examination of the witnesses. Consequently, self-proving affidavits are only effective if no one, including the court, objects to the admission or validity of the will. *In re Will of Westover*, 145 Misc. 2d 469, 546 N.Y.S.2d 937 (N.Y. Surr. 1989).

4. Can a probate court remove an executor, even one who was appointed under unusual circumstances, without first having a hearing on the matter?

When Doris Duke died she left an estate valued at over $1 billion. Ms. Duke's major domo was named the sole co-executor and under the will was given the discretion to appoint a co-executor, which he did. The major domo also inherited a large sum of money under the will, and was appointed trustee of a large charitable trust established by the will. He was granted temporary letters.

During the probate proceeding the major domo was accused of kidnapping, murder, fraud, and other acts disqualifying him as an executor. The New York surrogate summarily removed him as an executor, and he appealed. The appellate court decided that even under the unusual circumstances of this case, an executor cannot be removed without a hearing; to do otherwise would violate his constitutional rights. *In the Matter of Duke*, 7 N.Y.2d 465 (1996).

5. A man died leaving a small amount of personal property to one son, and everything else to his surviving spouse. Prior to his death, the decedent had the bulk of his property transferred to himself and his wife as joint tenants. The decedent had executed an earlier will, made before the property transfer, in which he left property to all of his children by a previous marriage. The disinherited children instituted a will contest, saying the will submitted to the court was obtained by undue influence, as was the title transfer. In their contest, the siblings neglected to include their brother, who was a beneficiary under the will in question.

The court dismissed the will contest on two grounds: first, the children failed to submit the earlier will in which they claimed they were left property; second, the legatee brother was an indispensable party to the suit, and because he was not joined in the action the contest could not be maintained. *Jones v. Jones, 770* S.W.2d 246 (Mo. Ct. App. 1988).

How does this decision differ from *D'Ambra v. Cole, supra*?

EXERCISES

1. Obtain copies of the appropriate probate court forms from your jurisdiction.
2. Complete the probate forms that would have to be filed if you died, and prepare all the appropriate probate forms for Kingston Lear based on the will drafted as an exercise in Chapter 5.
3. Draft a release form that you would use when estate property is distributed. As a starting point, obtain a sample from a formbook or the Internet.

4. How would you explain the entire estate administration process to the decedent's family? Prepare a tickler that you would use for this purpose.
5. Prepare a list of persons who might require a copy of the personal representative's letters before releasing the decedent's property.

ANALYTICAL PROBLEM

A self-proved will is submitted to probate. The decedent's sister, the only heir at law, contests the will and demands to examine the witnesses. The personal representative alleges that because the will is self-proved, the witnesses need not be called (calling the witnesses is an expense of the estate.) Argue the merits for each side.

8 Taxation

CHAPTER OVERVIEW

One of the most important functions performed by the paralegal with respect to the administration of a decedent's property is to assist the personal representative in the preparation of all of the tax forms incident to the winding up of an estate. It is the duty of the personal representative to see that all of the appropriate tax forms are filed and that any tax due is paid out of the estate funds. If the personal representative fails to file and to make timely payments of the taxes due, he or she is personally liable for all interest and penalties resulting from his negligence. Furthermore, should the estate be distributed to the heirs and beneficiaries before all taxes are paid, the personal representative is held personally liable for the tax itself.

In assisting the personal representative with respect to this tax aspect of estate administration, the legal assistant will work very closely with the attorney and the estate accountant. Although the paralegal is not usually responsible for the computation of the taxes nor responsible for making tax policy decisions, he or she is the person who keeps track of all of the assets and expenditures of the estate. For tax purposes, it is imperative that the estate assets be appropriately grouped according to the provisions of the various tax laws; in this manner the accountant can simply do the appropriate tally and see that the correct deductions are taken and taxes paid. Rather than computing the taxes due, the paralegal must correctly categorize the property left by the deceased.

Three different taxing authorities may become involved in the taxation of an estate: the federal government (the Internal Revenue Service), the state taxing authority, and any local tax authority, such as the city in which the decedent lived or owned property. The federal taxes that may be due fall into three general categories:

1. the individual income taxes of the decedent
2. the estate taxes
3. fiduciary income taxes

In addition, several states impose an inheritance tax, taxing the transfer of property from the decedent to the beneficiaries. Chapter 9 indicates which states impose such taxes.

Individual Income Taxes. The personal representative is given the responsibility of seeing that the final income tax returns of the deceased are filed, and any taxes due timely paid. These forms are the same ones that are filed on an annual basis by all taxpayers, but for the indication as the "Final Return" of the decedent. Federal, state, and sometimes local returns will have to be filed. The preparation of these forms follows the general pattern of all annual tax returns and is concerned with determining and recording all of the income the decedent received from the end of his last tax year until the day of his death. The paralegal will be responsible for seeing that all appropriate income information is received and given to the accountant for the preparation of the returns. The preparation of these returns is beyond the scope of this book and is appropriately covered in texts especially dealing with income taxation.

Estate Tax Returns. The personal representative is required to file both federal and state estate tax returns. There are some exceptions for particularly small estates; check the individual State tax requirements. Federal estate tax returns do not have to be filed for estates valued at under $675,000 for 2001, escalating to $1 million by year 2006. Even if no taxes are due, because the property remaining in the estate is minimal due to the effectiveness of the decedent's tax planning, the return must be completed and filed. The federal return will be discussed in detail below; state tax forms follow individual state law, and Chapter 9 provides the name and address of the appropriate state taxing authority for every jurisdiction. These state offices should be contacted directly for their forms and instructional booklets.

Fiduciary Income Tax Returns. If the estate is kept open long enough to generate income of its own, the estate is liable for the payment of taxes on such income. The fiduciary of the estate (the personal representative or the trustee, as the case may be) must file the return with the state and federal taxing authorities. The federal fiduciary income tax return is discussed below.

The purpose of this chapter is to familiarize the paralegal with all of the federal tax forms that must be filed to complete the administration of a decedent's estate. Because the tax laws of every state are different, see Chapter 9 to see where the appropriate state tax information can be obtained.

Federal Tax Law

There are three main sources of law involved in the preparation of the federal tax returns: the Internal Revenue Code of 1986, as amended; Revenue Rulings and Revenue Procedures established by the Internal Revenue Service; and judicial decisions of the courts.

The Internal Revenue Code (the "IRC" or "the Code") is the codified enactment of all federal tax laws, and is published in the United States Code. The Code is also published separately in a multivolume paperback set that is available at all legal bookstores. The Code establishes all of the rules and guidelines with respect to federal taxation, and incorporates specific tax acts, such as the Economic Recovery Tax Act of 1981 (ERTA) discussed in earlier chapters. As a companion to the Code, the Internal Revenue Service publishes Regulations in the Code of Federal Regulations that specify the Service's interpretation of the Code provisions. The Regulations also give practical examples of problems that arise in connection with each section of the Code. The Code and the Regulations, in concert, are the basis of the U.S. tax law.

Revenue Rulings (Rev Ruls) are cases decided internally by the IRS and published, with the specific taxpayers' identity hidden, in order to give guidance to the public with respect to the Service's interpretation of the Code and regulations. Revenue Rulings have the force of case law with respect to tax matters and are considered as precedent by both the IRS and the courts.

Revenue Procedures (Rev Procs) are Internal Revenue Service procedures for administering the tax laws. They are published to give guidance to the public on procedural matters. Similarly to Rev Ruls, Rev Procs are deemed to be binding as precedent on the Internal Revenue Service.

Revenue Rulings and Revenue Procedures are published officially in an IRS publication known as the Cumulative Bulletin (C.B.) several times each year. Additionally, the Rev Ruls and Rev Procs are published by various publishing houses such as Commerce Clearing House (CCH) and Prentice-Hall (P-H) in loose-leaf volumes updated weekly.

Finally, when litigation arises out of a federal tax matter, the decisions of the federal courts and the U.S. Tax Court provide judicial interpretations of the law. Federal court decisions are published in the federal reporters; U.S. Tax Court decisions are published in a reporter called the Tax Court Reports (TC).

The primary sources create and interpret the tax law, and should be consulted in case of problems with respect to the preparation of the tax forms. Fortunately, these sources are rarely needed to be called upon by the paralegal, but he or she must be aware of their existence as the basis of federal taxation.

As a practical matter, the legal assistant will be able to complete the appropriate federal tax returns simply by following the instructional booklets provided free by the IRS. The following section will discuss all of the most common federal estate tax forms.

Federal Tax Forms

Publication 559, *Survivors, Executors, and Administrators,* is an instructional booklet published by IRS and distributed free of charge by the Service. It indicates every tax form that may be required to be filed by the estate, gives samples of the tax forms and instructional problems, and provides a tickler (checklist) of all of the forms and states when each must be filed. This checklist appears in the Appendix. This section will discuss the most important of the federal estate tax forms.

SS-4: Application for Employer I.D. Number

The SS-4 must be filed by the personal representative as soon as possible. The estate itself is deemed to be a taxable entity, and as such must have a tax identification number, similar to the social security number used by individuals in the preparation of their tax documents. The SS-4 is filed with IRS, which then issues the estate a number that must be used on all returns, statements, and documents filed with respect to its tax liability.

In addition to the estate tax I.D., the personal representative should also obtain the social security numbers of all of the beneficiaries and personal representatives of the estate. Because the beneficiaries must be identified on the estate tax returns, the personal representative must have their I.D. numbers available for inclusion in the estate tax return.

Form 706–United States Estate and Generation Skipping Transfer Tax Return

Form 706 is the primary tax return for federal estate taxation. Its preparation is probably the most important tax responsibility of the personal representative. It is this form that requires the categorization of all of the assets and expenditures of the estate. IRS provides a special instruction booklet for the preparation of this form free of charge. It is a good idea to gather all of the IRS instructional booklets and read them *before* attempting to complete the tax return.

Form 706 must be filed nine months after the date of the death of the decedent. If there is going to be a problem in meeting this time limit, because of a potential will contest or the difficulty in finding the assets of the deceased, the personal representative can file Form 4768, Application for Extension of Time to File U.S. Estate Tax Return. This form must be filed as soon as possible so that IRS can rule on the application before the 706 is required to be filed (nine months after death).

Form 706 is divided into five main parts. Part 1 requires general information about the deceased: name, address, date of death, name of the personal representative, etc. This is just a simple identification section similar to the beginning of all federal and state tax returns.

Part 2 is the computation of the total tax due. This part of the form is dependent upon the schedules of assets and expenditures that must be attached to the return. There are 19 schedules that must be prepared in order to complete this part of the return; each of these schedules will be discussed in detail below.

Part 3 permits the personal representative to make certain tax elections with respect to the taxes due. This section merely requires affirmative or negative responses to the questions asked; the answers to the questions are determined by the tax planner, accountant, or attorney for the estate. The paralegal must get the responses from the appropriate professional for inclusion on the tax return.

The tax election in this part is primarily concerned with what is known as an **alternative valuation** for all of the assets of the estate, if such valuation will reduce the estate tax burden. The alternative valuation permits the value of *all* of the assets of the estate to be determined either by the value at the date of death or six months following the death. If the alternative valuation option is selected, it must apply to all of the assets; the personal representative cannot make the choice selectively. Remember, this alternative valuation is only used if it reduces the estate taxes (the property must have lost value during this time period).

Part 4 requires general information about the estate. As an attachment to this Part, the paralegal must affix a copy of the death certificate and indicate the name, tax I.D. number, relationship to the deceased, and amount received by each beneficiary of the estate. As mentioned above, this is one reason why the personal representative must get the social security numbers of all of the beneficiaries.

Finally, Part 5 is a recapitulation of all of the totals appearing on each of the 19 schedules that must be filed as part of the return. As can be seen, the body of the Form 706 is fairly simple and straightforward. The difficult aspect of this return is the preparation of all of the schedules. Generally, Schedules A through I cover all of the assets of the decedent, Schedules J through O indicate deductions from the gross estate, and the last three schedules provide tax credits for other taxes previously paid.

Form 706 Schedules Relating to Assets

Schedule A: Real Estate

Schedule A identifies the real estate owned by the decedent. This schedule includes real estate owned individually by the decedent, and the value of his or her share of any tenancies in common owned by him or her and another. The value of the real estate included on this schedule is to be the fair market value of the property, not what the property cost the decedent. Fair market value can be determined by recent sales of adjacent property, tax assessments, or valuation by experts in the field. The fair market value is also required to be calculated at the property's highest and best use. For instance, if the property could have a higher commercial value, but was left undeveloped by the decedent, the value for tax purposes would be the land's use as commercial real estate.

There may be some relief, however, for valuing the real estate at its highest and best use; IRS provides for what is known as a **special use valuation** for real estate if the assets of the estate are illiquid (not readily convertible to cash) and the higher valuation would force a sale of the realty to meet the tax burden. In this instance, the property may be valued at its current use provided the legatees do not change that use for a period of ten years after the death of the decedent. Note that this election is only permitted for property used in family farming and certain closely held businesses.

The value of the property includes all mortgages for which the decedent was personally liable. The mortgage itself will be computed as a debt of the estate on a later schedule. If the decedent was not personally liable for the mortgage, the amount of the Fair Market Value is reduced by the amount of the mortgage.

EXAMPLE:

Cornelia, the Lears' daughter, owns a vacation home with a fair market value of $200,000 (evidenced by the latest sale of adjacent property). Cornelia has a $50,000 mortgage on the property for which she is personally liable. Schedule A will value the house at $200,000, and the mortgage of $50,000 will appear as a debt of the estate later on.

If Cornelia was not personally liable for the mortgage, the value of the house on Schedule A would be $150,000 ($200,000 less the $50,000 mortgage), and the mortgage would appear nowhere else on the return.

The determination as to the personal liability of the decedent for the mortgage is dependent upon the terms of the mortgage agreement itself, and the attorney should make this decision.

For completion of this schedule, have the correct and complete addresses of the property and its description, and copies of all mortgages and evidences of fair market value of the realty. See the Sample Tax Form in the Appendix.

Be aware that the federal government imposes a tax lien on all real estate, and before title to the property can be transferred the personal representative must get a release from IRS. (Co-ops are considered real estate for the purpose of the tax lien.) The release is issued once the taxes on the property are paid. The government only imposes a lien on the real estate left by the decedent, not the personal property of the estate. The purpose of the lien is to insure that the government has property to attach to cover the estate tax liability.

Schedule B: Stocks and Bonds

Schedule B includes all stocks and bonds individually owned by the decedent, even if dividends and interest on the stocks and bonds were payable to someone else. The value that is to be placed on these assets depends on the type of security reported.

Publicly Traded Stocks and Bonds. If the assets are publicly traded, the value is determined to be the mean average of the security on the day of death. The mean value is the average mid-point of the high and low for that day (the closing price is irrelevant unless it represents the high or low). If the decedent died on the weekend, the value of the security is reflected as the average trading price for the two surrounding days.

EXAMPLES:

1. Acme, Inc. stock traded, on the day of death, at a low price of $4.00 per share and a high price of $4.80 per share. The mean value, for estate tax purposes, is $4.40 per share, regardless of the actual closing price of the stock.
2. Kingston dies on Saturday. His Acme stock traded at a low of $4.00 per share and a high of $5.00 per share on Friday, and a low of $4.20 and a high of $5.20 on Monday. Friday's average was $4.50 per share, and Monday's average was $4.70 per share. The average price of the share for Schedule B is $4.60—the average of Friday's and Monday's averages.

To obtain the trading prices and average value, the paralegal can either use the quotes from the *Wall Street Journal* or obtain a statement from the brokerage house handling the decedent's account. Evidence of the value should be attached to the schedule.

If the decedent dies after the record date for payment of a stock dividend but before the payment date, the value of the dividend is included in the value of the stock, but the dividend itself is considered income to the beneficiary of that security. This is known as **income in respect of a decedent (IRD)**. The beneficiary is responsible for income tax on that dividend, but may deduct any estate tax paid on the IRD. In this instance the dividend is taxed twice: as part of the gross estate and as income to the beneficiary.

EXAMPLE:

Kingston Lear died after the record date but before the payment date of a $2.00 per share dividend. That $2.00 per share is includable as part of the value of the stock for the estate taxes *and* is included as part of the income of the beneficiary of that stock in that tax year. Why? Because Kingston had a right to the value of the dividend as of the record date, but the money goes to the beneficiary.

Bonds are valued in the same manner as stocks, and interest accruing on the bonds is rated over the period from the last payment date until the date of death. All interest includable in this period is attributable to the estate.

Closely Held Stock. Because securities that are not publicly traded have no readily ascertainable value, the IRS is usually very suspicious of valuations placed on these shares. As a general rule, if the shareholders had a shareholders' agreement with a buy-sell provision (a clause requiring the company to repurchase the shares at a price established by conditions expressed in the contract itself), the Service may accept the price computed by reference to the agreement for the purpose of Schedule B. However, if there is no shareholders' agreement, it will be necessary to get an independent appraisal for the value of these closely held securities. Because these valuations are closely scrutinized by the IRS, it may behoove the estate to get several appraisals and use an average price for this stock. This type of security may create tax problems for the estate.

Co-operative Shares. Shares in co-operative residences are included on this schedule of Form 706, not Schedule A: Real Estate. The value placed on these shares is deemed to be the fair market value of the shares as reflected in recent sales of the stock. Include evidence of the recent sales as an attachment to Schedule B.

Treasury Bills. Treasury bills and other types of government securities are traded on the open market and are valued in the same manner as stocks and bonds indicated above.

Savings Bonds. Savings bonds (Series E Government Bonds) are taxed to the estate at their redemption value as of the date of death. The difference between this amount and the face value of the bond is included as income to the beneficiary of the bond. The redemption value is obtained by a letter from a bank or brokerage house that is attached to the schedule.

Brokerage Accounts. Any money market accounts managed by a brokerage firm are included in this schedule as stocks and bonds. The brokerage house will give a letter indicating the value of these accounts on the date of death.

Any stocks and bonds that are subject to the Uniform Gift to Minors Act (left to minors by the deceased) are reflected on Schedule G, not Schedule B.

Schedule C: Mortgages, Notes, and Cash

Schedule C includes evidences of monies owed to the decedent; the mortgages and notes included are ones in which the decedent was the mortgagee or promisee. Mortgages and notes are valued at their **discounted rate**. The discount rate is the amount that someone would pay for a note today, even though the note is not due for several years. Obviously the purchase price in this instance will not be the face value, since the purchaser has to wait to receive that amount. The discounted value that appears on this schedule is the amount a bank would be willing to pay for these evidences of indebtedness, and the tax preparer must get an order from a bank to indicate what that value is. This bank order is attached to the return.

EXAMPLE:

Oscar is the promisee of a $10,000 promissory note from Barney, evidencing the loan Oscar made to Barney to help him start a business. On Oscar's death, this note is discounted by the bank to $9,000, because the money isn't due for one more year.

Bank savings and checking accounts are valued at the date of death. Always obtain a letter from the bank indicating the amount in these accounts on the date of death.

Schedule D: Insurance on Decedent's Life

Although the proceeds from the life insurance policy on the decedent passes immediately to the beneficiary (Chapter 1), under certain circumstances the estate may be liable for estate taxes on the value of the policy. This occurs whenever the decedent's estate is named as the beneficiary or whenever the decedent retained **incidents of ownership** on the policy. Incidents of ownership include such rights as:

1. naming the estate as the beneficiary
2. retaining the right to change the beneficiary
3. having the right to surrender or cancel the policy
4. having the right to assign the policy
5. having the right to pledge the policy
6. having the right to borrow against the policy

Under these circumstances, because the decedent retains control over the policy and its proceeds, it is deemed to be taxable as part of his estate.

In addition to the foregoing, the value of the policy is included on Schedule D if the decedent transferred the life insurance policy within three years of death or had a life insurance policy as part of his or her employment benefit package and the employer changed the policy within three years of the decedent's death. The rationale for this is that the employer's ability to change the policy acts as an assignment by the employee to the employer, and is therefore considered to be a retained incident of ownership. The value of these policies is determined by the insurance company itself. The tax preparer must get Form 712 from the company that gives the value that is placed on the policy for Schedule D.

EXAMPLE:

Two years before Loretta's death, her employer changes insurance companies for the life insurance it provides its employees as part of its employee benefit package. At Loretta's death, the value of the policy is included as part of her taxable estate, even though the proceeds go directly to Evan.

Schedule E: Jointly Held Property

All property that was jointly held by the decedent is included at its full date of death value in the decedent's estate *unless* it can be proved that the surviving joint tenant contributed to the purchase of the property. If the surviving joint tenant can prove such participation in the acquisition of the property, only the portion attributable to the deceased is included on Schedule E.

For property that was jointly held by the decedent and the decedent's surviving spouse, one-half of the value of the property is included in the decedent's gross estate, regardless of the spouse's contribution.

The valuation follows the procedures for the valuation of all such types of property, real or personal.

EXAMPLES:

1. Kingston Lear was a tenant by the entirety with Donna in a summer home in Vermont. Because the surviving tenant is the decedent's spouse, only half of the value of this property is includable in Schedule E.
2. Kingston bought a house for his daughter Grace and put the title in both of their names as joint tenants. The entire value of this property is included in Schedule E because Grace, the surviving joint tenant, did not participate in the acquisition of the property.
3. Tom and his brother Ken bought an apartment building as joint tenants for investment purposes. If it can be proved that Ken paid for half of the property, only one-half is includable as part of Tom's taxable estate.
4. Hyacinth and her two sisters inherited their aunt's house as joint tenants. Only one-third of the value of the property is included as part of Hyacinth's estate because all three siblings inherited the property equally.

This schedule also includes the value of all property found in a jointly held safe deposit box, unless the surviving joint tenant can prove ownership of the stored property.

Schedule F: Other Miscellaneous Property

This is a catch-all Schedule for Form 706, and includes all tangible property not otherwise indicated on other Schedules. The property appearing on this schedule includes:

a) tangible property (jewelry, art, antiques, etc.)
b) unmatured life insurance held by the decedent on another's life (a policy Hyacinth took out on her father's life with herself as beneficiary)
c) income tax refunds
d) Social Security payments
e) annuity income
f) profit-sharing plans
g) interest in other estates or trusts, other than powers of appointment (the deceased is a beneficiary of an estate but died before distribution)
h) §2044 property (QTIP) (See Chapters 1 and 3.)

Schedule G: Transfers During Decedent's Life

Schedule G causes all property, other than incidental gifts, that the decedent transferred without compensation within three years of death to be included as part of the taxable estate. The paralegal must search the deceased's records to note any major transfers during this period that were not in some way paid for by the recipient, and, if the attorney determines that this property is to be included, value that property according to the methods of valuation discussed for similar types of property. Additionally, any property that the decedent transferred to a living trust within three years of death is included on this schedule.

EXAMPLE:

Nine months before his death, Kingston establishes a trust for his grandchildren. Property transferred to this trust is taxable as part of Kingston's estate because it was transferred within three years of his death and he retained incidents of ownership.

Schedule H: Powers of Appointment

If the deceased possessed a general power of appointment (Chapter 4), wherein he or she could have executed the power either in his own favor or in the favor of his or her estate, his or her creditors, or the creditors of his or her estate, then the value of the property incident to that power is included as part of his or her estate. On the other hand, if the power was a special power of appointment, wherein he or she could only exercise the power in favor of other named persons, the property is not considered part of the estate.

EXAMPLES:

1. By the terms of a trust established by his grandmother, Tom Poole has a power of appointment to select a successor beneficiary from among his cousin's children. Because the power could not be exercised in his favor, the property subject to the power is not part of Tom's estate.
2. Under her father's will, Hyacinth has the power to distribute the corpus of a trust to any of her father's children. Since she could select herself, this property is includable as part of Hyacinth's estate.

Schedule I: Annuities

Annuities that terminate on the death of the decedent are not included as part of his or her taxable estate. However, if the decedent purchases an annuity in which payments can be made to a survivor, the value of that annuity is included in the decedent's estate.

EXAMPLE:

Hyacinth took the money she inherited from her mother and bought an annuity policy for herself and her sisters. On Hyacinth's death, payment still goes to her surviving sisters. The value of the policy is included in Hyacinth's estate.

The value of the annuity is determined by obtaining a letter from the company issuing the annuity, and including that letter as an attachment to the schedule.

Form 706 Schedules Relating to Deductions

Schedule J: Funeral and Administrative Expenses

All reasonable expenses associated with the funeral service and burial, cremation, or other disposition of the decedent's body may be included in this schedule as a deduction from the taxable estate. However, these expenses are also permitted to be deducted from the decedent's final income tax return. This item cannot appear on both tax returns. The tax planner or accountant will decide on which form to take the deduction depending on the most favorable tax consequences for the estate.

Other administrative expenses, such as legal fees and court filing fees, are included on this schedule as deductions. Take careful note, however, that the fee for the attorney must be for legal matters in order to be deductible from the estate. Accounting fees are also deductible on the federal return, but may not be deductible on the state estate return. Each jurisdiction must be checked for the state deductibility of this item.

Also included on this schedule are any expenses incurred in keeping the estate intact during the administration, such as paying insurance on the property, rent, utility payments, fees for the safe deposit box, etc.

Schedule K: Debts of the Decedent

Because the estate is responsible for paying the reasonable debts of the decedent, and these debts diminish the value of the estate, they are deductible on this schedule. The schedule divides the debts into those that are secured and those that are unsecured. The **secured debts** include all mortgages and liens, and any other debts to which the decedent pledged estate property as collateral. The **unsecured debts** are real estate taxes owed, general bills and credit card payments, the cost of the last illness, and other miscellaneous expenses, that is, all amounts owed by the decedent at the date of his death. Remember, however, that the mortgages that are included on this schedule are only those for which the decedent was personally liable. (See the discussion of Schedule A above.)

Schedule L: Net Losses During Administration

Any losses to the estate, such as casualty, theft, or fire, are deductible from the taxable estate on this schedule. The paralegal should be sure to maintain records that can document the loss.

Schedule M: Bequests to Surviving Spouse

There is an unlimited deduction permitted for all property given to the surviving spouse. When the surviving spouse dies, the entire value of this property will be taxed at that time. The benefit of this unlimited deduction is obvious; however, under certain circumstances (for the benefit of children and grandchildren), it may be better to limit the amount of the deduction. The professional tax planner will have made this decision prior to the decedent's death, and certain of these considerations have been discussed in Chapters 1, 4, and 5.

EXAMPLE:

After making several gifts to her sons, Lottie Poole leaves the rest of her estate to her husband as a marital deduction. Everything left to the husband is a deduction from Lottie's taxable estate.

Schedule N: Qualified ESOP Sales

ESOP is short for **Employee Stock Ownership Plan**. The general provision with respect to ESOPs was repealed several years ago, but this schedule must still be completed if the client received stock pursuant to an employee stock ownership plan during the period in which the provision was in effect. If the estate does contain these ESOPs, consult with the appropriate tax advisor; ESOPs are too complicated for the purpose of this book, and the paralegal simply must gather the information from the tax professional working with the estate.

Schedule O: Charitable, Public, and Similar Gifts and Bequests

An unlimited deduction is permitted for all bequests to qualified charitable organizations organized pursuant to 501(c)(3) of the Internal Revenue Code. Most generally known charities are organized under 501(c)(3), and the organization or the IRS can tell the paralegal whether it is so organized if there is a question.

A problem under this schedule arises if the decedent left property other than cash to the charity, such as art or antiques. Because these items are considered unique, there may be a question with respect to a value IRS deems to be appropriate and acceptable. There are professionals who appraise this kind of property, and the estate will have to get an appraisal from such an expert to satisfy the IRS. Also, be aware that there is no guarantee that IRS will automatically accept such an appraisal as a valid valuation.

Form 706 Schedules Relating to Credits

Schedule P: Credit for Foreign Taxes Paid

A credit reduces the actual amount of taxes payable; a deduction reduces the value of the taxable property. Consequently, credits are beneficial in that they directly reduce the estate's tax burden.

IRS permits an estate tax credit for all foreign taxes paid by the estate. The paralegal must record these foreign taxes and attach proof of payment to the foreign government to Form 706.

Schedule Q: Credit for Tax on Prior Transfer

If the decedent's estate includes property that the decedent received as the result of being the beneficiary of someone else's estate within ten years before or two years after the decedent's death, there is a federal estate tax credit for the estate taxes paid on such property by the other estate. The credit is given on a sliding scale depending upon how long before the decedent's death the property was inherited. The credit for estate taxes paid is as follows:

When Acquired Before Death	*Credit for Taxes Paid*
Less than 2 years	100%
Between 3 and 4 years	80%
Between 5 and 6 years	60%
Between 7 and 8 years	40%
Between 9 and 10 years	20%

In order to take advantage of this credit, the paralegal must discover how the decedent acquired the property subject to the estate tax, whether it was previously taxed, and document the payment of those previous taxes.

EXAMPLE:

Hyacinth and her sisters inherited the house from their aunt five years before Fleur's death. The aunt's estate was too small to be taxable, and so Fleur's estate cannot take advantage of this tax credit, because the aunt's estate paid no estate taxes. Had the aunt's estate paid taxes on the house, Fleur's estate could take a credit of 60 percent of the taxes paid on the portion of the estate tax attributable to the house for her one-third share.

Schedule R: Generation Skipping Transfer

A Generation Skipping Transfer is an extremely complicated tax process and is most appropriately left up to the tax planning professional. The creation and taxation of generation skipping transfers have been discussed in Chapter 4. The paralegal must determine whether any property is subject to this provision and get the written advice of the tax professional for the information included on this Schedule. Clues that there might be property subject to this provision would be any trust indicating beneficiaries more than two generations removed from the deceased. See Chapter 4.

Schedule S: Excess Retirement Accumulations

This shedule only existed for a few years and has been repealed.

Form 1041—Fiduciary Income Tax Return

This tax form must be filed by all estates that produce income during the administration of the estate and prior to the distribution of the assets. Estates and trusts are taxed at the highest permitted individual tax rate, and so it behooves the personal representative to distribute the assets as soon as possible to avoid this tax obligation. However, it is the duty of every personal representative to see that the decedent's assets, while under his or her control, are productive and income-producing. Because this is the duty of the personal representative, the longer the assets are under his or her control, the greater the income should be to the estate, creating the need to complete the fiduciary return.

The Fiduciary Income Tax Return, Form 1041, must be filed if the estate earns more than $6,000 in income for the year or if there is a nonresident alien beneficiary of the estate. The personal representative must file a Notice of Fiduciary Relationship with the IRS with a copy of the court letters attached.

Like individuals, estates are taxed on a calendar year basis, but if it can be demonstrated that this would not be truly reflective of its income production, the estate may be able to file on a fiscal year basis. IRS Publication 559 mentioned above provides instructional examples for the preparation of this form. For the paralegal, the burden is to keep track of all income produced by the estate so that the information is available for the accountant.

Form 1040—U.S. Individual Income Tax Return

As indicated above, the personal representative is responsible for filing and paying the final income taxes of the decedent for income derived from the end of his last tax year until the date of his death. A discussion of the preparation of these forms is more appropriate for a treatise on individual income taxation, and these forms are usually handled by the decedent's accountant. The paralegal will assist the tax preparer of this form in gathering all documentation with respect to the decedent's income and expenses prior to death.

For samples of the tax forms discussed above, see Appendix B.

SITUATIONAL ANALYSIS

Because taxes are specifically dependent upon itemized property, it would be impossible to do a complete or effective situational analysis for our four families; however, a few brief words are in order.

Loretta Jones' estate is far too small to cause any federal tax problems. Because $600,000 can pass tax free, Loretta's estate would not be taxed.

The Bushes have also avoided most negative tax consequences. In their wills, Oscar and Hyacinth have left property valued at less than $600,000 to other people, and the remainder of their estates to the survivor as a marital deduction. In this fashion they have been able to avoid any federal tax liability.

The Lears, by transferring most of their property before death, in order to avoid Regina's inheriting anything, have also avoided federal tax liability, *provided* they survive the transfer by three years. Be aware, however, that some of the transfers previously described may have involved gift taxes at both the federal and state levels.

Tom Poole is our only tax-liable family. If he dies unmarried, and still individually possessed of all of his property, anything over the $600,000 exemption will be taxable. Additionally, his estate will probably be liable for state estate taxes.

CHAPTER SUMMARY

One of the primary responsibilities of a paralegal with respect to estate administration is the preparation of all of the various tax forms the personal representative is required to file on behalf of the decedent and the estate. Although most legal assistants are not expected to do the tax computation (that is the function of the estate accountant), the paralegal is expected to have all of the assets and expenditures of the estate appropriately grouped and recorded. It is from these records maintained by the paralegal that the tax returns are prepared. Furthermore, the legal assistant will keep track of all of the tax forms and the various due dates to guarantee that the forms are filed in a timely manner.

The most important of the tax forms that an estate will prepare is the Form 706, the federal estate tax return. For the purposes of this form, it is necessary to catalog assets according to the schedules attached to 706 and to maintain records of expenditures and taxes paid on behalf of the estate.

The paralegal must also acquire proof of the value of the estate assets, either by reference to external documents (e.g., newspapers, bank reports), certified appraisals, or by documents provided by the tax professional hired to handle the more complicated tax matters of the estate. For most estates, the preparation of the tax returns are fairly straightforward. The legal assistant can follow the following chart in order to help group the assets and expenditures for tax purposes:

Item	*Schedule*
Assets	
Annuities, if payments made to survivor	I
Brokerage accounts	B
Co-op shares	B
Debts owed decedent	C
Gifts to minors	G
Insurance on decedent's life, if he retained incidents of ownership	D
Jointly held property	E
Miscellaneous property	F
Mortgages	A & K
General power of appointment	H
Real estate individually owned	A
Savings bonds	B
Stocks & bonds publicly traded	B
Transfers within three years of death if decedent retained control	G
Treasury bills	B
Deductions	
Bequests to surviving spouse	J
Charitable bequests	O
Debts owed by decedent	K
ESOPs	N
Funeral & administrative expenses	J
Losses to estate during administration	L
Tax Credits	
Foreign death taxes paid	P
Generation skipping transfers	R
Property acquired within ten years of death from another estate	Q

In addition to Form 706, the paralegal is responsible for assisting the personal representative in preparing the final income tax return of the decedent, as well as making sure that any income accruing to the estate during the administration is reported to IRS.

By following the categories indicated above, the paralegal will be able to maintain all of the appropriate records for tax purposes. These same records will be used for the state tax returns that the estate will be required to file as well. For information regarding the state estate tax forms for any given jurisdiction, contact the state tax official indicated in the following chapter.

Key Terms

Alternative valuation: Rule permitting assets to be valued at date of death or sale, or six months later, whichever is less.
Credit: Permissible reduction in taxes payable.
Cumulative Bulletin: Official publication of IRS Revenue Rulings and Revenue Procedures.
Discount: Present value of securities that have not yet matured.
ESOP: Employee stock ownership plan.
Final return: Last income tax return of the decedent.
Form 706: Federal estate tax return.
Form 1040: Federal income tax return.
Form 1041: Federal fiduciary income tax return.
Incidents of ownership: Control a decedent keeps over the rights of a life insurance policy.
Income in respect of a decedent (IRD): Income received by a beneficiary that was due the decedent but wasn't paid to the decedent before death.
Inheritance tax: Tax imposed by some states on the transfer of property from a decedent.
Internal Revenue Code: Federal tax statute.
Internal Revenue Service: Federal agency that administers the tax laws.
Publication 559: IRS publication listing tax forms to be filed by executors and administrators.
Revenue Procedure: Official IRS procedure for complying with the tax laws.
Revenue Ruling: IRS internal case decision having precedential value.
Secured debt: Debt to which specific property has been pledged in case of default.
SS-4: Federal tax form used to acquire a tax I.D. number.
Tax credit: Deduction from taxes owed based on other taxes paid.
Tax deduction: Amount reducing value of taxable property.
United States Code: Published source of the federal statutes.
Unsecured debt: General obligation for which no specific property has been pledged in case of default.

Case Studies

1. What are the estate tax consequences when the proceeds of a life insurance policy on the decedent's life are payable to a corporation wholly owned by the decedent, and then to the decedent's estate pursuant to a stock redemption agreement? Are the insurance proceeds includable as an asset of the estate?

According to Rev. Rul. 82–85, 1982-C.B. 137, the proceeds from the insurance policy are not includable in the decedent's estate under Schedule D. Under this Ruling's facts, the corporation wholly owned by the decedent provided life insurance on the decedent's life, naming the corporation as the beneficiary. The purpose of the policy was to provide for payment to the decedent's estate for the value of his stock in the closely held company. Since the decedent retained no incident of ownership, the proceeds are not part of his estate under Schedule D.

However, since the insurance proceeds were used by the corporation to purchase the decedent's closely held stock, the proceeds are includable as the value of closely held stock under Schedule B. Because the agreement the decedent had with the corporation specified that the proceeds were to be used as a valuation tool for the repurchase of the stock, it is includable in this fashion.

2. Is a federal court bound by the decision of a state court with respect to federal estate tax liability?

In *Commissioner v. Estate of Bosch*, 387 U.S. 456 (1967), the decedent created a revocable trust under the laws of New York that provided that the income was to be paid to the decedent's wife during her lifetime, and that gave her a general power of appointment. Several years after the creation of the trust, but before the husband's death, the wife executed an instrument that purported to release her general power of appointment. When the husband died, the wife attempted to claim that her release was valid and therefore she was entitled to deduct the value of the trust from her husband's estate as a marital deduction.

The IRS disallowed the deduction. While an appeal was pending, the wife filed a petition in the New York state court which, among other items, declared her release of the general power of appointment to be valid under state law. The Tax Court accepted this ruling of the lower New York state court, but the U.S. Supreme Court disagreed.

In its decision, the U.S. Supreme Court held that only the decision of the highest court of a state would be binding in federal tax matters, but decisions of trial and intermediate state courts (lower courts) would have no effect with respect to federal estate tax liability. In other words, in order for the widow to be able to rely on a state court decision, the issue must be appealed to the highest court in the state; otherwise, federal courts are free to determine the federal estate tax liability without reference to lower state court decisions.

3. Valuing property always presents a problem for the preparer of the estate tax return. This is especially true if the property in question is closely held stock.

In *Ford v. Commissioner of Internal Revenue*, 53 F.3d 924 (8th Cir. 1995), the court had to determine whether closely held stock should be valued according to its book value and historical earnings or its net asset value. The lower court determined that the shares should be valued according to the government's contention, which was based on the net asset value. In affirming the decision, the appellate court held that such questions were questions of fact to be determined at the trial level, which determination will not be overturned absent clear error.

4. Pursuant to a divorce decree, a husband agreed in a judicial settlement to leave one-fourth of his net estate to each of his two children of the marriage. On the husband's death, the question arose as to whether such payments, as part of a divorce settlement, make the children creditors or beneficiaries of the estate. If the children are creditors, the estate can deduct one-half of its net assets as a debt of the decedent; if beneficiaries, the amount is included in the taxable estate.

The federal Court of Appeals held that the children were indeed creditors of the estate pursuant to a valid contractual obligation of the decedent, and therefore one-half of the net assets could be deducted as a claim against the estate. The court reasoned that had the decedent failed to fulfill this contractual obligation the children could certainly have sued as creditors. Therefore, the children should stand in the same position when the decedent did in fact fulfill his duty.

Does this mean that a person can avoid all federal estate taxes by contracting with presumptive beneficiaries before death to leave them property? Would these be valid contracts? *Beecher v. United States*, 280 F.2d 202 (3d Cir. 1960).

5. Persons often attempt to decrease the value of their estate by transferring property to family members while they are alive. Although this may prove to be excellent estate planning, in certain circumstances the IRS will look through these transactions and may include such transfers in the decedent's taxable estate.

This was true in *Estate of Musgrave v. United States*, 33 Fed. Cl. 657 (1995), where the decedent made "loans" to family members rather than outright gifts hoping to avoid both the gift and the estate tax. The court, and IRS, looked through these "transfers" and found that they were includable in the deceased's gross estate because in fact he had transferred nothing.

EXERCISES

1. Joseph Smith, a widower, died, survived by two sons, Henry and Ralph, and Ralph's daughter, Clare. In his will, he left all of his property equally to his two sons, with the exception of $25,000 that he left to his eight-year-old granddaughter and $2,000 that he left to the United Fund. Complete the appropriate federal estate tax returns using the following data:

Decedent:	Joseph Smith SS# 555-66-7777 123 Front Street Los Angeles, CA 90210
Born:	December 1, 1930
Died:	October 5, 1994

Executor: Henry Smith (same address as deceased)
Property: House at 123 Front Street, Los Angeles, CA, valued at $336,000, mortgage of $100,000 still due, for which decedent was personally liable
500 shares of Xerox stock, dividend of $200 payable to holder of record as of September 30, 1994, payable on October 15, 1994
Savings account at First Federal Bank: $37,802
Cash found in home: $950
Life insurance policy of $100,000 payable to Clare Smith, revocable by decedent
Safe deposit box at First Federal Bank containing jewelry worth $27,062
Household effects valued at $11,300
1990 Hyundai valued at $2,700
Expenses: Funeral expenses: $7,500
Executor's fee: $7,600
Attorney's fee: $5,000
Accountant's fee: $3,000
Court costs: $500
Visa card owing: $985
Mastercard owing: $200

What information is missing that you would need to complete the return?

2. Contact your state taxing authority (Chapter 9) and complete the appropriate state estate tax returns for Joseph Smith, above.

3. Using the library or the computer, research whether the following items are includable in the gross estate of a decedent for federal estate tax purposes:

a) bonus paid by employer to decedent's estate
b) value of crops growing on decedent's land
c) real estate sold and leased back by decedent
d) proceeds from flight insurance taken out by decedent prior to plane crash that killed her
e) leases held by decedent in which decedent could assign the leases

4. The personal representative of an estate wants to deduct attorneys' fees paid to lawyers representing certain residuary legatees in a state court proceeding to construe certain provisions of the will. The state court required the personal representative to reimburse these heirs for their legal expenses. Argue that these fees are deductible.

5. How would you detail for the IRS the value of a loss to the estate due to theft? Due to fire?

ANALYTICAL PROBLEM

A husband and wife executed reciprocal wills. The spouses died within six weeks of each other, the wife dying first. The wife's will was not submitted for probate by the time the husband died. Should the husband's estate include the wife's property left to him under her will? Discuss.

9 Comparison of Estate Law in the Different Jurisdictions

CHAPTER OVERVIEW

The purpose of this chapter is to introduce some state-specific material with respect to estate law. The following pages provide a brief glimpse at some of the requirements and idiosyncrasies of the different jurisdictions. Familiarity with the laws of the different states is important for the legal assistant's work.

One of the functions that a paralegal may be called upon to perform is to determine whether a will executed by a client in a state other than his or her current domicile will be found valid in the domiciliary state. Because society has become so transient, this can be an important consideration with respect to the disposition of someone's assets. Furthermore, a client may be the creditor of a person who dies in a different jurisdiction, and he would need to know the procedures for presenting his claims to the estate.

The following analysis is hardly extensive, and is included to direct the legal assistant to the primary areas of potential concern and the specific statutes and sections appropriate to those concerns in each state. Consider this section a précis, to be used before attempting a detailed analysis of the law of any one jurisdiction.

California

Execution

Pursuant to California Code Annotated, all persons over the age of 18 who are of sound mind may execute a will. §6100. The will must be signed by the testator or in the testator's name by some other person in the testator's presence and by the testator's direction. §6112. The testator need not see the witnesses sign, *In re Offil's Estate*, 96 Cal. App. 640 (1929), nor do the witnesses need to sign in each other's presence. *In re Armstrong's Estate*, 8 Cal. 2d 204 (1937). The testator may acknowledge his or her signature to the witnesses. §6101.

California permits nuncupative wills for a total property valued at no more than $1,000. *Brown v. United States*, 65 F.2d 65 (9th Cir. 1933). California also permits holographic wills under 6111. The holograph must be signed and have all material provisions in the testator's own hand. Although California permits a statutory will, §6200 et seq., a printed form cannot be used as a holograph.

California permits living wills under its provision for Durable Powers of Attorney, §22412. The Durable Power of Attorney must be executed by a competent adult and have two witnesses.

California is a community property state, and also has provisions for what it terms quasi-community property.

Administration

Personal representatives must have attained their majority, and be capable and fit to execute the duties of the office. §8402. Nonresidents may serve, provided they post a sufficient bond with the Superior Court. Unless waived, the court will fix a bond usually equal to the value of the estate plus the gross revenue of the estate. Accounting is mandatory in California.

Under its provisions for Small Estates, §6602, estates valued at under $20,000 may be administered by summary proceedings. Independent administration is permitted provided that the will affirmatively permits such administration.

Creditors must present their claims within four months after the letters have been granted or within 30 days if notice of administration is personally sent to them.

Tax and Miscellaneous Matters

California has a very complex statute. In addition to the foregoing, California has provisions in its statute for marital and premarital agreements under §5200. Property can go to a surviving spouse without any administration, and there are provisions for an affidavit procedure for estates valued at less than $10,000.

California imposes an estate tax. For information regarding state taxation contact:

Finance Department
1145 State Capital
Sacramento, California 95814

Maine

Execution

Under Art. 18-A of the Maine Revised Statutes Annotated, any person 18 years of age who is of sound mind may execute a will. §2-501. The will must be in writing, signed by the testator or in the testator's name by some other person in the testator's presence and by his direction, and must be signed by at least two persons each of whom witnessed either the signing or the testator's acknowledgment of the signature. §2-502. The witnesses must be competent, §2-502, and the will may be self-proving. §2-504.

Maine has a statutory will printed in its code, §2-514, and it permits holographs under §2-503. Nuncupative wills are only permitted for soldiers and sailors. Under Maine's provisions for durable powers of attorney a person may execute a living will. §5-701.

Administration

A personal representative must be at least 18 years old, competent, and resident in the state. §3-203. The Probate Court can impose a bond equal to the full value of the estate unless bond has been waived. Any person with an interest in the estate valued at $1,000 or more can request that the personal representative post a bond. Accounting is permissive in Maine. §3-1003.

Summary proceedings are permitted for small estates that do not exceed the value of the homestead, family allowance, and expenses, and informal proceedings are permitted under the auspices of the registrar, provided only one will has been filed for probate and there is no will contest. §3-102.

Creditors must present their claims within four months of notice of the appointment of the personal representative. §3-801.

Tax and Miscellaneous Matters

In order to inherit property a devisee must survive the decedent by 120 days. Anticontest clauses are unenforceable in Maine.

Maine imposes an estate tax. For information regarding state taxation contact:

Taxation Bureau
State House Station
Augusta, Maine 04333

Nevada

Execution

Under the Nevada Revised Statutes, any person over the age of 18 who is of sound mind may execute a will. §133.020. The will must be in writing, and the testator must sign in the presence of the witnesses who must also sign in the presence of the testator. §133.020. There must be two competent witnesses to the will, §133.040, and the will may be self-proving, §136.160.

Holographs are permitted under §133.090 if the will is entirely written, dated, and signed by the testator. The entire estate may be left by the holograph.

Nuncupative wills are allowed pursuant to §133.100 of the statute, but the limitations are that the testator be in his last illness, there be two witnesses asked for by the testator, and that no more than $1,000 worth of property is involved.

Section 449.535 of the statute permits living wills executed by persons over the age of 18, signed and witnessed by two competent witnesses. The statute provides a sample living will.

Nevada is a community property state which limits distribution by will.

Administration

The personal representative must be in his majority, competent, resident in the state, and cannot have been convicted of a felony. §138.020. Bond is discretionary with the court, §142.010, but accounting is mandatory.

Summary proceedings are permitted for estates valued at under $100,000, §141.010, and collection on affidavit is allowed for estates valued at under $20,000.

Creditors must present claims within 60 or 90 days of notice of administration.

Tax and Miscellaneous Matters

Hooray! Nevada has *no* estate, gift, or inheritance tax! For information regarding state taxation contact:
Taxation Department
Capitol Complex
Carson City, Nevada 89710

CHAPTER SUMMARY

As indicated above, there are far more similarities between the laws of the different jurisdictions than there are differences. Most well-drafted wills, with three witnesses, will stand up in almost every state.

The more important distinctions are in the area of estate administration, especially with respect to the publication of notices of administration, and the time allotted for the presentation of claims. It is imperative that the legal assistant be conversant with the different state requirements so as to be able to protect a client's interests.

EXERCISES

1. Which jurisdictions require more than two witnesses to execute a valid will?
2. How many states impose transfer taxes in addition to estate taxes? What are these states?
3. Which states permit holographs?
4. Are there any states that permit minors to be testators and/or witnesses?
5. Write a comparative analysis of the estate law of your state with any other state.

Appendix: Forms

California

204 Duties and Liabilities of Personal Representative
206A Proof of Subscribing Witness
213A Order for Probate
323 Proof of Holographic Instrument

Federal

Checklist of Forms and Due Dates
706 U.S. Estate (and Generation-Skipping Transfer) Tax Return Instructions for Form 706
709 U.S. Gift (and Generation-Skipping Transfer) Tax Return Instructions for Form 709
1041 U.S. Income Tax Return for Estates and Trusts
2848 Power of Attorney and Declaration of Representation
1310 Statement of Person Claiming Refund Due a Deceased Taxpayer

California Form 204: Duties and Liabilities of Personal Representative

TO COURT CLERK: This form is CONFIDENTIAL if local rule requires the Acknowledgment of Receipt to have a Social Security or driver's license number.

ATTORNEY OR PARTY WITHOUT ATTORNEY *(Name and Address)*: TELEPHONE NO.:	*FOR COURT USE ONLY*
ATTORNEY FOR *(Name)*:	
SUPERIOR COURT OF CALIFORNIA, COUNTY OF STREET ADDRESS: MAILING ADDRESS: CITY AND ZIP CODE: BRANCH NAME:	
ESTATE OF (NAME): DECEDENT	
DUTIES AND LIABILITIES OF PERSONAL REPRESENTATIVE and Acknowledgment of Receipt	CASE NUMBER:

DUTIES AND LIABILITIES OF PERSONAL REPRESENTATIVE

When you have been appointed by the court as personal representative of an estate, you become an officer of the court and assume certain duties and obligations. An attorney is best qualified to advise you about these matters. You should clearly understand the following:

1. MANAGING THE ESTATE'S ASSETS

a. Prudent investments
You must manage the estate assets with the care of a prudent person dealing with someone else's property. This means you must be cautious and you may not make any speculative investments.

b. Keep estate assets separate
You must keep the money and property in this estate separate from anyone else's, including your own. When you open a bank account for the estate, the account name must indicate that it is an estate account and not your personal account. Never deposit estate funds in your personal account or otherwise commingle them with anyone else's property. Securities in the estate must also be held in a name that shows they are estate property and not your personal property.

c. Interest-bearing accounts and other investments
Except for checking accounts intended for ordinary administration expenses, estate accounts must earn interest. You may deposit estate funds in insured accounts in financial institutions, but you should consult with an attorney before making other investments.

d. Other restrictions
There are many other restrictions on your authority to deal with estate property. You should not spend any of the estate's money unless you have received permission from the court or have been advised to do so by an attorney. You may reimburse yourself for official court costs paid by you to the county clerk and for the premium on your bond. Without prior order of the court, you may not pay fees to yourself or to your attorney, if you have one. If you do not obtain the court's permission when it is required, you may be removed as personal representative or you may be required to reimburse the estate from your own personal funds, or both. You should consult with an attorney concerning the legal requirements affecting sales, leases, mortgages, and investments of estate property.

2. INVENTORY OF ESTATE PROPERTY

a. Locate the estate's property
You must attempt to locate and take possession of all the decedent's property to be administered in the estate.

b. Determine the value of the property
You must arrange to have a court-appointed referee determine the value of the property unless the appointment is waived by the court. (You, rather than the referee, must determine the value of certain "cash items." An attorney can advise you about how to do this.)

c. File an inventory and appraisal
Within four months after your appointment as personal representative, you must file with the court an inventory and appraisal of all the assets in the estate.

(Continued on reverse)

California Form 204 (Continued)

ESTATE OF (NAME): DECEDENT	CASE NUMBER:

d. File a change of ownership
At the time you file the inventory and appraisal, you must also file a change of ownership statement with the county recorder or assessor in each county where the decedent owned real property at the time of death, as provided in section 480 of the California Revenue and Taxation Code.

3. NOTICE TO CREDITORS

You must mail a notice of administration to each known creditor of the decedent within four months after your appointment as personal representative. If the decedent received Medi-Cal assistance you must notify the State Director of Health Services within 90 days after appointment.

4. INSURANCE

You should determine that there is appropriate and adequate insurance covering the assets and risks of the estate. Maintain the insurance in force during the entire period of the administration.

5. RECORD KEEPING

a. Keep accounts
You must keep complete and accurate records of each financial transaction affecting the estate. You will have to prepare an account of all money and property you have received, what you have spent, and the date of each transaction. You must describe in detail what you have left after the payment of expenses.

b. Court review
Your account will be reviewed by the court. Save your receipts because the court may ask to review them. If you do not file your accounts as required, the court will order you to do so. You may be removed as personal representative if you fail to comply.

6. CONSULTING AN ATTORNEY

If you have an attorney, you should cooperate with the attorney at all times. You and your attorney are responsible for completing the estate administration as promptly as possible. **When in doubt, contact your attorney.**

NOTICE: This statement of duties and liabilities is a summary and is not a complete statement of the law. Your conduct as a personal representative is governed by the law itself and not by this summary.

ACKNOWLEDGMENT OF RECEIPT

1. I have petitioned the court to be appointed as a personal representative of the estate of *(specify)*:
2. I acknowledge that I have received a copy of this statement of the duties and liabilities of the office of personal representative.

Date:

.... (TYPE OR PRINT NAME) ▶ ______________________ (SIGNATURE OF PETITIONER)

*Social Security No.: ______________ *Driver's License No.: ______________

Date:

.... (TYPE OR PRINT NAME) ▶ ______________________ (SIGNATURE OF PETITIONER)

*Social Security No.: ______________ *Driver's License No.: ______________

Date:

.... (TYPE OR PRINT NAME) ▶ ______________________ (SIGNATURE OF PETITIONER)

*Social Security No.: ______________ *Driver's License No.: ______________

*Supply these numbers only if required to do so by local court rule. The law requires the court to keep this information CONFIDENTIAL. (Probate Code, § 8404(a).)

California Form 206A: Proof of Subscribing Witness

ATTORNEY OR PARTY WITHOUT ATTORNEY (*Name and Address*):	TELEPHONE NO.:	FOR COURT USE ONLY
ATTORNEY FOR (*Name*):		
SUPERIOR COURT OF CALIFORNIA, COUNTY OF STREET ADDRESS: MAILING ADDRESS: CITY AND ZIP CODE: BRANCH NAME:		
ESTATE OF (NAME): DECEDENT		
PROOF OF SUBSCRIBING WITNESS **(For decedents dying after December 31, 1984)**		CASE NUMBER:

1. I am one of the attesting witnesses to the instrument of which attachment 1 is a photographic copy. I have examined attachment 1 and my signature is on it.
   - a. ☐ The name of the decedent was signed in the presence of the attesting witnesses present at the same time by
     - ☐ the decedent personally.
     - ☐ another person in the decedent's presence and by the decedent's direction.
   - b. ☐ The decedent acknowledged in the presence of the attesting witnesses present at the same time that the decedent's name was signed by
     - ☐ the decedent personally.
     - ☐ another person in the decedent's presence and by the decedent's direction.
   - c. ☐ The decedent acknowledged in the presence of the attesting witnesses present at the same time that the instrument signed was decedent's
     - ☐ will.
     - ☐ codicil.
2. When I signed the instrument, I understood that it was decedent's ☐ will ☐ codicil.
3. I have no knowledge of any facts indicating that the instrument, or any part of it, was procured by duress, menace, fraud, or undue influence.

I declare under penalty of perjury under the laws of the State of California that the foregoing is true and correct.

Date:

.... (TYPE OR PRINT NAME) ▶ ____________________ (SIGNATURE OF WITNESS)

.... (ADDRESS)

ATTORNEY'S CERTIFICATION

(Check local court rules for requirements for certifying copies of wills and codicils)

I am an active member of The State Bar of California. I declare under penalty of perjury under the laws of the State of California that attachment 1 is a photographic copy of every page of the ☐ will ☐ codicil heretofore presented for probate.

Date:

.... (TYPE OR PRINT NAME) ▶ ____________________ (SIGNATURE OF ATTORNEY)

206A Form Approved by the Judicial Council of California DE-131 (New January 1, 1985)

PROOF OF SUBSCRIBING WITNESS
(Probate)

76P663S—RP067 – 1-85

California Form 213A: Order for Probate

ATTORNEY OR PARTY WITHOUT ATTORNEY *(Name and Address)*: TELEPHONE NO.:	*FOR COURT USE ONLY*
ATTORNEY FOR *(Name)*:	
SUPERIOR COURT OF CALIFORNIA, COUNTY OF STREET ADDRESS: MAILING ADDRESS: CITY AND ZIP CODE: BRANCH NAME:	
ESTATE OF (NAME): DECEDENT	
ORDER FOR PROBATE **ORDER APPOINTING** ☐ **Executor** ☐ **Administrator with Will Annexed** ☐ **Administrator** ☐ **Special Administrator** ☐ **Order Authorizing Independent Administration of Estate** ☐ **with full authority** ☐ **with limited authority**	CASE NUMBER:

1. Date of hearing: Time: Dept/Rm: Judge:

THE COURT FINDS

2. a. All notices required by law have been given.
   b. Decedent died on *(date)*:
      (1) ☐ a resident of the California county named above
      (2) ☐ a nonresident of California and left an estate in the county named above
   c. Decedent died
      (1) ☐ intestate
      (2) ☐ testate and decedent's will dated:
      and each codicil dated:
      was admitted to probate by Minute Order on *(date)*:

THE COURT ORDERS

3. *(Name)*:
   is appointed **personal representative:**
   a. ☐ Executor of the decedent's will
   b. ☐ Administrator with will annexed
   c. ☐ Administrator
   d. ☐ Special Administrator
      (1) ☐ with general powers
      (2) ☐ with special powers as specified in Attachment 3d
      (3) ☐ without notice of hearing

   and letters shall issue on qualification.

4. a. ☐ **Full authority** is granted to administer the estate under the Independent Administration of Estates Act.
   b. ☐ **Limited authority** is granted to administer the estate under the Independent Administration of Estates Act (there is no authority, without court supervision, to (1) sell or exchange real property or (2) grant an option to purchase real property or (3) borrow money with the loan secured by an encumbrance upon real property).
5. a. ☐ Bond is not required.
   b. ☐ Bond is fixed at: $ to be furnished by an authorized surety company or as otherwise provided by law.
   c. ☐ Deposits of: $ are ordered to be placed in a blocked account at *(specify institution and location)*:
   and receipts shall be filed. No withdrawals shall be made without a court order.

6. ☐ *(Name)*: is appointed probate referee.

Date:

JUDGE OF THE SUPERIOR COURT

7. ☐ Number of pages attached:

☐ Signature follows last attachment.

Form Approved by the Judicial Council of California DE-140 [Rev. July 1, 1988] **213A** ORDER FOR PROBATE 760051A-RP041 Probate Code, § 329

California Form 323: Proof of Holographic Instrument

ATTORNEY OR PARTY WITHOUT ATTORNEY *(Name and Address)* TELEPHONE NO	FOR COURT USE ONLY
ATTORNEY FOR *(Name)*	
SUPERIOR COURT OF CALIFORNIA, COUNTY OF STREET ADDRESS: MAILING ADDRESS: CITY AND ZIP CODE: BRANCH NAME	
ESTATE OF (NAME): DECEDENT	
PROOF OF HOLOGRAPHIC INSTRUMENT	CASE NUMBER:

1. I was acquainted with the decedent for the following number of years *(specify)*:

2. ☐ I was related to the decedent as *(specify)*:

3. I have personal knowledge of the decedent's handwriting which I acquired as follows:
   a. ☐ I saw the decedent write.
   b. ☐ I saw a writing purporting to be in the decedent's handwriting and upon which decedent acted or was charged. It was *(specify)*:

   c. ☐ I received letters in the due course of mail purporting to be from the decedent in response to letters I addressed and mailed to the decedent.
   d. ☐ Other *(specify other means of obtaining knowledge)*:

4. I have examined the attached copy of the instrument, and its handwritten provisions were written by and the instrument was signed by the hand of the decedent. *(Affix a copy of the instrument as attachment 4.)*

I declare under penalty of perjury under the laws of the State of California that the foregoing is true and correct.

Date:

.... ▶ ____________________
(TYPE OR PRINT NAME) (SIGNATURE)

....
(ADDRESS)

ATTORNEY'S CERTIFICATION

(Check local court rules for requirements for certifying copies of wills and codicils)

I am an active member of The State Bar of California. I declare under penalty of perjury under the laws of the State of California that attachment 4 is a photographic copy of every page of the holographic instrument heretofore presented for probate.

Date:

.... ▶ ____________________
(TYPE OR PRINT NAME) (SIGNATURE OF ATTORNEY)

323 Form Approved by the Judicial Council of California DE 135 (Rev. January 1, 1985) **PROOF OF HOLOGRAPHIC INSTRUMENT (Probate)** 76P157P—RP008 — 4-85

I.R.S. Checklist of Forms and Due Dates

TABLE A. Checklist Of Forms And Due Dates—For Executor, Administrator, Or Personal Representative

Form No.	Title	Due Date
SS-4	Application for Employer Identification Number	As soon as possible. The identification number must be included in returns, statements, or other documents.
56	Notice Concerning Fiduciary Relationship	As soon as all of the necessary information is available.
706	United States Estate (and Generation-Skipping Transfer) Tax Return	9 months after date of decedent's death.
706A	United States Additional Estate Tax Return	6 months after cessation or disposition of special-use valuation property.
706CE	Certification of Payment of Foreign Death Tax	9 months after decedent's death. To be filed with Form 706.
706GS (D)	Generation-Skipping Transfer Tax Return for Distributions	See form instructions.
706GS (D-1)	Notification of Distribution From A Generation-Skipping Trust	See form instructions.
706GS (T)	Generation-Skipping Transfer Tax Return for Terminations	See form instructions.
706NA	United States Estate (and Generation-Skipping Transfer) Tax Return, Estate of Nonresident Not a Citizen of the United States	9 months after date of decedent's death.
712	Life Insurance Statement	Part I to be filed with estate tax return.
1040	U.S. Individual Income Tax Return	Generally, April 15th of the year after death.
1040NR	U.S. Nonresident Alien Income Tax Return	15th day of 6th month after end of tax year.
1041	U.S. Fiduciary Income Tax Return	15th day of 4th month after end of estate's tax year.
1041-A	U.S. Information Return—Trust Accumulation of Charitable Amounts	15th day of 4th month after end of tax year.
1041-T	Allocation of Estimated Tax Payments to Beneficiaries	March 6th.
1041-ES	Estimated Income Tax for Fiduciaries	Generally, April 15, June 15, Sept. 15, and Jan. 15 for calendar-year filers.
1042	Annual Withholding Tax Return for U.S. Source Income of Foreign Persons	April 15th.
1042S	Foreign Person's U.S. Source Income Subject to Withholding	April 15th.
1310	Statement of Person Claiming Refund Due a Deceased Taxpayer	To be filed with Form 1040 or Form 1040NR if refund is due. If the person claiming the refund is a surviving spouse, filing a joint return with the decedent, this form is not required.
2758	Application for Extension of Time To File Certain Excise, Income, Information and Other Returns	Sufficiently early to permit IRS to consider the application and reply before the due date of Form 1041.
4768	Application for Extension of Time To File U.S. Estate (and Generation-Skipping Transfer) Tax Return and/or Pay Estate (and Generation-Skipping Transfer) Taxes	Sufficiently early to permit IRS to consider the application and reply before the estate tax due date.
4810	Request for Prompt Assessment Under Internal Revenue Code Section 6501(d)	As soon as possible after filing Form 1040 or Form 1041.
8300	Report of Cash Payments Over $10,000 Received in Trade or Business	15th day after the date of the transaction.
8822	Change of Address	As soon as the address is changed.

Note. A personal representative must report the termination of the estate, in writing, to the Internal Revenue Service. Form 56 may be used for this purpose.

I.R.S. Form 706—U.S. Estate (and Generation-Skipping Transfer) Tax Return

Form **706**
(Rev. July 1999)
Department of the Treasury
Internal Revenue Service

United States Estate (and Generation-Skipping Transfer) Tax Return

Estate of a citizen or resident of the United States (see separate instructions).
To be filed for decedents dying after December 31, 1998
For Paperwork Reduction Act Notice, see page 1 of the separate instructions.

OMB No. 1545-0015

Part 1.—Decedent and Executor

1a Decedent's first name and middle initial (and maiden name, if any)	1b Decedent's last name	2 Decedent's Social Security No.
3a Legal residence (domicile) at time of death (county, state, and ZIP code, or foreign country)	3b Year domicile established / 4 Date of birth	5 Date of death
6a Name of executor (see page 4 of the instructions)	6b Executor's address (number and street including apartment or suite no. or rural route; city, town, or post office; state; and ZIP code)	
6c Executor's social security number (see page 4 of the instructions)		
7a Name and location of court where will was probated or estate administered		7b Case number
8 If decedent died testate, check here ▶ ☐ and attach a certified copy of the will.	9 If Form 4768 is attached, check here ▶ ☐	
10 If Schedule R-1 is attached, check here ▶ ☐		

Part 2.—Tax Computation

1	Total gross estate less exclusion (from Part 5, Recapitulation, page 3, item 12)		1
2	Total allowable deductions (from Part 5, Recapitulation, page 3, item 23)		2
3	Taxable estate (subtract line 2 from line 1)		3
4	Adjusted taxable gifts (total taxable gifts (within the meaning of section 2503) made by the decedent after December 31, 1976, other than gifts that are includible in decedent's gross estate (section 2001(b)))		4
5	Add lines 3 and 4		5
6	Tentative tax on the amount on line 5 from Table A on page 12 of the instructions		6
7a	If line 5 exceeds $10,000,000, enter the lesser of line 5 or $17,184,000. If line 5 is $10,000,000 or less, skip lines 7a and 7b and enter -0- on line 7c	7a	
b	Subtract $10,000,000 from line 7a	7b	
c	Enter 5% (.05) of line 7b		7c
8	Total tentative tax (add lines 6 and 7c)		8
9	Total gift tax payable with respect to gifts made by the decedent after December 31, 1976. Include gift taxes by the decedent's spouse for such spouse's share of split gifts (section 2513) only if the decedent was the donor of these gifts and they are includible in the decedent's gross estate (see instructions)		9
10	Gross estate tax (subtract line 9 from line 8)		10
11	Maximum unified credit (applicable credit amount) against estate tax	11	
12	Adjustment to unified credit (applicable credit amount). (This adjustment may not exceed $6,000. See page 4 of the instructions.)	12	
13	Allowable unified credit (applicable credit amount) (subtract line 12 from line 11)		13
14	Subtract line 13 from line 10 (but do not enter less than zero)		14
15	Credit for state death taxes. Do not enter more than line 14. Figure the credit by using the amount on line 3 less $60,000. See Table B in the instructions and **attach credit evidence** (see instructions)		15
16	Subtract line 15 from line 14		16
17	Credit for Federal gift taxes on pre-1977 gifts (section 2012) (attach computation)	17	
18	Credit for foreign death taxes (from Schedule(s) P). (Attach Form(s) 706-CE.)	18	
19	Credit for tax on prior transfers (from Schedule Q)	19	
20	Total (add lines 17, 18, and 19)		20
21	Net estate tax (subtract line 20 from line 16)		21
22	Generation-skipping transfer taxes (from Schedule R, Part 2, line 10)		22
23	Total transfer taxes (add lines 21 and 22)		23
24	Prior payments. Explain in an attached statement	24	
25	United States Treasury bonds redeemed in payment of estate tax	25	
26	Total (add lines 24 and 25)		26
27	Balance due (or overpayment) (subtract line 26 from line 23)		27

Under penalties of perjury, I declare that I have examined this return, including accompanying schedules and statements, and to the best of my knowledge and belief, it is true, correct, and complete. Declaration of preparer other than the executor is based on all information of which preparer has any knowledge.

Signature(s) of executor(s) Date

Signature of preparer other than executor Address (and ZIP code) Date

Cat. No. 20548R

I.R.S. Form 706 (Continued)

Form 706 (Rev. 7-99)

Estate of:

Part 3—Elections by the Executor

Please check the "Yes" or "No" box for each question. (See instructions beginning on page 5.)		Yes	No
1 Do you elect alternate valuation?	1		
2 Do you elect special use valuation? If "Yes," you must complete and attach Schedule A-1.	2		
3 Do you elect to pay the taxes in installments as described in section 6166? If "Yes," you must attach the additional information described on page 8 of the instructions.	3		
4 Do you elect to postpone the part of the taxes attributable to a reversionary or remainder interest as described in section 6163?	4		

Part 4—General Information

(Note: *Please attach the necessary supplemental documents.* **You must attach the death certificate.)** *(See instructions on page 9.)*

Authorization to receive confidential tax information under Regs. sec. 601.504(b)(2)(i); to act as the estate's representative before the IRS; and to make written or oral presentations on behalf of the estate if return prepared by an attorney, accountant, or enrolled agent for the executor:

Name of representative (print or type)	State	Address (number, street, and room or suite no., city, state, and ZIP code)

I declare that I am the ☐ attorney/ ☐ certified public accountant/ ☐ enrolled agent (you must check the applicable box) for the executor and prepared this return for the executor. I am not under suspension or disbarment from practice before the Internal Revenue Service and am qualified to practice in the state shown above.

Signature	CAF number	Date	Telephone number

1 Death certificate number and issuing authority (attach a copy of the death certificate to this return).

2 Decedent's business or occupation. If retired, check here ▶ ☐ and state decedent's former business or occupation.

3 Marital status of the decedent at time of death:

☐ Married

☐ Widow or widower—Name, SSN, and date of death of deceased spouse ▶

☐ Single

☐ Legally separated

☐ Divorced—Date divorce decree became final ▶

4a Surviving spouse's name	4b Social security number	4c Amount received (see page 9 of the instructions)

5 Individuals (other than the surviving spouse), trusts, or other estates who receive benefits from the estate (do not include charitable beneficiaries shown in Schedule O) (see instructions). For Privacy Act Notice (applicable to individual beneficiaries only), see the Instructions for Form 1040.

Name of individual, trust, or estate receiving $5,000 or more	Identifying number	Relationship to decedent	Amount (see instructions)
All unascertainable beneficiaries and those who receive less than $5,000 ▶			
Total			

Please check the "Yes" or "No" box for each question.	Yes	No
6 Does the gross estate contain any section 2044 property (qualified terminable interest property (QTIP) from a prior gift or estate) (see page 9 of the instructions)?		

(continued on next page)

I.R.S. Form 706 (Continued)

Form 706 (Rev. 7-99)

Part 4—General Information *(continued)*

Please check the "Yes" or "No" box for each question.	Yes	No
7a Have Federal gift tax returns ever been filed? . . . . If "Yes," please attach copies of the returns, if available, and furnish the following information:		
7b Period(s) covered / **7c** Internal Revenue office(s) where filed		
If you answer "Yes" to any of questions 8–16, you must attach additional information as described in the instructions.		
8a Was there any insurance on the decedent's life that is not included on the return as part of the gross estate?		
b Did the decedent own any insurance on the life of another that is not included in the gross estate?		
9 Did the decedent at the time of death own any property as a joint tenant with right of survivorship in which **(a)** one or more of the other joint tenants was someone other than the decedent's spouse, and **(b)** less than the full value of the property is included on the return as part of the gross estate? If "Yes," you must complete and attach Schedule E		
10 Did the decedent, at the time of death, own any interest in a partnership or unincorporated business or any stock in an inactive or closely held corporation?		
11 Did the decedent make any transfer described in section 2035, 2036, 2037, or 2038 (see the instructions for Schedule G beginning on page 11 of the separate instructions)? If "Yes," you must complete and attach Schedule G		
12 Were there in existence at the time of the decedent's death:		
a Any trusts created by the decedent during his or her lifetime?		
b Any trusts not created by the decedent under which the decedent possessed any power, beneficial interest, or trusteeship?		
13 Did the decedent ever possess, exercise, or release any general power of appointment? If "Yes," you must complete and attach Schedule H		
14 Was the marital deduction computed under the transitional rule of Public Law 97-34, section 403(e)(3) (Economic Recovery Tax Act of 1981)? If "Yes," attach a separate computation of the marital deduction, enter the amount on item 20 of the Recapitulation, and note on item 20 "computation attached."		
15 Was the decedent, immediately before death, receiving an annuity described in the "General" paragraph of the instructions for Schedule I? If "Yes," you must complete and attach Schedule I		
16 Was the decedent ever the beneficiary of a trust for which a deduction was claimed by the estate of a pre-deceased spouse under section 2056(b)(7) and which is not reported on this return? If "Yes," attach an explanation.		

Part 5—Recapitulation

Item number	Gross estate		Alternate value	Value at date of death
1	Schedule A—Real Estate	1		
2	Schedule B—Stocks and Bonds.	2		
3	Schedule C—Mortgages, Notes, and Cash	3		
4	Schedule D—Insurance on the Decedent's Life (attach Form(s) 712) . . .	4		
5	Schedule E—Jointly Owned Property (attach Form(s) 712 for life insurance) .	5		
6	Schedule F—Other Miscellaneous Property (attach Form(s) 712 for life insurance)	6		
7	Schedule G—Transfers During Decedent's Life (att. Form(s) 712 for life insurance)	7		
8	Schedule H—Powers of Appointment	8		
9	Schedule I—Annuities	9		
10	Total gross estate (add items 1 through 9).	10		
11	Schedule U—Qualified Conservation Easement Exclusion	11		
12	Total gross estate less exclusion (subtract item 11 from item 10). Enter here and on line 1 of Part 2—Tax Computation	12		

Item number	Deductions		Amount
13	Schedule J—Funeral Expenses and Expenses Incurred in Administering Property Subject to Claims . . .	13	
14	Schedule K—Debts of the Decedent	14	
15	Schedule K—Mortgages and Liens	15	
16	Total of items 13 through 15	16	
17	Allowable amount of deductions from item 16 (see the instructions for item 17 of the Recapitulation) .	17	
18	Schedule L—Net Losses During Administration	18	
19	Schedule L—Expenses Incurred in Administering Property Not Subject to Claims	19	
20	Schedule M—Bequests, etc., to Surviving Spouse	20	
21	Schedule O—Charitable, Public, and Similar Gifts and Bequests	21	
22	Schedule T—Qualified Family-Owned Business Interest Deduction	22	
23	Total allowable deductions (add items 17 through 22). Enter here and on line 2 of the Tax Computation	23	

Page 3

I.R.S. Form 706 (Continued)

Form 706 (Rev. 7-99)

Estate of:

SCHEDULE A—Real Estate

- *For jointly owned property that must be disclosed on Schedule E, see the instructions on the reverse side of Schedule E.*
- *Real estate that is part of a sole proprietorship should be shown on Schedule F.*
- *Real estate that is included in the gross estate under section 2035, 2036, 2037, or 2038 should be shown on Schedule G.*
- *Real estate that is included in the gross estate under section 2041 should be shown on Schedule H.*
- *If you elect section 2032A valuation, you must complete Schedule A and Schedule A-1.*

Item number	Description	Alternate valuation date	Alternate value	Value at date of death
1				
Total from continuation schedules or additional sheets attached to this schedule . . .				
TOTAL. (Also enter on Part 5, Recapitulation, page 3, at item 1.)				

(If more space is needed, attach the continuation schedule from the end of this package or additional sheets of the same size.)
(See the instructions on the reverse side.)

I.R.S. Form 706 (Continued)

Form 706 (Rev. 7-99)

Instructions for Schedule A—Real Estate

If the total gross estate contains any real estate, you must complete Schedule A and file it with the return. On Schedule A list real estate the decedent owned or had contracted to purchase. Number each parcel in the left-hand column.

Describe the real estate in enough detail so that the IRS can easily locate it for inspection and valuation. For each parcel of real estate, report the area and, if the parcel is improved, describe the improvements. For city or town property, report the street and number, ward, subdivision, block and lot, etc. For rural property, report the township, range, landmarks, etc.

If any item of real estate is subject to a mortgage for which the decedent's estate is liable; that is, if the indebtedness may be charged against other property of the estate that is not subject to that mortgage, or if the decedent was personally liable for that mortgage, you must report the full value of the property in the value column. Enter the amount of the mortgage under "Description" on this schedule. The unpaid amount of the mortgage may be deducted on Schedule K.

If the decedent's estate is NOT liable for the amount of the mortgage, report only the value of the equity of redemption (or value of the property less the indebtedness) in the value column as part of the gross estate. Do not enter any amount less than zero. Do not deduct the amount of indebtedness on Schedule K.

Also list on Schedule A real property the decedent contracted to purchase. Report the full value of the property and not the equity in the value column. Deduct the unpaid part of the purchase price on Schedule K.

Report the value of real estate without reducing it for homestead or other exemption, or the value of dower, curtesy, or a statutory estate created instead of dower or curtesy.

Explain how the reported values were determined and attach copies of any appraisals.

Schedule A Examples

In this example, alternate valuation is not adopted; the date of death is January 1, 1999.

Item number	Description	Alternate valuation date	Alternate value	Value at date of death
1	House and lot, 1921 William Street NW, Washington, DC (lot 6, square 481). Rent of $2,700 due at end of each quarter, February 1, May 1, August 1, and November 1. Value based on appraisal, copy of which is attached			$108,000
	Rent due on item 1 for quarter ending November 1, 1998, but not collected at date of death			2,700
	Rent accrued on item 1 for November and December 1998			1,800
2	House and lot, 304 Jefferson Street, Alexandria, VA (lot 18, square 40). Rent of $600 payable monthly. Value based on appraisal, copy of which is attached			96,000
	Rent due on item 2 for December 1998, but not collected at date of death . . .			600

In this example, alternate valuation is adopted; the date of death is January 1, 1999.

Item number	Description	Alternate valuation date	Alternate value	Value at date of death
1	House and lot, 1921 William Street NW, Washington, DC (lot 6, square 481). Rent of $2,700 due at end of each quarter, February 1, May 1, August 1, and November 1. Value based on appraisal, copy of which is attached. Not disposed of within 6 months following death	7/1/99	90,000	$108,000
	Rent due on item 1 for quarter ending November 1, 1998, but not collected until February 1, 1999	2/1/99	2,700	2,700
	Rent accrued on item 1 for November and December 1998, collected on February 1, 1999	2/1/99	1,800	1,800
2	House and lot, 304 Jefferson Street, Alexandria, VA (lot 18, square 40). Rent of $600 payable monthly. Value based on appraisal, copy of which is attached. Property exchanged for farm on May 1, 1999	5/1/99	90,000	96,000
	Rent due on item 2 for December 1998, but not collected until February 1, 1999 .	2/1/99	600	600

I.R.S. Form 706 (Continued)

Instructions for Schedule A-1. Section 2032A Valuation

The election to value certain farm and closely held business property at its special use value is made by checking "Yes" to line 2 of Part 3, Elections by the Executor, Form 706. Schedule A-1 is used to report the additional information that must be submitted to support this election. In order to make a valid election, you must complete Schedule A-1 and attach all of the required statements and appraisals.

For definitions and additional information concerning special use valuation, see section 2032A and the related regulations.

Part 1. Type of Election

Estate and GST Tax Elections. If you elect special use valuation for the estate tax, you must also elect special use valuation for the GST tax and vice versa.

You must value each specific property interest at the same value for GST tax purposes that you value it at for estate tax purposes.

Protective Election. To make the protective election described in the separate instructions for line 2 of Part 3, Elections by the Executor, you must check this box, enter the decedent's name and social security number in the spaces provided at the top of Schedule A-1, and complete line 1 and column A of lines 3 and 4 of Part 2. For purposes of the protective election, list on line 3 all of the real property that passes to the qualified heirs even though some of the property will be shown on line 2 when the additional notice of election is subsequently filed. You need not complete columns B–D of lines 3 and 4. You need not complete any other line entries on Schedule A-1. Completing Schedule A-1 as described above constitutes a Notice of Protective Election as described in Regulations section 20.2032A-8(b).

Part 2. Notice of Election

Line 10. Because the special use valuation election creates a potential tax liability for the recapture tax of section 2032A(c), you must list each person who receives an interest in the specially valued property on Schedule A-1. If there are more than eight persons who receive interests, use an additional sheet that follows the format of line 10. In the columns "Fair market value" and "Special use value," you should enter the total respective values of all the specially valued property interests received by each person.

GST Tax Savings

To compute the additional GST tax due upon disposition (or cessation of qualified use) of the property, each "skip person" (as defined in the instructions to Schedule R) who receives an interest in the specially valued property must know the total GST tax savings on all of the interests in specially valued property received. This GST tax savings is the difference between the total GST tax that was imposed on all of the interests in specially valued property received by the skip person valued at their special use value and the total GST tax that would have been imposed on the same interests received by the skip person had they been valued at their fair market value.

Because the GST tax depends on the executor's allocation of the GST exemption and the grandchild exclusion, the skip person who receives the interests is unable to compute this GST tax savings. Therefore, for each skip person who receives an interest in specially valued property, you must attach worksheets showing the total GST tax savings attributable to all of that person's interests in specially valued property.

How To Compute the GST Tax Savings. Before computing each skip person's GST tax savings, you must complete Schedules R and R-1 for the entire estate (using the special use values).

For each skip person, you must complete two Schedules R (Parts 2 and 3 only) as worksheets, one showing the interests in specially valued property received by the skip person at their special use value and one showing the same interests at their fair market value.

If the skip person received interests in specially valued property that were shown on Schedule R-1, show these interests on the Schedule R, Parts 2 and 3 worksheets, as appropriate. Do not use Schedule R-1 as a worksheet.

Completing the Special Use Value Worksheets. On lines 2–4 and 6, enter -0-.

Completing the Fair Market Value Worksheets. *Lines 2 and 3, fixed taxes and other charges.* If valuing the interests at their fair market value (instead of special use value) causes any of these taxes and charges to increase, enter the increased amount (only) on these lines and attach an explanation of the increase. Otherwise, enter -0-.

Line 6—GST exemption. If you completed line 10 of Schedule R, Part 1, enter on line 6 the amount shown for the skip person on the *line 10 special use allocation schedule* you attached to Schedule R. If you did not complete line 10 of Schedule R, Part 1, enter -0- on line 6.

Total GST Tax Savings. For each skip person, subtract the tax amount on line 10, Part 2 of the special use value worksheet from the tax amount on line 10, Part 2 of the fair market value worksheet. This difference is the skip person's total GST tax savings.

Part 3. Agreement to Special Valuation Under Section 2032A

The agreement to special valuation by persons with an interest in property is required under section 2032A(a)(1)(B) and (d)(2) and must be signed by all parties who have any interest in the property being valued based on its qualified use as of the date of the decedent's death.

An interest in property is an interest that, as of the date of the decedent's death, can be asserted under applicable local law so as to affect the disposition of the specially valued property by the estate. Any person who at the decedent's death has any such interest in the property, whether present or future, or vested or contingent, must enter into the agreement. Included are owners of remainder and executory interests; the holders of general or special powers of appointment; beneficiaries of a gift over in default of exercise of any such power; joint tenants and holders of similar undivided interests when the decedent held only a joint or undivided interest in the property or when only an undivided interest is specially valued; and trustees of trusts and representatives of other entities holding title to, or holding any interests in the property. An heir who has the power under local law to caveat (challenge) a will and thereby affect disposition of the property is not, however, considered to be a person with an interest in property under section 2032A solely by reason of that right. Likewise, creditors of an estate are not such persons solely by reason of their status as creditors.

If any person required to enter into the agreement either desires that an agent act for him or her or cannot legally bind himself or herself due to infancy or other incompetency, or due to death before the election under section 2032A is timely exercised, a representative authorized by local law to bind the person in an agreement of this nature may sign the agreement on his or her behalf.

The Internal Revenue Service will contact the agent designated in the agreement on all matters relating to continued qualification under section 2032A of the specially valued real property and on all matters relating to the special lien arising under section 6324B. It is the duty of the agent as attorney-in-fact for the parties with interests in the specially valued property to furnish the IRS with any requested information and to notify the IRS of any disposition or cessation of qualified use of any part of the property.

I.R.S. Form 706 (Continued)

Form 706 (Rev. 7-99)

Checklist for Section 2032A Election. *If you are going to make the special use valuation election on Schedule A-1, please use this checklist to ensure that you are providing everything necessary to make a valid election.*

To have a valid special use valuation election under section 2032A, you must file, in addition to the Federal estate tax return, **(a)** a notice of election (Schedule A-1, Part 2), and **(b)** a fully executed agreement (Schedule A-1, Part 3). You must include certain information in the notice of election. To ensure that the notice of election includes all of the information required for a valid election, use the following checklist. The checklist is for your use only. Do not file it with the return.

1. Does the notice of election include the decedent's name and social security number as they appear on the estate tax return?

2. Does the notice of election include the relevant qualified use of the property to be specially valued?

3. Does the notice of election describe the items of real property shown on the estate tax return that are to be specially valued and identify the property by the Form 706 schedule and item number?

4. Does the notice of election include the fair market value of the real property to be specially valued and also include its value based on the qualified use (determined without the adjustments provided in section 2032A(b)(3)(B))?

5. Does the notice of election include the adjusted value (as defined in section 2032A(b)(3)(B)) of **(a)** all real property that both passes from the decedent and is used in a qualified use, without regard to whether it is to be specially valued, and **(b)** all real property to be specially valued?

6. Does the notice of election include **(a)** the items of personal property shown on the estate tax return that pass from the decedent to a qualified heir and that are used in qualified use and **(b)** the total value of such personal property adjusted under section 2032A(b)(3)(B)?

7. Does the notice of election include the adjusted value of the gross estate? (See section 2032A(b)(3)(A).)

8. Does the notice of election include the method used to determine the special use value?

9. Does the notice of election include copies of written appraisals of the fair market value of the real property?

10. Does the notice of election include a statement that the decedent and/or a member of his or her family has owned all of the specially valued property for at least 5 years of the 8 years immediately preceding the date of the decedent's death?

11. Does the notice of election include a statement as to whether there were any periods during the 8-year period preceding the decedent's date of death during which the decedent or a member of his or her family did not **(a)** own the property to be specially valued, **(b)** use it in a qualified use, or **(c)** materially participate in the operation of the farm or other business? (See section 2032A(e)(6).)

12. Does the notice of election include, for each item of specially valued property, the name of every person taking an interest in that item of specially valued property and the following information about each such person: **(a)** the person's address, **(b)** the person's taxpayer identification number, **(c)** the person's relationship to the decedent, and **(d)** the value of the property interest passing to that person based on both fair market value and qualified use?

13. Does the notice of election include affidavits describing the activities constituting material participation and the identity of the material participants?

14. Does the notice of election include a legal description of each item of specially valued property?

(In the case of an election made for qualified woodlands, the information included in the notice of election must include the reason for entitlement to the woodlands election.)

Any election made under section 2032A will not be valid unless a properly executed agreement (Schedule A-1, Part 3) is filed with the estate tax return. To ensure that the agreement satisfies the requirements for a valid election, use the following checklist.

1. Has the agreement been signed by each and every qualified heir having an interest in the property being specially valued?

2. Has every qualified heir expressed consent to personal liability under section 2032A(c) in the event of an early disposition or early cessation of qualified use?

3. Is the agreement that is actually signed by the qualified heirs in a form that is binding on all of the qualified heirs having an interest in the specially valued property?

4. Does the agreement designate an agent to act for the parties to the agreement in all dealings with the IRS on matters arising under section 2032A?

5. Has the agreement been signed by the designated agent and does it give the address of the agent?

I.R.S. Form 706 (Continued)

Form 706 (Rev. 7-99)

Estate of: | **Decedent's Social Security Number**

SCHEDULE A-1—Section 2032A Valuation

Part 1. Type of Election (Before making an election, see the checklist on page 7.):

☐ **Protective election (Regulations section 20.2032A-8(b)).** Complete Part 2, line 1, and column A of lines 3 and 4. (See instructions.)

☐ **Regular election.** Complete all of Part 2 (including line 11, if applicable) and Part 3. (See instructions.)

Before completing Schedule A-1, see the checklist on page 7 for the information and documents that must be included to make a valid election.

The election is not valid unless the agreement (i.e., Part 3—Agreement to Special Valuation Under Section 2032A)—

- Is signed by each and every qualified heir with an interest in the specially valued property, and
- Is attached to this return when it is filed.

Part 2. Notice of Election (Regulations section 20.2032A-8(a)(3))

Note: *All real property entered on lines 2 and 3 must also be entered on Schedules A, E, F, G, or H, as applicable.*

1 Qualified use—check one ▶ ☐ Farm used for farming, or

▶ ☐ Trade or business other than farming

2 Real property used in a qualified use, passing to qualified heirs, and to be specially valued on this Form 706.

A Schedule and item number from Form 706	B Full value (without section 2032A(b)(3)(B) adjustment)	C Adjusted value (with section 2032A(b)(3)(B) adjustment)	D Value based on qualified use (without section 2032A(b)(3)(B) adjustment)
Totals			

Attach a legal description of all property listed on line 2.

Attach copies of appraisals showing the column B values for all property listed on line 2.

3 Real property used in a qualified use, passing to qualified heirs, but not specially valued on this Form 706.

A Schedule and item number from Form 706	B Full value (without section 2032A(b)(3)(B) adjustment)	C Adjusted value (with section 2032A(b)(3)(B) adjustment)	D Value based on qualified use (without section 2032A(b)(3)(B) adjustment)
Totals			

If you checked "Regular election," you must attach copies of appraisals showing the column B values for all property listed on line 3.

(continued on next page)

I.R.S. Form 706 (Continued)

Form 706 (Rev. 7-99)

4 Personal property used in a qualified use and passing to qualified heirs.

A Schedule and item number from Form 706	B Adjusted value (with section 2032A(b)(3)(B) adjustment)	A (continued) Schedule and item number from Form 706	B (continued) Adjusted value (with section 2032A(b)(3)(B) adjustment)
		"Subtotal" from Col. B, below left	
Subtotal		**Total adjusted value**	

5 Enter the value of the total gross estate as adjusted under section 2032A(b)(3)(A). ▶

6 Attach a description of the method used to determine the special value based on qualified use.

7 Did the decedent and/or a member of his or her family own all property listed on line 2 for at least 5 of the 8 years immediately preceding the date of the decedent's death? ☐ **Yes** ☐ **No**

8 Were there any periods during the 8-year period preceding the date of the decedent's death during which the decedent or a member of his or her family:

	Yes	No
a Did not own the property listed on line 2 above?		
b Did not use the property listed on line 2 above in a qualified use?		
c Did not materially participate in the operation of the farm or other business within the meaning of section 2032A(e)(6)?		

If "Yes" to any of the above, you must attach a statement listing the periods. If applicable, describe whether the exceptions of sections 2032A(b)(4) or (5) are met.

9 Attach affidavits describing the activities constituting material participation and the identity and relationship to the decedent of the material participants.

10 Persons holding interests. Enter the requested information for each party who received any interest in the specially valued property. **(Each of the qualified heirs receiving an interest in the property must sign the agreement, and the agreement must be filed with this return.)**

	Name	Address
A		
B		
C		
D		
E		
F		
G		
H		

	Identifying number	Relationship to decedent	Fair market value	Special use value
A				
B				
C				
D				
E				
F				
G				
H				

You must attach a computation of the GST tax savings attributable to direct skips for each person listed above who is a skip person. (See instructions.)

11 Woodlands election. Check here ▶ ☐ if you wish to make a woodlands election as described in section 2032A(e)(13). Enter the Schedule and item numbers from Form 706 of the property for which you are making this election ▶

You must attach a statement explaining why you are entitled to make this election. The IRS may issue regulations that require more information to substantiate this election. You will be notified by the IRS if you must supply further information.

I.R.S. Form 706 (Continued)

Form 706 (Rev. 7-99)

Part 3. Agreement to Special Valuation Under Section 2032A

Estate of:	Date of Death	Decedent's Social Security Number

There cannot be a valid election unless:

- The agreement is executed by each and every one of the qualified heirs, and
- The agreement is included with the estate tax return when the estate tax return is filed.

We (list all qualified heirs and other persons having an interest in the property required to sign this agreement)

____

____,

being all the qualified heirs and ____

____,

being all other parties having interests in the property which is qualified real property and which is valued under section 2032A of the Internal Revenue Code, do hereby approve of the election made by ________________________,

Executor/Administrator of the estate of ________________________,

pursuant to section 2032A to value said property on the basis of the qualified use to which the property is devoted and do hereby enter into this agreement pursuant to section 2032A(d).

The undersigned agree and consent to the application of subsection (c) of section 2032A of the Code with respect to all the property described on line 2 of Part 2 of Schedule A-1 of Form 706, attached to this agreement. More specifically, the undersigned heirs expressly agree and consent to personal liability under subsection (c) of 2032A for the additional estate and GST taxes imposed by that subsection with respect to their respective interests in the above-described property in the event of certain early dispositions of the property or early cessation of the qualified use of the property. It is understood that if a qualified heir disposes of any interest in qualified real property to any member of his or her family, such member may thereafter be treated as the qualified heir with respect to such interest upon filing a Form 706-A and a new agreement.

The undersigned interested parties who are not qualified heirs consent to the collection of any additional estate and GST taxes imposed under section 2032A(c) of the Code from the specially valued property.

If there is a disposition of any interest which passes, or has passed to him or her, or if there is a cessation of the qualified use of any specially valued property which passes or passed to him or her, each of the undersigned heirs agrees to file a **Form 706-A,** United States Additional Estate Tax Return, and pay any additional estate and GST taxes due within 6 months of the disposition or cessation.

It is understood by all interested parties that this agreement is a condition precedent to the election of special use valuation under section 2032A of the Code and must be executed by every interested party even though that person may not have received the estate (or GST) tax benefits or be in possession of such property.

Each of the undersigned understands that by making this election, a lien will be created and recorded pursuant to section 6324B of the Code on the property referred to in this agreement for the adjusted tax differences with respect to the estate as defined in section 2032A(c)(2)(C).

As the interested parties, the undersigned designate the following individual as their agent for all dealings with the Internal Revenue Service concerning the continued qualification of the specially valued property under section 2032A of the Code and on all issues regarding the special lien under section 6324B. The agent is authorized to act for the parties with respect to all dealings with the Service on matters affecting the qualified real property described earlier. This authority includes the following:

- To receive confidential information on all matters relating to continued qualification under section 2032A of the specially valued real property and on all matters relating to the special lien arising under section 6324B.
- To furnish the Internal Revenue Service with any requested information concerning the property.
- To notify the Internal Revenue Service of any disposition or cessation of qualified use of any part of the property.
- To receive, but not to endorse and collect, checks in payment of any refund of Internal Revenue taxes, penalties, or interest.
- To execute waivers (including offers of waivers) of restrictions on assessment or collection of deficiencies in tax and waivers of notice of disallowance of a claim for credit or refund.
- To execute closing agreements under section 7121.

(continued on next page)

I.R.S. Form 706 (Continued)

Form 706 (Rev. 7-99)

Part 3. Agreement to Special Valuation Under Section 2032A *(Continued)*

Estate of:	Date of Death	**Decedent's Social Security Number**

• Other acts (specify) ▶ ______________________________

By signing this agreement, the agent agrees to provide the Internal Revenue Service with any requested information concerning this property and to notify the Internal Revenue Service of any disposition or cessation of the qualified use of any part of this property.

Name of Agent	Signature	Address

The property to which this agreement relates is listed in Form 706, United States Estate (and Generation-Skipping Transfer) Tax Return, and in the Notice of Election, along with its fair market value according to section 2031 of the Code and its special use value according to section 2032A. The name, address, social security number, and interest (including the value) of each of the undersigned in this property are as set forth in the attached Notice of Election.

IN WITNESS WHEREOF, the undersigned have hereunto set their hands at ______________________________,

this ________ day of ________ .

SIGNATURES OF EACH OF THE QUALIFIED HEIRS:

Signature of qualified heir	Signature of qualified heir
Signature of qualified heir	Signature of qualified heir
Signature of qualified heir	Signature of qualified heir
Signature of qualified heir	Signature of qualified heir
Signature of qualified heir	Signature of qualified heir
Signature of qualified heir	Signature of qualified heir

Signatures of other interested parties

Signatures of other interested parties

I.R.S. Form 706 (Continued)

Form 706 (Rev. 7-99)

Estate of:

SCHEDULE B—Stocks and Bonds

(For jointly owned property that must be disclosed on Schedule E, see the instructions for Schedule E.)

Item number	Description including face amount of bonds or number of shares and par value where needed for identification. Give 9-digit CUSIP number.	CUSIP number	Unit value	Alternate valuation date	Alternate value	Value at date of death
1						
Total from continuation schedules (or additional sheets) attached to this schedule . . .						
TOTAL. (Also enter on Part 5, Recapitulation, page 3, at item 2.)						

(If more space is needed, attach the continuation schedule from the end of this package or additional sheets of the same size.)
(The instructions to Schedule B are in the separate instructions.)

I.R.S. Form 706 (Continued)

Form 706 (Rev. 7-99)

Estate of:

SCHEDULE C—Mortgages, Notes, and Cash

(For jointly owned property that must be disclosed on Schedule E, see the instructions for Schedule E.)

Item number	Description	Alternate valuation date	Alternate value	Value at date of death
1				
	Total from continuation schedules (or additional sheets) attached to this schedule . .			
	TOTAL. (Also enter on Part 5, Recapitulation, page 3, at item 3.)			

(If more space is needed, attach the continuation schedule from the end of this package or additional sheets of the same size.)
(See the instructions on the reverse side.)

I.R.S. Form 706 (Continued)

Form 706 (Rev. 7-99)

Instructions for Schedule C.—Mortgages, Notes, and Cash

Complete Schedule C and file it with your return if the total gross estate contains any:

- mortgages,
- notes, or
- cash.

List on Schedule C:

- Mortgages and notes payable **to the decedent** at the time of death.
- Cash the decedent had at the date of death.

Do not list on Schedule C:

- Mortgages and notes payable **by the decedent.** (If these are deductible, list them on Schedule K.)

List the items on Schedule C in the following order:

- mortgages,
- promissory notes,
- contracts by decedent to sell land,
- cash in possession, and
- cash in banks, savings and loan associations, and other types of financial organizations.

What to enter in the "Description" column:

For mortgages, list:

- face value,
- unpaid balance,
- date of mortgage,
- date of maturity,
- name of maker,
- property mortgaged,
- interest dates, and
- interest rate.

Example to enter in "Description" column:

"Bond and mortgage of $50,000, unpaid balance: $24,000; dated: January 1, 1981; John Doe to Richard Roe; premises: 22 Clinton Street, Newark, NJ; due: January 1, 1999; interest payable at 10% a year--January 1 and July 1."

For promissory notes, list:

- in the same way as mortgages.

For contracts by the decedent to sell land, list:

- name of purchaser,
- contract date,
- property description,
- sale price,
- initial payment,
- amounts of installment payment,
- unpaid balance of principal, and
- interest rate.

For cash in possession, list:

- such cash separately from bank deposits.

For cash in banks, savings and loan associations, and other types of financial organizations, list:

- name and address of each financial organization,
- amount in each account,
- serial or account number,
- nature of account--checking, savings, time deposit, etc., and
- unpaid interest accrued from date of last interest payment to the date of death.

Important: If you obtain statements from the financial organizations, keep them for IRS inspection.

I.R.S. Form 706 (Continued)

Form 706 (Rev. 7-99)

Estate of:

SCHEDULE D—Insurance on the Decedent's Life

You must list **all** policies on the life of the decedent and attach a Form 712 for each policy.

Item number	Description	Alternate valuation date	Alternate value	Value at date of death
1				
Total from continuation schedules (or additional sheets) attached to this schedule . .				
TOTAL. (Also enter on Part 5, Recapitulation, page 3, at item 4.)				

(If more space is needed, attach the continuation schedule from the end of this package or additional sheets of the same size.)

(See the instructions on the reverse side.)

I.R.S. Form 706 (Continued)

Instructions for Schedule D—Insurance on the Decedent's Life

If you are required to file Form 706 and there was any insurance on the decedent's life, whether or not included in the gross estate, you must complete Schedule D and file it with the return.

Insurance you must include on Schedule D. Under section 2042 you must include in the gross estate:

- Insurance on the decedent's life receivable by or for the benefit of the estate; and
- Insurance on the decedent's life receivable by beneficiaries other than the estate, as described below.

The term "insurance" refers to life insurance of every description, including death benefits paid by fraternal beneficiary societies operating under the lodge system, and death benefits paid under no-fault automobile insurance policies if the no-fault insurer was unconditionally bound to pay the benefit in the event of the insured's death.

Insurance in favor of the estate. Include on Schedule D the full amount of the proceeds of insurance on the life of the decedent receivable by the executor or otherwise payable to or for the benefit of the estate. Insurance in favor of the estate includes insurance used to pay the estate tax, and any other taxes, debts, or charges that are enforceable against the estate. The manner in which the policy is drawn is immaterial as long as there is an obligation, legally binding on the beneficiary, to use the proceeds to pay taxes, debts, or charges. You must include the full amount even though the premiums or other consideration may have been paid by a person other than the decedent.

Insurance receivable by beneficiaries other than the estate. Include on Schedule D the proceeds of all insurance on the life of the decedent not receivable by or for the benefit of the decedent's estate if the decedent possessed at death any of the incidents of ownership, exercisable either alone or in conjunction with any person.

Incidents of ownership in a policy include:

- The right of the insured or estate to its economic benefits;
- The power to change the beneficiary;
- The power to surrender or cancel the policy;
- The power to assign the policy or to revoke an assignment;
- The power to pledge the policy for a loan;
- The power to obtain from the insurer a loan against the surrender value of the policy;
- A reversionary interest if the value of the reversionary interest was more than 5% of the value of the policy immediately before the decedent died. (An interest in an insurance policy is considered a reversionary interest if, for example, the proceeds become payable to the insured's estate or payable as the insured directs if the beneficiary dies before the insured.)

Life insurance not includible in the gross estate under section 2042 may be includible under some other section of the Code. For example, a life insurance policy could be transferred by the decedent in such a way that it would be includible in the gross estate under section 2036, 2037, or 2038. (See the instructions to Schedule G for a description of these sections.)

Completing the Schedule

You must list every policy of insurance on the life of the decedent, whether or not it is included in the gross estate.

Under "Description" list:

- Name of the insurance company and
- Number of the policy.

For every policy of life insurance listed on the schedule, you must request a statement on **Form 712,** Life Insurance Statement, from the company that issued the policy. Attach the Form 712 to the back of Schedule D.

If the policy proceeds are paid in one sum, enter the net proceeds received (from Form 712, line 24) in the value (and alternate value) columns of Schedule D. If the policy proceeds are not paid in one sum, enter the value of the proceeds as of the date of the decedent's death (from Form 712, line 25).

If part or all of the policy proceeds are not included in the gross estate, you must explain why they were not included.

I.R.S. Form 706 (Continued)

Form 706 (Rev. 7-99)

Estate of:

SCHEDULE E—Jointly Owned Property

(If you elect section 2032A valuation, you must complete Schedule E and Schedule A-1.)

PART 1.—Qualified Joint Interests—Interests Held by the Decedent and His or Her Spouse as the Only Joint Tenants (Section 2040(b)(2))

Item number	Description For securities, give CUSIP number.	Alternate valuation date	Alternate value	Value at date of death
	Total from continuation schedules (or additional sheets) attached to this schedule			
1a	Totals	**1a**		
1b	Amounts included in gross estate (one-half of line **1a**)	**1b**		

PART 2.—All Other Joint Interests

2a State the name and address of each surviving co-tenant. If there are more than three surviving co-tenants, list the additional co-tenants on an attached sheet.

	Name	Address (number and street, city, state, and ZIP code)
A.		
B.		
C.		

Item number	Enter letter for co-tenant	Description (including alternate valuation date if any) For securities, give CUSIP number.	Percentage includible	Includible alternate value	Includible value at date of death
		Total from continuation schedules (or additional sheets) attached to this schedule			
2b		Total other joint interests			
3		**Total includible joint interests** (add lines 1b and 2b). Also enter on Part 5, Recapitulation, page 3, at item 5			

(If more space is needed, attach the continuation schedule from the end of this package or additional sheets of the same size.)
(See the instructions on the reverse side.)

I.R.S. Form 706 (Continued)

Instructions for Schedule E. Jointly Owned Property

If you are required to file Form 706, you must complete Schedule E and file it with the return if the decedent owned any joint property at the time of death, whether or not the decedent's interest is includible in the gross estate.

Enter on this schedule all property of whatever kind or character, whether real estate, personal property, or bank accounts, in which the decedent held at the time of death an interest either as a joint tenant with right to survivorship or as a tenant by the entirety.

Do not list on this schedule property that the decedent held as a tenant in common, but report the value of the interest on Schedule A if real estate, or on the appropriate schedule if personal property. Similarly, community property held by the decedent and spouse should be reported on the appropriate Schedules A through I. The decedent's interest in a partnership should not be entered on this schedule unless the partnership interest itself is jointly owned. Solely owned partnership interests should be reported on Schedule F, "Other Miscellaneous Property."

Part 1—Qualified joint interests held by decedent and spouse. Under section 2040(b)(2), a joint interest is a qualified joint interest if the decedent and the surviving spouse held the interest as:

- Tenants by the entirety, or
- Joint tenants with right of survivorship if the decedent and the decedent's spouse are the only joint tenants.

Interests that meet either of the two requirements above should be entered in Part 1. Joint interests that do not meet either of the two requirements above should be entered in Part 2.

Under "Description," describe the property as required in the instructions for Schedules A, B, C, and F for the type of property involved. For example, jointly held stocks and bonds should be described using the rules given in the instructions to Schedule B.

Under "Alternate value" and "Value at date of death," enter the full value of the property.

Note: *You cannot claim the special treatment under section 2040(b) for property held jointly by a decedent and a surviving spouse who is not a U.S. citizen. You must report these joint interests on Part 2 of Schedule E, not Part 1.*

Part 2—Other joint interests. All joint interests that were not entered in Part 1 must be entered in Part 2.

For each item of property, enter the appropriate letter A, B, C, etc., from line 2a to indicate the name and address of the surviving co-tenant.

Under "Description," describe the property as required in the instructions for Schedules A, B, C, and F for the type of property involved.

In the "Percentage includible" column, enter the percentage of the total value of the property that you intend to include in the gross estate.

Generally, you must include the full value of the jointly owned property in the gross estate. However, the full value should not be included if you can show that a part of the property originally belonged to the other tenant or tenants and was never received or acquired by the other tenant or tenants from the decedent for less than adequate and full consideration in money or money's worth, or unless you can show that any part of the property was acquired with consideration originally belonging to the surviving joint tenant or tenants. In this case, you may exclude from the value of the property an amount proportionate to the consideration furnished by the other tenant or tenants. Relinquishing or promising to relinquish dower, curtesy, or statutory estate created instead of dower or curtesy, or other marital rights in the decedent's property or estate is not consideration in money or money's worth. See the Schedule A instructions for the value to show for real property that is subject to a mortgage.

If the property was acquired by the decedent and another person or persons by gift, bequest, devise, or inheritance as joint tenants, and their interests are not otherwise specified by law, include only that part of the value of the property that is figured by dividing the full value of the property by the number of joint tenants.

If you believe that less than the full value of the entire property is includible in the gross estate for tax purposes, you must establish the right to include the smaller value by attaching proof of the extent, origin, and nature of the decedent's interest and the interest(s) of the decedent's co-tenant or co-tenants.

In the "Includible alternate value" and "Includible value at date of death" columns, you should enter only the values that you believe are includible in the gross estate.

I.R.S. Form 706 (Continued)

Form 706 (Rev. 7-99)

Estate of:

SCHEDULE F—Other Miscellaneous Property Not Reportable Under Any Other Schedule

(For jointly owned property that must be disclosed on Schedule E, see the instructions for Schedule E.)
(If you elect section 2032A valuation, you must complete Schedule F and Schedule A-1.)

		Yes	No
1	Did the decedent at the time of death own any articles of artistic or collectible value in excess of $3,000 or any collections whose artistic or collectible value combined at date of death exceeded $10,000? . . . . If "Yes," submit full details on this schedule and attach appraisals.		
2	Has the decedent's estate, spouse, or any other person, received (or will receive) any bonus or award as a result of the decedent's employment or death? . . . . If "Yes," submit full details on this schedule.		
3	Did the decedent at the time of death have, or have access to, a safe deposit box? . . . . If "Yes," state location, and if held in joint names of decedent and another, state name and relationship of joint depositor. If any of the contents of the safe deposit box are omitted from the schedules in this return, explain fully why omitted.		

Item number	Description For securities, give CUSIP number.	Alternate valuation date	Alternate value	Value at date of death
1				
	Total from continuation schedules (or additional sheets) attached to this schedule . .			
	TOTAL. (Also enter on Part 5, Recapitulation, page 3, at item 6.)			

(If more space is needed, attach the continuation schedule from the end of this package or additional sheets of the same size.)
(See the instructions on the reverse side.)

I.R.S. Form 706 (Continued)

Instructions for Schedule F—Other Miscellaneous Property

You must complete Schedule F and file it with the return.

On Schedule F list all items that must be included in the gross estate that are not reported on any other schedule, including:

- Debts due the decedent (other than notes and mortgages included on Schedule C)
- Interests in business
- Insurance on the life of another (obtain and attach **Form 712,** Life Insurance Statement, for each policy)

Note for single premium or paid-up policies: *In certain situations, for example where the surrender value of the policy exceeds its replacement cost, the true economic value of the policy will be greater than the amount shown on line 56 of Form 712. In these situations, you should report the full economic value of the policy on Schedule F. See Rev. Rul. 78-137, 1978-1 C.B. 280 for details.*

- Section 2044 property (see **Decedent Who Was a Surviving Spouse** below)
- Claims (including the value of the decedent's interest in a claim for refund of income taxes or the amount of the refund actually received)
- Rights
- Royalties
- Leaseholds
- Judgments
- Reversionary or remainder interests
- Shares in trust funds (attach a copy of the trust instrument)
- Household goods and personal effects, including wearing apparel
- Farm products and growing crops
- Livestock
- Farm machinery
- Automobiles

If the decedent owned any interest in a partnership or unincorporated business, attach a statement of assets and liabilities for the valuation date and for the 5 years before the valuation date. Also attach statements of the net earnings for the same 5 years. You must account for goodwill in the valuation. In general, furnish the same information and follow the methods used to value close corporations. See the instructions for Schedule B.

All partnership interests should be reported on Schedule F unless the partnership interest, itself, is jointly owned. Jointly owned partnership interests should be reported on Schedule E.

If real estate is owned by the sole proprietorship, it should be reported on Schedule F and not on Schedule A. Describe the real estate with the same detail required for Schedule A.

Line 1. If the decedent owned at the date of death articles with artistic or intrinsic value (e.g., jewelry, furs, silverware, books, statuary, vases, oriental rugs, coin or stamp collections), check the "Yes" box on line 1 and provide full details. If any one article is valued at more than $3,000, or any collection of similar articles is valued at more than $10,000, attach an appraisal by an expert under oath and the required statement regarding the appraiser's qualifications (see Regulations section 20.2031-6(b)).

Decedent Who Was a Surviving Spouse

If the decedent was a surviving spouse, he or she may have received qualified terminable interest property (QTIP) from the predeceased spouse for which the marital deduction was elected either on the predeceased spouse's estate tax return or on a gift tax return, Form 709. The election was available for gifts made and decedents dying after December 31, 1981. List such property on Schedule F.

If this election was made and the surviving spouse retained his or her interest in the QTIP property at death, the full value of the QTIP property is includible in his or her estate, even though the qualifying income interest terminated at death. It is valued as of the date of the surviving spouse's death, or alternate valuation date, if applicable. Do not reduce the value by any annual exclusion that may have applied to the transfer creating the interest.

The value of such property included in the surviving spouse's gross estate is treated as passing from the surviving spouse. It therefore qualifies for the charitable and marital deductions on the surviving spouse's estate tax return if it meets the other requirements for those deductions.

For additional details, see Regulations section 20.2044-1.

I.R.S. Form 706 (Continued)

Form 706 (Rev. 7-99)

Estate of:

SCHEDULE G—Transfers During Decedent's Life

(If you elect section 2032A valuation, you must complete Schedule G and Schedule A-1.)

Item number	Description For securities, give CUSIP number.	Alternate valuation date	Alternate value	Value at date of death
A.	Gift tax paid by the decedent or the estate for all gifts made by the decedent or his or her spouse within 3 years before the decedent's death (section 2035(b))	X X X X X		
B.	Transfers includible under section 2035(a), 2036, 2037, or 2038:			
1				
	Total from continuation schedules (or additional sheets) attached to this schedule . .			
	TOTAL. (Also enter on Part 5, Recapitulation, page 3, at item 7.).			

SCHEDULE H—Powers of Appointment

(Include "5 and 5 lapsing" powers (section 2041(b)(2)) held by the decedent.)

(If you elect section 2032A valuation, you must complete Schedule H and Schedule A-1.)

Item number	Description	Alternate valuation date	Alternate value	Value at date of death
1				
	Total from continuation schedules (or additional sheets) attached to this schedule . .			
	TOTAL. (Also enter on Part 5, Recapitulation, page 3, at item 8.).			

(If more space is needed, attach the continuation schedule from the end of this package or additional sheets of the same size.)
(The instructions to Schedules G and H are in the separate instructions.)

I.R.S. Form 706 (Continued)

Form 706 (Rev. 7-99)

Estate of:

SCHEDULE I—Annuities

Note: *Generally, no exclusion is allowed for the estates of decedents dying after December 31, 1984 (see page 15 of the instructions).*

	Yes	No
A Are you excluding from the decedent's gross estate the value of a lump-sum distribution described in section 2039(f)(2)? . . . . If "Yes," you must attach the information required by the instructions.		

Item number	Description Show the entire value of the annuity before any exclusions.	Alternate valuation date	Includible alternate value	Includible value at date of death
1				
Total from continuation schedules (or additional sheets) attached to this schedule . .				
TOTAL. (Also enter on Part 5, Recapitulation, page 3, at item 9.)				

(If more space is needed, attach the continuation schedule from the end of this package or additional sheets of the same size.)

(The instructions to Schedule I are in the separate instructions.)

I.R.S. Form 706 (Continued)

Form 706 (Rev. 7-99)

Estate of:

SCHEDULE J—Funeral Expenses and Expenses Incurred in Administering Property Subject to Claims

Note: *Do not list on this schedule expenses of administering property not subject to claims. For those expenses, see the instructions for Schedule L.*

If executors' commissions, attorney fees, etc., are claimed and allowed as a deduction for estate tax purposes, they are not allowable as a deduction in computing the taxable income of the estate for Federal income tax purposes. They are allowable as an income tax deduction on Form 1041 if a waiver is filed to waive the deduction on Form 706 (see the Form 1041 instructions).

Item number	Description	Expense amount	Total amount
	A. Funeral expenses:		
1			
	Total funeral expenses . . . . ▶		
	B. Administration expenses:		
1	Executors' commissions—amount estimated/agreed upon/paid. (Strike out the words that do not apply.)		
2	Attorney fees—amount estimated/agreed upon/paid. (Strike out the words that do not apply.). .		
3	Accountant fees—amount estimated/agreed upon/paid. (Strike out the words that do not apply.).		
4	Miscellaneous expenses:	Expense amount	
	Total miscellaneous expenses from continuation schedules (or additional sheets) attached to this schedule		
	Total miscellaneous expenses . . . . ▶		

TOTAL. (Also enter on Part 5, Recapitulation, page 3, at item 13.) . . . . ▶

(If more space is needed, attach the continuation schedule from the end of this package or additional sheets of the same size.)
(See the instructions on the reverse side.)

I.R.S. Form 706 (Continued)

Instructions for Schedule J—Funeral Expenses and Expenses Incurred in Administering Property Subject to Claims

General. You must complete and file Schedule J if you claim a deduction on item 13 of Part 5, Recapitulation.

On Schedule J, itemize funeral expenses and expenses incurred in administering property subject to claims. List the names and addresses of persons to whom the expenses are payable and describe the nature of the expense. **Do not list expenses incurred in administering property not subject to claims on this schedule. List them on Schedule L instead.**

The deduction is limited to the amount paid for these expenses that is allowable under local law but may not exceed:

1. The value of property subject to claims included in the gross estate, plus

2. The amount paid out of property included in the gross estate but not subject to claims. This amount must actually be paid by the due date of the estate tax return.

The applicable local law under which the estate is being administered determines which property is and is not subject to claims. If under local law a particular property interest included in the gross estate would bear the burden for the payment of the expenses, then the property is considered property subject to claims.

Unlike certain claims against the estate for debts of the decedent (see the instructions for Schedule K in the separate instructions), you cannot deduct expenses incurred in administering property subject to claims on both the estate tax return and the estate's income tax return. If you choose to deduct them on the estate tax return, you cannot deduct them on a Form 1041 filed for the estate. Funeral expenses are only deductible on the estate tax return.

Funeral Expenses. Itemize funeral expenses on line A. Deduct from the expenses any amounts that were reimbursed, such as death benefits payable by the Social Security Administration and the Veterans Administration.

Executors' Commissions. When you file the return, you may deduct commissions that have actually been paid to you or that you expect will be paid. You may not deduct commissions if none will be collected. If the amount of the commissions has not been fixed by decree of the proper court, the deduction will be allowed on the final examination of the return, provided that:

- The District Director is reasonably satisfied that the commissions claimed will be paid;
- The amount entered as a deduction is within the amount allowable by the laws of the jurisdiction where the estate is being administered;
- It is in accordance with the usually accepted practice in that jurisdiction for estates of similar size and character.

If you have not been paid the commissions claimed at the time of the final examination of the return, you must support the amount you deducted with an affidavit or statement signed under the penalties of perjury that the amount has been agreed upon and will be paid.

You may not deduct a bequest or devise made to you instead of commissions. If, however, the decedent fixed by will the compensation payable to you for services to be rendered in the administration of the estate, you may deduct this amount to the extent it is not more than the compensation allowable by the local law or practice.

Do not deduct on this schedule amounts paid as trustees' commissions whether received by you acting in the capacity of a trustee or by a separate trustee. If such amounts were paid in administering property not subject to claims, deduct them on Schedule L.

Note: *Executors' commissions are taxable income to the executors. Therefore, be sure to include them as income on your individual income tax return.*

Attorney Fees. Enter the amount of attorney fees that have actually been paid or that you reasonably expect to be paid. If on the final examination of the return the fees claimed have not been awarded by the proper court and paid, the deduction will be allowed provided the District Director is reasonably satisfied that the amount claimed will be paid and that it does not exceed a reasonable payment for the services performed, taking into account the size and character of the estate and the local law and practice. If the fees claimed have not been paid at the time of final examination of the return, the amount deducted must be supported by an affidavit, or statement signed under the penalties of perjury, by the executor or the attorney stating that the amount has been agreed upon and will be paid.

Do not deduct attorney fees incidental to litigation incurred by the beneficiaries. These expenses are charged against the beneficiaries personally and are not administration expenses authorized by the Code.

Interest Expense. Interest expenses incurred after the decedent's death are generally allowed as a deduction if they are reasonable, necessary to the administration of the estate, and allowable under local law.

Interest incurred as the result of a Federal estate tax deficiency is a deductible administrative expense. Penalties are not deductible even if they are allowable under local law.

Note: *If you elect to pay the tax in installments under section 6166, you may* **not** *deduct the interest payable on the installments.*

Miscellaneous Expenses. Miscellaneous administration expenses necessarily incurred in preserving and distributing the estate are deductible. These expenses include appraiser's and accountant's fees, certain court costs, and costs of storing or maintaining assets of the estate.

The expenses of selling assets are deductible only if the sale is necessary to pay the decedent's debts, the expenses of administration, or taxes, or to preserve the estate or carry out distribution.

I.R.S. Form 706 (Continued)

Form 706 (Rev. 7-99)

Estate of:

SCHEDULE K—Debts of the Decedent, and Mortgages and Liens

Item number	Debts of the Decedent—Creditor and nature of claim, and allowable death taxes	Amount unpaid to date	Amount in contest	Amount claimed as a deduction
1				
	Total from continuation schedules (or additional sheets) attached to this schedule			
	TOTAL. (Also enter on Part 5, Recapitulation, page 3, at item 14.)			

Item number	Mortgages and Liens—Description	Amount
1		
	Total from continuation schedules (or additional sheets) attached to this schedule	
	TOTAL. (Also enter on Part 5, Recapitulation, page 3, at item 15.)	

(If more space is needed, attach the continuation schedule from the end of this package or additional sheets of the same size.)
(The instructions to Schedule K are in the separate instructions.)

I.R.S. Form 706 (Continued)

Form 706 (Rev. 7-99)

Estate of:

SCHEDULE L—Net Losses During Administration and Expenses Incurred in Administering Property Not Subject to Claims

Item number	Net losses during administration (**Note:** *Do not deduct losses claimed on a Federal income tax return.*)	Amount
1		
	Total from continuation schedules (or additional sheets) attached to this schedule	
	TOTAL. (Also enter on Part 5, Recapitulation, page 3, at item 18.)	

Item number	Expenses incurred in administering property not subject to claims (Indicate whether estimated, agreed upon, or paid.)	Amount
1		
	Total from continuation schedules (or additional sheets) attached to this schedule	
	TOTAL. (Also enter on Part 5, Recapitulation, page 3, at item 19.)	

(If more space is needed, attach the continuation schedule from the end of this package or additional sheets of the same size.)

 (The instructions to Schedule L are in the separate instructions.)

I.R.S. Form 706 (Continued)

Form 706 (Rev. 7-99)

Estate of:

SCHEDULE M—Bequests, etc., to Surviving Spouse

Election To Deduct Qualified Terminable Interest Property Under Section 2056(b)(7). If a trust (or other property) meets the requirements of qualified terminable interest property under section 2056(b)(7), and

a. The trust or other property is listed on Schedule M, and

b. The value of the trust (or other property) is entered in whole or in part as a deduction on Schedule M,

then unless the executor specifically identifies the trust (all or a fractional portion or percentage) or other property to be excluded from the election, the executor shall be deemed to have made an election to have such trust (or other property) treated as qualified terminable interest property under section 2056(b)(7).

If less than the entire value of the trust (or other property) that the executor has included in the gross estate is entered as a deduction on Schedule M, the executor shall be considered to have made an election only as to a fraction of the trust (or other property). The numerator of this fraction is equal to the amount of the trust (or other property) deducted on Schedule M. The denominator is equal to the total value of the trust (or other property).

Election To Deduct Qualified Domestic Trust Property Under Section 2056A. If a trust meets the requirements of a qualified domestic trust under section 2056A(a) and this return is filed no later than 1 year after the time prescribed by law (including extensions) for filing the return, and

a. The entire value of a trust or trust property is listed on Schedule M, and

b. The entire value of the trust or trust property is entered as a deduction on Schedule M,

then unless the executor specifically identifies the trust to be excluded from the election, the executor shall be deemed to have made an election to have the entire trust treated as qualified domestic trust property.

			Yes	No
1	Did any property pass to the surviving spouse as a result of a qualified disclaimer? . . . . *If "Yes," attach a copy of the written disclaimer required by section 2518(b).*	1		
2a	In what country was the surviving spouse born? ____			
b	What is the surviving spouse's date of birth? ____			
c	Is the surviving spouse a U.S. citizen?	2c		
d	If the surviving spouse is a naturalized citizen, when did the surviving spouse acquire citizenship? ____			
e	If the surviving spouse is not a U.S. citizen, of what country is the surviving spouse a citizen? ____			
3	**Election Out of QTIP Treatment of Annuities**—Do you elect under section 2056(b)(7)(C)(ii) **not** to treat as qualified terminable interest property any joint and survivor annuities that are included in the gross estate and would otherwise be treated as qualified terminable interest property under section 2056(b)(7)(C)? (see instructions)	3		

Item number	Description of property interests passing to surviving spouse	Amount
1		
	Total from continuation schedules (or additional sheets) attached to this schedule	

4	**Total** amount of property interests listed on Schedule M	4	
5a	Federal estate taxes payable out of property interests listed on Schedule M . .	5a	
b	Other death taxes payable out of property interests listed on Schedule M . . .	5b	
c	Federal and state GST taxes payable out of property interests listed on Schedule M	5c	
d	Add items 5a, b, and c	5d	
6	Net amount of property interests listed on Schedule M (subtract 5d from 4). Also enter on Part 5, Recapitulation, page 3, at item 20	6	

(If more space is needed, attach the continuation schedule from the end of this package or additional sheets of the same size.)
(See the instructions on the reverse side.)

I.R.S. Form 706 (Continued)

Examples of Listing of Property Interests on Schedule M

Item number	Description of property interests passing to surviving spouse	Amount
1	One-half the value of a house and lot, 256 South West Street, held by decedent and surviving spouse as joint tenants with right of survivorship under deed dated July 15, 1957 (Schedule E, Part I, item 1)	$132,500
2	Proceeds of Gibraltar Life Insurance Company policy No. 104729, payable in one sum to surviving spouse (Schedule D, item 3)	200,000
3	Cash bequest under Paragraph Six of will	100,000

Instructions for Schedule M—Bequests, etc., to Surviving Spouse (Marital Deduction)

General

You must complete Schedule M and file it with the return if you claim a deduction on item 20 of Part 5, Recapitulation.

The marital deduction is authorized by section 2056 for certain property interests that pass from the decedent to the surviving spouse. You may claim the deduction only for property interests that are included in the decedent's gross estate (Schedules A through I).

Note: *The marital deduction is generally not allowed if the surviving spouse is* ***not*** *a U.S. citizen. The marital deduction is allowed for property passing to such a surviving spouse in a "qualified domestic trust" or if such property is transferred or irrevocably assigned to such a trust before the estate tax return is filed. The executor must elect qualified domestic trust status on this return. See the instructions that follow, on pages 29–30, for details on the election.*

Property Interests That You May List on Schedule M

Generally, you may list on Schedule M all property interests that pass from the decedent to the surviving spouse and are included in the gross estate. However, you should not list any "Nondeductible terminable interests" (described below) on Schedule M unless you are making a QTIP election. The property for which you make this election must be included on Schedule M. See "Qualified terminable interest property" on the following page.

For the rules on common disaster and survival for a limited period, see section 2056(b)(3).

You may list on Schedule M only those interests that the surviving spouse takes:

1. As the decedent's legatee, devisee, heir, or donee;

2. As the decedent's surviving tenant by the entirety or joint tenant;

3. As an appointee under the decedent's exercise of a power or as a taker in default at the decedent's nonexercise of a power;

4. As a beneficiary of insurance on the decedent's life;

5. As the surviving spouse taking under dower or curtesy (or similar statutory interest); and

6. As a transferee of a transfer made by the decedent at any time.

Property Interests That You May Not List on Schedule M

You should not list on Schedule M:

1. The value of any property that does not pass from the decedent to the surviving spouse;

2. Property interests that are not included in the decedent's gross estate;

3. The full value of a property interest for which a deduction was claimed on Schedules J through L. The value of the property interest should be reduced by the deductions claimed with respect to it;

4. The full value of a property interest that passes to the surviving spouse subject to a mortgage or other encumbrance or an obligation of the surviving spouse. Include on Schedule M only the net value of the interest after reducing it by the amount of the mortgage or other debt;

5. Nondeductible terminable interests (described below);

6. Any property interest disclaimed by the surviving spouse.

Terminable Interests

Certain interests in property passing from a decedent to a surviving spouse are referred to as *terminable interests.* These are interests that will terminate or fail after the passage of time, or on the occurrence or nonoccurrence of some contingency. Examples are: life estates, annuities, estates for terms of years, and patents.

The ownership of a bond, note, or other contractual obligation, which when discharged would not have the effect of an annuity for life or for a term, is not considered a terminable interest.

Nondeductible terminable interests. A terminable interest is *nondeductible,* and should not be entered on Schedule M (unless you are making a QTIP election) if:

1. Another interest in the same property passed from the decedent to some other person for less than adequate and full consideration in money or money's worth; and

2. By reason of its passing, the other person or that person's heirs may enjoy part of the property after the termination of the surviving spouse's interest.

This rule applies even though the interest that passes from the decedent to a person other than the surviving spouse is not included in the gross estate, and regardless of when the interest passes. The rule also applies regardless of whether the surviving spouse's interest and the other person's interest pass from the decedent at the same time.

Property interests that are considered to pass to a person other than the surviving spouse are any property interest that: **(a)** passes under a decedent's will or intestacy; **(b)** was transferred by a decedent during life; or **(c)** is held by or passed on to any person as a decedent's joint tenant, as appointee under a decedent's exercise of a power, as taker in default at a decedent's release or nonexercise of a power, or as a beneficiary of insurance on the decedent's life.

For example, a decedent devised real property to his wife for life, with remainder to his children. The life interest that passed to the wife does not qualify for the marital deduction because it will terminate at her death and the children will thereafter possess or enjoy the property.

However, if the decedent purchased a joint and survivor annuity for himself and his wife who survived him, the value of the survivor's annuity, to the extent that it is included in the gross estate, qualifies for the marital deduction because even though the interest will terminate on the wife's death, no one else will possess or enjoy any part of the property.

The marital deduction is not allowed for an interest that the decedent directed the executor or a trustee to convert, after death, into a terminable interest for the surviving spouse. The marital deduction is not allowed for such an interest even if there was no interest

I.R.S. Form 706 (Continued)

in the property passing to another person and even if the terminable interest would otherwise have been deductible under the exceptions described below for life estate and life insurance and annuity payments with powers of appointment. For more information, see Regulations sections 20.2056(b)-1(f) and 20.2056(b)-1(g), Example (7).

If any property interest passing from the decedent to the surviving spouse may be paid or otherwise satisfied out of any of a group of assets, the value of the property interest is, for the entry on Schedule M, reduced by the value of any asset or assets that, if passing from the decedent to the surviving spouse, would be nondeductible terminable interests. Examples of property interests that may be paid or otherwise satisfied out of any of a group of assets are a bequest of the residue of the decedent's estate, or of a share of the residue, and a cash legacy payable out of the general estate.

Example: A decedent bequeathed $100,000 to the surviving spouse. The general estate includes a term for years (valued at $10,000 in determining the value of the gross estate) in an office building, which interest was retained by the decedent under a deed of the building by gift to a son. Accordingly, the value of the specific bequest entered on Schedule M is $90,000.

Life Estate With Power of Appointment in the Surviving Spouse. A property interest, whether or not in trust, will be treated as passing to the surviving spouse, and will not be treated as a nondeductible terminable interest if: **(a)** the surviving spouse is entitled for life to all of the income from the entire interest; **(b)** the income is payable annually or at more frequent intervals; **(c)** the surviving spouse has the power, exercisable in favor of the surviving spouse or the estate of the surviving spouse, to appoint the entire interest; **(d)** the power is exercisable by the surviving spouse alone and (whether exercisable by will or during life) is exercisable by the surviving spouse in all events; and **(e)** no part of the entire interest is subject to a power in any other person to appoint any part to any person other than the surviving spouse (or the surviving spouse's legal representative or relative if the surviving spouse is disabled. See Rev. Rul. 85-35, 1985-1 C.B. 328). If these five conditions are satisfied only for a specific portion of the entire interest, see the section 2056(b) regulations to determine the amount of the marital deduction.

Life Insurance, Endowment, or Annuity Payments, With Power of Appointment in Surviving Spouse. A property interest consisting of the entire proceeds under a life insurance, endowment, or annuity contract is treated as passing from the decedent to the surviving spouse, and will not be treated as a nondeductible terminable interest if: **(a)** the surviving spouse is entitled to receive the proceeds in installments, or is entitled to interest on them, with all amounts payable during the life of the spouse, payable only to the surviving spouse; **(b)** the installment or interest payments are payable annually, or more frequently, beginning not later than 13 months after the decedent's death; **(c)** the surviving spouse has the power, exercisable in favor of the surviving spouse or of the estate of the surviving spouse, to appoint all amounts payable under the contract; **(d)** the power is exercisable by the surviving spouse alone and (whether exercisable by will or during life) is exercisable by the surviving spouse in all events; and **(e)** no part of the amount payable under the contract is subject to a power in any other person to appoint any part to any person other than the surviving spouse. If these five conditions are satisfied only for a specific portion of the proceeds, see the section 2056(b) regulations to determine the amount of the marital deduction.

Charitable Remainder Trusts. An interest in a charitable remainder trust will **not** be treated as a nondeductible terminable interest if:

1. The interest in the trust passes from the decedent to the surviving spouse; and

2. The surviving spouse is the only beneficiary of the trust other than charitable organizations described in section 170(c).

A "charitable remainder trust" is either a charitable remainder annuity trust or a charitable remainder unitrust. (See section 664 for descriptions of these trusts.)

Election To Deduct Qualified Terminable Interests (QTIP)

You may elect to claim a marital deduction for qualified terminable interest property or property interests. You make the QTIP election simply by listing the qualified terminable interest property on Schedule M and deducting its value. You are presumed to have made the QTIP election if you list the property and deduct its value on Schedule M. If you make this election, the surviving spouse's gross estate will include the value of the "qualified terminable interest property." See the instructions for line 6 of General Information for more details. **The election is irrevocable.**

If you file a Form 706 in which you do not make this election, you may not file an amended return to make the election unless you file the amended return on or before the due date for filing the original Form 706.

The effect of the election is that the property (interest) will be treated as passing to the surviving spouse and will not be treated as a nondeductible terminable interest. All of the other marital deduction requirements must still be satisfied before you may make this election. For example, you may not make this election for property or property interests that are not included in the decedent's gross estate.

Qualified terminable interest property is property **(a)** that passes from the decedent, and **(b)** in which the surviving spouse has a qualifying income interest for life.

The surviving spouse has a *qualifying income interest for life* if the surviving spouse is entitled to all of the income from the property payable annually or at more frequent intervals, or has a usufruct interest for life in the property, and during the surviving spouse's lifetime no person has a power to appoint any part of the property to any person other than the surviving spouse. An annuity is treated as an income interest regardless of whether the property from which the annuity is payable can be separately identified.

Amendments to Regulations sections 20.2044-1, 20.2056(b)-7 and 20.2056(b)-10 clarify that an interest in property is eligible for QTIP treatment if the income interest is contingent upon the executor's election even if that portion of the property for which no election is made will pass to or for the benefit of beneficiaries other than the surviving spouse.

The QTIP election may be made for all or any part of qualified terminable interest property. A partial election must relate to a fractional or percentile share of the property so that the elective part will reflect its proportionate share of the increase or decline in the whole of the property when applying sections 2044 or 2519. Thus, if the interest of the surviving spouse in a trust (or other property in which the spouse has a qualified life estate) is qualified terminable interest property, you may make an election for a part of the trust (or other property) only if the election relates to a defined fraction or percentage of the entire trust (or other property). The fraction or percentage may be defined by means of a formula.

Qualified Domestic Trust Election (QDOT)

The marital deduction is allowed for transfers to a surviving spouse who is not a U.S. citizen only if the property passes to the surviving spouse in a "qualified domestic trust" (QDOT) or if

I.R.S. Form 706 (Continued)

Form 706 (Rev. 7-99)

such property is transferred or irrevocably assigned to a QDOT before the decedent's estate tax return is filed.

A QDOT is any trust:

1. That requires at least one trustee to be either an individual who is a citizen of the United States or a domestic corporation;

2. That requires that no distribution of corpus from the trust can be made unless such a trustee has the right to withhold from the distribution the tax imposed on the QDOT;

3. That meets the requirements of any applicable regulations; and

4. For which the executor has made an election on the estate tax return of the decedent.

Note: *For trusts created by an instrument executed before November 5, 1990, paragraphs **1** and **2** above will be treated as met if the trust instrument requires that all trustees be individuals who are citizens of the United States or domestic corporations.*

You make the QDOT election simply by listing the qualified domestic trust or the **entire value** of the trust property on Schedule M and deducting its value. You are presumed to have made the QDOT election if you list the trust or trust property and deduct its value on Schedule M. **Once made, the election is irrevocable.**

If an election is made to deduct qualified domestic trust property under section 2056A(d), the following information should be provided for each qualified domestic trust on an attachment to this schedule:

1. The name and address of every trustee;

2. A description of each transfer passing from the decedent that is the source of the property to be placed in trust; and

3. The employer identification number (EIN) for the trust.

The election must be made for an entire QDOT trust. In listing a trust for which you are making a QDOT election, unless you specifically identify the trust as not subject to the election, the election will be considered made for the entire trust.

The determination of whether a trust qualifies as a QDOT will be made as of the date the decedent's Form 706 is filed. If, however, judicial proceedings are brought before the Form 706's due date (including extensions) to have the trust revised to meet the QDOT requirements, then the determination will not be made until the court-ordered changes to the trust are made.

Line 1

If property passes to the surviving spouse as the result of a qualified disclaimer, check "Yes" and attach a copy of the written disclaimer required by section 2518(b).

Line 3

Section 2056(b)(7) creates an automatic QTIP election for certain joint and survivor annuities that are includible in the estate under section 2039. To qualify, only the surviving spouse can have the right to receive payments before the death of the surviving spouse.

The executor can elect out of QTIP treatment, however, by checking the "Yes" box on line 3. Once made, the election is irrevocable. If there is more than one such joint and survivor annuity, you are not required to make the election for all of them.

If you make the election out of QTIP treatment by checking "Yes" on line 3, you cannot deduct the amount of the annuity on Schedule M. If you do not make the election out, you must list the joint and survivor annuities on Schedule M.

Listing Property Interests on Schedule M

List each property interest included in the gross estate that passes from the decedent to the surviving spouse and for which a marital deduction is claimed. This includes otherwise nondeductible terminable interest property for which you are making a QTIP election. Number each item in sequence and describe each item in detail. Describe the instrument (including any clause or paragraph number) or provision of law under which each item passed to the surviving spouse. If possible, show where each item appears (number and schedule) on Schedules A through I.

In listing otherwise nondeductible property for which you are making a QTIP election, unless you specifically identify a fractional portion of the trust or other property as not subject to the election, the election will be considered made for all of the trust or other property.

Enter the value of each interest before taking into account the Federal estate tax or any other death tax. The valuation dates used in determining the value of the gross estate apply also on Schedule M.

If Schedule M includes a bequest of the residue or a part of the residue of the decedent's estate, attach a copy of the computation showing how the value of the residue was determined. Include a statement showing:

- The value of all property that is included in the decedent's gross estate (Schedules A through I) but is not a part of the decedent's probate estate, such as lifetime transfers, jointly owned property that passed to the survivor on decedent's death, and the insurance payable to specific beneficiaries.
- The values of all specific and general legacies or devises, with reference to the applicable clause or paragraph of the decedent's will or codicil. (If legacies are made to each member of a class; for example, $1,000 to each of decedent's employees, only the number in each class and the total value of property received by them need be furnished.)
- The date of birth of all persons, the length of whose lives may affect the value of the residuary interest passing to the surviving spouse.
- Any other important information such as that relating to any claim to any part of the estate not arising under the will.

Lines 5a, b, and c—The total of the values listed on Schedule M must be reduced by the amount of the Federal estate tax, the Federal GST tax, and the amount of state or other death and GST taxes paid out of the property interest involved. If you enter an amount for state or other death or GST taxes on lines 5b or 5c, identify the taxes and attach your computation of them.

Attachments. If you list property interests passing by the decedent's will on Schedule M, attach a certified copy of the order admitting the will to probate. If, when you file the return, the court of probate jurisdiction has entered any decree interpreting the will or any of its provisions affecting any of the interests listed on Schedule M, or has entered any order of distribution, attach a copy of the decree or order. In addition, the District Director may request other evidence to support the marital deduction claimed.

I.R.S. Form 706 (Continued)

Form 706 (Rev. 7-99)

Estate of:

SCHEDULE O—Charitable, Public, and Similar Gifts and Bequests

		Yes	No
1a	If the transfer was made by will, has any action been instituted to have interpreted or to contest the will or any of its provisions affecting the charitable deductions claimed in this schedule? If "Yes," full details must be submitted with this schedule.		
b	According to the information and belief of the person or persons filing this return, is any such action planned? If "Yes," full details must be submitted with this schedule.		
2	Did any property pass to charity as the result of a qualified disclaimer? If "Yes," attach a copy of the written disclaimer required by section 2518(b).		

Item number	Name and address of beneficiary	Character of institution	Amount
1			

Total from continuation schedules (or additional sheets) attached to this schedule			
3 Total		**3**	
4a Federal estate tax payable out of property interests listed above	**4a**		
b Other death taxes payable out of property interests listed above	**4b**		
c Federal and state GST taxes payable out of property interests listed above	**4c**		
d Add items 4a, b, and c		**4d**	
5 Net value of property interests listed above (subtract 4d from 3). Also enter on Part 5, Recapitulation, page 3, at item 21		**5**	

(If more space is needed, attach the continuation schedule from the end of this package or additional sheets of the same size.)
(The instructions to Schedule O are in the separate instructions.)

I.R.S. Form 706 (Continued)

Form 706 (Rev. 7-99)

Estate of:

SCHEDULE P—Credit for Foreign Death Taxes

List all foreign countries to which death taxes have been paid and for which a credit is claimed on this return.

If a credit is claimed for death taxes paid to more than one foreign country, compute the credit for taxes paid to one country on this sheet and attach a separate copy of Schedule P for each of the other countries.

The credit computed on this sheet is for the ....
(Name of death tax or taxes)

.... imposed in ....
(Name of country)

Credit is computed under the ....
(Insert title of treaty or "statute")

Citizenship (nationality) of decedent at time of death

(All amounts and values must be entered in United States money.)

1 Total of estate, inheritance, legacy, and succession taxes imposed in the country named above attributable to property situated in that country, subjected to these taxes, and included in the gross estate (as defined by statute)	1	
2 Value of the gross estate (adjusted, if necessary, according to the instructions for item 2)	2	
3 Value of property situated in that country, subjected to death taxes imposed in that country, and included in the gross estate (adjusted, if necessary, according to the instructions for item 3)	3	
4 Tax imposed by section 2001 reduced by the total credits claimed under sections 2010, 2011, and 2012 (see instructions)	4	
5 Amount of Federal estate tax attributable to property specified at item 3. (Divide item 3 by item 2 and multiply the result by item 4.)	5	
6 Credit for death taxes imposed in the country named above (the smaller of item 1 or item 5). Also enter on line 18 of Part 2, Tax Computation	6	

SCHEDULE Q—Credit for Tax on Prior Transfers

Part 1—Transferor Information

	Name of transferor	Social security number	IRS office where estate tax return was filed	Date of death
A				
B				
C				

Check here ▶ ☐ if section 2013(f) (special valuation of farm, etc., real property) adjustments to the computation of the credit were made (see page 18 of the instructions).

Part 2—Computation of Credit (see instructions beginning on page 18)

Item	Transferor			Total A, B, & C
	A	B	C	
1 Transferee's tax as apportioned (from worksheet, (line 7 ÷ line 8) × line 35 for each column)				
2 Transferor's tax (from each column of worksheet, line 20)				
3 Maximum amount before percentage requirement (for each column, enter amount from line 1 or 2, whichever is smaller)				
4 Percentage allowed (each column) (see instructions)	%	%	%	
5 Credit allowable (line 3 × line 4 for each column)				
6 TOTAL credit allowable (add columns A, B, and C of line 5). Enter here and on line 19 of Part 2, Tax Computation				

(The instructions to Schedules P and Q are in the separate instructions.)

I.R.S. Form 706 (Continued)

Form 706 (Rev. 7-99)

SCHEDULE R—Generation-Skipping Transfer Tax

Note: *To avoid application of the deemed allocation rules, Form 706 and Schedule R should be filed to allocate the GST exemption to trusts that may later have taxable terminations or distributions under section 2612 even if the form is not required to be filed to report estate or GST tax.*

The GST tax is imposed on taxable transfers of interests in property located ***outside the United States*** *as well as property located inside the United States.*

See instructions beginning on page 19.

Part 1—GST Exemption Reconciliation (Section 2631) and Section 2652(a)(3) (Special QTIP) Election

You no longer need to check a box to make a section 2652(a)(3) (special QTIP) election. If you list qualifying property in Part 1, line 9, below, you will be considered to have made this election. See page 21 of the separate instructions for details.

1 Maximum allowable GST exemption 1

2 Total GST exemption allocated by the decedent against decedent's lifetime transfers . 2

3 Total GST exemption allocated by the executor, using Form 709, against decedent's lifetime transfers 3

4 GST exemption allocated on line 6 of Schedule R, Part 2 4

5 GST exemption allocated on line 6 of Schedule R, Part 3 5

6 Total GST exemption allocated on line 4 of Schedule(s) R-1 6

7 Total GST exemption allocated to intervivos transfers and direct skips (add lines 2–6) 7

8 GST exemption available to allocate to trusts and section 2032A interests (subtract line 7 from line 1) 8

9 Allocation of GST exemption to trusts (as defined for GST tax purposes):

A Name of trust	B Trust's EIN (if any)	C GST exemption allocated on lines 2–6, above (see instructions)	D Additional GST exemption allocated (see instructions)	E Trust's inclusion ratio (optional—see instructions)

9D **Total.** May not exceed line 8, above 9D

10 GST exemption available to allocate to section 2032A interests received by individual beneficiaries (subtract line 9D from line 8). You must attach special use allocation schedule (see instructions) 10

(The instructions to Schedule R are in the separate instructions.)

I.R.S. Form 706 (Continued)

Form 706 (Rev. 7-99)

Estate of:

Part 2—Direct Skips Where the Property Interests Transferred Bear the GST Tax on the Direct Skips

Name of skip person	Description of property interest transferred	Estate tax value

1 Total estate tax values of all property interests listed above	1	
2 Estate taxes, state death taxes, and other charges borne by the property interests listed above .	2	
3 GST taxes borne by the property interests listed above but imposed on direct skips other than those shown on this Part 2 (see instructions)	3	
4 Total fixed taxes and other charges (add lines 2 and 3).	4	
5 Total tentative maximum direct skips (subtract line 4 from line 1)	5	
6 GST exemption allocated	6	
7 Subtract line 6 from line 5	7	
8 GST tax due (divide line 7 by 2.818182).	8	
9 Enter the amount from line 8 of Schedule R, Part 3	9	
10 **Total GST taxes payable by the estate** (add lines 8 and 9). Enter here and on line 22 of Part 2—Tax Computation, on page 1	10	

I.R.S. Form 706 (Continued)

Form 706 (Rev. 7-99)

Estate of:

Part 3—Direct Skips Where the Property Interests Transferred Do Not Bear the GST Tax on the Direct Skips

Name of skip person	Description of property interest transferred	Estate tax value

1 Total estate tax values of all property interests listed above	**1**	
2 Estate taxes, state death taxes, and other charges borne by the property interests listed above .	**2**	
3 GST taxes borne by the property interests listed above but imposed on direct skips other than those shown on this Part 3 (see instructions)	**3**	
4 Total fixed taxes and other charges (add lines 2 and 3).	**4**	
5 Total tentative maximum direct skips (subtract line 4 from line 1)	**5**	
6 GST exemption allocated	**6**	
7 Subtract line 6 from line 5	**7**	
8 GST tax due (multiply line 7 by .55). Enter here and on Schedule R, Part 2, line 9	**8**	

I.R.S. Form 706 (Continued)

SCHEDULE R-1 (Form 706) (Rev. July 1999) Department of the Treasury Internal Revenue Service	**Generation-Skipping Transfer Tax** Direct Skips From a Trust Payment Voucher	OMB No. 1545-0015

Executor: File one copy with Form 706 and send two copies to the fiduciary. Do not pay the tax shown. See the separate instructions.
Fiduciary: See instructions on the following page. Pay the tax shown on line 6.

Name of trust		**Trust's EIN**
Name and title of fiduciary	Name of decedent	
Address of fiduciary (number and street)	Decedent's SSN	Service Center where Form 706 was filed
City, state, and ZIP code	Name of executor	
Address of executor (number and street)	City, state, and ZIP code	
Date of decedent's death	Filing due date of Schedule R, Form 706 (with extensions)	

Part 1—Computation of the GST Tax on the Direct Skip

Description of property interests subject to the direct skip		Estate tax value
1 Total estate tax value of all property interests listed above	1	
2 Estate taxes, state death taxes, and other charges borne by the property interests listed above.	2	
3 Tentative maximum direct skip from trust (subtract line 2 from line 1)	3	
4 GST exemption allocated	4	
5 Subtract line 4 from line 3	5	
6 **GST tax due from fiduciary** (divide line 5 by 2.818182) **(See instructions if property will not bear the GST tax.)**	6	

Under penalties of perjury, I declare that I have examined this return, including accompanying schedules and statements, and to the best of my knowledge and belief, it is true, correct, and complete.

Signature(s) of executor(s) Date

Date

Signature of fiduciary or officer representing fiduciary Date

I.R.S. Form 706 (Continued)

Instructions for the Trustee

Introduction

Schedule R-1 (Form 706) serves as a payment voucher for the Generation-Skipping Transfer (GST) tax imposed on a direct skip from a trust, which you, the trustee of the trust, must pay. The executor completes the Schedule R-1 (Form 706) and gives you 2 copies. File one copy and keep one for your records.

How to pay

You can pay by check or money order.

- Make it payable to the "United States Treasury."
- Make the check or money order for the amount on line 6 of Schedule R-1.
- Write "GST Tax" and the trust's EIN on the check or money order.

Signature

You must sign the Schedule R-1 in the space provided.

What to mail

Mail your check or money order and the copy of Schedule R-1 that you signed.

Where to mail

Mail to the Service Center shown on Schedule R-1.

When to pay

The GST tax is due and payable 9 months after the decedent's date of death (shown on the Schedule R-1). You will owe interest on any GST tax not paid by that date.

Automatic extension

You have an automatic extension of time to file Schedule R-1 and pay the GST tax. The automatic extension allows you to file and pay by 2 months after the due date (with extensions) for filing the decedent's Schedule R (shown on the Schedule R-1).

If you pay the GST tax under the automatic extension, you will be charged interest (but no penalties).

Additional information

For more information, see Code section 2603(a)(2) and the instructions for Form 706, United States Estate (and Generation-Skipping Transfer) Tax Return.

I.R.S. Form 706 (Continued)

Form 706 (Rev. 7-99)

Estate of:

SCHEDULE T—Qualified Family-Owned Business Interest Deduction

For details on the deduction, including trades and businesses that do not qualify, see page 22 of the separate Instructions for Form 706.

Part 1—Election

Note: *The executor is deemed to have made the election under section 2057 if he or she files Schedule T and deducts any qualifying business interests from the gross estate.*

Part 2—General Qualifications

1 Did the decedent and/or a member of the decedent's family own the business interests listed on line 5 of this schedule for at least 5 of the 8 years immediately preceding the date of the decedent's death? . ☐ **Yes** ☐ **No**

2 Were there any periods during the 8-year period preceding the date of the decedent's death during which the decedent or a member of his or her family:

	Yes	No
a Did not own the business interests listed on this schedule?		
b Did not materially participate, within the meaning of section 2032A(e)(6), in the operation of the business to which such interests relate?.		

If "Yes" to either of the above, you must attach a statement listing the periods. If applicable, describe whether the exceptions of sections 2032A(b)(4) or (5) are met.

Attach affidavits describing the activities constituting material participation and the identity and relationship to the decedent of the material participants.

3 Check the applicable box(es). The qualified family-owned business interest(s) is:

☐ An interest as a proprietor in a trade or business carried on as a proprietorship.

☐ An interest in an entity, at least 50% of which is owned (directly or indirectly) by the decedent and members of the decedent's family.

☐ An interest in an entity, at least 70% of which is owned (directly or indirectly) by members of 2 families and at least 30% of which is owned (directly or indirectly) by the decedent and members of the decedent's family.

☐ An interest in an entity, at least 90% of which is owned (directly or indirectly) by members of 3 families and at least 30% of which is owned (directly or indirectly) by the decedent and members of the decedent's family.

4 Persons holding interests. Enter the requested information for each party who received any interest in the family-owned business. If any qualified heir is not a U.S. citizen, see the line 4 instructions beginning on page 23 of the separate instructions.

(Each of the qualified heirs receiving an interest in the business must sign the agreement that begins on the following page 40, and the agreement must be filed with this return.)

	Name	Address
A		
B		
C		
D		
E		
F		
G		
H		

	Identifying number	Relationship to decedent	Value of interest
A			
B			
C			
D			
E			
F			
G			
H			

I.R.S. Form 706 (Continued)

Form 706 (Rev. 7-99)

Part 3—Adjusted Value of Qualified Family-Owned Business Interests

5 Qualified family-owned business interests reported on this return.
Note: *All property listed on line 5 must also be entered on Schedules A, B, C, E, F, G, or H, as applicable.*

A Schedule and item number from Form 706	B Description of business interest and principal place of business	C Reported value

6 **Total** reported value			6	
7 Amount of claims or mortgages deductible under section 2053(a)(3) or (4) (see separate instructions)		7		
8a Enter the amount of any indebtedness on qualified residence of the decedent (see separate instructions)	8a			
b Enter the amount of any indebtedness used for educational or medical expenses (see separate instructions)	8b			
c Enter the amount of any indebtedness other than that listed on line 8a or 8b, but do not enter more than $10,000 (see separate instructions)	8c			
d Total (add lines 8a through 8c)		8d		
9 Subtract line 8d from line 7			9	
10 Adjusted value of qualified family-owned business interests (subtract line 9 from line 6)			10	

Part 4—Qualifying Estate

11 Includible gifts of qualified family-owned business interests (see separate instructions):				
a Amount of gifts taken into account under section 2001(b)(1)(B)		11a		
b Amount of such gifts excluded under section 2503(b)		11b		
c Add lines 11a and 11b			11c	
12 Add lines 10 and 11c			12	
13 Adjusted gross estate (see separate instructions):				
a Amount of gross estate	13a			
b Enter the amount from line 7	13b			
c Subtract line 13b from line 13a		13c		
d Enter the amount from line 11c	13d			
e Enter the amount of transfers, if any, to the decedent's spouse (see inst.)	13e			
f Enter the amount of other gifts (see inst.)	13f			
g Add the amounts on lines 13d, 13e, and 13f	13g			
h Enter any amounts from line 13g that are otherwise includible in the gross estate	13h			
i Subtract line 13h from line 13g		13i		
j Adjusted gross estate (add lines 13c and 13i)			13j	
14 Enter one-half of the amount on line 13j			14	

Note: *If line 12 does not exceed line 14, stop here; the estate does not qualify for the deduction. Otherwise, complete line 15.*

15 Net value of qualified family-owned business interests you elect to deduct (line 10 reduced by any marital or other deductions)—**DO NOT** enter more than $675,000—(see instructions) (attach schedule)—enter here and on Part 5, Recapitulation, page 3, at item 22	15	

I.R.S. Form 706 (Continued)

Form 706 (Rev. 7-99)

Part 5—Agreement to Family-Owned Business Interest Deduction Under Section 2057

Estate of:	Date of Death	Decedent's Social Security Number

There cannot be a valid election unless:

- The agreement is executed by each and every one of the qualified heirs, and
- The agreement is included with the estate tax return when the estate tax return is filed.

We (list all qualified heirs and other persons having an interest in the business required to sign this agreement)

____

____,

being all the qualified heirs and ____

____,

being all other parties having interests in the business(es) which are deducted under section 2057 of the Internal Revenue Code, do hereby approve of the election made by ____,

Executor/Administrator of the estate of ____,

pursuant to section 2057 to deduct said interests from the gross estate and do hereby enter into this agreement pursuant to section 2057(h).

The undersigned agree and consent to the application of subsection (f) of section 2057 of the Code with respect to all the qualified family-owned business interests deducted on Schedule T of Form 706, attached to this agreement. More specifically, the undersigned heirs expressly agree and consent to personal liability under subsection (c) of 2032A (as made applicable by section 2057(i)(3)(F) of the Code) for the additional estate tax imposed by that subsection with respect to their respective interests in the above-described business interests in the event of certain early dispositions of the interests or the occurrence of any of the disqualifying acts described in section 2057(f)(1) of the Code. It is understood that if a qualified heir disposes of any deducted interest to any member of his or her family, such member may thereafter be treated as the qualified heir with respect to such interest upon filing a new agreement and any other form required by the Internal Revenue Service.

The undersigned interested parties who are not qualified heirs consent to the collection of any additional estate tax imposed under section 2057(f) of the Code from the deducted interests.

If there is a disposition of any interest which passes or has passed to him or her, each of the undersigned heirs agrees to file the appropriate form and pay any additional estate tax due within 6 months of the disposition or other disqualifying act.

It is understood by all interested parties that this agreement is a condition precedent to the election of the qualified family-owned business deduction under section 2057 of the Code and must be executed by every interested party even though that person may not have received the estate tax benefits or be in possession of such property.

Each of the undersigned understands that by making this election, a lien will be created and recorded pursuant to section 6324B of the Code on the interests referred to in this agreement for the applicable percentage of the adjusted tax differences with respect to the estate as defined in section 2057(f)(2)(C).

As the interested parties, the undersigned designate the following individual as their agent for all dealings with the Internal Revenue Service concerning the continued qualification of the deducted property under section 2057 of the Code and on all issues regarding the special lien under section 6324B. The agent is authorized to act for all the parties with respect to all dealings with the Service on matters affecting the qualified interests described earlier. This authority includes the following:

- To receive confidential information on all matters relating to continued qualification under section 2057 of the deducted interests and on all matters relating to the special lien arising under section 6324B.
- To furnish the Service with any requested information concerning the interests.
- To notify the Service of any disposition or other disqualifying events specified in section 2057(f)(1) of the Code.
- To receive, but not to endorse and collect, checks in payment of any refund of Internal Revenue taxes, penalties, or interest.
- To execute waivers (including offers of waivers) of restrictions on assessment or collection of deficiencies in tax and waivers of notice of disallowance of a claim for credit or refund.
- To execute closing agreements under section 7121.

(continued on next page)

I.R.S. Form 706 (Continued)

Form 706 (Rev. 7-99)

Part 5. Agreement to Family-Owned Business Interest Deduction Under Section 2057 (continued)

Estate of:	Date of Death	**Decedent's Social Security Number**

• Other acts (specify) ▶ ______________________________

By signing this agreement, the agent agrees to provide the Internal Revenue Service with any requested information concerning the qualified business interests and to notify the Internal Revenue Service of any disposition or other disqualifying events with regard to said interests.

Name of Agent	Signature	Address

The interests to which this agreement relates are listed in Form 706, United States Estate (and Generation-Skipping Transfer) Tax Return, along with their fair market value according to section 2031 (or, if applicable, section 2032A) of the Code. The name, address, social security number, and interest (including the value) of each of the undersigned in this business(es) are as set forth in the attached Schedule T.

IN WITNESS WHEREOF, the undersigned have hereunto set their hands at ______________________________,

this __________ day of __________.

SIGNATURES OF EACH OF THE QUALIFIED HEIRS:

Signature of qualified heir	Signature of qualified heir
Signature of qualified heir	Signature of qualified heir
Signature of qualified heir	Signature of qualified heir
Signature of qualified heir	Signature of qualified heir
Signature of qualified heir	Signature of qualified heir
Signature of qualified heir	Signature of qualified heir

Signature(s) of other interested parties

Signature(s) of other interested parties

I.R.S. Form 706 (Continued)

Form 706 (Rev. 7-99)

Estate of:

SCHEDULE U. Qualified Conservation Easement Exclusion

Part 1—Election

Note: *The executor is deemed to have made the election under section 2031(c)(6) if he or she files Schedule U and excludes any qualifying conservation easements from the gross estate.*

Part 2—General Qualifications

1 Describe the land subject to the qualified conservation easement (see separate instructions) ____________

2 Did the decedent or a member of the decedent's family own the land described above during the 3-year period ending on the date of the decedent's death? . . . . ☐ **Yes** ☐ **No**

3 The land described above is located (check whichever applies) (see separate instructions):

☐ In or within 25 miles of an area which, on the date of the decedent's death, is a metropolitan area.

☐ In or within 25 miles of an area which, on the date of the decedent's death, is a national park or wilderness area.

☐ In or within 10 miles of an area which, on the date of the decedent's death, is an Urban National Forest.

4 Describe the conservation easement with regard to which the exclusion is being claimed (see separate instructions).

____

Part 3—Computation of Exclusion

5	Estate tax value of the land subject to the qualified conservation easement (see separate instructions)		5	
6	Date of death value of any easements granted prior to decedent's death and included on line 11 below (see instructions)	6		
7	Add lines 5 and 6	7		
8	Value of retained development rights on the land (see instructions)	8		
9	Subtract line 8 from line 7	9		
10	Multiply line 9 by 30% (.30).	10		
11	Value of qualified conservation easement for which the exclusion is being claimed (see instructions) . . . . **Note:** *If line 11 is less than line 10, continue with line 12. If line 11 is equal to or more than line 10, skip lines 12 through 14, enter ".40" on line 15, and complete the schedule.*	11		
12	Divide line 11 by line 9. Figure to 3 decimal places (e.g., .123) . . *If line 12 is equal to or less than .100, stop here; the estate does not qualify for the conservation easement exclusion.*	12		
13	Subtract line 12 from .300. Enter the answer in hundredths by rounding any thousandths up to the next higher hundredth (i.e., .030 = .03; but .031 = .04).	13		
14	Multiply line 13 by 2	14		
15	Subtract line 14 from .40	15		
16	Deduction under section 2055(f) for the conservation easement (see separate instructions)	16		
17	Amount of indebtedness on the land (see separate instructions)	17		
18	Total reductions in value (add lines 8, 16, and 17)		18	
19	Net value of land (subtract line 18 from line 5)		19	
20	Multiply line 19 by line 15		20	
21	Enter the smaller of line 20 or the exclusion limitation (see instructions). Also enter this amount on item 11, Part 5, Recapitulation, Page 3.		21	

I.R.S. Form 706 (Continued)

Form 706 (Rev. 7-99) (Make copies of this schedule before completing it if you will need more than one schedule.)

Estate of:

CONTINUATION SCHEDULE

Continuation of Schedule ______________________
(Enter letter of schedule you are continuing.)

Item number	Description For securities, give CUSIP number.	Unit value (Sch. B, E, or G only)	Alternate valuation date	Alternate value	Value at date of death or amount deductible
	TOTAL. (Carry forward to main schedule.)				

See the instructions on the reverse side.

I.R.S. Form 706 (Continued)

Form 706 (Rev. 7-99)

Instructions for Continuation Schedule

When you need to list more assets or deductions than you have room for on one of the main schedules, use the Continuation Schedule on page 43. It provides a uniform format for listing additional assets from Schedules A through I and additional deductions from Schedules J, K, L, M, and O.

Please keep the following points in mind:

- Use a separate Continuation Schedule for each main schedule you are continuing. Do not combine assets or deductions from different schedules on one Continuation Schedule.
- Make copies of the blank schedule before completing it if you expect to need more than one.
- Use as many Continuation Schedules as needed to list all the assets or deductions.
- Enter the letter of the schedule you are continuing in the space at the top of the Continuation Schedule.
- Use the *Unit value* column only if continuing Schedule B, E, or G. For all other schedules, use this space to continue the description.
- Carry the total from the Continuation Schedules forward to the appropriate line on the main schedule.

If continuing	Report	Where on Continuation Schedule
Schedule E, Pt. 2	*Percentage includible*	*Alternate valuation date*
Schedule K	*Amount unpaid to date*	*Alternate valuation date*
Schedule K	*Amount in contest*	*Alternate value*
Schedules J, L, M	*Description of deduction continuation*	*Alternate valuation date* **and** *Alternate value*
Schedule O	*Character of institution*	*Alternate valuation date* **and** *Alternate value*
Schedule O	*Amount of each deduction*	*Amount deductible*

Printed on recycled paper

☆ U. S. GOVERNMENT PRINTING OFFICE: 1999-715-015/69035

I.R.S.—Instructions for Form 706

Instructions for Form 706

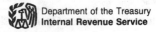

Department of the Treasury
Internal Revenue Service

(Revised July 1998)

United States Estate (and Generation-Skipping Transfer) Tax Return

For decedents dying after December 31, 1997, and before January 1, 1999.
Section references are to the Internal Revenue Code unless otherwise noted.

Paperwork Reduction Act Notice.— We ask for the information on this form to carry out the Internal Revenue laws of the United States. You are required to give us the information. We need it to ensure that you are complying with these laws and to allow us to figure and collect the right amount of tax.

You are not required to provide the information requested on a form that is subject to the Paperwork Reduction Act unless the form displays a valid OMB control number. Books or records relating to a form or its instructions must be retained as long as their contents may become material in the administration of any Internal Revenue law. Generally, tax returns and return information are confidential as required by section 6103.

The time needed to complete and file this form and related schedules will vary depending on individual circumstances. The estimated average times are:

Form	Recordkeeping	Learning about the law or the form	Preparing the form	Copying, assembling, and sending the form to the IRS
706	2 hr., 11 min.	1 hr., 25 min.	3 hr., 34 min.	49 min.
Sch. A	20 min.	16 min.	10 min.	20 min.
A-1	46 min.	25 min.	59 min.	49 min.
B	20 min.	16 min.	20 min.	20 min.
C	13 min.	2 min.	8 min.	20 min.
D	7 min.	6 min.	8 min.	20 min.
E	40 min.	7 min.	24 min.	20 min.
F	33 min.	8 min.	21 min.	20 min.
G	26 min.	23 min.	11 min.	14 min.
H	26 min.	7 min.	10 min.	14 min.
I	26 min.	27 min.	11 min.	20 min.
J	26 min.	7 min.	16 min.	20 min.
K	26 min.	10 min.	10 min.	20 min.
L	13 min.	5 min.	10 min.	20 min.
M	13 min.	29 min.	24 min.	20 min.
O	20 min.	11 min.	18 min.	17 min.
P	7 min.	14 min.	18 min.	14 min.
Q	7 min.	10 min.	11 min.	14 min.
Q Wksht.	7 min.	10 min.	59 min.	20 min.
R	20 min.	34 min.	1 hr., 1 min.	49 min.
R-1	7 min.	29 min.	24 min.	20 min.
T	1 hr., 12 min.	26 min.	1 hr., 14 min.	1 hr., 3 min.
U	20 min.	3 min.	29 min.	20 min.
Contin.	20 min.	3 min.	7 min.	20 min.

If you have comments concerning the accuracy of these time estimates or suggestions for making this form simpler, we would be happy to hear from you. You can write to the Tax Forms Committee, Western Area Distribution Center, Rancho Cordova, CA 95743-0001. **DO NOT** send the tax form to this address. Instead, see **Where To File** on page 2.

For Decedents Dying After	and	Before	Use Revision of Form 706 Dated
-------------		January 1, 1982	November 1981
December 31, 1981		October 23, 1986	November 1987
December 31, 1989		October 9, 1990	October 1988
October 8, 1990		January 1, 1998	April 1997

General Instructions

Changes To Note

Unified credit.— For the estates of decedents dying in 1998, the unified credit has increased to $202,050. Also, it is no longer phased out for large estates.

Family-owned business interest deduction.— Beginning with the estates of decedents dying in 1998, the executor can elect to deduct from the gross estate the value of certain qualified family-owned business interests. See new Schedule T and its separate instructions.

Conservation easement exclusion.— Beginning with the estates of decedents dying in 1998, the executor can elect to exclude from the gross estate a portion of the value of land subject to certain qualified conservation easements. See new Schedule U and its separate instructions.

Section 6166 election.— Beginning with the estates of decedents dying in 1998, the interest rates on installment payments of estate tax have changed, and the interest payments are no longer deductible by the estate. See the instructions for **Line 3—Installment Payments** on page 5.

Tax on excess accumulations.— The additional estate tax on excess accumulations has been repealed beginning with the estates of decedents dying in 1997, and Schedule S has been eliminated.

Purpose of Form

The executor of a decedent's estate uses Form 706 to figure the estate tax imposed by Chapter 11 of the Internal Revenue Code. This tax is levied on the entire taxable estate, not just on the share received by a particular beneficiary. Form 706 is also used to compute the generation-skipping transfer (GST) tax imposed by Chapter 13 on direct skips (transfers to skip persons of interests in property included in the decedent's gross estate).

Which Estates Must File

Form 706 must be filed by the executor for the estate of every U.S. citizen or resident whose gross estate, plus adjusted taxable gifts and specific exemption, is more than $625,000.

To determine whether you must file a return for the estate, add:

1. The adjusted taxable gifts (under section 2001(b)) made by the decedent after December 31, 1976;

2. The total specific exemption allowed under section 2521 (as in effect before its repeal by the Tax Reform Act of 1976) for gifts made by the decedent after September 8, 1976; and

3. The decedent's gross estate **valued at the date of death.**

Gross Estate

The gross estate includes all property in which the decedent had an interest (including real property outside the United States). It also includes:

- Certain transfers made during the decedent's life without an adequate and full consideration in money or money's worth;
- Annuities;
- The includible portion of joint estates with right of survivorship (see the instructions on the back of Schedule E);
- The includible portion of tenancies by the entirety (see the instructions on the back of Schedule E);
- Certain life insurance proceeds (even though payable to beneficiaries other than the estate)(see the instructions on the back of Schedule D);
- Property over which the decedent possessed a general power of appointment;
- Dower or curtesy (or statutory estate) of the surviving spouse;
- Community property to the extent of the decedent's interest as defined by applicable law.

I.R.S.—Instructions for Form 706 (Continued)

For more specific information, see the instructions for Schedules A through I.

U.S. Citizens or Residents; Nonresident Noncitizens

File Form 706 for the estates of decedents who were either U.S. citizens or U.S. residents at the time of death. For estate tax purposes, a resident is someone who had a domicile in the United States at the time of death. A person acquires a domicile by living in a place for even a brief period of time, as long as the person had no intention of moving from that place.

File **Form 706-NA,** United States Estate (and Generation-Skipping Transfer) Tax Return, Estate of nonresident not a citizen of the United States, for the estates of nonresident alien decedents (decedents who were neither U.S. citizens nor residents at the time of death).

Residents of U.S. Possessions

All references to citizens of the United States are subject to the provisions of sections 2208 and 2209, relating to decedents who were U.S. citizens and residents of a U.S. possession on the date of death. If such a decedent became a U.S. citizen only because of his or her connection with a possession, then the decedent is considered a nonresident alien decedent for estate tax purposes, and you should file Form 706-NA. If such a decedent became a U.S. citizen wholly independently of his or her connection with a possession, then the decedent is considered a U.S. citizen for estate tax purposes, and you should file Form 706.

Executor

The term "executor" means the executor, personal representative, or administrator of the decedent's estate. If none of these is appointed, qualified, and acting in the United States, every person in actual or constructive possession of any property of the decedent is considered an executor and must file a return.

When To File

You must file Form 706 to report estate and/or generation-skipping transfer tax within 9 months after the date of the decedent's death unless you receive an extension of time to file. Use **Form 4768,** Application for Extension of Time To File a Return and/or Pay U.S. Estate (and Generation-Skipping Transfer) Taxes, to apply for an extension of time to file. If you received an extension, attach a copy of it to Form 706.

Where To File

Unless the return is hand carried to the office of the District Director, please mail it to the Internal Revenue Service Center indicated below for the state where the **decedent was domiciled** at the time of death. If you are filing a return for the estate of a nonresident U.S. citizen, mail it to the Internal Revenue Service Center, Philadelphia, PA 19255, USA.

Where To File

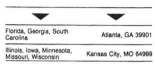

Florida, Georgia, South Carolina	Atlanta, GA 39901
Illinois, Iowa, Minnesota, Missouri, Wisconsin	Kansas City, MO 64999
New Jersey, New York (New York City and counties of Nassau, Rockland, Suffolk, and Westchester)	Holtsville, NY 00501
New York (all other counties), Connecticut, Maine, Massachusetts, New Hampshire, Rhode Island, Vermont	Andover, MA 05501
Delaware, District of Columbia, Maryland, Pennsylvania, Virginia	Philadelphia, PA 19255
Indiana, Kentucky, Michigan, Ohio, West Virginia	Cincinnati, OH 45999
Kansas, New Mexico, Oklahoma, Texas	Austin, TX 73301
Alaska, Arizona, California (counties of Alpine, Amador, Butte, Calaveras, Colusa, Contra Costa, Del Norte, El Dorado, Glenn, Humboldt, Lake, Lassen, Marin, Mendocino, Modoc, Napa, Nevada, Placer, Plumas, Sacramento, San Joaquin, Shasta, Sierra, Siskiyou, Solano, Sonoma, Sutter, Tehama, Trinity, Yolo, and Yuba), Colorado, Idaho, Montana, Nebraska, Nevada, North Dakota, Oregon, South Dakota, Utah, Washington, Wyoming	Ogden, UT 84201
California (all other counties), Hawaii	Fresno, CA 93888
Alabama, Arkansas, Louisiana, Mississippi, North Carolina, Tennessee	Memphis, TN 37501

Paying the Tax

The estate and GST taxes are due within 9 months after the date of the decedent's death unless an extension of time for payment has been granted, or unless you have properly elected under section 6166 to pay in installments, or under section 6163 to postpone the part of the tax attributable to a reversionary or remainder interest. These elections are made by checking lines 3 and 4 (respectively) of Part 3, Elections by the Executor, and attaching the required statements.

If the tax paid with the return is different from the balance due as figured on the return, explain the difference in an attached statement. If you have made prior payments to IRS or redeemed certain marketable United States Treasury bonds to pay the estate tax (see the last paragraph of the instructions to Schedule B), attach a statement to Form 706 including these facts. If an extension of time to pay has been granted, attach a copy of the approved Form 4768 to Form 706.

Make the check payable to the Internal Revenue Service. Please write the decedent's name, social security number, and "Form 706" on the check to assist us in posting it to the proper account.

Signature and Verification

If there is more than one executor, all listed executors must verify and sign the return. All executors are responsible for the return as filed and are liable for penalties provided for erroneous or false returns.

If two or more persons are liable for filing the return, they should all join together in filing one complete return. However, if they are unable to join in making one complete return, each is required to file a return disclosing all the information the person has in the case, including the name of every person holding an interest in the property and a full description of the property. If the appointed, qualified, and acting executor is unable to make a complete return, then every person holding an interest in the property must, on notice from the IRS, make a return regarding that interest.

The executor who files the return must, in every case, sign the declaration on page 1 under penalties of perjury. If the return is prepared by someone other than the person who is filing the return, the preparer must also sign at the bottom of page 1.

Amending Form 706

If you find that you must change something on a return that has already been filed, you should file another Form 706 and write "Supplemental Information" across the top of page 1 of the form. If you have already been notified that the return has been selected for examination, you should provide the additional information directly to the office conducting the examination.

Part 1

Line 2

Enter the social security number assigned specifically to the decedent. You cannot use the social security number assigned to the decedent's spouse. If the decedent did not have a social security number, the executor should obtain one for the decedent by filing **Form SS-5** with a local Social Security Administration office.

Line 6a—Name of Executor

If there is more than one executor, enter the name of the executor to be contacted by the IRS. List the other executors' names, addresses, and SSNs (if applicable) on an attached sheet.

Line 6b—Executor's Address

Use **Form 8822,** Change of Address, to report a change of the executor's address.

Line 6c—Executor's Social Security Number

Only individual executors should complete this line. If there is more than one individual executor, all should list their social security numbers on an attached sheet.

Supplemental Documents

You must attach the death certificate to the return.

If the decedent was a citizen or resident and died testate, attach a certified copy of the will to the return. If you cannot obtain a certified copy, attach a copy of the will and an explanation of why it is not certified. Other supplemental documents may be required as explained below. Examples include Forms 712, 709, 709-A, and 706-CE, trust and power of appointment instruments, death certificate, and state certification of payment of death taxes. If you do not file these documents with the return, the processing of the return will be delayed.

If the decedent was a U.S. citizen but not a resident of the United States, you must attach the following documents to the return: (1) a copy of the inventory of property and the schedule of liabilities, claims against the estate, and expenses of administration filed with the foreign court of probate jurisdiction, certified by a proper official of the court; (2) a copy of the return filed under the foreign inheritance, estate, legacy, succession tax, or other death tax act, certified by a proper official of the foreign tax department, if the estate is subject

I.R.S.—Instructions for Form 706 (Continued)

to such a foreign tax; and (3) if the decedent died testate, a certified copy of the will.

Rounding Off to Whole Dollars

You may show the money items on the return and accompanying schedules as whole-dollar amounts. To do so, drop any amount less than 50 cents and increase any amount from 50 cents through 99 cents to the next higher dollar.

Penalties

Late filing and late payment.— Section 6651 provides for penalties for both late filing and for late payment unless there is reasonable cause for the delay. The law also provides for penalties for willful attempts to evade payment of tax. The late filing penalty will not be imposed if the taxpayer can show that the failure to file a timely return is due to reasonable cause. Executors filing late (after the due date, including extensions) should attach an explanation to the return to show reasonable cause.

Valuation understatement.— Section 6662 provides a penalty for the underpayment of estate tax of $5,000 or more when the underpayment is attributable to valuation understatements. A valuation understatement occurs when the value of property reported on Form 706 is 50% or less of the actual value of the property.

This penalty increases to 40% if there is a **gross** valuation understatement. A gross valuation understatement occurs if any property on the return is valued at 25% or less of the value determined to be correct.

These penalties also apply to late filing, late payment, and underpayment of GST taxes.

Specific Instructions

You must file the first three pages of Form 706 and all required schedules. Schedules A through I must be filed, as appropriate, to support the entries in items 1 through 9 of the Recapitulation.

If you enter zero on any item of the Recapitulation, you need not file the schedule (except for Schedule F) referred to on that item.

If you claim an exclusion on item 11, you must complete and attach Schedule U.

If you claim any deductions on items 13 through 23 of the Recapitulation, you must complete and attach the appropriate schedules to support the claimed deductions.

If you claim the credits for foreign death taxes or tax on prior transfers, you must complete and attach Schedule P or Q.

Form 706 has 44 numbered pages. The pages are perforated so that you can remove them for copying and filing. When you complete the return, staple all the required pages together in the proper order.

Number the items you list on each schedule, beginning with 1 each time. Total the items listed on the schedule and its attachments, Continuation Schedules, etc. Enter the total of all attachments, Continuation Schedules, etc., at the bottom of the printed schedule, but do not carry the totals forward from one schedule to the next. Enter the total or totals for each schedule on the Recapitulation, page 3, Form 706.

Do not complete the "Alternate valuation date" or "Alternate value" columns of any schedule unless you elected alternate valuation on line 1 of Part 3, Elections by the Executor.

If there is not enough space on a schedule to list all the items, attach a Continuation Schedule (or additional sheets of the same size) to the back of the schedule. The Continuation Schedule is located at the end of the Form 706 package. You should photocopy the blank schedule before completing it if you will need more than one copy.

Instructions for Part 3.—Elections by the Executor

Line 1—Alternate Valuation

Unless you elect at the time you file the return to adopt alternate valuation as authorized by section 2032, you must value all property included in the gross estate on the date of the decedent's death. Alternate valuation cannot be applied to only a part of the property. You may elect special use valuation (line 2) in addition to alternate valuation.

You may not elect alternate valuation unless the election will decrease both the value of the gross estate and the total net estate and GST taxes due after application of all allowable credits.

You elect alternate valuation by checking "Yes" on line 1 and filing Form 706. Once made, the election may not be revoked. The election may be made on a late filed Form 706 provided it is not filed later than 1 year after the due date (including extensions).

If you elect alternate valuation, value the property that is included in the gross estate as of the applicable dates as follows:

1. Any property distributed, sold, exchanged, or otherwise disposed of or separated or passed from the gross estate by any method within 6 months after the decedent's death is valued on the date of distribution, sale, exchange, or other disposition, whichever occurs first. Value this property on the date it ceases to form a part of the gross estate, that is, on the date the title passes as the result of its sale, exchange, or other disposition.

2. Any property not distributed, sold, exchanged, or otherwise disposed of within the 6-month period is valued on the date 6 months after the date of the decedent's death.

3. Any property, interest, or estate that is "affected by mere lapse of time" is valued as of the date of decedent's death or on the date of its distribution, sale, exchange, or other disposition, whichever occurs first. However, you may change the date of death value to account for any change in value that is not due to a "mere lapse of time" on the date of its distribution, sale, exchange, or other disposition.

The property included in the alternate valuation and valued as of 6 months after the date of the decedent's death, or as of some intermediate date (as described above) is the property included in the gross estate on the date of the decedent's death. Therefore, you must first determine what property constituted the gross estate at the decedent's death.

Interest accrued to the date of the decedent's death on bonds, notes, and other interest-bearing obligations is property of the gross estate on the date of death and is included in the alternate valuation. Rent accrued to the date of the decedent's death on leased real or personal property is property of the gross estate on the date of death and is included in the alternate valuation.

Outstanding dividends that were declared to stockholders of record on or before the date of the decedent's death are considered property of the gross estate on the date of death, and are included in the alternate valuation. Ordinary dividends declared to stockholders of record after the date of the decedent's death are not property of the gross estate on the date of death and are not included in the alternate valuation. However, if dividends are declared to stockholders of record after the date of the decedent's death so that the shares of stock at the later valuation date do not reasonably represent the same property at the date of the decedent's death, include those dividends (except dividends paid from earnings of the corporation after the date of the decedent's death) in the alternate valuation.

As part of each Schedule A through I, you must show:

1. what property is included in the gross estate on the date of the decedent's death;

2. what property was distributed, sold, exchanged, or otherwise disposed of within the 6-month period after the decedent's death, and the dates of these distributions, etc. These two items should be entered in the "Description" column of each schedule. Briefly explain the status or disposition governing the alternate valuation date, such as: "Not disposed of within 6 months following death," "Distributed," "Sold," "Bond paid on maturity," etc. In this same column, describe each item of principal and includible income;

3. the date of death value, entered in the appropriate value column with items of principal and includible income shown separately; and

4. the alternate value, entered in the appropriate value column with items of principal and includible income shown separately. In the case of any interest or estate, the value of which is affected by lapse of time, such as patents, leaseholds, estates for the life of another, or remainder interests, the value shown under the heading "Alternate value" must be the adjusted value (i.e., the value as of the date of death with an adjustment reflecting any difference in its value as of the later date not due to lapse of time).

Distributions, sales, exchanges, and other dispositions of the property within the 6-month period after the decedent's death must be supported by evidence. If the court issued an order of distribution during that period, you must submit a certified copy of the order as part of the evidence. The District Director may require you to submit additional evidence if necessary.

If the alternate valuation method is used, the values of life estates, remainders, and similar interests are figured using the age of the recipient on the date of the decedent's death and the value of the property on the alternate valuation date.

Line 2—Special Use Valuation of Section 2032A

In general.— Under section 2032A, you may elect to value certain farm and closely held business real property at its farm or business use value rather than its fair market value. You may elect both special use valuation and alternate valuation.

To elect this valuation you must check "Yes" to line 2 and complete and attach Schedule A-1 and its required additional statements. You must file **Schedule A-1 and its required attachments with Form 706 for this election to be valid.** You may make the election on a late filed return so long as it is the first return filed.

The total value of the property valued under section 2032A may not be decreased from fair market value by more than $750,000.

Real property may qualify for the section 2032A election if:

1. The decedent was a U.S. citizen or resident at the time of death;

I.R.S.—Instructions for Form 706 (Continued)

2. The real property is located in the United States;

3. At the decedent's death the real property was used by the decedent or a family member for farming or in a trade or business, or was rented for such use by either the surviving spouse or a lineal descendant of the decedent to a family member on a net cash basis;

4. The real property was acquired from or passed from the decedent to a qualified heir of the decedent;

5. The real property was owned and used in a qualified manner by the decedent or a member of the decedent's family during 5 of the 8 years before the decedent's death;

6. There was material participation by the decedent or a member of the decedent's family during 5 of the 8 years before the decedent's death; and

7. The qualified property meets the following percentage requirements:

a. At least 50% of the adjusted value of the gross estate must consist of the adjusted value of real or personal property that was being used as a farm or in a closely held business and that was acquired from, or passed from, the decedent to a qualified heir of the decedent, and

b. At least 25% of the adjusted value of the gross estate must consist of the adjusted value of qualified farm or closely held business real property.

For this purpose, adjusted value is the value of property determined without regard to its special-use value. The value is reduced for unpaid mortgages on the property or any indebtedness against the property, if the full value of the decedent's interest in the property (not reduced by such mortgage or indebtedness) is included in the value of the gross estate. The adjusted value of the qualified real and personal property used in different businesses may be combined to meet the 50% and 25% requirements.

Qualified Real Property

Qualified use.— The term qualified use means the use of the property as a farm for farming purposes or the use of property in a trade or business other than farming. Trade or business applies only to the active conduct of a business. It does not apply to passive investment activities or the mere passive rental of property to a person other than a member of the decedent's family. Also, no trade or business is present in the case of activities not engaged in for profit.

Ownership.— To qualify as special-use property, the decedent or a member of the decedent's family must have owned and used the property in a qualified use for 5 of the last 8 years before the decedent's death. Ownership may be direct or indirect through a corporation, a partnership, or a trust.

If the ownership is indirect, the business must qualify as a closely held business under section 6166. The ownership, when combined with periods of direct ownership, must meet the requirements of section 6166 on the date of the decedent's death and for a period of time that equals at least 5 of the 8 years preceding death.

If the property was leased by the decedent to a closely held business, it qualifies as long as the business entity to which it was rented was a closely held business with respect to the decedent on the date of the decedent's death and for sufficient time to meet the "5 in 8 years" test explained above.

Structures and other real property improvements.— Qualified real property includes residential buildings and other structures and real property improvements regularly occupied or used by the owner or lessee of real property (or by the employees of the owner or lessee) to operate the farm or business. A farm residence which the decedent had occupied is considered to have been occupied for the purpose of operating the farm even when a family member and not the decedent was the person materially participating in the operation of the farm.

Qualified real property also includes roads, buildings, and other structures and improvements functionally related to the qualified use.

Elements of value such as mineral rights that are not related to the farm or business use are not eligible for special-use valuation.

Property acquired from the decedent.— Property is considered to have been acquired from or to have passed from the decedent if one of the following applies:

- The property is considered to have been acquired from or to have passed from the decedent under section 1014(b) (relating to basis of property acquired from a decedent).
- The property is acquired by any person from the estate.
- The property is acquired by any person from a trust, to the extent the property is includible in the gross estate.

Qualified heir.— A person is a qualified heir of property if he or she is a member of the decedent's family and acquired or received the property from the decedent. If a qualified heir disposes of any interest in qualified real property to any member of his or her family, that person will then be treated as the qualified heir with respect to that interest.

The term **member of the family** includes only:

1. An ancestor (parent, grandparent, etc.) of the individual;

2. The spouse of the individual;

3. The lineal descendant (child, stepchild, grandchild, etc.) of the individual, the individual's spouse, or a parent of the individual; or

4. The spouse, widow, or widower of any lineal descendant described above.

A legally adopted child of an individual is treated as a child of that individual by blood.

Material Participation

To elect special-use valuation, either the decedent or a member of his or her family must have materially participated in the operation of the farm or other business for at least 5 of the 8 years ending on the date of the decedent's death. The existence of material participation is a factual determination, but passively collecting rents, salaries, draws, dividends, or other income from the farm or other business does not constitute material participation. Neither does merely advancing capital and reviewing a crop plan and financial reports each season or business year.

In determining whether the required participation has occurred, disregard brief periods (e.g., 30 days or less) during which there was no material participation, as long as such periods were both preceded and followed by substantial periods (more than 120 days) during which there was uninterrupted material participation.

Retirement or disability.— If, on the date of death, the time period for material participation could not be met because the decedent had retired or was disabled, a substitute period may apply. The decedent must have retired on Social Security or been disabled for a continuous period ending with death. A person is disabled for this purpose if he or she was mentally or physically unable to materially participate in the operation of the farm or other business.

The substitute time period for material participation for these decedents is a period totaling at least 5 years out of the 8-year period that ended on the earlier of (1) the date the decedent began receiving social security benefits, or (2) the date the decedent became disabled.

Surviving spouse.— A surviving spouse who received qualified real property from the predeceased spouse is considered to have materially participated if he or she was engaged in the active management of the farm or other business. If the surviving spouse died within 8 years of the first spouse's death, you may add the period of material participation of the predeceased spouse to the period of active management by the surviving spouse to determine if the surviving spouse's estate qualifies for special-use valuation. To qualify for this, the property must have been eligible for special-use valuation in the predeceased spouse's estate, though it does not have to have been elected by that estate.

For additional details regarding material participation, see Regulations section 20.2032A-3(e).

Valuation Methods

The primary method of valuing special-use value property that is used for farming purposes is the annual gross cash rental method. If comparable gross cash rentals are not available, you can substitute comparable average annual net share rentals. If neither of these are available, or if you so elect, you can use the method for valuing real property in a closely held business.

Average annual gross cash rental.— Generally, the special-use value of property that is used for farming purposes is determined as follows:

1. Subtract the average annual state and local real estate taxes on actual tracts of comparable real property from the average annual gross cash rental for that same comparable property, and

2. Divide the result in **1** by the average annual effective interest rate charged for all new Federal Land Bank loans.

The computation of each average annual amount is based on the 5 most recent calendar years ending before the date of the decedent's death.

Gross cash rental.— Generally, gross cash rental is the total amount of cash received in a calendar year for the use of actual tracts of comparable farm real property in the same locality as the property being specially valued. You may not use appraisals or other statements regarding rental value or areawide averages of rentals. You may not use rents that are paid wholly or partly in kind, and the amount of rent may not be based on production. The rental must have resulted from an arm's-length transaction. Also, the amount of rent is not reduced by the amount of any expenses or liabilities associated with the farm operation or the lease.

Comparable property.— Comparable property must be situated in the same locality as the specially valued property as determined by generally accepted real property valuation rules. The determination of comparability is based on all the facts and circumstances. It is often necessary to value land in segments where there are different uses or land characteristics included in the specially valued land. The following list contains some of the factors considered in determining comparability.

- Similarity of soil.

I.R.S. — Instructions for Form 706 (Continued)

- Whether the crops grown would deplete the soil in a similar manner.
- Types of soil conservation techniques that have been practiced on the 2 properties.
- Whether the 2 properties are subject to flooding.
- Slope of the land.
- For livestock operations, the carrying capacity of the land.
- For timbered land, whether the timber is comparable.
- Whether the property as a whole is unified or segmented; if segmented, the availability of the means necessary for movement among the different sections.
- Number, types, and conditions of all buildings and other fixed improvements located on the properties and their location as it affects efficient management, use, and value of the property.
- Availability and type of transportation facilities in terms of costs and of proximity of the properties to local markets.

You must specifically identify on the return the property being used as comparable property. Use the type of descriptions used to list real property on Schedule A.

Effective interest rate.— To get the effective annual interest in effect for the year of death and the area in which the property is located, contact your IRS District Director.

Net share rental.— You may use average annual net share rental from comparable land only if there is no comparable land from which average annual gross cash rental can be determined. Net share rental is the difference between the gross value of produce received by the lessor from the comparable land and the cash operating expenses (other than real estate taxes) of growing the produce that, under the lease, are paid by the lessor. The production of the produce must be the business purpose of the farming operation. For this purpose, produce includes livestock.

The gross value of the produce is generally the gross amount received if the produce was disposed of in an arm's-length transaction within the period established by the Department of Agriculture for its price support program. Otherwise, the value is the weighted average price for which the produce sold on the closest national or regional commodities market. The value is figured for the date or dates on which the lessor received (or constructively received) the produce.

Valuing a real property interest in closely held business.— Use this method to determine the special-use valuation for qualifying real property used in a trade or business other than farming. You may also use this method for qualifying farm property if there is no comparable land or if you elect to use it. Under this method, the following factors are considered:

- The capitalization of income that the property can be expected to yield for farming or for closely held business purposes over a reasonable period of time with prudent management and traditional cropping patterns for the area, taking into account soil capacity, terrain configuration, and similar factors.
- The capitalization of the fair rental value of the land for farming or for closely held business purposes.
- The assessed land values in a state that provides a differential or use value assessment law for farmland or closely held business.
- Comparable sales of other farm or closely held business land in the same geographical area far enough removed from a metropolitan or resort area so that nonagricultural use is not a significant factor in the sales price.
- Any other factor that fairly values the farm or closely held business value of the property.

Making the Election

Include the words "section 2032A valuation" in the "Description" column of any Form 706 schedule if section 2032A property is included in the decedent's gross estate.

An election under section 2032A need not include all the property in an estate that is eligible for special use valuation, but sufficient property to satisfy the threshold requirements of section 2032A(b)(1)(B) must be specially valued under the election.

If joint or undivided interests (e.g., interests as joint tenants or tenants in common) in the same property are received from a decedent by qualified heirs, an election with respect to one heir's joint or undivided interest need not include any other heir's interest in the same property if the electing heir's interest plus other property to be specially valued satisfies the requirements of section 2032A(b)(1)(B).

If successive interests (e.g., life estates and remainder interests) are created by a decedent in otherwise qualified property, an election under section 2032A is available only with respect to that property (or part) in which qualified heirs of the decedent receive all of the successive interests, and such an election must include the interests of all of those heirs.

For example, if a surviving spouse receives a life estate in otherwise qualified property and the spouse's brother receives a remainder interest in fee, no part of the property may be valued pursuant to an election under section 2032A.

Where successive interests in specially valued property are created, remainder interests are treated as being received by qualified heirs only if the remainder interests are not contingent on surviving a nonfamily member or are not subject to divestment in favor of a nonfamily member.

Protective Election

You may make a protective election to specially value qualified real property. Under this election, whether or not you may ultimately use special use valuation depends upon values as finally determined (or agreed to following examination of the return) meeting the requirements of section 2032A.

To make a protective election, check "Yes" to line 2 and complete Schedule A-1 according to its instructions for "Protective Election."

If you make a protective election, you should complete this Form 706 by valuing all property at its fair market value. Do not use special use valuation. Usually, this will result in higher estate and GST tax liabilities than will be ultimately determined if special use valuation is allowed. **The protective election does not extend the time to pay the taxes shown on the return.** If you wish to extend the time to pay the taxes, you should file Form 4768 in adequate time *before* the return due date.

If it is found that the estate qualifies for special use valuation based on the values as finally determined (or agreed to following examination of the return), you must file an amended Form 706 (with a complete section 2032A election) within 60 days after the date of this determination. Complete the amended return using special use values under the rules of section 2032A, and complete Schedule A-1 and attach *all* of the required statements.

Additional Information

For definitions and additional information, see section 2032A and the related regulations.

Line 3—Installment Payments

If the gross estate includes an interest in a closely held business, you may be able to elect to pay part of the estate tax in installments.

The maximum amount that can be paid in installments is that part of the estate tax that is attributable to the closely held business. In general, that amount is the amount of tax that bears the same ratio to the total estate tax that the value of the closely held business included in the gross estate bears to the total gross estate.

Percentage requirements.— To qualify for installment payments, the value of the interest in the closely held business that is included in the gross estate must be more than 35% of the adjusted gross estate (the gross estate less expenses, indebtedness, taxes, and losses).

Interests in two or more closely held businesses are treated as an interest in a single business if at least 20% of the total value of each business is included in the gross estate. For this purpose, include any interest held by the surviving spouse that represents the surviving spouse's interest in a business held jointly with the decedent as community property or as joint tenants, tenants by the entirety, or tenants in common.

Value.— The value used for meeting the percentage requirements is the same value used for determining the gross estate. Therefore, if the estate is valued under alternate valuation or special use valuation, you must use those values to meet the percentage requirements.

Transfers before death.— Generally, gifts made before death are not included in the gross estate. However, the estate must meet the 35% requirement by both including and excluding in the gross estate any gifts made by the decedent within 3 years of death.

Passive assets.— In determining the value of a closely held business and whether the 35% requirement is met, do not include the value of any passive assets held by the business. A **passive asset** is any asset not used in carrying on a trade or business. Stock in another corporation is a passive asset unless the stock is treated as held by the decedent because of the election to treat holding company stock as business company stock, as discussed on page 6.

If a corporation owns at least 20% in value of the voting stock of another corporation, or the other corporation had no more than 15 shareholders and at least 80% of the value of the assets of each corporation is attributable to assets used in carrying on a trade or business, then these corporations will be treated as a single corporation, and the stock will not be treated as a passive asset. Stock held in the other corporation is not taken into account in determining the 80% requirement.

Interest in closely held business.— For purposes of the installment payment election, an interest in a closely held business means:

- Ownership of a trade or business carried on as a proprietorship.
- An interest as a partner in a partnership carrying on a trade or business if 20% or more of the total capital interest was included in the gross estate of the decedent or the partnership had no more than 15 partners.
- Stock in a corporation carrying on a trade or business if 20% or more in value of the voting stock of the corporation is included in the gross estate of the decedent or the corporation had no more than 15 shareholders.

The partnership or corporation must be carrying on a trade or business at the time of the decedent's death.

I.R.S. —Instructions for Form 706 (Continued)

In determining the number of partners or shareholders, a partnership or stock interest is treated as owned by one partner or shareholder if it is community property or held by a husband and wife as joint tenants, tenants in common, or as tenants by the entirety.

Property owned directly or indirectly by or for a corporation, partnership, estate, or trust is treated as owned proportionately by or for its shareholders, partners, or beneficiaries. For trusts, only beneficiaries with current interests are considered.

The interest in a closely held farm business includes the interest in the residential buildings and related improvements occupied regularly by the owners, lessees, and employees operating the farm.

Holding company stock.— The executor may elect to treat as business company stock the portion of any holding company stock that represents direct ownership (or indirect ownership through one or more other holding companies) in a business company. A **holding company** is a corporation holding stock in another corporation. A **business company** is a corporation carrying on a trade or business.

This election applies only to stock that is not readily tradable. For purposes of the 20% voting stock requirement, stock is treated as voting stock to the extent the holding company owns voting stock in the business company.

If the executor makes this election, the first installment payment is due when the estate tax return is filed. The 5-year deferral for payment of the tax, as discussed below under **Time for payment**, does not apply. In addition, the 2% interest rate, discussed below under **Interest computation**, will not apply.

Time for payment.— Under the installment method, the executor may elect to **defer** payment of the qualified estate tax, but not interest, for up to 5 years from the original payment due date. After the first installment of tax is paid, you must pay the remaining installments annually by the date one year after the due date of the preceding installment. There can be no more than 10 installment payments.

Interest on the unpaid portion of the tax is not deferred and must be paid annually. Interest must be paid at the same time as and as a part of each installment payment of the tax.

For information on the acceleration of payment when an interest in the closely held business is disposed of, see section 6166(g).

Interest computation.— A special interest rate applies to installment payments. The interest rate is 2% on the lesser of:

- $320,618, or
- The amount of the estate tax that is attributable to the closely held business and that is payable in installments.

Interest on the portion of the tax in excess of the 2% portion is figured at 45% of the annual rate of interest on underpayments. This rate is based on the Federal short-term rate and is announced quarterly by the IRS in the Internal Revenue Bulletin.

If you elect installment payments and the estate tax due is more than the maximum amount to which the 2% interest rate applies, each installment payment is deemed to comprise both tax subject to the 2% interest rate and tax subject to 45% of the regular underpayment rate. The amount of each installment that is subject to the 2% rate is the same as the percentage of total tax payable in installments that is subject to the 2% rate.

Important: *Beginning with the estates of decedents dying in 1998, the interest paid on installment payments is **not** deductible as an administrative expense of the estate.*

Making the election.— If you check this line to make a protective election, you should attach a notice of protective election as described in Regulations section 20.6166-1(d). If you check this line to make a final election, you should attach the notice of election described in Regulations section 20.6166-1(b).

In computing the adjusted gross estate under section 6166(b)(6) to determine whether an election may be made under section 6166, the net amount of any real estate in a closely held business must be used.

You may also elect to pay GST taxes in installments. See section 6166(i).

Line 4—Reversionary or Remainder Interests

For details of this election, see section 6163 and the related regulations.

Instructions for Part 4.— General Information (Pages 2 and 3)

Power of Attorney

Completing the authorization on page 2 of Form 706 will authorize one attorney, accountant, or enrolled agent to represent the estate and receive confidential tax information, but will not authorize the representative to enter into closing agreements for the estate. **If you wish to represent the estate, you must complete and sign the authorization.**

If you wish to authorize persons other than attorneys, accountants, and enrolled agents, or if you wish to authorize more than one person, to receive confidential information or represent the estate, you must complete and attach **Form 2848,** Power of Attorney and Declaration of Representative.

You must also complete and attach Form 2848 if you wish to authorize someone to enter into closing agreements for the estate.

If you wish only to authorize someone to inspect and/or receive confidential tax information (but not to represent you before the IRS), complete and file **Form 8821,**Tax Information Authorization.

Line 4

Complete line 4 whether or not there is a surviving spouse and whether or not the surviving spouse received any benefits from the estate. If there was no surviving spouse on the date of decedent's death, enter "None" in line 4a and leave lines 4b and 4c blank. The value entered in line 4c need not be exact. See the instructions for "Amount" under line 5, below.

Line 5

Name.— Enter the name of each individual, trust, or estate who received (or will receive) benefits of $5,000 or more from the estate directly as an heir, next-of-kin, devisee, or legatee; or indirectly (for example, as beneficiary of an annuity or insurance policy, shareholder of a corporation, or partner of a partnership that is an heir, etc.).

Identifying number.— Enter the social security number of each individual beneficiary listed. If the number is unknown, or the individual has no number, please indicate "unknown" or "none." For trusts and other estates, enter the employer identification number.

Relationship.— For each individual beneficiary enter the relationship (if known) to the decedent by reason of blood, marriage, or adoption. For trust or estate beneficiaries, indicate TRUST or ESTATE.

Amount.— Enter the amount actually distributed (or to be distributed) to each beneficiary including transfers during the decedent's life from Schedule G required to be included in the gross estate. The value to be entered need not be exact. A reasonable estimate is sufficient. For example, where precise values cannot readily be determined, as with certain future interests, a reasonable approximation should be entered. The total of these distributions should approximate the amount of gross estate reduced by funeral and administrative expenses, debts and mortgages, bequests to surviving spouse, charitable bequests, and any Federal and state estate and GST taxes paid (or payable) relating to the benefits received by the beneficiaries listed on lines 4 and 5.

All distributions of less than $5,000 to specific beneficiaries may be included with distributions to unascertainable beneficiaries on the line provided.

Line 6—Section 2044 Property

If you answered "Yes," these assets must be shown on Schedule F.

Section 2044 property is property for which a previous section 2056(b)(7) election (QTIP election) has been made, or for which a similar gift tax election (section 2523) has been made. For more information, see the instructions on the back of Schedule F.

Line 8—Insurance Not Included in the Gross Estate

If you checked "Yes" for either 8a or 8b, you must complete and attach Schedule D and attach a **Form 712,** Life Insurance Statement, for each policy and an explanation of why the policy or its proceeds are not includible in the gross estate.

Line 10—Partnership Interests and Stock in Close Corporations

If you answered "Yes" to line 10, you must include full details for partnerships and unincorporated businesses on Schedule F (Schedule E if the partnership interest is jointly owned). You must include full details for the stock of inactive or close corporations on Schedule B.

Value these interests using the rules of Regulations section 20.2031-2 (stocks) or 20.2031-3 (other business interests).

A "close corporation" is a corporation whose shares are owned by a limited number of shareholders. Often, one family holds the entire stock issue. As a result, little, if any, trading of the stock takes place. There is, therefore, no established market for the stock, and those sales that do occur are at irregular intervals and seldom reflect all the elements of a representative transaction as defined by the term "fair market value."

Line 12—Trusts

If you answered "Yes" to either 12a or 12b, you must attach a copy of the trust instrument for each trust.

You must complete Schedule G if you answered "Yes" to 12a and Schedule F if you answered "Yes" to 12b.

Line 14—Transitional Marital Deduction Computation

You must check "Yes" if property passes to the surviving spouse under a maximum marital deduction formula provision that meets the requirements of section 403(e)(3) of the Economic Recovery Tax Act of 1981 (P.L. 97-34; 95 Stat. 305).

I.R.S.—Instructions for Form 706 (Continued)

If you check "Yes" to line 14, you must compute the marital deduction under the rules that were in effect before the Economic Recovery Tax Act of 1981.

For a format for this computation, you should obtain the November 1981 revision of Form 706 and its instructions. The computation is items 19 through 26 of the Recapitulation. You should also apply the rules of Rev. Rul. 80-148, 1980-1 C.B. 207, if there is property that passes to the surviving spouse outside of the maximum marital deduction formula provision.

Instructions for Part 5.—Recapitulation (Page 3 of Form 706)

Gross Estate

Items 1 through 10.— You must make an entry in each of items 1 through 9. If the gross estate does not contain any assets of the type specified by a given item, enter zero for that item. Entering zero for any of items 1 through 9 is a statement by the executor, made under penalties of perjury, that the gross estate does not contain any includible assets covered by that item. Do not enter any amounts in the "Alternate value" column unless you elected alternate valuation on line 1 of Elections by the Executor on page 2.

Which schedules to attach for items 1 through 9.— You must attach Schedule F to the return and answer its questions even if you report no assets on it.

You must attach Schedules A, B, and C if the gross estate includes any Real Estate; Stocks and Bonds; or Mortgages, Notes, and Cash, respectively. You must attach Schedule D if the gross estate includes any Life Insurance or if you answered "Yes" to question 8a. You must attach Schedule E if the gross estate contains any Jointly Owned Property or if you answered "Yes" to question 9. You must attach Schedule G if the decedent made any of the lifetime transfers to be listed on that schedule or if you answered "Yes" to question 11 or 12a. You must attach Schedule H if you answered "Yes" to question 13. You must attach Schedule I if you answered "Yes" to question 15.

Exclusion

Item 11—Conservation easement exclusion.— You must complete and attach Schedule U (along with any required attachments) to claim the exclusion on this line.

Deductions

Items 13 through 23.— You must attach the appropriate schedules for the deductions you claim.

Item 17.— If item 16 is less than or equal to the value (at the time of the decedent's death) of the property subject to claims, enter the amount from item 16 on item 17.

If the amount on item 16 is more than the value of the property subject to claims, enter the greater of **(a)** the value of the property subject to claims, or **(b)** the amount actually paid at the time the return is filed.

In no event should you enter more on item 17 than the amount on item 16. See section 2053 and the related regulations for more information.

Instructions for Part 2.—Tax Computation (Page 1 of Form 706)

In general, the estate tax is figured by applying the unified rates shown in Table A to the total of transfers both during life and at death, and then subtracting the gift taxes. **You must complete the Tax Computation.**

Line 1

If you elected alternate valuation on line 1, Part 3, **Elections by the Executor,** enter the amount you entered in the "Alternate value" column of item 12 of Part 5, Recapitulation. Otherwise, enter the amount from the "Value at date of death" column.

Lines 4 and 9

Three worksheets are provided to help you compute the entries for these lines. You need not file these worksheets with your return but should keep them for your records. Worksheet TG allows you to reconcile the decedent's lifetime taxable gifts to compute totals that will be used for the line 4 and line 9 worksheets.

You must get all of the decedent's gift tax returns (**Form 709,** United States Gift (and Generation-Skipping Transfer) Tax Return) before you complete Worksheet TG. The amounts you will enter on Worksheet TG can usually be derived from these returns as filed. However, if any of the returns were audited by the IRS, you should use the amounts that were finally determined as a result of the audits.

In addition, you must include in column b of Worksheet TG any gifts in excess of the annual exclusion made by the decedent (or on behalf of the decedent under a power of attorney) but for which no Forms 709 were filed. You must make a reasonable inquiry as to the existence of any such gifts. The annual exclusion for 1977 through 1981 was $3,000 per donee per year and $10,000 for years after 1981.

Note: *In figuring the line 9 amount,* ***do not*** *include any tax paid or payable on gifts made before 1977. The line 9 amount is a hypothetical figure based only on gifts made after 1976 and used to calculate the estate tax.*

Special treatment of split gifts.— These special rules apply only if:

1. The decedent's spouse predeceased the decedent;

2. The decedent's spouse made gifts that were "split" with the decedent under the rules of section 2513;

3. The decedent was the "consenting spouse" for those split gifts, as that term is used on Form 709; and

4. The split gifts were included in the decedent's spouse's gross estate under section 2035.

If all four conditions above are met, *do not include* these gifts on line 4 of the Tax Computation and *do not include* the gift taxes payable on these gifts on line 9 of the Tax Computation. These adjustments are incorporated into the worksheets.

Line 7

Lines 7a–c are used to calculate the phaseout of the graduated rates. The phaseout applies only to estates in which the amount the tentative tax is computed on exceeds $10 million.

Line 12

If the decedent made gifts (including gifts made by the decedent's spouse and treated as made by the decedent by reason of gift splitting) after September 8, 1976, and before January 1, 1977, for which the decedent claimed a specific exemption, the unified credit on this estate tax return must be reduced. The reduction is figured by entering 20% of the specific exemption claimed for these gifts. (**Note:** *The specific exemption was allowed by section 2521 for gifts made before January 1, 1977.)*

If the decedent did not make any gifts between September 8, 1976, and January 1, 1977, or if the decedent made gifts during that period but did not claim the specific exemption, enter zero.

Line 15

You may take a credit on line 15 for estate, inheritance, legacy, or succession taxes paid as the result of the decedent's death to any state or the District of Columbia. However, see section 2053(d) and the related regulations for exceptions and limits if you elected to deduct the taxes from the value of the gross estate.

If you make a section 6166 election to pay the Federal estate tax in installments and make a similar election to pay the state death tax in installments, see Rev. Rul. 86-38, 1986-1 C.B. 296, for the method of computing the credit allowed with this Form 706.

If you have elected to extend the time to pay the tax on a reversionary or remainder interest, you may take a credit against that portion of the Federal estate tax for state death taxes attributable to the reversionary or remainder interest. The state death taxes must be paid and claimed before the expiration of the extended time for paying the estate tax.

The credit may not be more than the amount figured by using Table B on page 10, based on the value of the adjusted taxable estate. The adjusted taxable estate is the amount of the Federal taxable estate (line 3 of the Tax Computation) reduced by $60,000. You may claim an anticipated amount of credit and figure the Federal estate tax on the return before the state death taxes have been paid. However, the credit cannot be finally allowed unless you pay the state death taxes and claim the credit within 4 years after the return is filed (or later as provided by the Code if a petition is filed with the Tax Court of the United States, or if you have an extension of time to pay) and submit evidence that the tax has been paid. If you claim the credit for any state death tax that is later recovered, see Regulations section 20.2016-1 for the notice you are required to give the IRS within 30 days.

If you transfer property other than cash to the state in payment of state inheritance taxes, the amount you may claim as a credit is the lesser of the state inheritance tax liability discharged or the fair market value of the property on the date of the transfer.

For more details, see Rev. Rul. 86-117, 1986-2 C.B. 157.

You should send the following evidence to the IRS:

1. Certificate of the proper officer of the taxing state, or the District of Columbia, showing: (a) the total amount of tax imposed (before adding interest and penalties and before allowing discount); (b) the amount of discount allowed; (c) the amount of penalties and interest imposed or charged; (d) the total amount actually paid in cash; and (e) the date of payment.

2. Any additional proof the IRS specifically requests.

You should file the evidence requested above with the return if possible. Otherwise, send it as soon after you file the return as possible.

I.R.S.—Instructions for Form 706 (Continued)

Worksheet TG—Taxable Gifts Reconciliation

To be used for lines 4 and 9 of the Tax Computation

	a. Calendar year or calendar quarter	b. Total taxable gifts for period (see Note)	c. Taxable amount included in col. b for gifts included in the gross estate	d. Taxable amount included in col. b for gifts that qualify for "special treatment of split gifts" described above	e. Gift tax paid by decedent on gifts in col. d	f. Gift tax paid by decedent's spouse on gifts in col. c
Gifts made after June 6, 1932, and before 1977	1. Total taxable gifts made before 1977					
Gifts made after 1976						
2. Totals for gifts made after 1976						

Note: *For the definition of a taxable gift see section 2503. Ignore the old specific exemption. Follow Form 709. That is, include only the decedent's one-half of split gifts, whether the gifts were made by the decedent or the decedent's spouse. In addition to gifts reported on Form 709, you must include any taxable gifts in excess of the annual exclusion that were not reported on Form 709.*

Line 4 Worksheet—Adjusted Taxable Gifts Made After 1976

1. Taxable gifts made after 1976. Enter the amount from line 2, column b, Worksheet TG . . . . . .
2. Taxable gifts made after 1976 reportable on Schedule G. Enter the amount from line 2, column c, Worksheet TG . . . .
3. Taxable gifts made after 1976 that qualify for "special treatment." Enter the amount from line 2, column d, Worksheet TG . . . .
4. Add lines 2 and 3 . . . .
5. Adjusted taxable gifts. Subtract line 4 from line 1. Enter here and on line 4 of the Tax Computation of Form 706 . . . .

Line 17

You may take a credit for Federal gift taxes imposed by Chapter 12 of the Code, and the corresponding provisions of prior laws, on certain transfers the decedent made before January 1, 1977, that are included in the gross estate. The credit cannot be more than the amount figured by the following formula:

$$\frac{\text{Gross estate tax minus (the sum of the state death taxes and unified credit)}}{\text{Value of gross estate minus (the sum of the deductions for charitable, public, and similar gifts and bequests and marital deduction)}} \times \text{Value of included gift}$$

For more information, see the regulations under section 2012. This computation may be made using **Form 4808,** Computation of Credit for Gift Tax. Attach a copy of a completed Form 4808 or the computation of the credit. Also attach all available copies of Forms 709 filed by the decedent to help verify the amounts entered on lines 4, 9, and 17.

Line 25

You may not use these bonds to pay the GST tax.

Instructions for Schedule A.—Real Estate

See the reverse side of Schedule A on Form 706.

Instructions for Schedule B.—Stocks and Bonds

General

If the total gross estate contains any stocks or bonds, you must complete Schedule B and file it with the return.

On Schedule B list the stocks and bonds included in the decedent's gross estate. Number each item in the left-hand column. **Bonds that are exempt from Federal income tax are not exempt from estate tax unless specifically exempted by an estate tax provision of the Code.** Therefore, you should list these bonds on Schedule B.

Public housing bonds includible in the gross estate must be included at their full value.

If you paid any estate, inheritance, legacy, or succession tax to a foreign country on any stocks or bonds included in this schedule, group those stocks and bonds together and label them "Subjected to Foreign Death Taxes."

List interest and dividends on each stock or bond separately. Indicate as a separate item dividends that have not been collected at death, but which are payable to the decedent or the estate because the decedent was a stockholder of record on the date of death. However, if the stock is being traded on an exchange and is selling ex-dividend on the date of the decedent's death, do not include the amount of the dividend as a separate item. Instead, add it to the ex-dividend quotation in determining the fair market value of the stock on the date of the decedent's death. Dividends declared on shares of stock before the death of the decedent but payable to stockholders of record on a date after the decedent's death are not includible in the gross estate for Federal estate tax purposes.

Description

For stocks indicate:

- Number of shares
- Whether common or preferred
- Issue
- Par value where needed for identification
- Price per share
- Exact name of corporation
- Principal exchange upon which sold, if listed on an exchange
- 9-digit CUSIP number

For bonds indicate:

- Quantity and denomination
- Name of obligor
- Date of maturity
- Interest rate
- Interest due date
- Principal exchange, if listed on an exchange
- 9-digit CUSIP number

If the stock or bond is unlisted, show the company's principal business office.

The CUSIP (Committee on Uniform Security Identification Procedure) number is a nine-digit number that is assigned to all stocks and bonds traded on major exchanges and many unlisted securities. Usually, the CUSIP number is printed on the face of the stock certificate. If the CUSIP number is not printed on the certificate, it may be obtained through the company's transfer agent.

Valuation

List the fair market value of the stocks or bonds. The fair market value of a stock or bond

I.R.S.—Instructions for Form 706 (Continued)

Line 9 Worksheet—Gift Tax on Gifts Made After 1976

a. Calendar year or calendar quarter	b. Total taxable gifts for prior periods (from Form 709, Tax Computation, line 2)	c. Taxable gifts for this period (from Form 709, Tax Computation, line 1) (see below)	d. Tax payable using Table A (on page 10) (see below)	e. Unused unified credit for this period (see below)	f. Tax payable for this period (subtract col. e from col. d)
Total pre-1977 taxable gifts. Enter the amount from line 1, Worksheet TG					

1. Total gift taxes payable on gifts made after 1976 (combine the amounts in column f)	
2. Gift taxes paid by the decedent on gifts that qualify for "special treatment." Enter the amount from line 2, column e, Worksheet TG on page 8	
3. Subtract line 2 from line 1	
4. Gift tax paid by decedent's spouse on split gifts included on Schedule G. Enter the amount from line 2, column f, Worksheet TG on page 8	
5. Add lines 3 and 4. Enter here and on line 9 of the Tax Computation of Form 706	

Columns b and c.—*In addition to gifts reported on Form 709, you must include in these columns any taxable gifts in excess of the annual exclusion that were not reported on Form 709.*

Column d.—To figure the "tax payable" for this column, you must use Table A in these instructions, *as it applies to the year of the decedent's death rather than to the year the gifts were actually made.* To compute the entry for col. d, you should figure the "tax payable" on the amount in col. b and subtract it from the "tax payable" on the amounts in cols. b and c added together. Enter the difference in col. d.

"Tax payable" as used here is an hypothetical amount and does not necessarily reflect tax actually paid. Figure "tax payable" only on gifts made after 1976. Do not include any tax paid or payable on gifts made before 1977. Pre-1977 gifts are listed only to exclude them from the calculation.

If the amount in columns b and c combined exceeds $10 million *for any given calendar year,* then you must calculate the tax in column d for that year using the Form 709 revision in effect for the *year of the decedent's death.*

To calculate the tax, enter the amount for the appropriate year from column c of the worksheet on line 1 of the Tax Computation of the Form 709. Enter the amount from column b on line 2 of the Tax Computation. Complete the Tax Computation through the tax due before any reduction for the unified credit and enter that amount in column d, above.

Column e.—To figure the unused unified credit, use the unified credit in effect for the year the gift was made. This amount should be on line 12 of the Tax Computation of the Form 709 filed for the gift.

(whether listed or unlisted) is the mean between the highest and lowest selling prices quoted on the valuation date. If only the closing selling prices are available, then the fair market value is the mean between the quoted closing selling price on the valuation date and on the trading day before the valuation date. To figure the fair market value if there were no sales on the valuation date:

1. Find the mean between the highest and lowest selling prices on the nearest trading date before and the nearest trading date after the valuation date. Both trading dates must be reasonably close to the valuation date.

2. Prorate the difference between the mean prices to the valuation date.

3. Add or subtract (whichever applies) the prorated part of the difference to or from the mean price figured for the nearest trading date before the valuation date.

If no actual sales were made reasonably close to the valuation date, make the same computation using the mean between the bona fide bid and asked prices instead of sales prices. If actual sales prices or bona fide bid and asked prices are available within a reasonable period of time before the valuation date but not after the valuation date, or vice versa, use the mean between the highest and lowest sales prices or bid and asked prices as the fair market value.

For example, assume that sales of stock nearest the valuation date (June 15) occurred 2 trading days before (June 13) and 3 trading days after (June 18). On those days the mean sale prices per share were $10 and $15, respectively. Therefore, the price of $12 is considered the fair market value of a share of stock on the valuation date. If, however, on June 13 and 18, the mean sale prices per share were $15 and $10, respectively, the fair market value of a share of stock on the valuation date is $13.

If only closing prices for bonds are available, see Regulations section 20.2031-2(b).

Apply the rules in the section 2031 regulations to determine the value of inactive stock and stock in close corporations. Send with the schedule complete financial and other data used to determine value, including balance sheets (particularly the one nearest to the valuation date) and statements of the net earnings or operating results and dividends paid for each of the 5 years immediately before the valuation date.

Securities reported as of no value, nominal value, or obsolete should be listed last. Include the address of the company and the state and date of the incorporation. Attach copies of correspondence or statements used to determine the "no value."

If the security was listed on more than one stock exchange, use either the records of the exchange where the security is principally traded or the composite listing of combined exchanges, if available, in a publication of general circulation. In valuing listed stocks and bonds, you should carefully check accurate records to obtain values for the applicable valuation date.

If you get quotations from brokers, or evidence of the sale of securities from the officers of the issuing companies, attach to the schedule copies of the letters furnishing these quotations or evidence of sale.

See Rev. Rul. 69-489, 1969-2 C.B. 172, for the special valuation rules for certain marketable U.S. Treasury Bonds (issued before March 4, 1971). These bonds, commonly called "flower bonds," may be redeemed at par plus accrued interest in payment of the tax at any Federal Reserve bank, the office of the Treasurer of the United States, or the Bureau of the Public Debt, as explained in Rev. Proc. 69-18, 1969-2 C.B. 300.

Instructions for Schedule C.—Mortgages, Notes, and Cash

See the reverse side of Schedule C on Form 706.

Instructions for Schedule D.—Insurance on the Decedent's Life

See the reverse side of Schedule D on Form 706.

Instructions for Schedule E.—Jointly Owned Property

See the reverse side of Schedule E on Form 706.

Instructions for Schedule F.—Other Miscellaneous Property

See the reverse side of Schedule F on Form 706.

Instructions for Schedule G.—Transfers During Decedent's Life

You must complete Schedule G and file it with the return if the decedent made any of the transfers described in **1** through **5** beginning on page 11, or if you answered "Yes" on line 11 or 12a of Part 4, General Information.

Note: *Beginning with the estates of decedents dying after August 5, 1997:*

I.R.S.—Instructions for Form 706 (Continued)

Table A—Unified Rate Schedule

Column A Taxable amount over	Column B Taxable amount not over	Column C Tax on amount in column A	Column D Rate of tax on excess over amount in column A
			(Percent)
0	$10,000	0	18
$10,000	20,000	$1,800	20
20,000	40,000	3,800	22
40,000	60,000	8,200	24
60,000	80,000	13,000	26
80,000	100,000	18,200	28
100,000	150,000	23,800	30
150,000	250,000	38,800	32
250,000	500,000	70,800	34
500,000	750,000	155,800	37
750,000	1,000,000	248,300	39
1,000,000	1,250,000	345,800	41
1,250,000	1,500,000	448,300	43
1,500,000	2,000,000	555,800	45
2,000,000	2,500,000	780,800	49
2,500,000	3,000,000	1,025,800	53
3,000,000	....	1,290,800	55

Table B Worksheet

Federal Adjusted Taxable Estate

1	Federal taxable estate (from Tax Computation, Form 706, line 3)	$
2	Adjustment	60,000
3	Federal adjusted taxable estate. Subtract line 2 from line 1. Use this amount to compute maximum credit for state death taxes in Table B.	

Table B

Computation of Maximum Credit for State Death Taxes

(Based on Federal adjusted taxable estate computed using the worksheet above.)

(1) Adjusted taxable estate equal to or more than—	(2) Adjusted taxable estate less than—	(3) Credit on amount in column (1)	(4) Rate of credit on excess over amount in column (1)	(1) Adjusted taxable estate equal to or more than—	(2) Adjusted taxable estate less than—	(3) Credit on amount in column (1)	(4) Rate of credit on excess over amount in column (1)
			(Percent)				(Percent)
0	$40,000	0	None	2,040,000	2,540,000	106,800	8.0
$40,000	90,000	0	0.8	2,540,000	3,040,000	146,800	8.8
90,000	140,000	$400	1.6	3,040,000	3,540,000	190,800	9.6
140,000	240,000	1,200	2.4	3,540,000	4,040,000	238,800	10.4
240,000	440,000	3,600	3.2	4,040,000	5,040,000	290,800	11.2
440,000	640,000	10,000	4.0	5,040,000	6,040,000	402,800	12.0
640,000	840,000	18,000	4.8	6,040,000	7,040,000	522,800	12.8
840,000	1,040,000	27,600	5.6	7,040,000	8,040,000	650,800	13.6
1,040,000	1,540,000	38,800	6.4	8,040,000	9,040,000	786,800	14.4
1,540,000	2,040,000	70,800	7.2	9,040,000	10,040,000	930,800	15.2
				10,040,000	....	1,082,800	16.0

Examples showing use of Schedule B

Example where the alternate valuation is not adopted; date of death, January 1, 1998

Item number	Description including face amount of bonds or number of shares and par value where needed for identification. Give CUSIP number.	Unit value	Alternate valuation date	Alternate value	Value at date of death
1	$60,000-Arkansas Railroad Co. first mortgage 4%, 20-year bonds, due 2000. Interest payable quarterly on Feb. 1, May 1, Aug. 1 and Nov. 1; N.Y. Exchange, CUSIP No. XXXXXXXXX	100	....	....	60,000
	Interest coupons attached to bonds, item 1, due and payable on Nov. 1, 1997, but not cashed at date of death	....	....	....	600
	Interest accrued on item 1, from Nov. 1, 1997, to Jan. 1, 1998 . .	....	....	....	400
2	500 shares Public Service Corp., common; N.Y. Exchange, CUSIP No. XXXXXXXXX	110	....	....	55,000
	Dividend on item 2 of $2 per share declared Dec. 10, 1997, payable on Jan. 10, 1998, to holders of record on Dec. 30, 1997	....	....	....	1,000

I.R.S.—Instructions for Form 706 (Continued)

Example where the alternate valuation is adopted; date of death, January 1, 1998

Item number	Description including face amount of bonds or number of shares and par value where needed for identification. Give CUSIP number.	Unit value	Alternate valuation date	Alternate value	Value at date of death
1	$60,000-Arkansas Railroad Co. first mortgage 4%, 20-year bonds, due 2000. Interest payable quarterly on Feb. 1, May 1, Aug. 1 and Nov. 1; N.Y. Exchange, CUSIP No. XXXXXXXXX	100	....	....	60,000
	$30,000 of item 1 distributed to legatees on Apr. 1, 1998	99	4/1/98	29,700	....
	$30,000 of item 1 sold by executor on May 2, 1998	98	5/2/98	29,400	....
	Interest coupons attached to bonds, item 1, due and payable on Nov. 1, 1997, but not cashed at date of death. Cashed by executor on Feb. 1, 1998	....	2/1/98	600	600
	Interest accrued on item 1, from Nov. 1, 1997, to Jan. 1, 1998. Cashed by executor on Feb. 1, 1998	....	2/1/98	400	400
2	500 shares of Public Service Corp., common; N.Y. Exchange, CUSIP No. XXXXXXXXX	110	....	....	55,000
	Not disposed of within 6 months following death	90	7/1/98	45,000	....
	Dividend on item 2 of $2 per share declared Dec. 10, 1997, and paid on Jan. 10, 1998, to holders of record on Dec. 30, 1997	....	1/10/98	1,000	1,000

(Continued from page 9)

• *If the decedent made a transfer from a trust, and*

• *At the time of the transfer, the transfer was from a portion of the trust that was owned by the grantor under section 676 (other than by reason of section 672(e)) by reason of a power in the grantor,*

then for purposes of sections 2035 and 2038, the transfer is treated as made directly by the decedent. Any such transfer within the annual gift tax exclusion is not includible in the gross estate.

Five types of transfers should be reported on this schedule:

1. Certain gift taxes (section 2035(b)).—Enter at item A of the Schedule the total value of the gift taxes that were paid by the decedent or the estate on gifts made by the decedent or the decedent's spouse within 3 years before death.

The date of the gift, not the date of payment of the gift tax, determines whether a gift tax paid is included in the gross estate under this rule. Therefore, you should carefully examine the Forms 709 filed by the decedent and the decedent's spouse to determine what part of the total gift taxes reported on them was attributable to gifts made within 3 years before death. For example, if the decedent died on July 10, 1998, you should examine gift tax returns for 1998, 1997, 1996, and 1995. However, the gift taxes on the 1995 return that are attributable to gifts made before July 10, 1995, are not included in the gross estate.

Attach an explanation of how you computed the includible gift taxes if you do not include in the gross estate the entire gift taxes shown on any Form 709 filed for gifts made within 3 years of death. Also attach copies of any pertinent gift tax returns filed by the decedent's spouse for gifts made within 3 years of death.

2. Other transfers within 3 years before death (section 2035(a)).— These transfers include *only* the following:

• Any transfer by the decedent with respect to a life insurance policy within 3 years before death.

• Any transfer within 3 years before death of a retained section 2036 life estate, section 2037 reversionary interest, or section 2038 power to revoke, etc., if the property subject to the life estate, interest, or power would have been included in the gross estate had the decedent continued to possess the life estate, interest, or power until death.

These transfers are reported on Schedule G regardless of whether a gift tax return was required to be filed for them when they were made. However, the amount includible and the information required to be shown for the transfers are determined:

• For insurance on the life of the decedent using the instructions to Schedule D. (Attach Forms 712.)

• For insurance on the life of another using the instructions to Schedule F. (Attach Forms 712.)

• For sections 2036, 2037, and 2038 transfers, using paragraphs **3**, **4**, and **5** of these instructions.

3. Transfers with retained life estate (section 2036).—These are transfers by the decedent in which the decedent retained an interest in the transferred property. The transfer can be in trust or otherwise, but excludes bona fide sales for adequate and full consideration.

Interests or rights. Section 2036 applies to the following retained interests or rights:

• The right to income from the transferred property.

• The right to the possession or enjoyment of the property.

• The right, either alone or with any person, to designate the persons who shall receive the income from, or possess or enjoy the property.

Retained voting rights. Transfers with a retained life estate also include transfers of stock in a "controlled corporation" after June 22, 1976, if the decedent retained or acquired voting rights in the stock. If the decedent retained direct or indirect voting rights in a controlled corporation, the decedent is considered to have retained enjoyment of the transferred property. A corporation is a "controlled corporation" if the decedent owned (actually or constructively) or had the right (either alone or with any other person) to vote at least 20% of the total combined voting power of all classes of stock. See section 2036(b). If these voting rights ceased or were relinquished within 3 years before the decedent's death, the corporate interests are included in the gross estate as if the decedent had actually retained the voting rights until death.

The amount includible in the gross estate is the value of the transferred property at the time of the decedent's death. If the decedent kept or reserved an interest or right to only a part of the transferred property, the amount includible in the gross estate is a corresponding part of the entire value of the property.

A retained life estate does not have to be legally enforceable. What matters is that a substantial economic benefit was retained. For example, if a mother transferred title to her home to her daughter but with the informal understanding that she was to continue living there until her death, the value of the home would be includible in the mother's estate even if the agreement would not have been legally enforceable.

4. Transfers taking effect at death (section 2037).—A transfer that takes effect at the decedent's death is one under which possession or enjoyment can be obtained only by surviving the decedent. A transfer is not treated as one that takes effect at the decedent's death unless the decedent retained a reversionary interest (defined below) in the property that immediately before the decedent's death had a value of more than 5% of the value of the transferred property. If the transfer was made before October 8, 1949, the reversionary interest must have arisen by the express terms of the instrument of transfer.

A *reversionary interest* is generally any right under which the transferred property will or may be returned to the decedent or the decedent's estate. It also includes the possibility that the transferred property may become subject to a power of disposition by the decedent. It does not matter if the right arises by the express terms of the instrument of transfer or by operation of law. For this purpose, reversionary interest **does not** include the possibility the income alone from the property may return to the decedent or become subject to the decedent's power of disposition.

5. Revocable transfers (section 2038).—The gross estate includes the value of transferred property in which the enjoyment of the transferred property was subject at decedent's death to any change through the exercise of a power to alter, amend, revoke, or terminate. A decedent's power to change the beneficiaries and to hasten or increase any beneficiary's enjoyment of the property are examples of this.

It does not matter whether the power was reserved at the time of the transfer, whether it arose by operation of law, or was later created or conferred. The rule applies regardless of the source from which the power was acquired, and regardless of whether the power was exercisable by the decedent alone or with any person (and regardless of whether that person

I.R.S.—Instructions for Form 706 (Continued)

had a substantial adverse interest in the transferred property).

The capacity in which the decedent could use a power has no bearing. If the decedent gave property in trust and was the trustee with the power to revoke the trust, the property would be included in his or her gross estate. For transfers or additions to an irrevocable trust after October 28, 1979, the transferred property is includible if the decedent reserved the power to remove the trustee at will and appoint another trustee.

If the decedent relinquished within 3 years before death any of the includible powers described above, figure the gross estate as if the decedent had actually retained the powers until death.

Only the part of the transferred property that is subject to the decedent's power is included in the gross estate.

For more detailed information on which transfers are includible in the gross estate, see the Estate Tax Regulations.

Special Valuation Rules for Certain Lifetime Transfers

Code sections 2701–2704 provide rules for valuing certain transfers to family members.

Section 2701 deals with the transfer of an interest in a corporation or partnership while retaining certain distribution rights, or a liquidation, put, call, or conversion right.

Section 2702 deals with the transfer of an interest in a trust while retaining any interest other than a qualified interest. In general, a qualified interest is a right to receive certain distributions from the trust at least annually, or a noncontingent remainder interest if all of the other interests in the trust are distribution rights specified in section 2702.

Section 2703 provides rules for the valuation of property transferred to a family member but subject to an option, agreement, or other right to acquire or use the property at less than fair market value. It also applies to transfers subject to restrictions on the right to sell or use the property.

Finally, section 2704 provides that in certain cases the lapse of a voting or liquidation right in a family-owned corporation or partnership will result in a deemed transfer.

These rules have potential consequences for the valuation of property in an estate. If the decedent (or any member of his or her family) was involved in any such transactions, see Code sections 2701–2704 and the related regulations for additional details.

How To Complete Schedule G

All transfers (other than outright transfers not in trust and bona fide sales) made by the decedent at any time during life must be reported on the Schedule regardless of whether you believe the transfers are subject to tax. If the decedent made any transfers not described in the instructions above, the transfers should not be shown on Schedule G. Instead, attach a statement describing these transfers: list the date of the transfer, the amount or value of the transferred property, and the type of transfer.

Complete the schedule for each transfer that is included in the gross estate under sections 2035(a), 2036, 2037, and 2038 as described beginning on page 9.

In the "Item number" column, number each transfer consecutively beginning with 1. In the "Description" column, list the name of the transferee, the date of the transfer, and give a complete description of the property. Transfers included in the gross estate should be valued on the date of the decedent's death or, if alternate valuation is adopted, according to section 2032.

If only part of the property transferred meets the terms of section 2035(a), 2036, 2037, or 2038, then only a corresponding part of the value of the property should be included in the value of the gross estate. If the transferee makes additions or improvements to the property, the increased value of the property at the valuation date should not be included on Schedule G. However, if only a part of the value of the property is included, enter the value of the whole under the column headed "Description" and explain what part was included.

Attachments.— If a transfer, by trust or otherwise, was made by a written instrument, attach a copy of the instrument to the Schedule. If of public record, the copy should be certified; if not of record, the copy should be verified.

Instructions for Schedule H.—Powers of Appointment

You must complete Schedule H and file it with the return if you answered "Yes" to line 13 of Part 4, General Information.

On Schedule H include in the gross estate:

1. The value of property for which the decedent possessed a general power of appointment on the date of his or her death; and

2. The value of property for which the decedent possessed a general power of appointment which he or she exercised or released before death by disposing of it in such a way that if it were a transfer of property owned by the decedent, the property would be includible in the decedent's gross estate as a transfer with a retained life estate, a transfer taking effect at death, or a revocable transfer.

With the above exceptions, property subject to a power of appointment is not includible in the gross estate if the decedent released the power completely and the decedent held no interest in or control over the property.

If the failure to exercise a general power of appointment results in a lapse of the power, the lapse is treated as a release only to the extent that the value of the property that could have been appointed by the exercise of the lapsed power is more than the greater of $5,000 or 5% of the total value, at the time of the lapse, of the assets out of which, or the proceeds of which, the exercise of the lapsed power could have been satisfied.

Powers of Appointment

A power of appointment determines who will own or enjoy the property subject to the power and when they will own or enjoy it. The power must be created by someone other than the decedent. It does not include a power created or held on property transferred by the decedent.

A power of appointment includes all powers which are in substance and effect powers of appointment regardless of how they are identified and regardless of local property laws. For example, if a settlor transfers property in trust for the life of his wife, with a power in the wife to appropriate or consume the principal of the trust, the wife has a power of appointment.

Some powers do not in themselves constitute a power of appointment. For example, a power to amend only administrative provisions of a trust that cannot substantially affect the beneficial enjoyment of the trust property or income is not a power of appointment. A power to manage, invest, or control assets, or to allocate receipts and disbursements, when exercised only in a fiduciary capacity, is not a power of appointment.

General power of appointment.— A general power of appointment is a power that is exercisable in favor of the decedent, the decedent's estate, the decedent's creditors, or the creditors of the decedent's estate, **except**:

1. A power to consume, invade, or appropriate property for the benefit of the decedent that is limited by an ascertainable standard relating to health, education, support, or maintenance of the decedent.

2. A power exercisable by the decedent only in conjunction with **(a)** the creator of the power, or **(b)** a person who has a substantial interest in the property subject to the power, which is adverse to the exercise of the power in favor of the decedent.

A part of a power is considered a general power of appointment if the power:

1. May only be exercised by the decedent in conjunction with another person; and

2. Is also exercisable in favor of the other person (in addition to being exercisable in favor of the decedent, the decedent's creditors, the decedent's estate, or the creditors of the decedent's estate).

The part to include in the gross estate as a general power of appointment is figured by dividing the value of the property by the number of persons (including the decedent) in favor of whom the power is exercisable.

Date power was created.— Generally, a power of appointment created by will is considered created on the date of the testator's death.

A power of appointment created by an inter vivos instrument is considered created on the date the instrument takes effect. If the holder of a power exercises it by creating a second power, the second power is considered as created at the time of the exercise of the first.

Attachments

If the decedent ever possessed a power of appointment, attach a certified or verified copy of the instrument granting the power and a certified or verified copy of any instrument by which the power was exercised or released. You must file these copies even if you contend that the power was not a general power of appointment, and that the property is not otherwise includible in the gross estate.

Instructions for Schedule I.—Annuities

You must complete Schedule I and file it with the return if you answered "Yes" to question 15 of Part 4, General Information.

Enter on Schedule I every annuity that meets all of the conditions under **General,** below, and every annuity described in paragraphs **a–h** of **Annuities Under Approved Plans,** even if the annuities are wholly or partially excluded from the gross estate.

See the instructions for line 3 of Schedule M for a discussion regarding the QTIP treatment of certain joint and survivor annuities.

General

In general, you must include in the gross estate all or part of the value of any annuity that meets the following requirements:

- It is receivable by a beneficiary following the death of the decedent and by reason of surviving the decedent;
- The annuity is under a contract or agreement entered into after March 3, 1931;
- The annuity was payable to the decedent (or the decedent possessed the right to receive the

I.R.S.—Instructions for Form 706 (Continued)

annuity) either alone or in conjunction with another, for the decedent's life or for any period not ascertainable without reference to the decedent's death or for any period that did not in fact end before the decedent's death;

- The contract or agreement is not a policy of insurance on the life of the decedent.

These rules apply to all types of annuities, including pension plans, individual retirement arrangements, and purchased commercial annuities.

An annuity contract that provides periodic payments to a person for life and ceases at the person's death is not includible in the gross estate. Social Security benefits are not includible in the gross estate even if the surviving spouse receives benefits.

An annuity or other payment that is not includible in the decedent's or the survivor's gross estate as an annuity may still be includible under some other applicable provision of the law. For example, see **Powers of Appointment** on page 12.

If the decedent retired before January 1, 1985, see **Annuities Under Approved Plans** below for rules that allow the exclusion of part or all of certain annuities.

Part Includible

If the decedent contributed only part of the purchase price of the contract or agreement, include in the gross estate only that part of the value of the annuity receivable by the surviving beneficiary that the decedent's contribution to the purchase price of the annuity or agreement bears to the total purchase price.

For example, if the value of the survivor's annuity was $20,000 and the decedent had contributed three-fourths of the purchase price of the contract, the amount includible is $15,000 (3/4 × $20,000).

Except as provided under **Annuities Under Approved Plans,** contributions made by the decedent's employer to the purchase price of the contract or agreement are considered made by the decedent if they were made by the employer because of the decedent's employment. For more information, see section 2039.

Definitions

Annuity.— The term "annuity" includes one or more payments extending over any period of time. The payments may be equal or unequal, conditional or unconditional, periodic or sporadic.

Examples.— The following are examples of contracts (but not necessarily the only forms of contracts) for annuities that must be included in the gross estate.

1. A contract under which the decedent immediately before death was receiving or was entitled to receive, for the duration of life, an annuity with payments to continue after death to a designated beneficiary, if surviving the decedent.

2. A contract under which the decedent immediately before death was receiving or was entitled to receive, together with another person, an annuity payable to the decedent and the other person for their joint lives, with payments to continue to the survivor following the death of either.

3. A contract or agreement entered into by the decedent and employer under which the decedent immediately before death and following retirement was receiving, or was entitled to receive, an annuity payable to the decedent for life and after the decedent's death to a designated beneficiary, if surviving the decedent, whether the payments after the decedent's death are fixed by the contract or subject to an option or election exercised or exercisable by the decedent. However, see **Annuities Under Approved Plans,** below.

4. A contract or agreement entered into by the decedent and the decedent's employer under which at the decedent's death, before retirement, or before the expiration of a stated period of time, an annuity was payable to a designated beneficiary, if surviving the decedent. However, see **Annuities Under Approved Plans,** below.

5. A contract or agreement under which the decedent immediately before death was receiving, or was entitled to receive, an annuity for a stated period of time, with the annuity to continue to a designated beneficiary, surviving the decedent, upon the decedent's death and before the expiration of that period of time.

6. An annuity contract or other arrangement providing for a series of substantially equal periodic payments to be made to a beneficiary for life or over a period of at least 36 months after the date of the decedent's death under an individual retirement account, annuity, or bond as described in section 2039(e) (before its repeal by P.L. 98-369).

Payable to the decedent.— An annuity or other payment **was payable** to the decedent if, at the time of death, the decedent was in fact receiving an annuity or other payment, with or without an enforceable right to have the payments continued.

Right to receive an annuity.— The decedent had the **right to receive** an annuity or other payment if, immediately before death, the decedent had an enforceable right to receive payments at some time in the future, whether or not at the time of death the decedent had a present right to receive payments.

Annuities Under Approved Plans

The following rules relate to whether part or all of an otherwise includible annuity may be excluded. These rules have been repealed and apply only if the decedent either:

1. On December 31, 1984, was both a participant in the plan and in pay status (i.e., had received at least one benefit payment on or before December 31, 1984), and had irrevocably elected the form of the benefit before July 18, 1984; **OR**

2. Had separated from service before January 1, 1985, and did not change the form of benefit before death.

The amount excluded cannot exceed $100,000 unless either of the following conditions is met:

1. On December 31, 1982, the decedent was both a participant in the plan and in pay status (i.e., had received at least one benefit payment on or before December 31, 1982), and the decedent irrevocably elected the form of the benefit before January 1, 1983; **OR**

2. The decedent separated from service before January 1, 1983, and did not change the form of benefit before death.

Approved Plans

Approved plans may be separated into two categories:

- Pension, profit-sharing, stock bonus, and other similar plans, and
- Individual retirement arrangements (IRAs), and retirement bonds

Different exclusion rules apply to the two categories of plans.

Pension, etc., plans.— The following plans are approved plans for the exclusion rules:

a. An employees' trust (or under a contract purchased by an employees' trust) forming part of a pension, stock bonus, or profit-sharing plan that met all the requirements of section 401(a), either at the time of the decedent's separation from employment (whether by death or otherwise) or at the time of the termination of the plan (if earlier).

b. A retirement annuity contract purchased by the employer (but not by an employees' trust) under a plan that, at the time of the decedent's separation from employment (by death or otherwise), or at the time of the termination of the plan (if earlier), was a plan described in section 403(a).

c. A retirement annuity contract purchased for an employee by an employer that is an organization referred to in section 170(b)(1)(A)(ii) or (vi), or that is a religious organization (other than a trust), and that is exempt from tax under section 501(a).

d. Chapter 73 of Title 10 of the United States Code.

e. A bond purchase plan described in section 405 (before its repeal by P.L. 98-369, effective for obligations issued after December 31, 1983.)

Exclusion rules for pension, etc., plans.— If an annuity under an "approved plan" described in **a–e** above is receivable by a beneficiary other than the executor and the decedent made no contributions under the plan toward the cost, no part of the value of the annuity, subject to the $100,000 limitation (if applicable), is includible in the gross estate.

If the decedent made a contribution under a plan described in **a–e** above toward the cost, include in the gross estate on this schedule that proportion of the value of the annuity which the amount of the decedent's contribution under the plan bears to the total amount of all contributions under the plan. The remaining value of the annuity is excludable from the gross estate subject to the $100,000 limitation (if applicable). For the rules to determine whether the decedent made contributions to the plan, see Regulations section 20.2039.

IRAs and retirement bonds.— The following plans are approved plans for the exclusion rules:

f. An individual retirement account described in section 408(a);

g. An individual retirement annuity described in section 408(b);

h. A retirement bond described in section 409(a)(before its repeal by P.L. 98-369).

Exclusion rules for IRAs and retirement bonds.— These plans are approved plans only if they provide for a series of substantially equal periodic payments made to a beneficiary for life, or over a period of at least 36 months after the date of the decedent's death.

Subject to the $100,000 limitation, if applicable, if an annuity under a "plan" described in **f–h** above is receivable by a beneficiary other than the executor, the entire value of the annuity is excludable from the gross estate even if the decedent made a contribution under the plan.

However, if any payment to or for an account or annuity described in paragraph **f, g,** or **h** above was not allowable as an income tax deduction under section 219 (and was not a rollover contribution as described in section 2039(e) before its repeal by P.L. 98-369), include in the gross estate on this schedule that proportion of the value of the annuity which the amount not allowable as a deduction under section 219 and not a rollover contribution bears to the total amount paid to or for such account or annuity. For more information, see Regulations section 20.2039-5.

Rules applicable to all approved plans.— The following rules apply to all approved plans described in paragraphs **a–h** above.

If any part of an annuity under a "plan" described in **a–h** above is receivable by the executor, it is generally includible in the gross

I.R.S. — Instructions for Form 706 (Continued)

estate on this schedule to the extent that it is receivable by the executor in that capacity. In general, the annuity is receivable by the executor if it is to be paid to the executor or if there is an agreement (expressed or implied) that it will be applied by the beneficiary for the benefit of the estate (such as in discharge of the estate's liability for death taxes or debts of the decedent, etc.) or that its distribution will be governed to any extent by the terms of the decedent's will or the laws of descent and distribution.

If data available to you does not indicate whether the plan satisfies the requirements of section 401(a), 403(a), 408(a), 408(b), or 409(a), you may obtain that information from the District Director of Internal Revenue for the district where the employer's principal place of business is located.

Line A—Lump Sum Distribution Election

The election pertaining to the lump sum distribution from qualified plans (approved plans) excludes from the gross estate all or part of the lump sum distribution that would otherwise be includible. When the recipient makes the election to take a lump sum distribution and include it in his or her income tax, the amount excluded from the gross estate is the portion attributable to the employer contributions. The portion, if any, attributable to the employee-decedent's contributions is always includible. The actual election is made by the recipient of the distribution by taking the lump sum distribution and by treating it as taxable on his or her income tax return as described in Regulations section 20.2039-4(d). The election is irrevocable. However, you may not compute the gross estate in accordance with this election unless you check "Yes" to line A and attach the name, address, and identifying number of the recipients of the lump sum distributions. See Regulations section 20.2039-4.

How To Complete the Schedule

In describing an annuity, give the name and address of the grantor of the annuity. Specify if the annuity is under an approved plan. If it is under an approved plan, you must state the ratio of the decedent's contribution to the total purchase price of the annuity. If the decedent was employed at the time of death and an annuity as described in paragraph 4 of **Annuity Defined,** on page 13, became payable to any beneficiary because the beneficiary survived the decedent, you must state the ratio of the decedent's contribution to the total purchase price of the annuity.

If an annuity under an individual retirement account or annuity became payable to any beneficiary because that beneficiary survived the decedent and is payable to the beneficiary for life or for at least 36 months following the decedent's death, you must state the ratio of the amount paid for the individual retirement account or annuity that was not allowable as an income tax deduction under section 219 (other than a rollover contribution) to the total amount paid for the account or annuity. If the annuity is payable out of a trust or other fund, the description should be sufficiently complete to fully identify it. If the annuity is payable for a term of years, include the duration of the term and the date on which it began, and if payable for the life of a person other than the decedent, include the date of birth of that person. If the annuity is wholly or partially excluded from the gross estate, enter the amount excluded under "Description" and explain how you computed the exclusion.

Instructions for Schedule J.—Funeral Expenses and Expenses Incurred in Administering Property Subject to Claims

See the reverse side of Schedule J on Form 706.

Instructions for Schedule K.—Debts of the Decedent and Mortgages and Liens

You must complete and attach Schedule K if you claimed deductions on either item 14 or item 15 of Part 5, Recapitulation.

Income vs. estate tax deduction.— Taxes, interest, and business expenses accrued at the date of the decedent's death are deductible both on Schedule K and as deductions in respect of the decedent on the income tax return of the estate.

If you choose to deduct medical expenses of the decedent only on the estate tax return, they are fully deductible as claims against the estate. If, however, they are claimed on the decedent's final income tax return under section 213(c), they may not also be claimed on the estate tax return. In this case, you also may not deduct on the estate tax return any amounts that were not deductible on the income tax return because of the percentage limitations.

Debts of the Decedent

List under "Debts of the Decedent" only valid debts the decedent owed at the time of death. List any indebtedness secured by a mortgage or other lien on property of the gross estate under the heading "Mortgages and Liens." If the amount of the debt is disputed or the subject of litigation, deduct only the amount the estate concedes to be a valid claim. Enter the amount in contest in the column provided.

Generally, if the claim against the estate is based on a promise or agreement, the deduction is limited to the extent that the liability was contracted bona fide and for an adequate and full consideration in money or money's worth. However, any enforceable claim based on a promise or agreement of the decedent to make a contribution or gift (such as a pledge or a subscription) to or for the use of a charitable, public, religious, etc., organization is deductible to the extent that the deduction would be allowed as a bequest under the statute that applies.

Certain claims of a former spouse against the estate based on the relinquishment of marital rights are deductible on Schedule K. For these claims to be deductible, all of the following conditions must be met:

- The decedent and the decedent's spouse must have entered into a written agreement relative to their marital and property rights.
- The decedent and the spouse must have been divorced before the decedent's death and the divorce must have occurred within the 3-year period beginning on the date 1 year before the agreement was entered into. It is not required that the agreement be approved by the divorce decree.
- The property or interest transferred under the agreement must be transferred to the decedent's spouse in settlement of the spouse's marital rights.

You may not deduct a claim made against the estate by a remainderman relating to section 2044 property. Section 2044 property is described in the instructions to line 6 of Part 4, General Information, on page 6.

Include in this schedule notes unsecured by mortgage or other lien and give full details, including name of payee, face and unpaid balance, date and term of note, interest rate, and date to which interest was paid before death. Include the exact nature of the claim as well as the name of the creditor. If the claim is for services performed over a period of time, state the period covered by the claim. Example: Edison Electric Illuminating Co., for electric service during December 1997, $150.

If the amount of the claim is the unpaid balance due on a contract for the purchase of any property included in the gross estate, indicate the schedule and item number where you reported the property. If the claim represents a joint and separate liability, give full facts and explain the financial responsibility of the co-obligor.

Property and income taxes.— The deduction for property taxes is limited to the taxes accrued before the date of the decedent's death. Federal taxes on income received during the decedent's lifetime are deductible, but taxes on income received after death are not deductible.

Keep all vouchers or original records for inspection by the Internal Revenue Service.

Allowable death taxes.— If you elect to take a deduction under section 2053(d) rather than a credit under section 2011 or section 2014, the deduction is subject to the limitations described in section 2053(d) and its regulations. If you have difficulty figuring the deduction, you may request a computation of it. Send your request within a reasonable amount of time before the due date of the return to the Commissioner of Internal Revenue, Washington, DC 20224. Attach to your request a copy of the will and relevant documents, a statement showing the distribution of the estate under the decedent's will, and a computation of the state or foreign death tax showing the amount payable by charity.

Mortgages and Liens

List under "Mortgages and Liens" only obligations secured by mortgages or other liens on property that you included in the gross estate at its full value or at a value that was undiminished by the amount of the mortgage or lien. If the debt is enforceable against other property of the estate not subject to the mortgage or lien, or if the decedent was personally liable for the debt, you must include the full value of the property subject to the mortgage or lien in the gross estate under the appropriate schedule and may deduct the mortgage or lien on the property on this schedule.

However, if the decedent's estate is not liable, include in the gross estate only the value of the equity of redemption (or the value of the property less the amount of the debt), and do not deduct any portion of the indebtedness on this schedule.

Notes and other obligations secured by the deposit of collateral, such as stocks, bonds, etc., also should be listed under "Mortgages and Liens."

Description

Include under the "Description" column the particular schedule and item number where the property subject to the mortgage or lien is reported in the gross estate.

Include the name and address of the mortgagee, payee, or obligee, and the date and term of the mortgage, note, or other agreement by which the debt was established. Also include the face amount, the unpaid balance,

I.R.S.—Instructions for Form 706 (Continued)

the rate of interest, and date to which the interest was paid before the decedent's death.

Instructions for Schedule L.—Net Losses During Administration and Expenses Incurred in Administering Property Not Subject to Claims

You must complete Schedule L and file it with the return if you claim deductions on either item 18 or item 19 of Part 5, Recapitulation.

Net Losses During Administration

You may deduct only those losses from thefts, fires, storms, shipwrecks, or other casualties that occurred during the settlement of the estate. You may deduct only the amount not reimbursed by insurance or otherwise.

Describe in detail the loss sustained and the cause. If you received insurance or other compensation for the loss, state the amount collected. Identify the property for which you are claiming the loss by indicating the particular schedule and item number where the property is included in the gross estate.

If you elect alternate valuation, do not deduct the amount by which you reduced the value of an item to include it in the gross estate.

Do not deduct losses claimed as a deduction on a Federal income tax return or depreciation in the value of securities or other property.

Expenses Incurred in Administering Property Not Subject to Claims

You may deduct expenses incurred in administering property that is included in the gross estate but that is not subject to claims. You may only deduct these expenses if they were paid before the section 6501 period of limitations for assessment expired.

The expenses deductible on this schedule are usually expenses incurred in the administration of a trust established by the decedent before death. They may also be incurred in the collection of other assets or the transfer or clearance of title to other property included in the decedent's gross estate for estate tax purposes, but not included in the decedent's probate estate.

The expenses deductible on this schedule are limited to those that are the result of settling the decedent's interest in the property or of vesting good title to the property in the beneficiaries. Expenses incurred on behalf of the transferees (except those described above) are not deductible. Examples of deductible and nondeductible expenses are provided in Regulations section 20.2053-8.

List the names and addresses of the persons to whom each expense was payable and the nature of the expense. Identify the property for which the expense was incurred by indicating the schedule and item number where the property is included in the gross estate. If you do not know the exact amount of the expense, you may deduct an estimate, provided that the amount may be verified with reasonable certainty and will be paid before the period of limitations for assessment (referred to above) expires. Keep all vouchers and receipts for inspection by the Internal Revenue Service.

Instructions for Schedule M.—Bequests, etc. to Surviving Spouse (Marital Deduction)

See pages 28 through 30 of Form 706 for these instructions.

Instructions for Schedule O.—Charitable, Public, and Similar Gifts and Bequests

General

You must complete Schedule O and file it with the return if you claim a deduction on item 21 of the Recapitulation.

You can claim the charitable deduction allowed under section 2055 for the value of property in the decedent's gross estate that was transferred by the decedent during life or by will to or for the use of any of the following:

- The United States, a state, a political subdivision of a state, or the District of Columbia, for exclusively public purposes;
- Any corporation or association organized and operated exclusively for religious, charitable, scientific, literary, or educational purposes, including the encouragement of art, or to foster national or international amateur sports competition (but only if none of its activities involve providing athletic facilities or equipment, unless the organization is a qualified amateur sports organization) and the prevention of cruelty to children and animals, as long as no part of the net earnings benefits any private individual and no substantial activity is undertaken to carry on propaganda, or otherwise attempt to influence legislation or participate in any political campaign on behalf of any candidate for public office;
- A trustee or a fraternal society, order or association operating under the lodge system, if the transferred property is to be used exclusively for religious, charitable, scientific, literary, or educational purposes, or for the prevention of cruelty to children or animals, and no substantial activity is undertaken to carry on propaganda or otherwise attempt to influence legislation, or participate in any political campaign on behalf of any candidate for public office;
- Any veterans organization incorporated by an Act of Congress or any of its departments, local chapters, or posts, for which none of the net earnings benefits any private individual; or
- A foreign government or its political subdivision when the use of such property is limited exclusively to charitable purposes.

For this purpose, certain Indian tribal governments are treated as states and transfers to them qualify as deductible charitable contributions. See Rev. Proc. 83-87, 1983-2 C.B. 606, as modified and supplemented by subsequent Revenue Procedures, for a list of qualifying Indian tribal governments.

You may also claim a charitable contribution deduction for a qualifying conservation easement granted **after** the decedent's death under the provisions of section 2031(c)(9).

The charitable deduction is allowed for amounts that are transferred to charitable organizations as a result of either a qualified disclaimer (see **Line 2** below) or the complete termination of a power to consume, invade, or appropriate property for the benefit of an individual. It does not matter whether termination occurs because of the death of the individual or in any other way. The termination must occur within the period of time (including extensions) for filing the decedent's estate tax return and before the power has been exercised.

The deduction is limited to the amount actually available for charitable uses. Therefore, if under the terms of a will or the provisions of local law, or for any other reason, the Federal estate tax, the Federal GST tax, or any other estate, GST, succession, legacy, or inheritance tax is payable in whole or in part out of any bequest, legacy, or devise that would otherwise be allowed as a charitable deduction, the amount you may deduct is the amount of the bequest, legacy, or devise reduced by the total amount of the taxes.

If you elected to make installment payments of the estate tax, and the interest is payable out of property transferred to charity, you must reduce the charitable deduction by an estimate of the maximum amount of interest that will be paid on the deferred tax.

For split-interest trusts (or pooled income funds) enter in the "Amount" column the amount treated as passing to the charity. Do not enter the entire amount that passes to the trust (fund).

If you are deducting the value of the residue or a part of the residue passing to charity under the decedent's will, attach a copy of the computation showing how you determined the value, including any reduction for the taxes described above.

Also include:

1. A statement that shows the values of all specific and general legacies or devises for both charitable and noncharitable uses. For each legacy or devise, indicate the paragraph or section of the decedent's will or codicil that applies. (If legacies are made to each member of a class (e.g., $1,000 to each of the decedent's employees), show only the number of each class and the total value of property they received.)

2. The date of birth of all life tenants or annuitants, the length of whose lives may affect the value of the interest passing to charity under the decedent's will.

3. A statement showing the value of all property that is included in the decedent's gross estate but does not pass under the will, such as transfers, jointly owned property that passed to the survivor on decedent's death, and insurance payable to specific beneficiaries.

4. Any other important information such as that relating to any claim, not arising under the will, to any part of the estate (e.g., a spouse claiming dower or curtesy, or similar rights).

Line 2

The charitable deduction is allowed for amounts that are transferred to charitable organizations as a result of a qualified disclaimer. To be a qualified disclaimer, a refusal to accept an interest in property must meet the conditions of section 2518. These are explained in Regulations sections 25.2518-1 through 25.2518-3. If property passes to a charitable beneficiary as the result of a qualified disclaimer, check the "Yes" box on line 2 and attach a copy of the written disclaimer required by section 2518(b).

Attachments

If the charitable transfer was made by will, attach a certified copy of the order admitting the will to probate, in addition to the copy of the will. If the charitable transfer was made by any other written instrument, attach a copy. If the instrument is of record, the copy should be certified; if not, the copy should be verified.

Value

The valuation dates used in determining the value of the gross estate apply also on Schedule O.

I.R.S.—Instructions for Form 706 (Continued)

Instructions for Schedule P.—Credit for Foreign Death Taxes

General

If you claim a credit on line 18 of Part 2, Tax Computation, you must complete Schedule P and file it with the return. **You must attach Form(s) 706-CE, Certificate of Payment of Foreign Death Tax, to support any credit you claim.**

If the foreign government refuses to certify Form 706-CE, you must file it directly with the District Director as instructed on the Form 706-CE. See Form 706-CE for instructions on how to complete the form and for a description of the items that must be attached to the form when the foreign government refuses to certify it.

The credit for foreign death taxes is allowable only if the decedent was a citizen or resident of the United States. However, see section 2053(d) and the related regulations for exceptions and limitations if the executor has elected, in certain cases, to deduct these taxes from the value of the gross estate. For a resident, not a citizen, who was a citizen or subject of a foreign country for which the President has issued a proclamation under section 2014(h), the credit is allowable only if the country of which the decedent was a national allows a similar credit to decedents who were U.S. citizens residing in that country.

The credit is authorized either by statute or by treaty. If a credit is authorized by a treaty, whichever of the following is the most beneficial to the estate is allowed: **(a)** the credit computed under the treaty; **(b)** the credit computed under the statute; or **(c)** the credit computed under the treaty, plus the credit computed under the statute for death taxes paid to each political subdivision or possession of the treaty country that are not directly or indirectly creditable under the treaty. Under the statute, the credit is authorized for all death taxes (national and local) imposed in the foreign country. Whether local taxes are the basis for a credit under a treaty depends upon the provisions of the particular treaty.

If a credit for death taxes paid in more than one foreign country is allowable, a separate computation of the credit must be made for each foreign country. The copies of Schedule P on which the additional computations are made should be attached to the copy of Schedule P provided in the return.

The total credit allowable in respect to any property, whether subjected to tax by one or more than one foreign country, is limited to the amount of the Federal estate tax attributable to the property. The anticipated amount of the credit may be computed on the return, but the credit cannot finally be allowed until the foreign tax has been paid and a Form 706-CE evidencing payment is filed. Section 2014(g) provides that for credits for foreign death taxes, each U.S. possession is deemed a foreign country.

Convert death taxes paid to the foreign country into U.S. dollars by using the rate of exchange in effect at the time each payment of foreign tax is made.

If a credit is claimed for any foreign death tax that is later recovered, see Regulations section 20.2016-1 for the notice required within 30 days.

Limitation period

The credit for foreign death taxes is limited to those taxes that actually were paid and for which a credit was claimed within the later of the 4 years after the filing of the estate tax return, or before the date of expiration of any extension of time for payment of the Federal estate tax, or 60 days after a final decision of the Tax Court on a timely filed petition for a redetermination of a deficiency.

Credit Under the Statute

For the credit allowed by the statute, the question of whether particular property is situated in the foreign country imposing the tax is determined by the same principles that would apply in determining whether similar property of a nonresident not a U.S. citizen is situated within the United States for purposes of the Federal estate tax. See the instructions for Form 706-NA.

Computation of Credit Under the Statute

Item 1.— Enter the amount of the estate, inheritance, legacy, and succession taxes paid to the foreign country and its possessions or political subdivisions, attributable to property that is **(a)** situated in that country, **(b)** subjected to these taxes, and **(c)** included in the gross estate. The amount entered at item 1 should not include any tax paid to the foreign country with respect to property not situated in that country and should not include any tax paid to the foreign country with respect to property not included in the gross estate. If only a part of the property subjected to foreign taxes is both situated in the foreign country and included in the gross estate, it will be necessary to determine the portion of the taxes attributable to that part of the property. Also attach the computation of the amount entered at item 1.

Item 2.— Enter the value of the gross estate less the total of the deductions on items 20 and 21 of Part 5, Recapitulation.

Item 3.— Enter the value of the property situated in the foreign country that is subjected to the foreign taxes and included in the gross estate, less those portions of the deductions taken on Schedules M and O that are attributable to the property.

Item 4.— Subtract line 17, Part 2, Form 706 from line 16, Part 2, Form 706, and enter the balance at item 4 of Schedule P.

Credit Under Treaties

If you are reporting any items on this return based on the provisions of a death tax treaty, you may have to attach a statement to this return disclosing the return position that is treaty based. See Regulations section 301.6114-1 for details.

In general.— If the provisions of a treaty apply to the estate of a U.S. citizen or resident, a credit is authorized for payment of the foreign death tax or taxes specified in the treaty. Treaties with death tax conventions are in effect with the following countries: Australia, Austria, Canada, Denmark, Finland, France, Germany, Greece, Ireland, Italy, Japan, Netherlands, Norway, Republic of South Africa, Sweden, Switzerland, and the United Kingdom.

A credit claimed under a treaty is in general computed on Schedule P in the same manner as the credit is computed under the statute with the following principal exceptions:

- The situs rules contained in the treaty apply in determining whether property was situated in the foreign country;
- The credit may be allowed only for payment of the death tax or taxes specified in the treaty (but see the instructions above for credit under the statute for death taxes paid to each political subdivision or possession of the treaty country that are not directly or indirectly creditable under the treaty);
- If specifically provided, the credit is proportionately shared for the tax applicable to property situated outside both countries, or that was deemed in some instances situated within both countries; and
- The amount entered at item 4 of Schedule P is the amount shown on line 16 of Part 2, Tax Computation, less the total of the amounts on lines 17 and 19 of the Tax Computation. (If a credit is claimed for tax on prior transfers, it will be necessary to complete Schedule Q before completing Schedule P.) For examples of computation of credits under the treaties, see the applicable regulations.

Computation of credit in cases where property is situated outside both countries or deemed situated within both countries.— See the appropriate treaty for details.

Instructions for Schedule Q.—Credit for Tax on Prior Transfers

General

You must complete Schedule Q and file it with the return if you claim a credit on line 19 of Part 2, Tax Computation.

The term "transferee" means the decedent for whose estate this return is filed. If the transferee received property from a transferor who died within 10 years before, or 2 years after, the transferee, a credit is allowable on this return for all or part of the Federal estate tax paid by the transferor's estate with respect to the transfer. There is no requirement that the property be identified in the estate of the transferee or that it exist on the date of the transferee's death. It is sufficient for the allowance of the credit that the transfer of the property was subjected to Federal estate tax in the estate of the transferor and that the specified period of time has not elapsed. A credit may be allowed with respect to property received as the result of the exercise or nonexercise of a power of appointment when the property is included in the gross estate of the donee of the power.

If the transferee was the transferor's surviving spouse, no credit is allowed for property received from the transferor to the extent that a marital deduction was allowed to the transferor's estate for the property. There is no credit for tax on prior transfers for Federal gift taxes paid in connection with the transfer of the property to the transferee.

If you are claiming a credit for tax on prior transfers on Form 706-NA, you should first complete and attach the Recapitulation from Form 706 before computing the credit on Schedule Q from Form 706.

Section 2056(d)(3) contains specific rules for allowing a credit for certain transfers to a spouse who was not a U.S. citizen where the property passed outright to the spouse, or to a "qualified domestic trust."

Property

The term "property" includes any interest (legal or equitable) of which the transferee received the beneficial ownership. The transferee is considered the beneficial owner of property over which the transferee received a general power of appointment. Property does not include interests to which the transferee received only a bare legal title, such as that of a trustee. Neither does it include an interest in property over which the transferee received a power of appointment that is not a general power of appointment. In addition to interests in which the transferee received the complete ownership, the credit may be allowed for annuities, life estates, terms for years,

I.R.S.—Instructions for Form 706 (Continued)

remainder interests (whether contingent or vested), and any other interest that is less than the complete ownership of the property, to the extent that the transferee became the beneficial owner of the interest.

Maximum Amount of the Credit

The maximum amount of the credit is the smaller of:

1. The amount of the estate tax of the transferor's estate attributable to the transferred property, or

2. The amount by which **(a)** an estate tax on the transferee's estate determined without the credit for tax on prior transfers, exceeds **(b)** an estate tax on the transferee's estate determined by excluding from the gross estate the net value of the transfer. If credit for a particular foreign death tax may be taken under either the statute or a death duty convention, and on this return the credit actually is taken under the convention, then no credit for that foreign death tax may be taken into consideration in computing estate tax **(a)** or estate tax **(b)** above.

Percent Allowable

Where transferee predeceased the transferor.— If not more than 2 years elapsed between the dates of death, the credit allowed is 100% of the maximum amount. If more than 2 years elapsed between the dates of death, no credit is allowed.

Where transferor predeceased the transferee.— The percent of the maximum amount that is allowed as a credit depends on the number of years that elapsed between dates of death. It is determined using the following table:

Period of Time Exceeding	Not Exceeding	Percent Allowable
-----	2 years	100
2 years	4 years	80
4 years	6 years	60
6 years	8 years	40
8 years	10 years	20
10 years	-----	none

How To Compute the Credit

A worksheet is provided on the last page of these instructions to allow you to compute the limits before completing Schedule Q. Transfer the appropriate amounts from the worksheet to Schedule Q as indicated on the schedule. You do not need to file the worksheet with your Form 706, but should keep it for your records.

Cases involving transfers from two or more transferors.— Part I of the worksheet and Schedule Q enable you to compute the credit for as many as three transferors. The number of transferors is irrelevant to Part II of the worksheet. If you are computing the credit for more than three transferors, use more than one worksheet and Schedule Q, Part I, and combine the totals for the appropriate lines.

Section 2032A additional tax.— If the *transferor's* estate elected special use valuation and the additional estate tax of section 2032A(c) was imposed at any time up to 2 years after the death of the *decedent for whom you are filing this return,* check the box on Schedule Q. On lines 1 and 9 of the worksheet, include the property subject to the additional estate tax at its fair market value rather than its special use value. On line 10 of the worksheet, include the additional estate tax paid as a Federal estate tax paid.

How To Complete the Worksheet

Most of the information to complete Part I of the worksheet should be obtained from the transferor's Form 706.

Line 5.— Enter on line 5 the applicable marital deduction claimed for the transferor's estate (from the transferor's Form 706).

Lines 10–18.— Enter on these lines the appropriate taxes paid by the transferor's estate.

If the transferor's estate elected to pay the Federal estate tax in installments, enter on line 10 only the total of the installments that have actually been paid at the time you file this Form 706. See Rev. Rul. 83-15, 1983-1 C.B. 224, for more details. Do not include as estate tax any tax attributable to section 4980A, before its repeal by the Taxpayer Relief Act of 1997.

Line 21.— Add lines 13, 15, 17, and 18 of Part 2, Tax Computation, of this Form 706 and subtract this total from line 10 of the Tax Computation. Enter the result on line 21 of the worksheet.

Line 26.— If you computed the marital deduction on this Form 706 using the rules that were in effect before the Economic Recovery Tax Act of 1981 (as described in the instructions to line 14 of Part 4 of General Information), enter on line 26 the lesser of:

- The marital deduction you claimed on line 20 of Part 5 of the Recapitulation; or
- 50% of the "reduced adjusted gross estate."

If you computed the marital deduction using the unlimited marital deduction in effect for decedents dying after 1981, for purposes of determining the marital deduction for the reduced gross estate, see Rev. Rul. 90-2, 1990-1 C.B. 170. To determine the "reduced adjusted gross estate," subtract the amount on line 25 of the Schedule Q worksheet from the amount on line 24 of the worksheet. If community property is included in the amount on line 24 of the worksheet, compute the reduced adjusted gross estate using the rules of Regulations section 20.2056(c)-2 and Rev. Rul. 76-311, 1976-2 C.B. 261.

Instructions for Schedules R and R-1.— Generation-Skipping Transfer Tax

Introduction and Overview

Schedule R is used to compute the generation-skipping transfer (GST) tax that is payable by the estate. Schedule R-1 (Form 706) is used to compute the GST tax that is payable by certain trusts that are includible in the gross estate.

The GST tax that is to be reported on Form 706 is imposed only on "direct skips occurring at death." Unlike the estate tax, which is imposed on the value of the entire taxable estate regardless of who receives it, the GST tax is imposed only on the value of interests in property, wherever located, that actually pass to certain transferees, who are referred to as "skip persons."

For purposes of Form 706, the property interests transferred must be includible in the gross estate before they are subject to the GST tax. Therefore, the first step in computing the GST tax liability is to determine the property interests includible in the gross estate by completing Schedules A–I of Form 706.

The second step is to determine who the skip persons are. To do this, assign each transferee to a generation and determine whether each transferee is a "natural person" or a "trust" for GST purposes.

The third step is to determine which skip persons are transferees of "interests in property." If the skip person is a natural person, anything transferred is an interest in property. If the skip person is a trust, make this determination using the rules under **Interest in Property** on page 18. These first three steps are described in detail under the heading **Determining Which Transfers Are Direct Skips.**

The fourth step is to determine whether to enter the transfer on Schedule R or on Schedule R-1. See the rules under the heading **Dividing Direct Skips Between Schedules R and R-1.**

The fifth step is to complete Schedules R and R-1 using the **How To Complete** instructions on page 19, for each schedule.

Determining Which Transfers Are Direct Skips

Effective dates.— The rules below apply **only** for the purpose of determining if a transfer is a direct skip that should be reported on Schedule R or R-1 of Form 706.

In general.— The GST tax is effective for the estates of decedents dying after October 22, 1986.

Irrevocable trusts.— The GST tax will not apply to any transfer under a trust that was irrevocable on September 25, 1985, but only to the extent that the transfer was not made out of corpus added to the trust after September 25, 1985. An addition to the corpus after that date will cause a proportionate part of future income and appreciation to be subject to the GST tax. For more information, see Regulations section 26.2601-1(b)(1)(ii).

Mental disability.— If, on October 22, 1986, the decedent was under a mental disability to change the disposition of his or her property and did not regain the competence to dispose of property before death, the GST tax will not apply to any property included in the gross estate (other than property transferred on behalf of the decedent during life and after October 21, 1986). The GST tax will also not apply to any transfer under a trust to the extent that the trust consists of property included in the gross estate (other than property transferred on behalf of the decedent during life and after October 21, 1986).

The term "mental disability" means the decedent's mental incompetence to execute an instrument governing the disposition of his or her property, whether or not there has been an adjudication of incompetence and whether or not there has been an appointment of any other person charged with the care of the person or property of the transferor.

If the decedent had been adjudged mentally incompetent, a copy of the judgment or decree must be filed with this return.

If the decedent had not been adjudged mentally incompetent, the executor must file with the return a certification from a qualified physician stating that in his opinion the decedent had been mentally incompetent at all times on and after October 22, 1986, and that the decedent had not regained the competence to modify or revoke the terms of the trust or will prior to his death or a statement as to why no such certification may be obtained from a physician.

Direct skip.— The GST tax reported on Form 706 and Schedule R-1 (Form 706) is imposed only on direct skips. For purposes of Form 706, a direct skip is a transfer that is:

1. Subject to the estate tax,

2. Of an interest in property, and

3. To a skip person.

All three requirements must be met before the transfer is subject to the GST tax. A transfer is subject to the estate tax if you are required to list it on any of Schedules A–I of Form 706. To determine if a transfer is of an interest in property and to a skip person, you must first determine if the transferee is a natural person or a trust as defined below.

I.R.S.—Instructions for Form 706 (Continued)

Trust.— For purposes of the GST tax, a trust includes not only an explicit trust (as defined in **Special Rule for Trusts Other than Explicit Trusts** below), but also any other arrangement (other than an estate) which, although not explicitly a trust, has substantially the same effect as a trust. For example, trust includes life estates with remainders, terms for years, and insurance and annuity contracts.

Substantially separate and independent shares of different beneficiaries in a trust are treated as separate trusts.

Interest in property.— If a transfer is made to a natural person, it is always considered a transfer of an interest in property for purposes of the GST tax.

If a transfer is made to a trust, a person will have an interest in the property transferred to the trust if that person either has a present right to receive income or corpus from the trust (such as an income interest for life) or is a permissible current recipient of income or corpus from the trust (e.g., may receive income or corpus at the discretion of the trustee).

Skip person.— A transferee who is a natural person is a skip person if that transferee is assigned to a generation that is two or more generations below the generation assignment of the decedent. See **Determining the Generation of a Transferee,** below.

A transferee who is a trust is a skip person if all the interests in the property (as defined above) transferred to the trust are held by skip persons. Thus, whenever a non-skip person has an interest in a trust, the trust will not be a skip person even though a skip person also has an interest in the trust.

A trust will also be a skip person if there are no interests in the property transferred to the trust held by any person, and future distributions or terminations from the trust can be made only to skip persons.

Non-skip person.— A non-skip person is any transferee who is not a skip person.

Determining the generation of a transferee.— Generally, a generation is determined along family lines as follows:

1. Where the beneficiary is a lineal descendant of a grandparent of the decedent (for example, the decedent's cousin, niece, nephew, etc.), the number of generations between the decedent and the beneficiary is determined by subtracting the number of generations between the grandparent and the decedent from the number of generations between the grandparent and the beneficiary.

2. Where the beneficiary is a lineal descendant of a grandparent of a spouse (or former spouse) of the decedent, the number of generations between the decedent and the beneficiary is determined by subtracting the number of generations between the grandparent and the spouse (or former spouse) from the number of generations between the grandparent and the beneficiary.

3. A person who at any time was married to a person described in **1** or **2** above is assigned to the generation of that person. A person who at any time was married to the decedent is assigned to the decedent's generation.

4. A relationship by adoption or half-blood is treated as a relationship by whole-blood.

5. A person who is not assigned to a generation according to **1, 2, 3,** or **4** above is assigned to a generation based on his or her birth date, as follows:

a. A person who was born not more than 12½ years after the decedent is in the decedent's generation.

b. A person born more than 12½ years, but not more than 37½ years, after the decedent is in the first generation younger than the decedent.

c. A similar rule applies for a new generation every 25 years.

If more than one of the rules for assigning generations applies to a transferee, that transferee is generally assigned to the youngest of the generations that would apply.

If an estate, trust, partnership, corporation, or other entity (other than certain charitable organizations and trusts described in sections 511(a)(2) and 511(b)(2)) is a transferee, then each person who indirectly receives the property interests through the entity is treated as a transferee and is assigned to a generation as explained in the above rules. However, this look-thru rule does not apply for the purpose of determining whether a transfer to a trust is a direct skip.

Generation assignment where intervening parent is dead.— A special rule may apply in the case of the death of a parent of the transferee. For terminations, distributions, and transfers after December 31, 1997, the existing rule that applied to grandchildren of the decedent has been extended to apply to other lineal descendants.

If property is transferred to an individual who is a descendant of a parent of the transferor, and that individual's parent (who is a lineal descendant of the parent of the transferor) is dead at the time the transfer is subject to gift or estate tax, then for purposes of generation assignment, the individual is treated as if he or she is a member of the generation that is one generation below the lower of:

- the transferor's generation, or
- the generation assignment of the youngest living ancestor of the individual, who is also a descendant of the parent of the transferor.

The same rules apply to the generation assignment of any descendant of the individual.

This rule **does not** apply to a transfer to an individual who is not a lineal descendant of the transferor if the transferor has any living lineal descendants.

If any transfer of property to a trust would have been a direct skip except for this generation assignment rule, then the rule also applies to transfers from the trust attributable to such property.

Charitable organizations.— Charitable organizations and trusts described in sections 511(a)(2) and 511(b)(2) are assigned to the decedent's generation. Transfers to such organizations are therefore not subject to the GST tax.

Charitable remainder trusts.— Transfers to or in the form of charitable remainder annuity trusts, charitable remainder unitrusts, and pooled income funds are not considered made to skip persons and, therefore, are not direct skips even if all of the life beneficiaries are skip persons.

Estate tax value.— Estate tax value is the value shown on Schedules A–I of this Form 706.

Examples.— The rules above can be illustrated by the following examples:

Example 1.— Under the will, the decedent's house is transferred to the decedent's daughter for her life with the remainder passing to her children. This transfer is made to a "trust" even though there is no explicit trust instrument. The interest in the property transferred (the present right to use the house) is transferred to a nonskip person (the decedent's daughter). Therefore, the trust is not a skip person because there is an interest in the transferred property that is held by a non-skip person. The transfer is not a direct skip.

Example 2.— The will bequeaths $100,000 to the decedent's grandchild. This transfer is a direct skip that is not made in trust and should be shown on Schedule R.

Example 3.— The will establishes a trust that is required to accumulate income for 10 years and then pay its income to the decedent's grandchildren for the rest of their lives and, upon their deaths, distribute the corpus to the decedent's great-grandchildren. Because the trust has no current beneficiaries, there are no present interests in the property transferred to the trust. All of the persons to whom the trust can make future distributions (including distributions upon the termination of interests in property held in trust) are skip persons (i.e., the decedent's grandchildren and great-grandchildren). Therefore, the trust itself is a skip person and you should show the transfer on Schedule R.

Example 4.— The will establishes a trust that is to pay all of its income to the decedent's grandchildren for 10 years. At the end of 10 years, the corpus is to be distributed to the decedent's children. All of the interests in this trust are held by skip persons. Therefore, the trust is a skip person and you should show this transfer on Schedule R. You should show the estate tax value of all the property transferred to the trust even though the trust has some ultimate beneficiaries who are non-skip persons.

Dividing Direct Skips Between Schedules R and R-1

Report all generation-skipping transfers on Schedule R unless the rules below specifically provide that they are to be reported on Schedule R-1.

Under section 2603(a)(2), the GST tax on direct skips from a trust (as defined for GST tax purposes above) is to be paid by the trustee and not by the estate. Schedule R-1 serves as a notification from the executor to the trustee that a GST tax is due.

For a direct skip to be reportable on Schedule R-1, the trust must be includible in the decedent's gross estate.

If the decedent was the surviving spouse life beneficiary of a marital deduction power of appointment (or QTIP) trust created by the decedent's spouse, then transfers caused by reason of the decedent's death from that trust to skip persons are direct skips required to be reported on Schedule R-1.

If a direct skip is made "from a trust" under these rules, it is reportable on Schedule R-1 even if it is also made "to a trust" rather than to an individual.

Similarly, if property in a trust (as defined for GST tax purposes on page 17) is included in the decedent's gross estate under section 2035, 2036, 2037, 2038, 2039, 2041, or 2042 and such property is, by reason of the decedent's death, transferred to skip persons, the transfers are direct skips required to be reported on Schedule R-1.

Special rule for trusts other than explicit trusts.— An **explicit trust** is a trust as defined in Regulations section 301.7701-4(a) as "an arrangement created by a will or by an inter vivos declaration whereby trustees take title to property for the purpose of protecting or conserving it for the beneficiaries under the ordinary rules applied in chancery or probate courts." Direct skips from explicit trusts are required to be reported on Schedule R-1 regardless of their size unless the executor is also a trustee (see page 19).

Direct skips from trusts that are trusts for GST tax purposes but are not explicit trusts are to be shown on Schedule R-1 only if the total of all tentative maximum direct skips from the

I.R.S.—Instructions for Form 706 (Continued)

entity is $250,000 or more. If this total is less than $250,000, the skips should be shown on Schedule R. For purposes of the $250,000 limit, "tentative maximum direct skips" is the amount you would enter on line 5 of Schedule R-1 if you were to file that schedule.

A liquidating trust (such as a bankruptcy trust) under Regulations section 301.7701-4(d) is not treated as an explicit trust for the purposes of this special rule.

If the proceeds of a life insurance policy are includible in the gross estate and are payable to a beneficiary who is a skip person, the transfer is a direct skip from a trust that is not an explicit trust. It should be reported on Schedule R-1 if the total of all the tentative maximum direct skips from the company is $250,000 or more. Otherwise, it should be reported on Schedule R.

Similarly, if an annuity is includible on Schedule I and its survivor benefits are payable to a beneficiary who is a skip person, then the estate tax value of the annuity should be reported as a direct skip on Schedule R-1 if the total tentative maximum direct skips from the entity paying the annuity is $250,000 or more.

Executor as trustee.— If any of the executors of the decedent's estate are trustees of the trust, then all direct skips with respect to that trust must be shown on Schedule R and not on Schedule R-1 even if they would otherwise have been required to be shown on Schedule R-1. This rule applies even if the trust has other trustees who are not executors of the decedent's estate.

How To Complete Schedules R and R-1

Valuation.— Enter on Schedules R and R-1 the estate tax value of the property interests subject to the direct skips. If you elected alternate valuation (section 2032) and/or special use valuation (section 2032A), you must use the alternate and/or special use values on Schedules R and R-1.

How To Complete Schedule R

Part 1—GST exemption reconciliation.— Part 1, line 6 of both Parts 2 and 3, and line 4 of Schedule R-1 are used to allocate the decedent's $1 million GST exemption. This allocation is made by filing Form 706. Once made, the allocation is irrevocable. You are not required to allocate all of the decedent's GST exemption. However, the portion of the exemption that you do not allocate will be allocated by IRS under the deemed allocation at death rules of section 2632(c).

Special QTIP election.— In the case of property for which a marital deduction is allowed to the decedent's estate under section 2056(b)(7) (QTIP election), section 2652(a)(3) allows you to treat such property for purposes of the GST tax as if the election to be treated as qualified terminable interest property had not been made.

The 2652(a)(3) election must include the value of all property in the trust for which a QTIP election was allowed under section 2056(b)(7).

If a section 2652(a)(3) election is made, then the decedent will for GST tax purposes be treated as the transferor of all the property in the trust for which a marital deduction was allowed to the decedent's estate under section 2056(b)(7). In this case, the executor of the decedent's estate may allocate part or all of the decedent's GST exemption to the property.

You make the election simply by listing qualifying property on line 9 of Part 1.

Line 2.— These allocations will have been made either on Forms 709 filed by the decedent or on Notices of Allocation made by the decedent for inter vivos transfers that were not direct skips but to which the decedent allocated the GST exemption. These allocations by the decedent are irrevocable.

Line 3.— Make an entry on this line if you are filing Form(s) 709 for the decedent and wish to allocate any exemption.

Lines 4, 5, and 6.— These lines represent your allocation of the GST exemption to direct skips made by reason of the decedent's death. Complete Parts 2 and 3 and Schedule R-1 before completing these lines.

Line 9.— Line 9 is used to allocate the remaining unused GST exemption (from line 8) and to help you compute the trust's inclusion ratio. Line 9 is a Notice of Allocation for allocating the GST exemption to trusts as to which the decedent is the transferor and from which a generation-skipping transfer could occur after the decedent's death. If line 9 is not completed, the deemed allocation at death rules will apply to allocate the decedent's remaining unused GST exemption, first to property that is the subject of a direct skip occurring at the decedent's death, and then to trusts as to which the decedent is the transferor. If you wish to avoid the application of the deemed allocation rules, you should enter on line 9 every trust (except certain trusts entered on Schedule R-1, as described below) to which you wish to allocate any part of the decedent's GST exemption. Unless you enter a trust on line 9, the unused GST exemption will be allocated to it under the deemed allocation rules.

If a trust is entered on Schedule R-1, the amount you entered on line 4 of Schedule R-1 serves as a Notice of Allocation and you need not enter the trust on line 9 unless you wish to allocate more than the Schedule R-1, line 4 amount to the trust. However, you must enter the trust on line 9 if you wish to allocate any of the unused GST exemption amount to it. Such an additional allocation would not ordinarily be appropriate in the case of a trust entered on Schedule R-1 when the trust property passes outright (rather than to another trust) at the decedent's death. However, where section 2032A property is involved it may be appropriate to allocate additional exemption amounts to the property. See the instructions for line 10.

Note: *To avoid application of the deemed allocation rules, Form 706 and Schedule R should be filed to allocate the exemption to trusts that may later have taxable terminations or distributions under section 2612 even if the form is not required to be filed to report estate or GST tax.*

Line 9, column C.— Enter the GST exemption included on lines 2–6 above that was allocated to the trust.

Line 9, column D.— The line 8 amount is to be allocated in column D of line 9. This amount may be allocated to transfers into trusts that are not otherwise reported on Form 706. For example, the line 8 amount may be allocated to an inter vivos trust established by the decedent during his or her lifetime and not included in the gross estate. This allocation is made by identifying the trust on line 9 and making an allocation to it using column D. If the trust is not included in the gross estate, value the trust as of the date of death. You should inform the trustee of each trust listed on line 9 of the total GST exemption you allocated to the trust. The trustee will need this information to compute the GST tax on future distributions and terminations.

Line 9, column E—trust's inclusion ratio.— The trustee must know the trust's inclusion ratio to figure the trust's GST tax for future distributions and terminations. You are not required to inform the trustee of the inclusion ratio and may not have enough information to compute it. Therefore, you are not required to make an entry in column E. However, column E and the worksheet below are provided to assist you in computing the inclusion ratio for the trustee if you wish to do so.

You should inform the trustee of the amount of the GST exemption you allocated to the trust. Line 9, columns C and D may be used to compute this amount for each trust.

This worksheet will compute an accurate inclusion ratio only if the decedent was the only settlor of the trust. You should use a separate worksheet for each trust (or separate share of a trust that is treated as a separate trust).

1	Total estate and gift tax value of all of the property interests that passed to the trust	______
2	Estate taxes, state death taxes, and other charges actually recovered from the trust	______
3	GST taxes imposed on direct skips to skip persons other than this trust and borne by the property transferred to this trust	______
4	GST taxes actually recovered from this trust (from Schedule R, Part 2, line 8 or Schedule R-1, line 6)	______
5	Add lines 2–4	______
6	Subtract line 5 from line 1	______
7	Add columns C and D of line 9	______
8	Divide line 7 by line 6	______
9	Trust's inclusion ratio. Subtract line 8 from 1.000	______

Line 10—Special use allocation.— For skip persons who receive an interest in section 2032A special use property, you may allocate more GST exemption than the direct skip amount to reduce the additional GST tax that would be due when the interest is later disposed of or qualified use ceases. See Schedule A-1 of this Form 706 for more details about this additional GST tax.

Enter on line 10 the total additional GST exemption you are allocating to all skip persons who received any interest in section 2032A property. Attach a special use allocation schedule listing each such skip person and the amount of the GST exemption allocated to that person.

If you do not allocate the GST exemption, it will be automatically allocated under the deemed allocation at death rules. To the extent any amount is not so allocated it will be automatically allocated (under regulations to be published) to the earliest disposition or cessation that is subject to the GST tax. Under certain circumstances, post-death events may cause the decedent to be treated as a transferor for purposes of Chapter 13.

Line 10 may be used to set aside an exemption amount for such an event. You must attach a schedule listing each such event and the amount of exemption allocated to that event.

Parts 2 and 3.— Use Part 2 to compute the GST tax on transfers in which the property interests transferred are to bear the GST tax on the transfers. Use Part 3 to report the GST tax on transfers in which the property interests transferred do not bear the GST tax on the transfers.

Section 2603(b) requires that unless the governing instrument provides otherwise, the GST tax is to be charged to the property constituting the transfer. Therefore, you will usually enter all of the direct skips on Part 2.

You may enter a transfer on Part 3 only if the will or trust instrument directs, by specific reference, that the GST tax is not to be paid from the transferred property interests.

Part 2—Line 3.— Enter -0- on this line unless the will or trust instrument specifies that the GST taxes will be paid by property other than that constituting the transfer (as described above). Enter on line 3 the total of the GST

I.R.S. — Instructions for Form 706 (Continued)

taxes shown on Part 3 and Schedule(s) R-1 that are payable out of the property interests shown on Part 2, line 1.

Part 2—Line 6.— Do not enter more than the amount on line 5. Additional allocations may be made using Part 1.

Part 3—Line 3.— See the instructions to Part 2, line 3, on page 19. Enter only the total of the GST taxes shown on Schedule(s) R-1 that are payable out of the property interests shown on Part 3, line 1.

Part 3—Line 6.— See the instructions to Part 2, line 6, above.

How To Complete Schedule R-1

Filing due date.— Enter the due date of Schedule R, Form 706. You must send the copies of Schedule R-1 to the fiduciary by this date.

Line 4.— Do not enter more than the amount on line 3. If you wish to allocate an additional GST exemption, you must use Schedule R, Part 1. Making an entry on line 4 constitutes a Notice of Allocation of the decedent's GST exemption to the trust.

Line 6.— If the property interests entered on line 1 will not bear the GST tax, multiply line 6 by 55% (.55).

Signature.— The executor(s) must sign Schedule R-1 in the same manner as Form 706. See **Signature and Verification** on page 2.

Filing Schedule R-1.— Attach one copy of each Schedule R-1 that you prepare to Form 706. Send two copies of each Schedule R-1 to the fiduciary.

Schedule T.—Qualified Family-Owned Business Interest Deduction

Under section 2057, you may elect to deduct the value of certain family-owned business interests from the gross estate. You make the election by filing Schedule T, attaching all required statements, and deducting the value of the qualifying business interests on Part 5, Recapitulation, page 3, at item 22. You can only deduct the value of property that you have also reported on Schedule A, B, C, F, G, or H of Form 706.

For the estates of decedents dying in 1998, the amount of the deduction cannot exceed the lesser of:

- The adjusted value of the qualified family-owned business interests of the decedent otherwise includible in the gross estate, or
- $675,000.

General Requirements

Business interests may qualify for the exclusion if the following requirements are met:

- The decedent was a citizen or resident of the United States at the date of death.
- The business interests are includible in the gross estate.
- The interests must have passed to or been acquired by a qualified heir from the decedent.
- The adjusted value of the qualified family-owned business interests must exceed 50% of the adjusted gross estate (see below for a discussion of these terms).
- The interest must be in a trade or business that has its principal place of business in the United States.
- The business interest was owned by the decedent or a member of the decedent's family during 5 of the 8 years before the decedent's death.
- For 5 of the 8 years before the decedent's death, there was material participation by the decedent or a member of the decedent's family in the business to which the ownership interest relates.

Qualified Family-Owned Business Interest

In general.— To qualify for the deduction, the business interest must be either an interest as a proprietor in a trade or business carried on as a proprietorship, or an interest in an entity carrying on a trade or business in which:

- At least 50% of the entity is owned by the decedent or members of the decedent's family.
- At least 70% of the entity is owned by members of 2 families, and at least 30% is owned by the decedent or members of the decedent's family. Or,
- At least 90% of the entity is owned by members of 3 families, and at least 30% is owned by the decedent or members of the decedent's family.

In all cases, ownership may be either direct or indirect.

Ownership rules.— Ownership of the business interest may either be direct, or indirect through a corporation, partnership, or a trust. An interest owned, directly or indirectly, by or for such an entity is considered owned proportionately by or for the entity's shareholders, partners, or beneficiaries. A person is the beneficiary of a trust only if he or she has a present interest in the trust.

Corporations.— Ownership of a corporation is determined by holding stock that has the appropriate percentage of the total combined voting power of all classes of stock entitled to vote and the appropriate percentage of the total value of shares of all classes of stock.

Partnerships.— Ownership of a partnership is based on owning the appropriate percentage of the capital interest in the partnership.

Tiered entities.— For the purpose of determining ownership of a business under section 2057, if the decedent, a member of the decedent's family, any qualified heir, or any member of the qualified heir's family owns an interest in a business, and by reason of that ownership the person is treated as owning an interest in any other business, the ownership interest in the other business is disregarded in determining the ownership interest in the first business. Likewise, you must apply the ownership rules separately in determining ownership of the other business.

Limitations

"Qualified family-owned business interests" shall **not** include the following:

- Any interest in a trade or business if its principal place of business is located outside the United States.
- Any interest in an entity if the stock or debt of the entity (or a controlled group of which the entity is a member) was readily tradable on an established securities market or secondary market at any time within 3 years of the date of the decedent's death.
- Any interest in a trade or business (excluding banks and domestic building and loan associations) if more than 35% of its adjusted ordinary gross income for the taxable year that includes the date of the decedent's death would qualify as personal holding company income (as defined in section 2057(e)(2)(C)) if such trade or business was a corporation.
- The portion of an interest in a trade or business that is attributable to:

1. Cash and/or marketable securities in excess of the reasonably expected day-to-day working capital needs, and

2. Any other assets (other than assets held in the active conduct of a bank or domestic building and loan) which produce or are held for the production of personal holding company income and most types of foreign personal holding company income. See section 2057(e)(2)(D) for more information.

Net cash lease.— If the decedent leased property on a net cash basis to a member of the decedent's family, income from the lease is not considered personal holding company income for this purpose, and the property is not considered an asset producing or held for the production of personal holding company income. However, if the income or property would have been personal holding company income or property if the decedent had engaged directly in the activities of the lessee, then this net cash lease rule does not apply.

Qualified Heir

A person is a qualified heir of property if he or she is a member of the decedent's family and acquired or received the interest from the decedent.

If a qualified heir disposes of any qualified family-owned business interest to any member of his or her family, that person will then be treated as the qualified heir with respect to that interest.

The term member of the family includes only:

- An ancestor (parent, grandparent, etc.) of the individual;
- The spouse of the individual;
- The lineal descendent (child, stepchild, grandchild, etc.) of the individual, the individual's spouse, or a parent of the individual; and
- The spouse, widow, or widower of any lineal descendent described above.

A legally adopted child of an individual is treated as a child of that individual by blood.

For the purpose of this deduction, qualified heir also includes any active employee of the trade or business to which the qualified family-owned business interest relates if the employee has been employed by the trade or business for a period of at least 10 years before the date of the decedent's death.

Interests Acquired From the Decedent

An interest in a business is considered to have been acquired from or to have passed from the decedent if one or more of the following apply:

- The interest is considered to have been acquired from or to have passed from the decedent under section 1014(b) (relating to basis of property acquired from a decedent).
- The interest is acquired by any person from the estate.
- The interest is acquired by any person from a trust, to the extent the property is includible in the gross estate.

Material Participation

To make the section 2057 election, either the decedent or a member of the decedent's family must have materially participated in the trade or business to which the ownership interest relates for at least 5 of the 8 years ending on the date of the decedent's death.

The existence of material participation is a factual determination, and the types of activities and financial risks that will support a finding of material participation will vary with the mode of ownership. No single factor is determinative of the presence of material participation, but physical work and participation in management decisions are the principal factors to be considered. Passively collecting rents, salaries, draws, dividends, or other income from the

I.R.S.—Instructions for Form 706 (Continued)

trade or business does not constitute material participation. Neither does merely advancing capital and reviewing business plans and financial reports each business year.

For more information on material participation, see page 4 of these instructions and Regulations section 20.2032A-3.

Specific Instructions

Line 4

If any qualified heir is not a U.S. citizen, the ownership interest he or she receives must pass, be acquired, or be held in a qualified trust. See section 2057(g) for details. If any qualified heir listed on line 4 is not a U.S. citizen, indicate along with their address "citizen of _______," filling-in the appropriate country.

Line 5

List on line 5 **all** qualified family-owned business interests included in the gross estate, even if they will not be included in the deduction because, for example, they pass to the surviving spouse and are deducted on Schedule M rather than Schedule T (see the instructions for line 15 below).

Line 7

Enter on line 7 the amount, if any, deductible from the gross estate as claims against the estate or indebtedness of the estate reported elsewhere on this Form 706. Do not include funeral or administrative expenses on this line.

Line 8a

Enter the amount of any indebtedness that is both:

- Included on line 7, and
- Indebtedness on a residence of the decedent that qualifies for the mortgage interest deduction under section 163(h)(3).

Line 8b

Enter the amount of any indebtedness:

- That is included on line 7, and
- The proceeds of which were used to pay educational or medical expenses of the decedent, the decedent's spouse, or the decedent's dependents.

Line 8c

Enter the amount of any other indebtedness included on line 7 but not on lines 8a or 8b, but **DO NOT** enter more than $10,000.

Line 11a

Enter on this line the amount of gifts, if any, that were:

- Included on line 4 of Part 2, page 1, Form 706;
- Of qualified family-owned business interests;
- From the decedent to members of the decedent's family **other than** the decedent's spouse; and
- Continuously held by such members of the decedent's family from the date of the gift to the date of the decedent's death.

Line 11b

Enter the amount, if any, of gifts that would have been included on line 11a except that they were excluded under the gift tax annual exclusion of section 2503(b).

Line 13a

Enter the amount from item 12, Part 5, Recapitulation.

Line 13e

Enter any amounts (other than de minimis amounts) transferred from the decedent to the decedent's spouse (determined at the time of the transfer) and within 10 years of the date of the decedent's death. At the time this form went to print, the IRS had not issued guidelines on what constitutes a de minimis amount.

Line 13f

Enter the amount of any other gifts:

- That are not included on lines 13d or 13e;
- That were from the decedent;
- That were made within 3 years of the date of the decedent's death; and
- That were **not** both gifts to members of the decedent's family and excluded under the annual gift tax exclusion of section 2503(b).

Line 13h

Enter the amounts, if any, from lines 13d, 13e, or 13f, that are otherwise included in the gross estate (e.g., under section 2035).

Line 15

The interests listed on line 5 above are used to qualify the estate for the section 2057 deduction. You may choose, however, not to deduct on Schedule T all of the trade or business interests that are listed on line 5. For example, if a trade or business interest that is a qualified family-owned business interest passes to the surviving spouse and you choose to deduct it on Schedule M, you may **not** deduct on Schedule T the part of its value deducted on Schedule M. Or, you may simply choose not to include a particular trade or business interest in the section 2057 election.

Report on line 15, only the value of those trade or business interests listed on line 5 for which you are making the section 2057 election.

Also, you must reduce the amount of the Schedule T deduction by the amount of any Federal estate or GST tax and any state inheritance taxes paid out of, and any other deductions claimed with respect to, the interests that you elect to deduct on Schedule T.

Attach a schedule showing the following:

- Identify each trade or business interest from line 5 for which you are making the section 2057 election and the amount being deducted.
- Specify the amount, if any, of the interests for which you are making the election that is deducted on Schedule M.
- List for each trade or business interest the type and amount of any taxes paid out of that interest.
- List for each trade or business interest the type and amount of any other deductions claimed with respect to that interest.

If there are no such reductions, enter the amount from line 10 on line 15.

Schedule U.—Qualified Conservation Easement Exclusion

Under section 2031(c), you may elect to exclude a portion of the value of land that is subject to a qualified conservation easement. You make the election by filing Schedule U with all of the required information and excluding the applicable value of the land that is subject to the easement on Part 5, Recapitulation, page 3, at item 11. To elect the exclusion, you must include on Schedule A, B, E, F, G, or H, as appropriate, the decedent's interest in the land that is subject to the exclusion. You must make the election on a timely filed Form 706, including extensions.

For the estates of decedents dying in 1998, the exclusion is the lesser of:

- The applicable percentage of the value of land (after certain reductions) subject to a qualified conservation easement, or
- $100,000.

Once made, the election is irrevocable.

General Requirements

Qualified Land

Land may qualify for the exclusion if all of the following requirements are met:

- The decedent or a member of the decedent's family must have owned the land for the 3-year period ending on the date of the decedent's death.
- No later than the date the election is made, a qualified conservation easement on the land has been made by the decedent, a member of the decedent's family, the executor of the decedent's estate, or the trustee of a trust that holds the land.
- The land is located:

1. In or within 25 miles of an area which, on the date of the decedent's death, is a metropolitan area, as defined by the Office of Management and Budget;

2. In or within 25 miles of an area which, on the date of the decedent's death, is a national park or wilderness area designated as part of the National Wilderness Preservation System (unless it has been determined that such land is not under significant development pressure); or

3. In or within 10 miles of an area which, on the date of the decedent's death, is an Urban National Forest, as designated by the Forest Service.

Member of Family

Members of the decedent's family include the decedent's spouse; ancestors; lineal descendants of the decedent, of the decedent's spouse, and of the parents of the decedent; and the spouse of any lineal descendant. A legally adopted child of an individual is considered a child of the individual by blood.

Indirect Ownership of Land

The qualified conservation easement exclusion applies if the land is owned indirectly through a partnership, corporation, or trust, if the decedent owned (directly or indirectly) at least 30% of the entity. For the rules on determining ownership of an entity, see the Schedule T instructions under **Qualified Family-Owned Business Interest.**

Qualified Conservation Easement

A qualified conservation easement is one that would qualify as a qualified conservation contribution under section 170(h). It must be a contribution:

- Of a qualified real property interest;
- To a qualified organization; and
- Exclusively for conservation purposes.

Qualified real property interest.— The term qualified real property interest means any of the following:

- The entire interest of the donor, other than a qualified mineral interest;
- A remainder interest; or
- A restriction granted in perpetuity on the use that may be made of the real property. The restriction must include a prohibition on more than a de minimis use for commercial recreational activity.

I.R.S.—Instructions for Form 706 (Continued)

Qualified organization.— Qualified organizations include:

- The United States, a possession of the United States, a state (or the District of Columbia), or a political subdivision of them, as long as the gift is for exclusively public purposes.
- A domestic entity that meets the general requirements for qualifying as a charity under section 170(c)(2) and which generally receives a substantial amount of its support from a government unit or from the general public.
- Any entity that qualifies under section 170(h)(3)(B).

Conservation purpose.— The term conservation purpose means:

- The preservation of land areas for outdoor recreation by, or the education of, the public;
- The protection of a relatively natural habitat of fish, wildlife, or plants, or a similar ecosystem; or
- The preservation of open space (including farmland and forest land) where such preservation is for the scenic enjoyment of the general public, or pursuant to a clearly delineated Federal, state, or local conservation policy and will yield a significant public benefit.

Specific Instructions

Line 1

If the land is reported as one or more item numbers on a Form 706 schedule, simply list the schedule and item numbers. If the land subject to the easement comprises only part of an item, however, list the schedule and item number and describe the part subject to the easement. See the instructions for Schedule A for information on how to describe the land.

Line 4

Using the general rules for describing real estate, provide enough information so the IRS can value the easement. Give the date the easement was granted and by whom it was granted.

Line 5

Enter on this line the gross value at which the land was reported on the applicable asset schedule on this Form 706. Do not reduce the value by the amount of any mortgage outstanding. Report the estate tax value even if the easement was granted by the decedent (or someone other than the decedent) prior to the decedent's death.

Line 6

The amount on line 6 should be the date of death value of any qualifying conservation easements granted prior to the decedent's death, whether granted by the decedent or someone other than the decedent, for which the exclusion is being elected.

Line 8

You must reduce the land value by the value of any development rights retained by the donor in the conveyance of the easement. A development right is any right to use the land for any commercial purpose that is not subordinate to **and** directly supportive of the use of the land as a farm for farming purposes.

You do not have to make this reduction if everyone with an interest in the land (regardless of whether in possession) agrees to permanently extinguish the retained development right. The agreement must be filed with this return and must include the following information and terms:

1. A statement that the agreement is made pursuant to IRC section 2031(c)(5).

2. A list of all persons in being holding an interest in the land that is subject to the qualified conservation easement. Include each person's name, address, tax identifying number, relationship to the decedent, and a description of their interest.

3. The items of real property shown on the estate tax return that are subject to the qualified conservation easement (identified by schedule and item number).

4. A description of the retained development right that is to be extinguished.

5. A clear statement of consent that is binding on all parties under applicable local law:

- To take whatever action is necessary to permanently extinguish the retained development rights listed in the agreement; and
- To be personally liable for additional taxes under IRC section 2031(c)(5)(C) if this agreement is not implemented by the earlier of:
  - The date that is 2 years after the date of the decedent's death, or
  - The date of sale of the land subject to the qualified conservation easement.

6. A statement that in the event this agreement is not timely implemented, that they will report the additional tax on whatever return is required by the IRS and will file the return and pay the additional tax by the last day of the 6th month following the applicable date described above.

All parties to the agreement must sign the agreement.

For an example of an agreement containing some of the same terms, see Schedule A-1 (Form 706).

Line 11

Enter the total value of the qualified conservation easements on which the exclusion is based. This could include easements granted by the decedent (or someone other than the decedent) prior to the decedent's death, easements granted by the decedent that take effect at death, easements granted by the executor after the decedent's death, or some combination of these.

Important: *Use the value of the easement as of the date of death, even if the easement was granted prior to the date of death.*

Explain how this value was determined and attach copies of any appraisals. Normally, the appropriate way to value a conservation easement is to determine the fair market value of the land both before and after the granting of the easement, with the difference being the value of the easement.

You must reduce the reported value of the easement by the amount of any consideration received for the easement. If the date of death value of the easement is different than the value at the time the consideration was received, you must reduce the value of the easement by the same proportion that the consideration received bears to the value of the easement at the time it was granted. For example, assume the value of the easement at the time it was granted was $100,000 and $10,000 was received in consideration for the easement. If the easement was worth $150,000 at the date of death, you must reduce the value of the easement by $15,000 ($10,000/$100,000 × $150,000) and report the value of the easement on line 11 as $135,000.

Line 16

If a charitable contribution deduction for this land has been taken on Schedule O, enter the amount of the deduction here. If the easement was granted after the decedent's death, a contribution deduction may be taken on Schedule O, if it otherwise qualifies, as long as no income tax deduction was or will be claimed for the contribution by any person or entity.

Line 17

You must reduce the value of the land by the amount of any acquisition indebtedness on the land at the date of the decedent's death. Acquisition indebtedness includes the unpaid amount of:

- Any indebtedness incurred by the donor in acquiring the property;
- Any indebtedness incurred before the acquisition if the indebtedness would not have been incurred but for the acquisition;
- Any indebtedness incurred after the acquisition if the indebtedness would not have been incurred but for the acquisition and the incurrence of the indebtedness was reasonably foreseeable at the time of the acquisition; and
- The extension, renewal, or refinancing of acquisition indebtedness.

I.R.S.—Instructions for Form 706 (Continued)

Worksheet for Schedule Q—Credit for Tax on Prior Transfers

Part I Transferor's tax on prior transfers

Item	Transferor (From Schedule Q) A	B	C	Total for all transfers (line 8 only)
1. Gross value of prior transfer to this transferee				
2. Death taxes payable from prior transfer				
3. Encumbrances allocable to prior transfer				
4. Obligations allocable to prior transfer				
5. Marital deduction applicable to line 1 above, as shown on transferor's Form 706				
6. **Total** *(Add lines 2, 3, 4, and 5)*				
7. **Net value of transfers** *(Subtract line 6 from line 1)*				
8. **Net value of transfers** *(Add columns A, B, and C of line 7)*				
9. Transferor's taxable estate				
10. Federal estate tax paid				
11. State death taxes paid				
12. Foreign death taxes paid				
13. Other death taxes paid				
14. **Total taxes paid** *(Add lines 10, 11, 12, and 13)*				
15. **Value of transferor's estate** *(Subtract line 14 from line 9)*				
16. Net Federal estate tax paid on transferor's estate				
17. Credit for gift tax paid on transferor's estate with respect to pre-1977 gifts (section 2012)				
18. Credit allowed transferor's estate for tax on prior transfers from prior transferor(s) who died within 10 years before death of decedent				
19. **Tax on transferor's estate** *(Add lines 16, 17, and 18)*				
20. Transferor's tax on prior transfers ((Line 7 ÷ line 15) × line 19 of respective estates)				

Part II Transferee's tax on prior transfers

Item			Amount
21. Transferee's actual tax before allowance of credit for prior transfers *(see instructions)*			
22. Total gross estate of transferee *(from line 1 of the Tax Computation, page 1, Form 706)*			
23. Net value of all transfers *(from line 8 of this worksheet)*			
24. Transferee's reduced gross estate *(subtract line 23 from line 22)*			
25. Total debts and deductions (not including marital and charitable deductions) *(items 17, 18, and 19 of the Recapitulation, page 3, Form 706)*			
26. Marital deduction *(from item 20, Recapitulation, page 3, Form 706) (see instructions)*			
27. Charitable bequests *(from item 21, Recapitulation, page 3, Form 706)*			
28. Charitable deduction proportion ([line 23 ÷ (line 22–line 25)] × line 27)			
29. Reduced charitable deduction *(subtract line 28 from line 27)*			
30. Transferee's deduction as adjusted *(add lines 25, 26, and 29)*			
31. (a) Transferee's reduced taxable estate *(subtract line 30 from line 24)*			
(b) Adjusted taxable gifts			
(c) Total reduced taxable estate *(add lines 31(a) and 31(b))*			
32. Tentative tax on reduced taxable estate			
33. (a) Post-1976 gift taxes paid			
(b) Unified credit			
(c) Section 2011 state death tax credit			
(d) Section 2012 gift tax credit			
(e) Section 2014 foreign death tax credit			
(f) Total credits *(add lines 33(a) through 33(e))*			
34. Net tax on reduced taxable estate *(subtract line 33(f) from line 32)*			
35. Transferee's tax on prior transfers *(subtract line 34 from line 21)*			

*U.S. Government Printing Office: 1998 — 615-015/63307

Printed on recycled paper

I.R.S. Form 709: U.S. Gift (and Generation-Skipping Transfer) Tax Return

Form **709** — **United States Gift (and Generation-Skipping Transfer) Tax Return** — OMB No. 1545-0020

(Section 6019 of the Internal Revenue Code) (For gifts made during calendar year 1999)

1999

Department of the Treasury
Internal Revenue Service

▶ **See separate instructions. For Privacy Act Notice, see the Instructions for Form 1040.**

Part 1—General Information

1 Donor's first name and middle initial	2 Donor's last name	3 **Donor's social security number**
4 Address (number, street, and apartment number)		5 Legal residence (domicile) (county and state)
6 City, state, and ZIP code		7 Citizenship

		Yes	No
8	If the donor died during the year, check here ▶ ☐ and enter date of death ______ , ______		
9	If you received an extension of time to file this Form 709, check here ▶ ☐ and attach the Form 4868, 2688, 2350, or extension letter		
10	Enter the total number of separate donees listed on Schedule A—count each person only once. ▶		
11a	Have you (the donor) previously filed a Form 709 (or 709-A) for any other year? If the answer is "No," do not complete line 11b		
11b	If the answer to line 11a is "Yes," has your address changed since you last filed Form 709 (or 709-A)?		
12	Gifts by husband or wife to third parties.—Do you consent to have the gifts (including generation-skipping transfers) made by you and by your spouse to third parties during the calendar year considered as made one-half by each of you? (See instructions.) (If the answer is "Yes," the following information must be furnished and your spouse must sign the consent shown below. **If the answer is "No," skip lines 13–18 and go to Schedule A.**)		
13	Name of consenting spouse — **14** SSN		
15	Were you married to one another during the entire calendar year? (see instructions)		
16	If the answer to 15 is "No," check whether ☐ married ☐ divorced or ☐ widowed, and give date (see instructions) ▶		
17	Will a gift tax return for this calendar year be filed by your spouse?		

18 **Consent of Spouse**—I consent to have the gifts (and generation-skipping transfers) made by me and by my spouse to third parties during the calendar year considered as made one-half by each of us. We are both aware of the joint and several liability for tax created by the execution of this consent.

Consenting spouse's signature ▶ **Date** ▶

Part 2—Tax Computation

1	Enter the amount from Schedule A, Part 3, line 15	1		
2	Enter the amount from Schedule B, line 3	2		
3	Total taxable gifts (add lines 1 and 2)	3		
4	Tax computed on amount on line 3 (see Table for Computing Tax in separate instructions)	4		
5	Tax computed on amount on line 2 (see Table for Computing Tax in separate instructions)	5		
6	Balance (subtract line 5 from line 4)	6		
7	Maximum unified credit (nonresident aliens, see instructions)	7	211,300	00
8	Enter the unified credit against tax allowable for all prior periods (from Sch. B, line 1, col. C)	8		
9	Balance (subtract line 8 from line 7)	9		
10	Enter 20% (.20) of the amount allowed as a specific exemption for gifts made after September 8, 1976, and before January 1, 1977 (see instructions)	10		
11	Balance (subtract line 10 from line 9)	11		
12	Unified credit (enter the smaller of line 6 or line 11)	12		
13	Credit for foreign gift taxes (see instructions)	13		
14	Total credits (add lines 12 and 13)	14		
15	Balance (subtract line 14 from line 6) (do not enter less than zero)	15		
16	Generation-skipping transfer taxes (from Schedule C, Part 3, col. H, Total)	16		
17	Total tax (add lines 15 and 16)	17		
18	Gift and generation-skipping transfer taxes prepaid with extension of time to file	18		
19	If line 18 is less than line 17, enter BALANCE DUE (see instructions)	19		
20	If line 18 is greater than line 17, enter AMOUNT TO BE REFUNDED	20		

Attach check or money order here.

Under penalties of perjury, I declare that I have examined this return, including any accompanying schedules and statements, and to the best of my knowledge and belief it is true, correct, and complete. Declaration of preparer (other than donor) is based on all information of which preparer has any knowledge.

Donor's signature ▶ Date ▶

Preparer's signature (other than donor) ▶ Date ▶

Preparer's address (other than donor) ▶

For Paperwork Reduction Act Notice, see page 8 of the separate instructions for this form. Cat. No. 16783M Form **709** (1999)

I.R.S. Form 709 (Continued)

Form 709 (1999) Page 2

SCHEDULE A **Computation of Taxable Gifts** (Including Transfers in Trust)

A Does the value of any item listed on Schedule A reflect any valuation discount? If the answer is "Yes," see instructions . . Yes ☐ No ☐

B ☐ ◄ Check here if you elect under section 529(c)(2)(B) to treat any transfers made this year to a qualified state tuition program as made ratably over a 5-year period beginning this year. See instructions. Attach explanation.

Part 1—Gifts Subject Only to Gift Tax. *Gifts less political organization, medical, and educational exclusions—see instructions*

A Item number	B • Donee's name and address • Relationship to donor (if any) • Description of gift • If the gift was made by means of a trust, enter trust's identifying number and attach a copy of the trust instrument • If the gift was of securities, give CUSIP number	C Donor's adjusted basis of gift	D Date of gift	E Value at date of gift
1				

Total of Part 1 (add amounts from Part 1, column E) . . . . ▶

Part 2—Gifts That are Direct Skips and are Subject to Both Gift Tax and Generation-Skipping Transfer Tax. You must list the gifts in chronological order. *Gifts less political organization, medical, and educational exclusions—see instructions. (Also list here direct skips that are subject only to the GST tax at this time as the result of the termination of an "estate tax inclusion period." See instructions.)*

A Item number	B • Donee's name and address • Relationship to donor (if any) • Description of gift • If the gift was made by means of a trust, enter trust's identifying number and attach a copy of the trust instrument • If the gift was of securities, give CUSIP number	C Donor's adjusted basis of gift	D Date of gift	E Value at date of gift
1				

Total of Part 2 (add amounts from Part 2, column E) . . . . ▶

Part 3—Taxable Gift Reconciliation

1	Total value of gifts of donor (add totals from column E of Parts 1 and 2)	1	
2	One-half of items .... attributable to spouse (see instructions)	2	
3	Balance (subtract line 2 from line 1)	3	
4	Gifts of spouse to be included (from Schedule A, Part 3, line 2 of spouse's return—see instructions) . .	4	
	If any of the gifts included on this line are also subject to the generation-skipping transfer tax, check here ▶ ☐ and enter those gifts also on Schedule C, Part 1.		
5	Total gifts (add lines 3 and 4)	5	
6	Total annual exclusions for gifts listed on Schedule A (including line 4, above) (see instructions) . . .	6	
7	Total included amount of gifts (subtract line 6 from line 5)	7	
Deductions (see instructions)			
8	Gifts of interests to spouse for which a marital deduction will be claimed, based on items .... of Schedule A 8		
9	Exclusions attributable to gifts on line 8 9		
10	Marital deduction—subtract line 9 from line 8 10		
11	Charitable deduction, based on items ....less exclusions . . 11		
12	Total deductions—add lines 10 and 11	12	
13	Subtract line 12 from line 7	13	
14	Generation-skipping transfer taxes payable with this Form 709 (from Schedule C, Part 3, col. H, Total) .	14	
15	Taxable gifts (add lines 13 and 14). Enter here and on line 1 of the Tax Computation on page 1 . . .	15	

(If more space is needed, attach additional sheets of same size.) Form **709** (1999)

I.R.S. Form 709 (Continued)

Form 709 (1999) Page **3**

SCHEDULE A Computation of Taxable Gifts *(continued)*

16 Terminable Interest (QTIP) Marital Deduction. (See instructions for line 8 of Schedule A.)

If a trust (or other property) meets the requirements of qualified terminable interest property under section 2523(f), and

a. The trust (or other property) is listed on Schedule A, and

b. The value of the trust (or other property) is entered in whole or in part as a deduction on line 8, Part 3 of Schedule A,

then the donor shall be deemed to have made an election to have such trust (or other property) treated as qualified terminable interest property under section 2523(f).

If less than the entire value of the trust (or other property) that the donor has included in Part 1 of Schedule A is entered as a deduction on line 8, the donor shall be considered to have made an election only as to a fraction of the trust (or other property). The numerator of this fraction is equal to the amount of the trust (or other property) deducted on line 10 of Part 3, Schedule A. The denominator is equal to the total value of the trust (or other property) listed in Part 1 of Schedule A.

If you make the QTIP election (see instructions for line 8 of Schedule A), the terminable interest property involved will be included in your spouse's gross estate upon his or her death (section 2044). If your spouse disposes (by gift or otherwise) of all or part of the qualifying life income interest, he or she will be considered to have made a transfer of the entire property that is subject to the gift tax (see Transfer of Certain Life Estates on page 3 of the instructions).

17 Election Out of QTIP Treatment of Annuities

☐ ◀ Check here if you elect under section 2523(f)(6) **NOT** to treat as qualified terminable interest property any joint and survivor annuities that are reported on Schedule A and would otherwise be treated as qualified terminable interest property under section 2523(f). (See instructions.)

Enter the item numbers (from Schedule A) for the annuities for which you are making this election ▶

SCHEDULE B Gifts From Prior Periods

If you answered "Yes" on line 11a of page 1, Part 1, see the instructions for completing Schedule B. If you answered "No," skip to the Tax Computation on page 1 (or Schedule C, if applicable).

A Calendar year or calendar quarter (see instructions)	B Internal Revenue office where prior return was filed	C Amount of unified credit against gift tax for periods after December 31, 1976	D Amount of specific exemption for prior periods ending before January 1, 1977	E Amount of taxable gifts

1	Totals for prior periods (without adjustment for reduced specific exemption)	1			
2	Amount, if any, by which total specific exemption, line 1, column D, is more than $30,000			2	
3	Total amount of taxable gifts for prior periods (add amount, column E, line 1, and amount, if any, on line 2). (Enter here and on line 2 of the Tax Computation on page 1.)			3	

(If more space is needed, attach additional sheets of same size.) Form **709** (1999)

I.R.S. Form 709 (Continued)

SCHEDULE C Computation of Generation-Skipping Transfer Tax

Note: *Inter vivos direct skips that are completely excluded by the GST exemption must still be fully reported (including value and exemptions claimed) on Schedule C.*

Part 1—Generation-Skipping Transfers

A Item No. (from Schedule A, Part 2, col. A)	B Value (from Schedule A, Part 2, col. E)	C Split Gifts (enter ½ of col. B) (see instructions)	D Subtract col. C from col. B	E Nontaxable portion of transfer	F Net Transfer (subtract col. E from col. D)
1					
2					
3					
4					
5					
6					

If you elected gift splitting and your spouse was required to file a separate Form 709 (see the instructions for "Split Gifts"), you must enter all of the gifts shown on Schedule A, Part 2, of your spouse's Form 709 here. In column C, enter the item number of each gift in the order it appears in column A of your spouse's Schedule A, Part 2. We have preprinted the prefix "S-" to distinguish your spouse's item numbers from your own when you complete column A of Schedule C, Part 3. In column D, for each gift, enter the amount reported in column C, Schedule C, Part 1, of your spouse's Form 709.	Split gifts from spouse's Form 709 (enter item number)	Value included from spouse's Form 709	Nontaxable portion of transfer	Net transfer (subtract col. E from col. D)
	S-			
	S-			
	S-			
	S-			
	S-			
	S-			
	S-			
	S-			

Part 2—GST Exemption Reconciliation (Section 2631) and Section 2652(a)(3) Election

Check box ▶ ☐ if you are making a section 2652(a)(3) (special QTIP) election (see instructions)

Enter the item numbers (from Schedule A) of the gifts for which you are making this election ▶ ....

1	Maximum allowable exemption (see instructions)	1	
2	Total exemption used for periods before filing this return	2	
3	Exemption available for this return (subtract line 2 from line 1)	3	
4	Exemption claimed on this return (from Part 3, col. C total, below)	4	
5	Exemption allocated to transfers not shown on Part 3, below. **You must attach a Notice of Allocation.** (See instructions.)	5	
6	Add lines 4 and 5	6	
7	Exemption available for future transfers (subtract line 6 from line 3)	7	

Part 3—Tax Computation

A Item No. (from Schedule C, Part 1)	B Net transfer (from Schedule C, Part 1, col. F)	C GST Exemption Allocated	D Divide col. C by col. B	E Inclusion Ratio (subtract col. D from 1.000)	F Maximum Estate Tax Rate	G Applicable Rate (multiply col. E by col. F)	H Generation-Skipping Transfer Tax (multiply col. B by col. G)
1					55% (.55)		
2					55% (.55)		
3					55% (.55)		
4					55% (.55)		
5					55% (.55)		
6					55% (.55)		
					55% (.55)		
					55% (.55)		
					55% (.55)		
					55% (.55)		
Total exemption claimed. Enter here and on line 4, Part 2, above. May not exceed line 3, Part 2, above			**Total generation-skipping transfer tax.** Enter here, on line 14 of Schedule A, Part 3, and on line 16 of the Tax Computation on page 1				

(If more space is needed, attach additional sheets of same size.) Printed on recycled paper

*U.S. Government Printing Office: 1999 — 461-004/10090

I.R.S.—Instructions for Form 709

1999

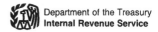

Department of the Treasury
Internal Revenue Service

Instructions for Form 709

United States Gift (and Generation-Skipping Transfer) Tax Return

(For gifts made during calendar year 1999.)
For Privacy Act Notice, see the Instructions for Form 1040.
Section references are to the Internal Revenue Code unless otherwise noted.

If you are filing this form solely to elect gift-splitting for gifts of not more than $20,000 per donee, you may be able to use **Form 709–A,** United States Short Form Gift Tax Return, instead of this form. See **Who Must File** on page 2 and **When the Consenting Spouse Must Also File a Gift Tax Return** beginning on page 4.

For Gifts Made After	and	Before	Use Revision of Form 709 Dated
— — —		January 1, 1982	November 1981
December 31, 1981		January 1, 1987	January 1987
December 31, 1986		January 1, 1989	December 1988
December 31, 1988		January 1, 1990	December 1989
December 31, 1989		October 9, 1990	October 1990
October 8, 1990		January 1, 1992	November 1991
December 31, 1992		January 1, 1998	December 1996

Changes To Note

- For gifts made in 1999, the unified credit has increased to $211,300.
- For gifts made to spouses who are not U.S. citizens, the annual exclusion has increased to $101,000. See page 3.
- The generation-skipping transfer (GST) lifetime exemption has increased to $1,010,000. See page 7.

General Instructions

Note: *If you meet all of the following requirements, you are **not** required to file Form 709:*

1. *You made no gifts during the year to your spouse;*
2. *You gave no more than $10,000 during the year to any one donee; and*
3. *All of the gifts you made were of present interests.*

*For additional information, see **Transfers Not Subject to the Gift Tax** below and **Who Must File** on page 2.*

Purpose of Form

Use Form 709 to report the following:

- Transfers subject to the Federal gift and certain generation-skipping transfer (GST) taxes and to figure the tax, if any, due on those transfers, and
- Allocation of the lifetime GST exemption to property transferred during the transferor's lifetime. (For more details, see the instructions for **Part—2 GST Exemption Reconciliation** starting on page 7, and Regulations section 26.2632-1.)

All gift and GST taxes are computed and filed on a calendar year basis regardless of your income tax accounting period.

Transfers Subject to the Gift Tax

Generally, the Federal gift tax applies to any transfer by gift of real or personal property, whether tangible or intangible, that you made directly or indirectly, in trust, or by any other means to a donee.

The gift tax applies not only to the gratuitous transfer of any kind of property, but also to sales or exchanges, not made in the ordinary course of business, where money or money's worth is exchanged but the value of the money (or property) or money's worth received is less than the value of what is sold or exchanged. The gift tax is in addition to any other tax, such as Federal income tax, paid or due on the transfer.

The exercise or release of a general power of appointment may be a gift by the individual possessing the power. General powers of appointment are those in which the holders of the power can appoint the property subject to the power to themselves, their creditors, their estates, or the creditors of their estates. To qualify as a power of appointment, it must be created by someone other than the holder of the power.

The gift tax may also apply to the forgiveness of a debt, to interest-free or below market interest rate loans, to the assignment of the benefits of an insurance policy, to certain property settlements in divorce cases, and to the giving up of some amount of annuity in exchange for the creation of a survivor annuity.

Bonds that are exempt from Federal income taxes are not exempt from Federal gift taxes.

Code sections 2701 and 2702 provide rules for determining whether certain transfers to a family member of interests in corporations, partnerships, and trusts are gifts. The rules of section 2704 determine whether the lapse of any voting or liquidation right is a gift.

Transfers Not Subject to the Gift Tax

Three types of transfers are not subject to the gift tax. These are transfers to political organizations and payments that qualify for the educational and medical exclusions. These transfers are not "gifts" as that term is used on Form 709 and its instructions. You need not file a Form 709 to report these transfers and should not list them on Schedule A of Form 709 if you do file Form 709.

Political organizations. The gift tax does not apply to a transfer to a political organization (defined in section 527(e)(1)) for the use of the organization.

Educational exclusion. The gift tax does not apply to an amount you paid on behalf of an individual to a qualifying domestic or foreign educational organization as tuition for the education or training of the individual. A *qualifying educational organization* is one that normally maintains a regular faculty and curriculum and normally has a regularly enrolled body of pupils or students in attendance at the place where its educational activities are regularly carried on. See section 170(b)(1)(A)(ii) and its regulations.

The payment must be made directly to the qualifying educational organization and it must be for tuition. No educational exclusion is allowed for amounts paid for books, supplies, room and board, or other similar expenses that do not constitute direct tuition costs. To the extent that the payment to the educational institution was for something other than tuition, it is a gift to the individual for whose benefit it was made, and may be offset by the annual exclusion if it is otherwise available.

Contributions to a qualified state tuition program on behalf of a designated beneficiary do not qualify for the educational exclusion.

Medical exclusion. The gift tax does not apply to an amount you paid on behalf of an individual to a person or institution that provided medical care for the individual. The payment must be to the care provider. The medical care must meet the requirements of section 213(d) (definition of medical care for income tax deduction purposes). Medical care includes expenses incurred for the diagnosis, cure, mitigation, treatment, or prevention of disease, or for the purpose of affecting any structure or function of the body, or for transportation primarily for and essential to medical care. Medical care also includes amounts paid for medical insurance on behalf of any individual.

The medical exclusion does not apply to amounts paid for medical care that are reimbursed by the donee's insurance. If payment for a medical expense is reimbursed by the donee's insurance company, your payment for that expense, to the extent of the reimbursed amount, is not eligible for the medical exclusion and you have made a gift to the donee.

To the extent that the payment was for something other than medical care, it is a gift to the individual on whose behalf the payment was made, and may be offset by the annual exclusion if it is otherwise available.

The medical and educational exclusions are allowed without regard to the relationship between you and the donee. For examples illustrating these exclusions, see Regulations section 25.2503-6.

Qualified disclaimers. A donee's refusal to accept a gift is called a disclaimer. If a person makes a qualified disclaimer with respect to any interest in property, the property will be treated as if it had never been transferred to

I.R.S.—Instructions for Form 709 (Continued)

that person. Accordingly, the disclaimant is not regarded as making a gift to the person who receives the property because of the qualified disclaimer.

Requirements. To be a qualified disclaimer, a refusal to accept an interest in property must meet the following conditions:

1. The refusal must be in writing;

2. The refusal must be received by the donor, the legal representative of the donor, the holder of the legal title to the property to which the interest relates or the person in possession of the property within 9 months after the later of **(a)** the day on which the transfer creating the interest is made, or **(b)** the day on which the disclaimant reaches age 21;

3. The disclaimant must not have accepted the interest or any of its benefits;

4. As a result of the refusal, the interest must pass without any direction from the disclaimant to either **(a)** the spouse of the decedent, or **(b)** a person other than the disclaimant; and

5. The refusal must be irrevocable and unqualified.

The 9-month period for making the disclaimer generally is determined separately for each taxable transfer. For gifts, the period begins on the date the transfer is a completed transfer for gift tax purposes. For a transfer by will, it begins on the date of the decedent's death.

Transfers Subject to the Generation-Skipping Transfer Tax

You must report on Form 709 the GST tax imposed on inter vivos direct skips. (See Regulations section 26.2662-1(b) for instructions on how to report other generation-skipping transfers.) An *inter vivos direct skip* is a transfer made during the donor's lifetime that is: **(a)** subject to the gift tax; **(b)** of an interest in property; and **(c)** made to a skip person. (See page 5.)

A transfer is *subject to the gift tax* if it is required to be reported on Schedule A of Form 709 under the rules contained in the gift tax portions of these instructions, including the split gift rules. Therefore, transfers made to political organizations, transfers that qualify for the medical or educational exclusions, transfers that are fully excluded under the annual exclusion, and most transfers made to your spouse are not subject to the GST tax.

Transfers subject to the GST tax are described in further detail in the instructions for Schedule A on page 4.

Important: *Certain transfers, particularly transfers to a trust, that are not subject to gift tax and are therefore not subject to the GST tax on Form 709 may be subject to the GST tax at a later date. This is true even if the transfer is less than the $10,000 annual exclusion. In this instance, you may want to apply a GST exemption amount to the transfer on this return or on a Notice of Allocation. For more information, see* ***Part 2—GST Exemption Reconciliation*** *on page 7.*

Transfers Subject to an "Estate Tax Inclusion Period"

If property that is transferred by gift in a GST direct skip would have been includible in the donor's estate if the donor had died immediately after the transfer (other than by reason of the donor having died within 3 years of making the gift), the direct skip will be treated as having been made at the end of the "estate tax inclusion period" (ETIP) rather than at the time it was actually made. For details, see section 2642(f).

Report the gift portion of such a transfer in Schedule A, Part 1, at the time of the actual transfer. Report the GST portion in Schedule A, Part 2, but only at the close of the ETIP. Use Form 709 only to report those transfers where the ETIP closed due to something other than the donor's death. If the ETIP closed as the result of the donor's death, report the transfer on Form 706.

If you are filing this Form 709 solely to report transfers subject to an ETIP, complete the form as you normally would with the following exceptions:

1. Write "ETIP" at the top of page 1;

2. Complete only lines 1–4, 6, 8, and 9 of Part 1, General Information;

3. Complete Schedule A, Part 2, as explained in the instructions for that schedule on page 6;

4. Complete Column B of Schedule C, Part 1, as explained in the instructions for that schedule on page 7;

5. Complete only lines 14 and 15 of Schedule A, Part 3. (Also list here direct skips that are subject only to the GST tax as the result of the termination of an "estate tax inclusion period." See instructions for Schedule C on page 7.)

Section 2701 Elections

The special valuation rules of section 2701 contain three elections that you must make with Form 709.

1. A transferor may elect to treat a qualified payment right he or she holds (and all other rights of the same class) as other than a qualified payment right.

2. A person may elect to treat a distribution right held by that person in a controlled entity as a qualified payment right.

3. An interest holder may elect to treat as a taxable event the payment of a qualified payment that occurs more than 4 years after its due date.

The elections described in **1** and **2** must be made on the Form 709 that is filed by the transferor to report the transfer that is being valued under section 2701. The elections are made by attaching a statement to Form 709. For information on what must be in the statement and for definitions and other details on the elections, see section 2701 and Regulations section 25.2701-2(c).

The election described in **3** may be made by attaching a statement to either a timely or a late filed Form 709 filed by the recipient of the qualified payment for the year the payment is received. If the election is made on a timely filed return, the taxable event is deemed to occur on the date the qualified payment is received. If it is made on a late filed return, the taxable event is deemed to occur on the first day of the month immediately preceding the month in which the return is filed. For information on what must be in the statement and for definitions and other details on this election, see section 2701 and Regulations section 25.2701-4(d).

All of the elections are revocable only with the consent of the IRS.

Who Must File

Only individuals are required to file gift tax returns. If a trust, estate, partnership, or corporation makes a gift, the individual beneficiaries, partners, or stockholders are considered donors and may be liable for the gift and GST taxes.

The donor is responsible for paying the gift tax. However, if the donor does not pay the tax, the person receiving the gift may have to pay the tax.

If a donor dies before filing a return, the donor's executor must file the return.

A married couple may not file a joint gift tax return. However, see **Split Gifts—Gifts by Husband or Wife to Third Parties** on page 3.

If a gift is of community property, it is considered made one-half by each spouse. For example, a gift of $100,000 of community property is considered a gift of $50,000 made by each spouse, and each spouse must file a gift tax return.

Likewise, each spouse must file a gift tax return if they have made a gift of property held by them as joint tenants or tenants by the entirety.

Citizens or Residents of the United States

If you are a citizen or resident of the United States, you must file a gift tax return (whether or not any tax is ultimately due) in the following situations:

Gifts to your spouse. Except as described below, you **do not** have to file a gift tax return to report gifts to your spouse regardless of the amount of these gifts and regardless of whether the gifts are present or future interests.

You must file a gift tax return if your spouse is **not** a U.S. citizen and the total gifts you made to your spouse during the year exceed $101,000, or if you made any gift of a terminable interest that does not meet the exception described in **Life estate with power of appointment** on page 7.

You must also file a gift tax return to make the QTIP (Qualified Terminable Interest Property) election described on page 7.

Gifts to donees other than your spouse. You must file a gift tax return if you gave gifts to any such donee that are not fully excluded under the $10,000 annual exclusion (as described below). Thus, you must file a gift tax return to report any gift of a future interest (regardless of amount) or to report gifts to any donee that total more than $10,000 for the year.

Gifts to charities. If the only gifts you made during the year are deductible as gifts to charities, you **do not** need to file a return as long as you transferred your entire interest in the property to qualifying charities. If you transferred only a partial interest, or transferred part of your interest to someone other than a charity, you must still file a return.

If you are required to file a return to report noncharitable gifts and you made gifts to charities, you must include all of your gifts to charities on the return.

Gift splitting. You must file a gift tax return to split gifts (regardless of their amount) with your spouse as described in the **Specific Instructions** for Part 1 on page 3.

The term *citizen of the United States* includes a person who, at the time of making the gift:

- Was domiciled in a possession of the United States;
- Was a U.S. citizen; and
- Became a U.S. citizen for a reason other than being a citizen of a U.S. possession or being born or residing in a possession.

Annual Exclusion

The first $10,000 of gifts of present interests to each donee during the calendar year is subtracted from total gifts in figuring the amount of taxable gifts. For a gift in trust, each beneficiary of the trust is treated as a separate donee for purposes of the annual exclusion.

I.R.S.—Instructions for Form 709 (Continued)

All of the gifts made during the calendar year to a donee are **fully excluded under the annual exclusion** if they are all gifts of *present interests* and if they total $10,000 or less.

Note: *For gifts made to spouses who are* **not** *U.S.* ***citizens,*** *the annual exclusion has been increased to $101,000, provided the additional $91,000 gift would otherwise qualify for the gift tax marital deduction (as described in the line 8 instructions on page 6).*

A gift of a *future interest* cannot be excluded under the annual exclusion.

A gift is considered a *present interest* if the donee has all immediate rights to the use, possession, and enjoyment of the property and income from the property. A gift is considered a *future interest* if the donee's rights to the use, possession, and enjoyment of the property and income from the property will not begin until some future date. Future interests include reversions, remainders, and other similar interests or estates.

Note: *A contribution to a qualified state tuition plan on behalf of a designated beneficiary is considered a gift of a present interest.*

A gift to a minor is considered a present interest if all of the following conditions are met:

1. Both the property and its income may be expended by, or for the benefit of, the minor before the minor reaches age 21;

2. All remaining property and its income must pass to the minor on the minor's 21st birthday; and

3. If the minor dies before the age of 21, the property and its income will be payable either to the minor's estate or to whomever the minor may appoint under a general power of appointment.

The gift of a present interest to more than one donee as joint tenants qualifies for the annual exclusion for each donee.

Nonresident Aliens

Nonresident aliens are subject to gift and GST taxes for gifts of tangible property situated in the United States. Under certain circumstances, they are also subject to gift and GST taxes for gifts of intangible property. (See section 2501(a).)

If you are a nonresident alien who made a gift subject to gift tax, you must file a gift tax return if: **(a)** you gave *any* gifts of future interests; or **(b)** your gifts of present interests to *any donee* other than your spouse total more than $10,000; or **(c)** your outright gifts to your spouse who is not a U.S. citizen total more than $101,000.

When To File

Form 709 is an annual return.

Generally, you must file the 1999 Form 709 on or after January 1 but not later than April 17, 2000.

If the donor died during 1999, the executor must file the donor's 1999 Form 709 not later than the earlier of: **(a)** the due date (with extensions) for filing the donor's estate tax return; or **(b)** April 17, 2000. Under this rule, the 1999 Form 709 may be due before April 17, 2000, if the donor died before July 15, 1999. If the donor died after July 14, 1999, the due date (without extensions) is April 17, 2000. If no estate tax return is required to be filed, the due date for the 1999 Form 709 (without extensions) is April 17, 2000. For more information, see Regulations section 25.6075-1.

Extension of Time To File

There are two methods of extending the time to file the gift tax return. *Neither method extends the time to pay the gift or GST taxes.* If you want an extension of time to pay the gift or GST taxes, you must request that separately. (See Regulations section 25.6161-1.)

By letter. You can request an extension of time to file your gift tax return by writing to the district director or service center for your area. You must explain the reasons for the delay. You **MUST** use a letter to request an extension of time to file your gift tax return unless you are also requesting an extension to file your income tax return.

By extending the time to file your income tax return. Any extension of time granted for filing your calendar year Federal income tax return will also extend the time to file any gift tax return. Income tax extensions are made by using Form 4868, 2688, or 2350, which have checkboxes for Form 709. See Form 4868 to get an automatic 4-month extension by phone using a credit card to pay part or all of the Federal income tax (but not gift or GST taxes) you expect to owe for 1999. You may only use one of these forms to extend the time for filing your gift tax return if you are also requesting an extension of time to file your income tax return.

Where To File

File Form 709 with the Internal Revenue Service Center where you would file your Federal income tax return. See the Form 1040 instructions for a list of filing locations.

Penalties

The law provides for penalties for both late filing of returns and late payment of tax unless you have reasonable cause. There are also penalties for valuation understatements that cause an underpayment of the tax, willful failure to file a return on time, and willful attempt to evade or defeat payment of tax.

The late filing penalty will not be imposed if the taxpayer can show that the failure to file a timely return is due to reasonable cause. Those filing late (after the due date, including extensions) should attach an explanation to the return to show reasonable cause.

A valuation understatement occurs when the reported value of property entered on Form 709 is 50% or less of the actual value of the property.

Joint Tenancy

If you buy property with your own funds and the title to such property is held by yourself and the donee as joint tenants with right of survivorship and if either you or the donee may give up those rights by severing your interest, you have made a gift to the donee in the amount of half the value of the property.

If you create a joint bank account for yourself and the donee (or a similar kind of ownership by which you can get back the entire fund without the donee's consent), you have made a gift to the donee when the donee draws on the account for his or her own benefit. The amount of the gift is the amount that the donee took out without any obligation to repay you. If you buy a U.S. savings bond registered as payable to yourself or the donee, there is a gift to the donee when he or she cashes the bond without any obligation to account to you.

Transfer of Certain Life Estates

If you received a qualifying terminable interest (see page 7) from your spouse for which a marital deduction was elected on your spouse's estate or gift tax return, you will be subject to the gift (and GST, if applicable) tax if you dispose of all or part of your life income interest (by gift, sale, or otherwise).

The entire value of the property involved less: **(a)** the amount you received on the disposition, and **(b)** the amount (if any) of the life income interest you retained after the transfer will be treated as a taxable gift. That portion of the property's value that is attributable to the remainder interest is a gift of a future interest for which no annual exclusion is allowed. To the extent you made a gift of the life income interest, you may claim an annual exclusion, treating the person to whom you transferred the interest as the donee for purposes of computing the annual exclusion.

Specific Instructions

Part I—General Information

Split Gifts—Gifts by Husband or Wife to Third Parties

A married couple may not file a joint gift tax return.

However, if after reading the instructions below, you and your spouse agree to split your gifts, you should file both of your individual gift tax returns together (i.e., in the same envelope) to avoid correspondence from the IRS.

If you and your spouse agree, all gifts (including gifts of property held with your spouse as joint tenants or tenants by the entirety) either of you make to third parties during the calendar year will be considered as made one-half by each of you if:

- You and your spouse were married to one another at the time of the gift;
- If divorced or widowed after the gift, you did not remarry during the rest of the calendar year;
- Neither of you was a nonresident alien at the time of the gift; and
- You did not give your spouse a general power of appointment over the property interest transferred.

If you transferred property partly to your spouse and partly to third parties, you can only split the gifts if the interest transferred to the third parties is ascertainable at the time of the gift.

If you meet these requirements and want your gifts to be considered made one-half by you and one-half by your spouse, check the "Yes" box on line 12, page 1; complete lines 13 through 17; and have your spouse sign the consent on line 18. If you are not married or do not wish to split gifts, skip to Schedule A.

Line 15. If you were married to one another for the entire calendar year, check the "Yes" box and skip to line 17. If you were married for only part of the year, check the "No" box and go to line 16.

Line 16. Check the box that explains the change in your marital status during the year and give the date you were married, divorced, or widowed.

Consent of Spouse

To have your gifts (and generation-skipping transfers) considered as made one-half by each of you, your spouse must sign the consent. The consent may generally be signed at any time after the end of the calendar year. However, there are two exceptions:

1. The consent may not be signed after April 15 following the end of the year in which the gift was made. (But, if neither you nor your spouse has filed a gift tax return for the year on or before that date, the consent must be made on the first gift tax return for the year filed by either of you.)

I.R.S.—Instructions for Form 709 (Continued)

2. The consent may not be signed after a notice of deficiency for the gift or GST tax for the year has been sent to either you or your spouse.

The executor for a deceased spouse or the guardian for a legally incompetent spouse may sign the consent.

The consent is effective for the entire calendar year; therefore, all gifts made by both you and your spouse to third parties during the calendar year (while you were married) must be split.

If the consent is effective, the liability for the entire gift and GST taxes of each spouse is joint and several.

When the Consenting Spouse Must Also File a Gift Tax Return

If the spouses elect gift splitting (described under **Split Gifts** on page 3), then both the donor spouse and the consenting spouse must each file separate gift tax returns unless all the requirements of either **Exception 1** or **2** below are met.

Exception 1. During the calendar year:

- Only one spouse made any gifts;
- The total value of these gifts to each third-party donee does not exceed $20,000; and
- All of the gifts were of present interests.

Exception 2. During the calendar year:

- Only one spouse (the donor spouse) made gifts of more than $10,000 but not more than $20,000 to any third-party donee;
- The only gifts made by the other spouse (the consenting spouse) were gifts of not more than $10,000 to third-party donees other than those to whom the donor spouse made gifts; and
- All of the gifts by both spouses were of present interests.

If either **Exception 1** or **2** is met, only the donor spouse must file a return and the consenting spouse signifies consent on that return. This return may be made on **Form 709-A,** United States Short Form Gift Tax Return. This form is much easier to complete than Form 709, and you should consider filing it whenever either of the above **exceptions** is met and the gifts consist entirely of present interests in tangible personal property, cash, U.S. Savings Bonds, or stocks and bonds listed on a stock exchange.

Specific instructions for **Part 2—Tax Computation** are continued on page 8. Because you must complete Schedules A, B, and C to fill out Part 2, you will find instructions for these schedules below.

Schedule A—Computation of Taxable Gifts

Do not enter on Schedule A any gift or part of a gift that qualifies for the political organization, educational, or medical exclusions. In the instructions below, "gifts" means gifts (or parts of gifts) that do not qualify for the political organization, educational, or medical exclusions.

Valuation Discounts

If the value of any gift you report in either Part 1 or Part 2 of Schedule A reflects a discount for lack of marketability, a minority interest, a fractional interest in real estate, blockage, market absorption, or for any other reason, answer "Yes" to the question at the top of Schedule A. Also, attach an explanation giving the factual basis for the claimed discounts and the amount of the discounts taken.

Qualified State Tuition Programs

If your total 1999 contributions to a qualified state tuition plan on behalf of any individual beneficiary exceed $10,000, then for purposes of the annual exclusion you may elect under section 529(c)(2)(B) to treat up to $50,000 of your total contributions as having been made ratably over a 5-year period beginning in 1999.

You must report in 1999 the entire amount of the contribution in excess of $50,000.

You make the election by checking the box on line B at the top of Schedule A. The election must be made for the calendar year in which the contribution is made. Also attach an explanation that includes the following:

- The total amount contributed per individual beneficiary;
- The amount for which the election is being made;
- The name of the individual for whom the contribution was made.

If you make this election, report only 1/5 (20%) of your total contributions (up to $50,000) on the 1999 Form 709. You must then report an additional 20% of the total in each of the succeeding 4 years. If you are electing gift splitting for the contributions, apply the gift-splitting rules before applying these rules. In this case, both spouses must make the section 529(c)(2)(B) election on their respective returns.

Note: *Contributions to qualified state tuition plans do not qualify for the educational exclusion.*

How To Complete Schedule A

After you determine which gifts you made are subject to the gift tax and therefore should be listed on Schedule A, you must divide these gifts between those subject only to the gift tax (gifts made to nonskip persons—see page 5) and those subject to both the gift and GST taxes (gifts made to skip persons—see page 5). Gifts made to nonskip persons are entered in Part 1. Gifts made to skip persons are entered in Part 2.

If you need more space, attach a separate sheet using the same format as Schedule A.

Gifts to Donees Other Than Your Spouse

You must always enter all gifts of *future interests* that you made during the calendar year regardless of their value.

If you do not elect gift splitting. If the total gifts of *present interests* to any donee are more than $10,000 in the calendar year, then you must enter *all such gifts* that you made during the year to or on behalf of that donee, including those gifts that will be excluded under the annual exclusion. If the total is $10,000 or less, you need not enter on Schedule A any gifts (except gifts of future interests) that you made to that donee.

If you elect gift splitting. Enter on Schedule A the entire value of every gift you made during the calendar year while you were married, even if the gift's value will be less than $10,000 after it is split on line 2 of Part 3.

Gifts to Your Spouse

You do not need to enter any of your gifts to your spouse on Schedule A unless you gave a gift of a terminable interest to your spouse, you gave a gift of a future interest to your spouse as described below, or your spouse was not a citizen of the United States at the time of the gift.

Terminable interest. Terminable interests are defined in the instructions to line 8. If all the terminable interests you gave to your spouse qualify as life estates with power of appointment (defined on page 7) you do not need to enter any of them on Schedule A.

However, if you gave your spouse *any* terminable interest that does not qualify as a life estate with power of appointment, you must report on Schedule A *all* gifts of terminable interests you made to your spouse during the year.

You should not report any gifts you made to your spouse who is a U.S. citizen that are not terminable interests (except as described under **Future interest** below); however, you must report all terminable interests, whether or not they can be deducted.

Charitable remainder trusts. If you make a gift to a charitable remainder trust and your spouse is the only noncharitable beneficiary (other than yourself), the interest you gave to your spouse is not considered a terminable interest and, therefore, should not be shown on Schedule A. For definitions and rules concerning these trusts, see section 2056(b)(8)(B) and Regulations section 20.2055-2.

Future interest. Generally, you should not report gifts of future interests to your spouse unless the future interest is also a terminable interest that is required to be reported as described above. However, if you gave a gift of a future interest to your spouse and you are required to report the gift on Form 709 because you gave the present interest to a donee other than your spouse, then you should enter the entire gift, including the future interest given to your spouse, on Schedule A. You should use the rules under **Gifts Subject to Both Gift and GST Taxes,** below, to determine whether to enter the gift on Schedule A, Part 1 or Part 2.

Non-U.S. citizen spouse donee. If your spouse is not a U.S. citizen and you gave him or her a gift of a future interest, you must report on Schedule A all gifts to your spouse for the year. If all gifts to your spouse were present interests, do not report on Schedule A any gifts to your spouse if the total of such gifts for the year does not exceed $101,000 and all gifts in excess of $10,000 would qualify for a marital deduction if your spouse were a U.S. citizen (see the instructions for Schedule A, Part 3, line 8, on page 6). If the gifts exceed $101,000, you must report all of the gifts even though some may be excluded.

Gifts Subject to Both Gift and GST Taxes

Direct Skip

The GST tax you must report on Form 709 is that imposed only on inter vivos direct skips. An "inter vivos direct skip" is a gift that **(a)** is subject to the gift tax, **(b)** is an interest in property, and **(c)** is made to a skip person. All three requirements must be met before the gift is subject to the GST tax.

A gift is "subject to the gift tax" if you are required to list it on Schedule A of Form 709 (as described above). However, if you make a nontaxable gift (which is a direct skip) to a trust for the benefit of an individual, this transfer is also subject to the GST tax unless:

1. During the lifetime of the beneficiary, no corpus or income may be distributed to anyone other than the beneficiary; and

2. If the beneficiary dies before the termination of the trust, the assets of the trust will be included in the gross estate of the beneficiary.

Note: *If the property transferred in the direct skip would have been includible in the donor's estate if the donor had died immediately after the transfer, see* **Transfers Subject to an "Estate Tax Inclusion Period"** *on page 2.*

I.R.S.—Instructions for Form 709 (Continued)

To determine if a gift "is of an interest in property" and "is made to a skip person," you must first determine if the donee is a "natural person" or a "trust" as defined below.

Trust

For purposes of the GST tax, trust includes not only an explicit trust, but also any other arrangement (other than an estate) that although not explicitly a trust, has substantially the same effect as a trust. For example, trust includes life estates with remainders, terms for years, and insurance and annuity contracts. A transfer of property that is conditional on the occurrence of an event is a transfer in trust.

Interest in Property

If a gift is made to a "natural person," it is always considered a gift of an interest in property for purposes of the GST tax.

If a gift is made to a trust, a natural person will have an interest in the property transferred to the trust if that person either has a present right to receive income or corpus from the trust (such as an income interest for life) or is a permissible current recipient of income or corpus from the trust (e.g., possesses a general power of appointment).

Skip Person

A donee who is a natural person is a skip person if that donee is assigned to a generation that is two or more generations below the generation assignment of the donor. See **Determining the Generation of a Donee** below.

A donee that is a trust is a skip person if all the interests in the property transferred to the trust (as defined above) are held by skip persons.

A trust will also be a skip person if there are no interests in the property transferred to the trust held by any person, and future distributions or terminations from the trust can be made only to skip persons.

NonSkip Person

A nonskip person is any donee who is not a skip person.

Determining the Generation of a Donee

Generally, a generation is determined along family lines as follows:

1. If the donee is a lineal descendant of a grandparent of the donor (e.g., the donor's cousin, niece, nephew, etc.), the number of generations between the donor and the descendant (donee) is determined by subtracting the number of generations between the grandparent and the donor from the number of generations between the grandparent and the descendant (donee).

2. If the donee is a lineal descendant of a grandparent of a spouse (or former spouse) of the donor, the number of generations between the donor and the descendant (donee) is determined by subtracting the number of generations between the grandparent and the spouse (or former spouse) from the number of generations between the grandparent and the descendant (donee).

3. A person who at any time was married to a person described in **1** or **2** above is assigned to the generation of that person. A person who at any time was married to the donor is assigned to the donor's generation.

4. A relationship by adoption or half-blood is treated as a relationship by whole-blood.

5. A person who is not assigned to a generation according to **1, 2, 3,** or **4** above is assigned to a generation based on his or her birth date as follows:

a. A person who was born not more than 12½ years after the donor is in the donor's generation.

b. A person born more than 12½ years, but not more than 37½ years, after the donor is in the first generation younger than the donor.

c. Similar rules apply for a new generation every 25 years.

If more than one of the rules for assigning generations applies to a donee, that donee is generally assigned to the youngest of the generations that would apply.

If an estate or trust, partnership, corporation, or other entity (other than certain charitable organizations and trusts described in sections 511(a)(2) and 511(b)(2) and governmental entities) is a donee, then each person who indirectly receives the gift through the entity is treated as a donee and is assigned to a generation as explained in the above rules.

Charitable organizations and trusts described in sections 511(a)(2) and 511(b)(2) and governmental entities are assigned to the donor's generation. Transfers to such organizations are therefore not subject to the GST tax. These gifts should always be listed in Part 1 of Schedule A.

Charitable Remainder Trusts

Gifts in the form of charitable remainder annuity trusts, charitable remainder unitrusts, and pooled income funds are not transfers to skip persons and therefore are not direct skips. You should always list these gifts in Part 1 of Schedule A even if all of the life beneficiaries are skip persons.

Generation Assignment Where Intervening Parent Is Dead

If you made a gift to your grandchild and at the time you made the gift, the grandchild's parent (who is your or your spouse's or your former spouse's child) is dead, then for purposes of generation assignment, your grandchild is considered to be your child rather than your grandchild. Your grandchild's children will be treated as your grandchildren rather than your great-grandchildren.

This rule is also applied to your lineal descendants below the level of grandchild. For example, if your grandchild is dead, your great-grandchildren who are lineal descendants of the dead grandchild are considered your grandchildren for purposes of the GST tax.

This special rule may also apply in other cases of the death of a parent of the transferee. Beginning with gifts made in 1998, the existing rule that applies to grandchildren of the decedent has been extended to apply to other lineal descendants.

If property is transferred to an individual who is a descendant of a parent of the transferor and that individual's parent (who is a lineal descendant of the parent of the transferor) is dead at the time the transfer is subject to gift or estate tax, then for purposes of generation assignment, the individual is treated as if he or she is a member of the generation that is one generation below the lower of:

- the transferor's generation, or
- the generation assignment of the youngest living ancestor of the individual who is also a descendant of the parent of the transferor.

The same rules apply to the generation assignment of any descendant of the individual.

This rule **does not** apply to a transfer to an individual who is not a lineal descendant of the transferor if the transferor has any living lineal descendants.

If any transfer of property to a trust would have been a direct skip except for this generation assignment rule, then the rule also applies to transfers from the trust attributable to such property.

Examples

The generation-skipping transfer rules can be illustrated by the following examples:

Example 1. You give your house to your daughter for her life with the remainder then passing to her children. This gift is made to a "trust" even though there is no explicit trust instrument. The interest in the property transferred (the present right to use the house) is transferred to a nonskip person (your daughter). Therefore, the trust is not a skip person because there is an interest in the transferred property that is held by a nonskip person. The gift is not a direct skip and you should list it in Part 1 of Schedule A. (However, on the death of the daughter, a termination of her interest in the trust will occur that may be subject to the generation-skipping transfer tax. See the instructions for line 5, Part 2, Schedule C (on page 8) for a discussion of how to allocate GST exemption to such a trust.)

Example 2. You give $100,000 to your grandchild. This gift is a direct skip that is not made in trust. You should list it in Part 2 of Schedule A.

Example 3. You establish a trust that is required to accumulate income for 10 years and then pay its income to your grandchildren for their lives and upon their deaths distribute the corpus to their children. Because the trust has no current beneficiaries, there are no present interests in the property transferred to the trust. All of the persons to whom the trust can make future distributions (including distributions upon the termination of interests in property held in trust) are skip persons (i.e., your grandchildren and great-grandchildren). Therefore, the trust itself is a skip person and you should list the gift in Part 2 of Schedule A.

Example 4. You establish a trust that pays all of its income to your grandchildren for 10 years. At the end of 10 years, the corpus is to be distributed to your children. Since for this purpose interests in trusts are defined only as present interests, all of the interests in this trust are held by skip persons (the children's interests are future interests). Therefore, the trust is a skip person and you should list the entire amount you transferred to the trust in Part 2 of Schedule A even though some of the trust's ultimate beneficiaries are nonskip persons.

Part 1—Gifts Subject Only to Gift Tax

List gifts subject only to the gift tax in Part 1. Generally, all of the gifts you made to your spouse (that are required to be listed, as described earlier), to your children, and to charitable organizations are not subject to the GST tax and should, therefore, be listed only in Part 1.

Group the gifts in four categories: gifts made to your spouse; gifts made to third parties that are to be split with your spouse; charitable gifts (if you are not splitting gifts with your spouse); and other gifts. If a transfer results in gifts to two or more individuals (such as a life estate to one with remainder to the other), list the gift to each separately.

Number and describe all gifts (including charitable, public, and similar gifts) in the columns provided in Schedule A. Describe each gift in enough detail so that the property can be easily identified, as explained below.

For real estate provide:

- A legal description of each parcel;
- The street number, name, and area if the property is located in a city; and
- A short statement of any improvements made to the property.

I.R.S.—Instructions for Form 709 (Continued)

For bonds, give:

- The number of bonds transferred;
- The principal amount of each bond;
- Name of obligor;
- Date of maturity;
- Rate of interest;
- Date or dates when interest is payable;
- Series number if there is more than one issue;
- Exchanges where listed or, if unlisted, give the location of the principal business office of the corporation; and
- CUSIP number. The CUSIP number is a nine-digit number assigned by the American Banking Association to traded securities.

For stocks:

- Give number of shares;
- State whether common or preferred;
- If preferred, give the issue, par value, quotation at which returned, and exact name of corporation;
- If unlisted on a principal exchange, give location of principal business office of corporation, state in which incorporated, and date of incorporation;
- If listed, give principal exchange; and
- CUSIP number. The CUSIP number is a nine-digit number assigned by the American Banking Association to traded securities.

For interests in property based on the length of a person's life, give the date of birth of the person.

For life insurance policies, give the name of the insurer and the policy number.

Clearly identify in the description column which gifts create the opening of an estate tax inclusion period (ETIP) as described under **Transfers Subject to an "Estate Tax Inclusion Period"** on page 2. Describe the interest that is creating the ETIP. You may not allocate the GST exemption to these transfers until the close of the ETIP. See the instructions for Schedule C on page 7.

Donor's Adjusted Basis of Gifts

Show the basis you would use for income tax purposes if the gift were sold or exchanged. Generally, this means cost plus improvements, less applicable depreciation, amortization, and depletion.

For more information on adjusted basis, see **Pub. 551,** Basis of Assets.

Date and Value of Gift

The value of a gift is the fair market value of the property on the date the gift is made. The fair market value is the price at which the property would change hands between a willing buyer and a willing seller, when neither is forced to buy or to sell, and when both have reasonable knowledge of all relevant facts. Fair market value may not be determined by a forced sale price, nor by the sale price of the item in a market other than that in which the item is most commonly sold to the public. The location of the item must be taken into account wherever appropriate.

The fair market value of a stock or bond (whether listed or unlisted) is the mean between the highest and lowest selling prices quoted on the valuation date. If only the closing selling prices are available, then the fair market value is the mean between the quoted closing selling price on the valuation date and on the trading day before the valuation date. To figure the fair market value if there were no sales on the valuation date, see the instructions for Schedule B of Form 706.

Stock of close corporations or inactive stock must be valued on the basis of net worth, earnings, earning and dividend capacity, and other relevant factors.

Generally, the best indication of the value of real property is the price paid for the property in an arm's-length transaction on or before the valuation date. If there has been no such transaction, use the comparable sales method. In comparing similar properties, consider differences in the date of the sale, and the size, condition, and location of the properties, and make all appropriate adjustments.

The value of all annuities, life estates, terms for years, remainders, or reversions is generally the present value on the date of the gift.

Sections 2701 and 2702 provide special valuation rules to determine the amount of the gift when a donor transfers an equity interest in a corporation or partnership (section 2701) or makes a gift in trust (section 2702). The rules only apply if, immediately after the transfer, the donor (or an applicable family member) holds an applicable retained interest in the corporation or partnership, or retains an interest in the trust. For details, see sections 2701 and 2702, and their regulations.

Supplemental Documents

To support the value of your gifts, you must provide information showing how it was determined.

For stock of close corporations or inactive stock, attach balance sheets, particularly the one nearest the date of the gift, and statements of net earnings or operating results and dividends paid for each of the 5 preceding years.

For each life insurance policy, attach **Form 712,** Life Insurance Statement.

Note for single premium or paid-up policies: *In certain situations, for example, where the surrender value of the policy exceeds its replacement cost, the true economic value of the policy will be greater than the amount shown on line 56 of Form 712. In these situations, report the full economic value of the policy on Schedule A. See Rev. Rul. 78-137, 1978-1 C.B. 280 for details.*

If the gift was made by means of a trust, attach a certified or verified copy of the trust instrument to the return on which you report your **first** transfer to the trust. You do not need to attach the trust to returns on which you report subsequent transfers to the trust, unless the trust provisions have been revised.

Also attach any appraisal used to determine the value of real estate or other property.

If you do not attach this information, you must include in Schedule A full information to explain how the value was determined.

Part 2—Gifts That are Direct Skips and are Subject to Both Gift Tax and Generation-Skipping Transfer Tax

List in Part 2 only those gifts that are subject to both the gift and GST taxes. **You must list the gifts in Part 2 in the chronological order that you made them.** Number, describe, and value the gifts as described in the instructions for Part 1 above.

If you made a gift in trust, list the entire gift as one line entry in Part 2. Enter the entire value of the property transferred to the trust even if the trust has nonskip person future beneficiaries.

How to report GST transfers after the close of an ETIP. If you are reporting a generation-skipping transfer that was subject to an "estate tax inclusion period" (ETIP) (provided the ETIP closed as a result of something other than the death of the transferor—see Form 706), and you are also reporting gifts made during the year, complete Schedule A as you normally would with the following changes:

Report the transfer subject to an ETIP on Schedule A, Part 2.

1. Column B. In addition to the information already requested, describe the interest that is closing the ETIP; explain what caused the interest to terminate; and list the year the gift portion of the transfer was reported and its item number on Schedule A of the Form 709 that was originally filed to report the gift portion of the ETIP transfer.

2. Column D. Give the date the ETIP closed rather than the date of the initial gift.

3. Column E. Enter "N/A" in Column E.

The value is entered only in Column B, Part 1, Schedule C. See the instructions for Schedule C.

Part 3—Taxable Gift Reconciliation

If you have made no gifts yourself and are filing this return only to report gifts made by your spouse but which are being split with you, skip lines 1–3 and enter your share of the split gifts on line 4.

Line 2. If you are not splitting gifts with your spouse, skip this line and enter the amount from line 1 on line 3. If you are splitting gifts with your spouse, show half of the gifts you made to third parties on line 2. On the dotted line indicate which numbered items from Parts 1 and 2 of Schedule A you treated this way. Generally, if you elect to split your gifts, you must split **ALL** gifts made by you and your spouse to third-party donees. The only exception is if you gave your spouse a general power of appointment over a gift you made.

Line 4. If you are not splitting gifts, skip this line and go to line 5. If you gave all of the gifts, and your spouse is only filing to show his or her half of those gifts, you need not enter any gifts on line 4 of your return or include your spouse's half anywhere else on your return. Your spouse should enter the amount from Schedule A, line 2, of your return on Schedule A, line 4, of his or her return.

If both you and your spouse make gifts for which a return is required, the amount each of you shows on Schedule A, line 2, of his or her return must be shown on Schedule A, line 4, of the other's return.

Line 6. Enter the total annual exclusions you are claiming for the gifts listed on Schedule A (including gifts listed on line 4). See **Annual Exclusion** on page 2. If you split a gift with your spouse, the annual exclusion you claim against that gift may not be more than your half of the gift.

Deductions

Line 8. Enter on line 8 all of the gifts to your spouse that you listed on Schedule A and for which you are claiming a marital deduction. **Do not enter any gift that you did not include on Schedule A.** On the dotted line on line 8, indicate which numbered items from Schedule A are gifts to your spouse for which you are claiming the marital deduction.

Do not enter on line 8 any gifts to your spouse who was not a U.S. citizen at the time of the gift.

You may deduct all gifts of nonterminable interests made during this time that you entered on Schedule A regardless of amount, and certain gifts of terminable interests as outlined below.

Terminable interests. Generally, you cannot take the marital deduction if the gift to your spouse is a terminable interest. In most instances, a terminable interest is nondeductible if someone other than the donee spouse will have an interest in the property following the termination of the donee spouse's interest. Some examples of terminable interests are:

I.R.S.—Instructions for Form 709 (Continued)

• A life estate;
• An estate for a specified number of years; or
• Any other property interest that after a period of time will terminate or fail.

If you transfer an interest to your spouse as sole joint tenant with yourself or as a tenant by the entirety, the interest is not considered a terminable interest just because the tenancy may be severed.

Life estate with power of appointment. You may deduct, without an election, a gift of a terminable interest if all four requirements below are met:

1. Your spouse is entitled for life to all of the income from the entire interest;

2. The income is paid yearly or more often;

3. Your spouse has the unlimited power, while he or she is alive or by will, to appoint the entire interest in all circumstances; and

4. No part of the entire interest is subject to another person's power of appointment (except to appoint it to your spouse).

If either the right to income or the power of appointment given to your spouse pertains only to a **specific portion** of a property interest, the marital deduction is allowed only to the extent that the rights of your spouse meet all 4 of the above conditions. For example, if your spouse is to receive all of the income from the entire interest, but only has a power to appoint one-half of the entire interest, then only one-half qualifies for the marital deduction.

A partial interest in property is treated as a specific portion of an entire interest only if the rights of your spouse to the income and to the power constitute a fractional or percentile share of the entire property interest. This means that the interest or share will reflect any increase or decrease in the value of the entire property interest. If the spouse is entitled to receive a specified sum of income annually, the capital amount that would produce such a sum will be considered the specific portion from which the spouse is entitled to receive the income.

Election to deduct qualified terminable interest property (QTIP). You may *elect* to deduct a gift of a terminable interest if it meets requirements **1**, **2**, and **4** above, even though it does not meet requirement **3**.

You make this election simply by listing the qualified terminable interest property on Schedule A and deducting its value on line 8, Part 3, Schedule A. There is no longer a box to check to make the election. You are presumed to have made the election for all qualified property that you both list and deduct on Schedule A. You may not make the election on a late filed Form 709.

Line 9. Enter the amount of the annual exclusions that were claimed for the gifts you listed on line 8.

Line 11. You may deduct from the total gifts made during the calendar year all gifts you gave to or for the use of:

• The United States, a state or political subdivision of a state or the District of Columbia, for exclusively public purposes;
• Any corporation, trust, community chest, fund, or foundation organized and operated only for religious, charitable, scientific, literary, or educational purposes, or to prevent cruelty to children or animals, or to foster national or international amateur sports competition (if none of its activities involve providing athletic equipment (unless it is a qualified amateur sports organization)), as long as no part of the earnings benefits any one person, no substantial propaganda is produced, and no lobbying or campaigning for any candidate for public office is done;
• A fraternal society, order, or association operating under a lodge system, if the transferred property is to be used only for religious, charitable, scientific, literary, or educational purposes, including the encouragement of art and the prevention of cruelty to children or animals;
• Any war veterans' organization organized in the United States (or any of its possessions), or any of its auxiliary departments or local chapters or posts, as long as no part of any of the earnings benefits any one person.

On line 11, show your total charitable, public, or similar gifts (minus annual exclusions allowed). On the dotted line, indicate which numbered items from the top of Schedule A (or line 4) are charitable gifts.

Line 14. If you will pay GST tax with this return on any direct skips reported on this return, the amount of that GST tax is also considered a gift and must be added to your other gifts reported on this return.

If you entered gifts on Part 2, or if you and your spouse elected gift splitting and your spouse made gifts subject to the GST tax that you are required to show on your Form 709, complete Schedule C, and enter on line 14 the total of Schedule C, Part 3, column H. Otherwise, enter zero on line 14.

Line 17. Section 2523(f)(6) creates an automatic QTIP election for gifts of joint and survivor annuities where the spouses are the only possible recipients of the annuity prior to the death of the last surviving spouse.

The donor spouse can elect out of QTIP treatment, however, by checking the box on line 17 and entering the item number from Schedule A for the annuities for which you are making the election. Any annuities entered on line 17 cannot also be entered on line 8 of Schedule A, Part 3. Any such annuities that are not listed on line 17 must be entered on line 8 of Part 3, Schedule A. If there is more than one such joint and survivor annuity, you are not required to make the election for all of them. Once made, the election is irrevocable.

Schedule B—Gifts From Prior Periods

If you did not file gift tax returns for previous periods, check the "No" box on line 11a of Part 1, page 1, and skip to the Tax Computation on page 1. (However, be sure to complete Schedule C, if applicable.) If you filed gift tax returns for previous periods, check the "Yes" box on line 11a and complete Schedule B by listing the years or quarters in chronological order as described below. If you need more space, attach a separate sheet using the same format as Schedule B.

If you filed returns for gifts made before 1971 or after 1981, show the calendar years in column A. If you filed returns for gifts made after 1970 and before 1982, show the calendar quarters.

In column B, identify the Internal Revenue Service office where you filed the returns. If you have changed your name, be sure to list any other names under which the returns were filed. If there was any other variation in the names under which you filed, such as the use of full given names instead of initials, please explain.

In column E, show the correct amount (the amount finally determined) of the taxable gifts for each earlier period.

Schedule C—Computation of Generation-Skipping Transfer Tax

Part 1—Generation-Skipping Transfers

You must enter in Part 1 all of the gifts you listed in Part 2 of Schedule A in that order and using those same values.

Column B. Transfers subject to an ETIP. If you are reporting a generation-skipping transfer that occurred because of the close of an "estate tax inclusion period" (ETIP), complete column B for such transfer as follows:

1. Provided the GST exemption is being allocated on a timely filed gift tax return, enter the value as of the close of the ETIP;

2. If the exemption is being allocated after the due date (including extensions) for the gift tax return on which the transfer should be reported, enter the value as of the time the exemption allocation was made.

Column C. If you elected gift splitting, enter half the value of each gift entered in column B. If you did not elect gift splitting, enter zero in column C.

Column E. You are allowed to claim the gift tax annual exclusion currently allowable with respect to your reported direct skips (other than certain direct skips to trusts), using the rules and limits discussed earlier for the gift tax annual exclusion. However, you must allocate the exclusion on a gift-by-gift basis for GST computation purposes. You must allocate the exclusion to each gift to the maximum allowable amount and in chronological order, beginning with the earliest gift that qualifies for the exclusion. Be sure that you do not claim a total exclusion of more than $10,000 per donee.

Note: *You may not claim any annual exclusion for a direct skip made to a trust unless the trust meets the requirements discussed under* **Direct Skip** *on page 4.*

Part 2—GST Exemption Reconciliation

Line 1. Every donor is allowed a lifetime GST exemption. The amount of the exemption is indexed for inflation and is published annually by the IRS in a revenue procedure. For transfers made through 1998, the GST exemption is $1 million. For transfers made in 1999, the exemption is $1,010,000.

The $10,000 increase can only be allocated to transfers made during or after calendar year 1999.

Example. A donor had made $1.5 million in GST transfers through 1998 and had allocated all $1 million of the exemption to those transfers. In 1999, the donor makes a $5,000 taxable generation-skipping transfer. The donor can allocate $5,000 of exemption to the 1999 transfer but cannot allocate the unused $5,000 of exemption to pre-1999 transfers.

You should keep a record of your transfers and exemption allocations to make sure that any future increases are allocated correctly.

Enter on line 1 of Part 2 the maximum GST exemption you are allowed. This will not necessarily be the highest indexed amount if you have made no GST transfer during the year of the increase. For example, if your last GST transfer was in 1998, your maximum GST exemption would be $1,000,000, not $1,010,000.

The donor can apply this exemption to inter vivos transfers (i.e., transfers made during the donor's life) on Form 709. The executor can apply the exemption on Form 706 to transfers taking effect at death. An allocation is irrevocable.

I.R.S.—Instructions for Form 709 (Continued)

In the case of inter vivos direct skips, a portion of the donor's unused exemption is automatically allocated to the transferred property unless the donor elects otherwise. To elect out of the automatic application of exemption, you must file Form 709 and attach a statement to it clearly describing the transaction and the extent to which the automatic allocation is not to apply. Reporting a direct skip on a timely filed Form 709 and paying the GST tax on the transfer will qualify as such a statement.

Special QTIP election. If you have elected QTIP treatment for any gifts in trust listed on Schedule A, Part 1, then you may make an election on Schedule C to treat the entire trust as non-QTIP for purposes of the GST tax. The election must be made for the entire trust that contains the particular gift involved on this return. Be sure to identify by item number the specific gift for which you are making this special QTIP election.

Line 5. You may wish to allocate your exemption to transfers made in trust that are not direct skips. For example, if you transferred property to a trust that has your children as its present beneficiaries and your grandchildren and great-grandchildren as future beneficiaries, the transfer was not a direct skip because the present interests in the trust are held by nonskip persons. **However, future terminations and distributions made from this trust would be subject to the GST tax.**

You may elect to reduce the trust's inclusion ratio by allocating part or all of your exemption to the transfer. Because this transfer would be entered on Schedule A, Part 1, it will not be shown on Schedule C.

In other cases you may wish to allocate your exemption to a trust that is not involved in a transfer listed on Schedule A or C. For example, if your only gift for the year was $10,000 transferred to a trust that had your children as present beneficiaries and your grandchildren as future beneficiaries, you would not be required to file Form 709 for the year. However, future distributions from the trust or the termination of the trust may result in GST tax being due. In this case, you may want to allocate GST exemption to the transfer at the time of the transfer.

To allocate your exemption to such transfers, attach a statement to this Form 709 and entitle it "Notice of Allocation." You may file one Notice of Allocation and consolidate on it all of your Schedule A, Part 1, transfers, plus all transfers not appearing on Form 709, to which you wish to allocate your exemption. The notice must contain the following for each trust:

- Clearly identify the trust, including the trust's EIN, if known;
- The item number(s) from column A, Schedule A, Part 1, of the gifts to that trust (if applicable);
- The values shown in column E, Schedule A, Part 1, for the gifts (adjusted to account for split gifts, if any, reported on Schedule A, Part 3, line 2) (or, if the allocation is late, the value of the trust assets at the time of the allocation);
- The amount of your GST exemption allocated to each gift (or a statement that you are allocating exemption by means of a formula such as "an amount necessary to produce an inclusion ratio of zero"); and
- The inclusion ratio of the trust after the allocation.

Total the exemption allocations and enter this total on line 5.

Note: *Where the property involved in such a transfer is subject to an estate tax inclusion period because it would be includible in the donor's estate if the donor died immediately after the transfer (other than by reason of the donor having died within 3 years of making the gift), you cannot allocate the GST exemption at the time of the transfer but must wait until the end of the estate tax inclusion period. For details, see* **Transfers Subject to an "Estate Tax Inclusion Period"** *on page 2, and section 2642(f).*

Part 3—Tax Computation

You must enter in Part 3 every gift you listed in Part 1 of Schedule C.

Column C. You are not required to allocate your available exemption. You may allocate some, all, or none of your available exemption, as you wish, among the gifts listed in Part 3 of Schedule C. However, the total exemption claimed in column C may not exceed the amount you entered on line 3 of Part 2 of Schedule C.

You may enter an amount in column C that is greater than the amount you entered in column B.

Column D. Carry your computation to three decimal places (e.g., "1.000").

Part 2—Tax Computation (Page 1 of Form)

Line 7. If you are a citizen or resident of the United States, you must take any available unified credit against gift tax. Nonresident aliens may not claim the unified credit. If you are a nonresident alien, delete the $211,300 entry and write in zero on line 11.

Line 10. Enter 20% of the amount allowed as a specific exemption for gifts made after September 8, 1976, and before January 1, 1977. (These amounts will be among those listed in column D of Schedule B, for gifts made in the third and fourth quarters of 1976.)

Line 13. Gift tax conventions are in effect with Australia, Austria, Denmark, France, Germany, Japan, Sweden, and the United Kingdom. If you are claiming a credit for payment of foreign gift tax, figure the credit on an attached sheet and attach evidence that the foreign taxes were paid. See the applicable convention for details of computing the credit.

Line 19. Make your check or money order payable to "United States Treasury" and write the donor's social security number on it. You may not use an overpayment on Form 1040 to offset the gift and GST taxes owed on Form 709.

Signature. As a donor, you must sign the return. If you pay another person, firm, or corporation to prepare your return, that person must also sign the return as preparer unless he or she is your regular full-time employee.

Paperwork Reduction Act Notice. We ask for the information on this form to carry out the Internal Revenue laws of the United States. You are required to give us the information. We need it to ensure that you are complying with these laws and to allow us to figure and collect the right amount of tax.

You are not required to provide the information requested on a form that is subject to the Paperwork Reduction Act unless the form displays a valid OMB control number. Books or records relating to a form or its instructions must be retained as long as their contents may become material in the administration of any Internal Revenue law. Generally, tax returns and return information are confidential, as required by section 6103.

The time needed to complete and file this form will vary depending on individual circumstances. The estimated average time is:

Recordkeeping	40 min.
Learning about the law or the form	1 hr., 5 min.
Preparing the form	1 hr., 54 min.
Copying, assembling, and sending the form to the IRS	1 hr., 3 min.

If you have comments concerning the accuracy of these time estimates or suggestions for making this form simpler, we would be happy to hear from you. You can write to the Tax Forms Committee, Western Area Distribution Center, Rancho Cordova, CA 95743-0001. **DO NOT** send the tax form to this office. Instead, see **Where To File** on page 3.

Table for Computing Tax

Column A	Column B	Column C	Column D
Taxable amount over—	Taxable amount not over—	Tax on amount in Column A	Rate of tax on excess over amount in Column A
-----	$10,000	-----	18%
$10,000	20,000	$1,800	20%
20,000	40,000	3,800	22%
40,000	60,000	8,200	24%
60,000	80,000	13,000	26%
80,000	100,000	18,200	28%
100,000	150,000	23,800	30%
150,000	250,000	38,800	32%
250,000	500,000	70,800	34%
500,000	750,000	155,800	37%
750,000	1,000,000	248,300	39%
1,000,000	1,250,000	345,800	41%
1,250,000	1,500,000	448,300	43%
1,500,000	2,000,000	555,800	45%
2,000,000	2,500,000	780,800	49%
2,500,000	3,000,000	1,025,800	53%
3,000,000	10,000,000	1,290,800	55%
10,000,000	17,184,000	5,140,800	60%
17,184,000	-----	9,451,200	55%

Printed on recycled paper

I.R.S. Form 1041: U.S. Income Tax Return for Estates and Trusts

Form **1041** Department of the Treasury—Internal Revenue Service

U.S. Income Tax Return for Estates and Trusts **1999**

For calendar year 1999 or fiscal year beginning , 1999, and ending , OMB No. 1545-0092

A Type of entity:
- ☐ Decedent's estate
- ☐ Simple trust
- ☐ Complex trust
- ☐ Grantor type trust
- ☐ Bankruptcy estate–Ch. 7
- ☐ Bankruptcy estate–Ch. 11
- ☐ Pooled income fund

B Number of Schedules K-1 attached (see instructions) ▶

Name of estate or trust (If a grantor type trust, see page 8 of the instructions.)

Name and title of fiduciary

Number, street, and room or suite no. (If a P.O. box, see page 8 of the instructions.)

City or town, state, and ZIP code

C **Employer identification number**

D Date entity created

E Nonexempt charitable and split-interest trusts, check applicable boxes (see page 10 of the instructions):
- ☐ Described in section 4947(a)(1)
- ☐ Not a private foundation
- ☐ Described in section 4947(a)(2)

F Check applicable boxes: ☐ Initial return ☐ Final return ☐ Amended return ☐ Change in fiduciary's name ☐ Change in fiduciary's address

G Pooled mortgage account (see page 10 of the instructions): ☐ Bought ☐ Sold Date:

Income

1	Interest income	1	
2	Ordinary dividends	2	
3	Business income or (loss) (attach Schedule C or C-EZ (Form 1040))	3	
4	Capital gain or (loss) (attach Schedule D (Form 1041))	4	
5	Rents, royalties, partnerships, other estates and trusts, etc. (attach Schedule E (Form 1040))	5	
6	Farm income or (loss) (attach Schedule F (Form 1040))	6	
7	Ordinary gain or (loss) (attach Form 4797)	7	
8	Other income. List type and amount	8	
9	**Total income.** Combine lines 1 through 8 ▶	9	

Deductions

10	Interest. Check if Form 4952 is attached ▶ ☐	10	
11	Taxes	11	
12	Fiduciary fees	12	
13	Charitable deduction (from Schedule A, line 7)	13	
14	Attorney, accountant, and return preparer fees	14	
15a	Other deductions NOT subject to the 2% floor (attach schedule)	15a	
b	Allowable miscellaneous itemized deductions subject to the 2% floor	15b	
16	**Total.** Add lines 10 through 15b	16	
17	Adjusted total income or (loss). Subtract line 16 from line 9. Enter here and on Schedule B, line 1 ▶	17	
18	Income distribution deduction (from Schedule B, line 15) (attach Schedules K-1 (Form 1041))	18	
19	Estate tax deduction (including certain generation-skipping taxes) (attach computation)	19	
20	Exemption	20	
21	**Total deductions.** Add lines 18 through 20 ▶	21	

Tax and Payments

22	Taxable income. Subtract line 21 from line 17. If a loss, see page 14 of the instructions	22	
23	**Total tax** (from Schedule G, line 8)	23	
24	**Payments: a** 1999 estimated tax payments and amount applied from 1998 return	24a	
b	Estimated tax payments allocated to beneficiaries (from Form 1041-T)	24b	
c	Subtract line 24b from line 24a	24c	
d	Tax paid with extension of time to file: ☐ Form 2758 ☐ Form 8736 ☐ Form 8800	24d	
e	Federal income tax withheld. If any is from Form(s) 1099, check ▶ ☐	24e	
	Other payments: **f** Form 2439 ; **g** Form 4136 ; Total ▶	24h	
25	**Total payments.** Add lines 24c through 24e, and 24h ▶	25	
26	Estimated tax penalty (see page 15 of the instructions)	26	
27	**Tax due.** If line 25 is smaller than the total of lines 23 and 26, enter amount owed	27	
28	**Overpayment.** If line 25 is larger than the total of lines 23 and 26, enter amount overpaid	28	
29	Amount of line 28 to be: **a Credited to 2000 estimated tax** ▶ ; **b Refunded** ▶	29	

Please Sign Here

Under penalties of perjury, I declare that I have examined this return, including accompanying schedules and statements, and to the best of my knowledge and belief, it is true, correct, and complete. Declaration of preparer (other than fiduciary) is based on all information of which preparer has any knowledge.

Signature of fiduciary or officer representing fiduciary | Date | EIN of fiduciary if a financial institution (see page 5 of the instructions)

Paid Preparer's Use Only

Preparer's signature | Date | Check if self-employed ▶ ☐ | **Preparer's SSN or PTIN**

Firm's name (or yours if self-employed) and address | EIN ▶ | ZIP code ▶

For Paperwork Reduction Act Notice, see the separate instructions. Cat. No. 11370H Form **1041** (1999)

I.R.S. Form 1041 (Continued)

Form 1041 (1999) Page 2

Schedule A **Charitable Deduction.** Do not complete for a simple trust or a pooled income fund.

1	Amounts paid or permanently set aside for charitable purposes from gross income (see page 15)	1	
2	Tax-exempt income allocable to charitable contributions (see page 16 of the instructions)	2	
3	Subtract line 2 from line 1	3	
4	Capital gains for the tax year allocated to corpus and paid or permanently set aside for charitable purposes	4	
5	Add lines 3 and 4	5	
6	Section 1202 exclusion allocable to capital gains paid or permanently set aside for charitable purposes (see page 16 of the instructions)	6	
7	**Charitable deduction.** Subtract line 6 from 5. Enter here and on page 1, line 13	7	

Schedule B **Income Distribution Deduction**

1	Adjusted total income (from page 1, line 17) (see page 16 of the instructions)	1	
2	Adjusted tax-exempt interest	2	
3	Total net gain from Schedule D (Form 1041), line 16, column (1) (see page 16 of the instructions)	3	
4	Enter amount from Schedule A, line 4 (reduced by any allocable section 1202 exclusion).	4	
5	Capital gains for the tax year included on Schedule A, line 1 (see page 16 of the instructions)	5	
6	Enter any gain from page 1, line 4, as a negative number. If page 1, line 4, is a loss, enter the loss as a positive number	6	
7	**Distributable net income (DNI).** Combine lines 1 through 6. If zero or less, enter -0-	7	
8	If a complex trust, enter accounting income for the tax year as determined under the governing instrument and applicable local law [8]		
9	Income required to be distributed currently	9	
10	Other amounts paid, credited, or otherwise required to be distributed	10	
11	Total distributions. Add lines 9 and 10. If greater than line 8, see page 17 of the instructions	11	
12	Enter the amount of tax-exempt income included on line 11	12	
13	Tentative income distribution deduction. Subtract line 12 from line 11	13	
14	Tentative income distribution deduction. Subtract line 2 from line 7. If zero or less, enter -0-	14	
15	**Income distribution deduction.** Enter the smaller of line 13 or line 14 here and on page 1, line 18	15	

Schedule G **Tax Computation** (see page 17 of the instructions)

1	**Tax: a** ☐ Tax rate schedule or ☐ Schedule D (Form 1041)	1a			
	b Tax on lump-sum distributions (attach Form 4972)	1b			
	c Total. Add lines 1a and 1b ▶			1c	
2a	Foreign tax credit (attach Form 1116)	2a			
b	Check: ☐ Nonconventional source fuel credit ☐ Form 8834	2b			
c	General business credit. Enter here and check which forms are attached: ☐ Form 3800 or ☐ Forms (specify) ▶	2c			
d	Credit for prior year minimum tax (attach Form 8801)	2d			
3	**Total credits.** Add lines 2a through 2d ▶			3	
4	Subtract line 3 from line 1c			4	
5	Recapture taxes. Check if from: ☐ Form 4255 ☐ Form 8611			5	
6	Alternative minimum tax (from Schedule I, line 39)			6	
7	Household employment taxes. Attach Schedule H (Form 1040)			7	
8	**Total tax.** Add lines 4 through 7. Enter here and on page 1, line 23 ▶			8	

Other Information

		Yes	No
1	Did the estate or trust receive tax-exempt income? If "Yes," attach a computation of the allocation of expenses. Enter the amount of tax-exempt interest income and exempt-interest dividends ▶ $		
2	Did the estate or trust receive all or any part of the earnings (salary, wages, and other compensation) of any individual by reason of a contract assignment or similar arrangement?		
3	At any time during calendar year 1999, did the estate or trust have an interest in or a signature or other authority over a bank, securities, or other financial account in a foreign country? See page 18 of the instructions for exceptions and filing requirements for Form TD F 90-22.1. If "Yes," enter the name of the foreign country ▶		
4	During the tax year, did the estate or trust receive a distribution from, or was it the grantor of, or transferor to, a foreign trust? If "Yes," the estate or trust may have to file Form 3520. See page 19 of the instructions		
5	Did the estate or trust receive, or pay, any qualified residence interest on seller-provided financing? If "Yes," see page 19 for required attachment		
6	If this is an estate or a complex trust making the section 663(b) election, check here (see page 19) ▶ ☐		
7	To make a section 643(e)(3) election, attach Schedule D (Form 1041), and check here (see page 19) ▶ ☐		
8	If the decedent's estate has been open for more than 2 years, attach an explanation for the delay in closing the estate, and check here ▶ ☐		
9	Are any present or future trust beneficiaries skip persons? See page 19 of the instructions		

Form **1041** (1999)

I.R.S. Form 1041 (Continued)

Form 1041 (1999) Page 3

Schedule I — Alternative Minimum Tax (see pages 19 through 24 of the instructions)

Part I—Estate's or Trust's Share of Alternative Minimum Taxable Income

1	Adjusted total income or (loss) (from page 1, line 17)			1	
2	Net operating loss deduction. Enter as a positive amount			2	
3	Add lines 1 and 2			3	
4	**Adjustments and tax preference items:**				
a	Interest	4a			
b	Taxes	4b			
c	Miscellaneous itemized deductions (from page 1, line 15b)	4c			
d	Refund of taxes	4d	( )		
e	Depreciation of property placed in service after 1986	4e			
f	Circulation and research and experimental expenditures	4f			
g	Mining exploration and development costs	4g			
h	Long-term contracts entered into after February 28, 1986	4h			
i	Amortization of pollution control facilities	4i			
j	Installment sales of certain property	4j			
k	Adjusted gain or loss (including incentive stock options)	4k			
l	Certain loss limitations	4l			
m	Tax shelter farm activities	4m			
n	Passive activities	4n			
o	Beneficiaries of other trusts or decedent's estates	4o			
p	Tax-exempt interest from specified private activity bonds	4p			
q	Depletion	4q			
r	Accelerated depreciation of real property placed in service before 1987	4r			
s	Accelerated depreciation of leased personal property placed in service before 1987	4s			
t	Intangible drilling costs	4t			
u	Other adjustments	4u			
5	Combine lines 4a through 4u			5	
6	Add lines 3 and 5			6	
7	Alternative tax net operating loss deduction (see page 22 of the instructions for limitations)			7	
8	Adjusted alternative minimum taxable income. Subtract line 7 from line 6. Enter here and on line 13 **Note:** *Complete Part II below before going to line 9.*			8	
9	Income distribution deduction from line 27 below	9			
10	Estate tax deduction (from page 1, line 19)	10			
11	Add lines 9 and 10			11	
12	Estate's or trust's share of alternative minimum taxable income. Subtract line 11 from line 8			12	

If line 12 is:

- $22,500 or less, stop here and enter -0- on Schedule G, line 6. The estate or trust is not liable for the alternative minimum tax.
- Over $22,500, but less than $165,000, go to line 28.
- $165,000 or more, enter the amount from line 12 on line 34 and go to line 35.

Part II—Income Distribution Deduction on a Minimum Tax Basis

13	Adjusted alternative minimum taxable income (from line 8)	13	
14	Adjusted tax-exempt interest (other than amounts included on line 4p)	14	
15	Total net gain from Schedule D (Form 1041), line 16, column (1). If a loss, enter -0-	15	
16	Capital gains for the tax year allocated to corpus and paid or permanently set aside for charitable purposes (from Schedule A, line 4)	16	
17	Capital gains paid or permanently set aside for charitable purposes from gross income (see page 23 of the instructions)	17	
18	Capital gains computed on a minimum tax basis included on line 8	18	( )
19	Capital losses computed on a minimum tax basis included on line 8. Enter as a positive amount	19	
20	Distributable net alternative minimum taxable income (DNAMTI). Combine lines 13 through 19. If zero or less, enter -0-	20	
21	Income required to be distributed currently (from Schedule B, line 9)	21	
22	Other amounts paid, credited, or otherwise required to be distributed (from Schedule B, line 10)	22	
23	Total distributions. Add lines 21 and 22	23	
24	Tax-exempt income included on line 23 (other than amounts included on line 4p)	24	
25	Tentative income distribution deduction on a minimum tax basis. Subtract line 24 from line 23	25	
26	Tentative income distribution deduction on a minimum tax basis. Subtract line 14 from line 20. If zero or less, enter -0-	26	
27	**Income distribution deduction on a minimum tax basis.** Enter the smaller of line 25 or line 26. Enter here and on line 9	27	

Form **1041** (1999)

I.R.S. Form 1041 (Continued)

Form 1041 (1999) Page 4

Part III—Alternative Minimum Tax

28	Exemption amount	28	$22,500 00
29	Enter the amount from line 12 . . . 29		
30	Phase-out of exemption amount . . . 30 $75,000 00		
31	Subtract line 30 from line 29. If zero or less, enter -0- . . . 31		
32	Multiply line 31 by 25% (.25)	32	
33	Subtract line 32 from line 28. If zero or less, enter -0-	33	
34	Subtract line 33 from line 29	34	
35	If the estate or trust completed Schedule D (Form 1041) and has an amount on line 24 or 26 (or would have had an amount on either line if Part V had been completed) (as refigured for the AMT, if necessary), go to Part IV below to figure line 35. **All others:** If line 34 is— • $175,000 or less, multiply line 34 by 26% (.26). • Over $175,000, multiply line 34 by 28% (.28) and subtract $3,500 from the result	35	
36	Alternative minimum foreign tax credit (see page 23 of instructions)	36	
37	Tentative minimum tax. Subtract line 36 from line 35	37	
38	Enter the tax from Schedule G, line 1a (minus any foreign tax credit from Schedule G, line 2a).	38	
39	**Alternative minimum tax.** Subtract line 38 from line 37. If zero or less, enter -0-. Enter here and on Schedule G, line 6	39	

Part IV—Line 35 Computation Using Maximum Capital Gains Rates

Caution: *If the estate or trust did not complete Part V of Schedule D (Form 1041), complete lines 19 through 26 of Schedule D (as refigured for the AMT, if necessary) before completing this part.*

40	Enter the amount from line 34	40	
41	Enter the amount from Schedule D (Form 1041), line 26 (as refigured for AMT, if necessary) . . . 41		
42	Enter the amount from Schedule D (Form 1041), line 24 (as refigured for AMT, if necessary) . . . 42		
43	Add lines 41 and 42. If zero or less, enter -0- . . . 43		
44	Enter the amount from Schedule D (Form 1041), line 21 (as refigured for AMT, if necessary) . . . 44		
45	Enter the **smaller** of line 43 or line 44	45	
46	Subtract line 45 from line 40. If zero or less, enter -0-	46	
47	If line 46 is $175,000 or less, multiply line 46 by 26% (.26). Otherwise, multiply line 46 by 28% (.28) and subtract $3,500 from the result ▶	47	
48	Enter the amount from Schedule D (Form 1041), line 35 (as figured for the regular tax)	48	
49	Enter the **smallest** of line 40, line 41, or line 48	49	
50	Multiply line 49 by 10% (.10) ▶	50	
51	Enter the **smaller** of line 40 or line 41	51	
52	Enter the amount from line 49	52	
53	Subtract line 52 from line 51. If zero or less, enter -0-	53	
54	Multiply line 53 by 20% (.20) ▶	54	
55	Enter the amount from line 40	55	
56	Add lines 46, 49, and 53	56	
57	Subtract line 56 from line 55	57	
58	Multiply line 57 by 25% (.25) ▶	58	
59	Add lines 47, 50, 54, and 58	59	
60	If line 40 is $175,000 or less, multiply line 40 by 26% (.26). Otherwise, multiply line 40 by 28% (.28) and subtract $3,500 from the result	60	
61	Enter the **smaller** of line 59 or line 60 here and on line 35 ▶	61	

*U.S.GPO:1999-456-252 Printed on recycled paper Form **1041** (1999)

I.R.S. Form 2848: Power of Attorney and Declaration of Representative

Form **2848** (Rev. February 1993) Department of the Treasury Internal Revenue Service

Power of Attorney and Declaration of Representative

▶ For Paperwork Reduction and Privacy Act Notice, see the instructions.

OMB No. 1545-0150 Expires 2-29-96

Part I **Power of Attorney** (Please type or print.)

1 Taxpayer Information (Taxpayer(s) must sign and date this form on page 2, line 9.)

Taxpayer name(s) and address	**Social security number(s)**	**Employer identification number**
		Plan number (if applicable)
	Daytime telephone number ( )	

hereby appoint(s) the following representative(s) as attorney(s)-in-fact:

2 Representative(s) (Representative(s) must sign and date this form on page 2, Part II.)

Name and address	CAF No. .... Telephone No. ( ) .... Fax No. ( ) .... Check if new: Address ☐ Telephone No. ☐
Name and address	CAF No. .... Telephone No. ( ) .... Fax No. ( ) .... Check if new: Address ☐ Telephone No. ☐
Name and address	CAF No. .... Telephone No. ( ) .... Fax No. ( ) .... Check if new: Address ☐ Telephone No. ☐

to represent the taxpayer(s) before the Internal Revenue Service for the following tax matters:

3 Tax Matters

Type of Tax (Income, Employment, Excise, etc.)	Tax Form Number (1040, 941, 720, etc.)	Year(s) or Period(s)

4 Specific Use Not Recorded on Centralized Authorization File (CAF).— If the power of attorney is for a specific use not recorded on CAF, please check this box. (See **Line 4—Specific Uses Not Recorded on CAF** on page 3.) . . . . . ▶ ☐

5 Acts Authorized.—The representatives are authorized to receive and inspect confidential tax information and to perform any and all acts that I (we) can perform with respect to the tax matters described in line 3, for example, the authority to sign any agreements, consents, or other documents. The authority does not include the power to receive refund checks (see line 6 below) or the power to sign certain returns (see **Line 5—Acts Authorized** on page 4).

List any specific additions or deletions to the acts otherwise authorized in this power of attorney: ....

....

....

Note: *In general, an unenrolled preparer of tax returns cannot sign any document for a taxpayer. See Revenue Procedure 81-38, printed as Pub. 470, for more information.*

Note: *The tax matters partner/person of a partnership or S corporation is not permitted to authorize representatives to perform certain acts. See the instructions for more information.*

6 Receipt of Refund Checks.—If you want to authorize a representative named in line 2 to receive, **BUT NOT TO ENDORSE OR CASH**, refund checks, initial here ____________ and list the name of that representative below.

Name of representative to receive refund check(s) ▶

Cat. No. 11980J Form **2848** (Rev. 2-93)

I.R.S. Form 2848 (Continued)

Form 2848 (Rev. 2-93) Page 2

7 Notices and Communications.—Notices and other written communications will be sent to the first representative listed in line 2.

a If you also want the second representative listed to receive such notices and communications, check this box . . . . ▶ ☐

b If you do not want any notices or communications sent to your representative, check this box . . . . ▶ ☐

8 Retention/Revocation of Prior Power(s) of Attorney.—The filing of this power of attorney automatically revokes all earlier power(s) of attorney on file with the Internal Revenue Service for the same tax matters and years or periods covered by this document. If you do not want to revoke a prior power of attorney, check here . . . . ▶ ☐

YOU MUST ATTACH A COPY OF ANY POWER OF ATTORNEY YOU WANT TO REMAIN IN EFFECT.

9 Signature of Taxpayer(s).—If a tax matter concerns a joint return, **both** husband and wife must sign if joint representation is requested, otherwise, see the instructions. If signed by a corporate officer, partner, guardian, tax matters partner/person, executor, receiver, administrator, or trustee on behalf of the taxpayer, I certify that I have the authority to execute this form on behalf of the taxpayer.

▶ IF THIS POWER OF ATTORNEY IS NOT SIGNED AND DATED, IT WILL BE RETURNED.

Signature .... Date .... Title (if applicable)

Print Name

Signature .... Date .... Title (if applicable)

Print Name

Part II Declaration of Representative

Under penalties of perjury, I declare that:

- I am not currently under suspension or disbarment from practice before the Internal Revenue Service;
- I am aware of regulations contained in Treasury Department Circular No. 230 (31 CFR, Part 10), as amended, concerning the practice of attorneys, certified public accountants, enrolled agents, enrolled actuaries, and others;
- I am authorized to represent the taxpayer(s) identified in Part I for the tax matter(s) specified there; and
- I am one of the following:

a Attorney—a member in good standing of the bar of the highest court of the jurisdiction shown below.

b Certified Public Accountant—duly qualified to practice as a certified public accountant in the jurisdiction shown below.

c Enrolled Agent—enrolled as an agent under the requirements of Treasury Department Circular No. 230.

d Officer—a bona fide officer of the taxpayer organization.

e Full-Time Employee—a full-time employee of the taxpayer.

f Family Member—a member of the taxpayer's immediate family (i.e., spouse, parent, child, brother, or sister).

g Enrolled Actuary—enrolled as an actuary by the Joint Board for the Enrollment of Actuaries under 29 U.S.C. 1242 (the authority to practice before the Service is limited by section 10.3(d)(1) of Treasury Department Circular No. 230).

h Unenrolled Return Preparer—an unenrolled return preparer under section 10.7(a)(7) of Treasury Department Circular No. 230.

▶ If this declaration of representative is not signed and dated, the power of attorney will be returned.

Designation —Insert above letter (**a–h**)	Jurisdiction (state) or Enrollment Card No.	Signature	Date

I.R.S. Form 2848 (Continued)

Privacy Act and Paperwork Reduction Act Notice.—We ask for the information on this form to carry out the Internal Revenue laws of the United States. Form 2848 is provided by the IRS for your convenience and its use is voluntary. If you choose to designate a representative to act on your behalf, under section 6109 you must disclose your social security number (SSN) or your employer identification number (EIN). The principal purpose of this disclosure is to secure proper identification of the taxpayer. We also need this information to gain access to your tax information in our files and properly respond to your request. If you do not disclose this information, the IRS may suspend processing the power of attorney and may not be able to fill your request until you provide the number.

The time needed to complete and file this form will vary depending on individual circumstances. The estimated average time is: **Recordkeeping,** 20 min.; **Learning about the law or the form,** 29 min.; **Preparing the form,** 29 min.; **Copying, assembling, and sending the form to the IRS,** 35 min.

If you have comments concerning the accuracy of these time estimates or suggestions for making this form more simple, we would be happy to hear from you. You can write to both the **Internal Revenue Service,** Washington, DC 20224, Attention: IRS Reports Clearance Officer, T:FP; and the **Office of Management and Budget,** Paperwork Reduction Project (1545-0150), Washington, DC 20503. **DO NOT** send this form to either of these offices. Instead, see **Filing the Power of Attorney** below.

General Instructions

Section references are to the Internal Revenue Code unless otherwise noted.

Purpose of Form.—Form 2848 may be used to grant authority to an individual to represent you before the IRS and to receive tax information. You may file this form ONLY if you want to name a person(s) to represent you and that person is a "person recognized to practice before the Service." Persons recognized to practice before the Service are listed in Part II, Declaration of Representative, items **a–h.** Any person who is not listed in **a–h** of Part II is not authorized to practice before the IRS under the provisions of Treasury Department Circular No. 230 and therefore cannot act as your representative. However, you can use **Form 8821,** Tax Information Authorization, to authorize any person (or an organization) to receive and inspect confidential tax return information under the provisions of section 6103. For additional information about this or any other matter concerning practice before the IRS, get **Pub. 216,** Conference and Practice Requirements.

Fiduciaries.—A fiduciary (trustee, executor, administrator, receiver, or guardian) stands in the position of a taxpayer and acts as the taxpayer. Therefore, a fiduciary does not act as a representative and should not file a power of attorney. **Form 56,** Notice Concerning Fiduciary Relationship, should be filed to notify the IRS of the existence of a fiduciary relationship. If a fiduciary wishes to authorize an individual to represent or perform certain acts on behalf of the entity, a power of attorney must be filed and signed by the fiduciary acting in the position of the taxpayer.

Authority Granted.—This power of attorney authorizes the individual(s) named to perform any and all acts you can perform, such as signing consents extending the time to assess tax, recording the interview, or executing waivers agreeing to a tax adjustment. Delegating authority or substituting another representative must be specifically stated on line 5. However, the authority granted to an unenrolled preparer may not exceed that allowed under Revenue Procedure 81-38, printed as **Pub. 470,** Limited Practice Without Enrollment.

The power to sign tax returns can only be granted in limited situations. See **Line 5—Acts Authorized** on page 4 for more information.

Filing the Power of Attorney.—File the original, photocopy, or facsimile transmission (fax) of the power of attorney with each IRS office with which you deal. If you choose to file a power of attorney by fax, you must first be sure that the appropriate IRS office is equipped to accept fax transmissions. If the power of attorney is filed for a matter currently pending before an office of the IRS, such as an examination, file the power of attorney with that office. Otherwise, file it with the service center where the related return was, or will be, filed. Refer to the instructions for the related tax return for the service center addresses.

Substitute Form 2848.—If you want to prepare and use a substitute Form 2848, get **Pub. 1167,** Substitute Printed, Computer-Prepared, and Computer-Generated Tax Forms and Schedules. If your substitute Form 2848 is approved, the form approval number must be printed in the lower left margin of each substitute Form 2848 you file with the IRS.

Specific Instructions

Part I—Power of Attorney

Line 1—Taxpayer Information.—

Individuals.—Enter your name, SSN (and/or EIN, if applicable), and street address in the space provided. If a joint return is involved, and you and your spouse are designating the same representative(s), also enter your spouse's name and SSN, and your spouse's address if different from yours.

Corporations, partnerships, or associations.—Enter the name, EIN, and business address. If this form is being prepared for corporations filing a consolidated tax return (Form 1120), do not attach a list of subsidiaries to this form. Only the parent corporation information is required in line 1. Also, line 3 should only list Form 1120 in the Tax Form Number column. A subsidiary must file its own Form 2848 for returns that are required to be filed separately from the consolidated return, such as **Form 720,** Quarterly Federal Excise Tax Return, and **Form 941,** Employer's Quarterly Federal Tax Return.

Employee plan.—Enter the plan name, EIN of the plan sponsor, three-digit plan number, and business address of the sponsor.

Trust.—Enter the name, title, and address of the trustee, and the name and EIN of the trust.

Estate.—Enter the name, title, and address of the decedent's executor/personal representative, and the name and identification number of the estate. The identification number for an estate includes both the EIN, if the estate has one, and the decedent's SSN.

Line 2—Representative(s).—Enter the name of your representative(s). Only individuals may be named as representatives. Please use the identical name on all submissions. If you want to name more than three representatives, indicate so on this line and attach a list of additional representatives to the form.

Enter the nine-digit Centralized Authorization File (CAF) number for each representative. If a CAF number has not been assigned, enter "None," and the IRS will issue one directly to your representative. The CAF number is a unique nine-digit identification number (not the SSN, EIN, or enrollment card number) that the IRS assigns to representatives. The CAF number is not an indication of authority to practice. The representative should use the assigned CAF number on all future powers of attorney. CAF numbers will not be assigned for employee plans and exempt organizations application requests (EP/EO).

Check the appropriate box to indicate if either the address or telephone number is new since a CAF number was assigned. Enter your representative's fax telephone number, if available.

If the representative is a former employee of the Federal Government, he or she must be aware of the post-employment restrictions contained in 18 U.S.C., section 207 and in Treasury Department Circular No. 230, section 10.26. Criminal penalties are provided for violation of the statutory restrictions, and the Director of Practice is authorized to take disciplinary action against the practitioner.

Line 3—Tax Matters.—Enter the type of tax, the tax form number, and the years or period(s). For example, you may list "income tax, Form 1040" for calendar year "1992" and "Excise tax, Form 720" for the "1st, 2nd, 3rd, and 4th quarters of 1992." A general reference to "All years," "All periods," or "All taxes" is **not** acceptable. Any power of attorney with such general reference will be returned. You may list any tax years or periods that have already ended as of the date you sign the power of attorney. However, the number of future tax periods that can be recorded on the CAF is limited to returns with due dates within 3 years of your signature on Form 2848. If the matter relates to estate tax, enter the date of the taxpayer's death instead of the year or period. If the type of tax, tax form number, or years or periods does not apply to the matter (i.e., representation for a penalty or filing a ruling request or determination), specifically describe on this line the matter to which the power of attorney pertains and enter "Not Applicable" in the appropriate column(s).

Line 4—Specific Uses Not Recorded on CAF.—Generally, the IRS records all powers of attorney on the CAF system. However, a power of attorney will not be recorded on the CAF if it does not relate to a specific tax period or it is for a specific issue. Examples of specific issues include but are not limited to the following: **(a)** civil penalty issues, **(b)** trust fund recovery penalty, **(c)** request for a private letter ruling, **(d)** application for an EIN, **(e)** claims filed on **Form 843,** Claim for Refund and Request for Abatement,

I.R.S. Form 2848 (Continued)

(f) corporation dissolutions, **(g)** a request to change accounting methods, and **(h)** a request to change accounting periods. Check the specific use box on line 4 if the power of attorney is for a use that will not be listed on the CAF. If the box on line 4 is checked, the representative should bring a copy of the power of attorney to each meeting with the IRS. A specific use power of attorney will not automatically revoke any prior powers of attorney.

Line 5—Acts Authorized.—If you want to modify the acts that your named representative(s) can perform, describe any specific additions or deletions in the space provided. The authority to substitute another representative or delegate authority must be specifically stated on line 5.

If you want to authorize your representative to sign an income tax return, this authorization must be specifically listed and the requirements of Regulations section 1.6012-1(a)(5) must be satisfied. In general, this regulation only permits a representative to sign your return if you are unable to make the return by reason of: **(a)** disease or injury, **(b)** continuous absence from the United States (including Puerto Rico), for a period of at least 60 days prior to the date required by law for filing the return, or **(c)** specific permission is requested of and granted by the district director for other good cause.

If you want to authorize a person other than a representative (an agent) to sign an income tax return, you must

1. Complete the information on lines 1–3,

2. Check the box on line 4, and

3. Write the following on line 5:

"This power of attorney is being filed pursuant to Regulation 1.6012(a)(5), reason (a), (b), or (c), which requires a power of attorney to be attached to a return if a return is signed by an agent. No other acts on behalf of the taxpayer are authorized."

Reasons (a), (b), and (c) are defined above. The agent does not complete Part II, Declaration of Representative.

If any representative you name is an unenrolled return preparer, the acts that person can perform on your behalf are limited by Revenue Procedure 81-38 (Pub. 470). In general, an unenrolled return preparer is permitted to appear as your representative only before revenue agents and examining officers of the Examination Division and the EP/EO Division and is not permitted to represent you before other offices (i.e., Collection Division or Appeals Division) of the IRS. Also, an unenrolled return preparer is not permitted to extend the statutory period, execute waivers, delegate authority, or substitute another representative.

Tax Matters Partner/Person.—The tax matters partner/person (TMP)(as defined in sections 6231(a)(7) and 6244) is authorized to perform various acts on behalf of the partnership or S corporation. The following are examples of acts performed by the TMP that **cannot** be delegated to the representative: **(a)** binding nonnotice partners to a settlement agreement under section 6224 and, under certain circumstances, binding all partners or shareholders to a settlement agreement under Tax Court Rule 248; **(b)** filing a petition for readjustment of partnership or subchapter S items in the Tax Court, District Court, or Claims Court, under sections 6226 and 6244, based on the issuance of a notice of final partnership administrative adjustment or notice of final S corporation administrative adjustment by the IRS; **(c)** filing a request for administrative adjustment on behalf of the partnership or S corporation under sections 6227 and 6244; **(d)** filing a petition for adjustment of partnership items with respect to an administrative request in the Tax Court, District Court, or Claims Court, under sections 6228 and 6244; and **(e)** extending the statute of limitations on assessment of any tax attributable to partnership or subchapter S items (and affected items) under sections 6229 and 6244.

Line 6—Receipt of Refund Checks.—If you want to authorize your representative to receive, but not endorse, refund checks on your behalf, you must initial and enter the name of that person in the space provided. Section 10.31 of Treasury Department Circular No. 230 prohibits an attorney, CPA, or enrolled agent, any of whom is an income tax return preparer, from endorsing or otherwise negotiating a tax refund check.

Line 7—Notices and Communications.—Notices and other written communications will be sent to the first representative listed. Also, if you want the second representative listed to receive such communications, check box **(a)** on line 7. The IRS will send notices only to two representatives.

However, if you do not want any notices or communications sent to your representative, you must check box **(b)** on line 7.

If this form is being filed for a private letter ruling, the taxpayer can request that the original letter ruling be sent to the representative. A statement must be attached to Form 2848 stating this.

Line 8—Retention/Revocation of Prior Power(s) of Attorney.—If there is any existing power(s) of attorney you do not want to revoke, check the box on this line and attach a copy of the power(s) of attorney.

If you want to revoke an existing power of attorney and do not want to name a new representative, send a copy of the previously executed power of attorney to each IRS office where the power of attorney was filed. The copy of the power of attorney must have a current signature of the taxpayer under the signature already on line 9. Write "REVOKE" across the top of the form. If you do not have a copy of the power of attorney you want to revoke, send a statement to each IRS office where you filed the power of attorney. The statement of revocation must indicate that the authority of the power of attorney is revoked and must be signed by the taxpayer. Also, the name and address of each recognized representative whose authority is revoked must be listed.

A representative can withdraw from representation by filing a statement with each office of the IRS where the power of attorney was filed. The statement must be signed by the representative and identify the name and address of the taxpayer(s) and tax matter(s) from which the representative is withdrawing. Include your CAF No. on the statement if one has been assigned to you.

The filing of a Form 2848 will not revoke any Form 8821 that is in effect.

Line 9—Signature of Taxpayer(s).—

Individuals.—You must sign and date the power of attorney. If a joint return has been filed and both husband and wife will be represented by the same individual(s), both must sign the power of attorney unless one spouse authorizes the other, in writing, to sign for both. In that case, attach a copy of the authorization. However, if a joint return has been filed and husband and wife will be represented by different individuals, each taxpayer must execute his or her own power of attorney on a separate Form 2848.

Corporations or associations.—An officer having authority to bind the taxpayer must sign. However, the tax matters person may sign on behalf of an S corporation.

Partnerships.—All partners must sign unless one partner is authorized to act in the name of the partnership. A partner is authorized to act in the name of the partnership if, under state law, the partner has authority to bind the partnership. A copy of such authorization must be attached. For purposes of executing Form 2848, the tax matters partner is authorized to act in the name of the partnership. For dissolved partnerships, see Regulations section 601.503(c)(6).

Other.—If the taxpayer is a dissolved corporation, deceased, insolvent, or a person for whom or by whom a fiduciary (a trustee, guarantor, receiver, executor, or administrator) has been appointed, see Regulations section 601.503(d).

Part II—Declaration of Representative

The representative(s) you name must sign and date this declaration and enter the designation (i.e., items **a–h**) under which he or she is authorized to practice before the IRS. In addition, the representative(s) must list the following in the "Jurisdiction" column:

- **a** Attorney—Enter the two-letter abbreviation for the state (e.g., "NY" for New York) in which admitted to practice.
- **b** Certified Public Accountant—Enter the two-letter abbreviation for the state (e.g., "CA" for California) in which licensed to practice.
- **c** Enrolled Agent—Enter the enrollment card number issued by the Director of Practice.
- **d** Officer—Enter the title of the officer (i.e., President, Vice President, or Secretary).
- **e** Full-Time Employee—Enter title or position (e.g., Comptroller or Accountant).
- **f** Family Member—Enter the relationship to taxpayer (i.e., spouse, parent, child, brother, or sister).
- **g** Enrolled Actuary—Enter the enrollment card number issued by the Joint Board for the Enrollment of Actuaries.
- **h** Unenrolled Return Preparer—Enter the two-letter abbreviation for the state (e.g., "KY" for Kentucky) in which the return was prepared.

*U.S. Government Printing Office: 1993 — 343-034/80193

I.R.S. Form 1310: Statement of Person Claiming Refund Due a Deceased Taxpayer

Form **1310** (Rev. March 1995) Department of the Treasury Internal Revenue Service

Statement of Person Claiming Refund Due a Deceased Taxpayer

▶ **See instructions below and on back.**

OMB No. 1545-0073

Attachment Sequence No. **87**

Tax year decedent was due a refund:

Calendar year , or other tax year beginning , 19 , and ending , 19

Please type or print			
	Name of decedent	Date of death	**Decedent's social security number**
	Name of person claiming refund		
	Home address (number and street). If you have a P.O. box, see instructions.		Apt. no.
	City, town or post office, state, and ZIP code. If you have a foreign address, see instructions.		

Part I **Check the box that applies to you.** Check only one box. **Be sure to complete Part III below.**

A ☐ Surviving spouse requesting reissuance of a refund check. See instructions.

B ☐ Court-appointed or certified personal representative. You may have to attach a court certificate showing your appointment. See instructions.

C ☐ Person, **other** than A or B, claiming refund for the decedent's estate. Also, complete Part II. You may have to attach a copy of the proof of death. See instructions.

Part II **Complete this part only if you checked the box on line C above.**

		Yes	No
1	Did the decedent leave a will?		
2a	Has a court appointed a personal representative for the estate of the decedent?		
b	If you answered **"No"** to 2a, will one be appointed?		
	If you answered **"Yes"** to 2a or 2b, the personal representative must file for the refund.		
3	As the person claiming the refund for the decedent's estate, will you pay out the refund according to the laws of the state where the decedent was a legal resident?		
	If you answered **"No"** to 3, a refund cannot be made until you submit a court certificate showing your appointment as personal representative or other evidence that you are entitled under state law to receive the refund.		

Part III **Signature and verification. All filers must complete this part.**

I request a refund of taxes overpaid by or on behalf of the decedent. Under penalties of perjury, I declare that I have examined this claim, and to the best of my knowledge and belief, it is true, correct, and complete.

Signature of person claiming refund ▶ **Date** ▶

Paperwork Reduction Act Notice

We ask for the information on this form to carry out the Internal Revenue laws of the United States. You are required to give us the information. We need it to ensure that you are complying with these laws and to allow us to figure and collect the right amount of tax.

The time needed to complete and file this form will vary depending on individual circumstances. The estimated average time is:

Recordkeeping . . . . 7 min.
Learning about the law or the form . . . . 3 min.
Preparing the form . . . . 16 min.
Copying, assembling, and sending the form to the IRS . . . . 17 min.

If you have comments concerning the accuracy of these time estimates or suggestions for making this form simpler, we would be happy to hear from you. You can write to the **Internal Revenue Service,** Attention: Tax Forms Committee, PC:FP, Washington, DC 20224. **DO NOT** send the form to this address.

General Instructions

Purpose of Form

Use Form 1310 to claim a refund on behalf of a deceased taxpayer.

Who Must File

If you are claiming a refund on behalf of a deceased taxpayer, you must file Form 1310 unless **either** of the following applies:

- You are a surviving spouse filing an original or amended joint return with the decedent, OR
- You are a personal representative (see back of form) filing an original Form 1040, Form 1040A, Form 1040EZ, or Form 1040NR for the decedent and a court certificate showing your appointment is attached to the return.

Example. Assume Mr. Green died on January 4 before filing his tax return. On April 3 of the same year, you were appointed by the court as the personal representative for Mr. Green's estate and you file Form 1040 for Mr. Green. You do not need to file Form 1310 to claim the refund on Mr. Green's tax return. However, you must attach to his return a copy of the court certificate showing your appointment.

Cat. No. 11566B Form **1310** (Rev. 3-95)

I.R.S. Form 1310 (Continued)

Personal Representative

For purposes of this form, a personal representative is the executor or administrator of the decedent's estate, as certified or appointed by the court. A copy of the decedent's will **cannot** be accepted as evidence that you are the personal representative.

Additional Information

For more details, see **Death of Taxpayer** in the index to the Form 1040, Form 1040A, or Form 1040EZ instructions, or get **Pub. 559,** Survivors, Executors, and Administrators.

Specific Instructions

P.O. Box

If your post office does not deliver mail to your home and you have a P.O. box, show your box number instead of your home address.

Foreign Address

If your address is outside the United States or its possessions or territories, enter the information on the line for "City, town or post office, state, and ZIP code" in the following order: city, province or state, postal code, and the name of the country. **Do not** abbreviate the country name.

Line A

Check the box on line A if you received a refund check in your name and your deceased spouse's name. You can return the joint-name check with Form 1310 to your local IRS office or the service center where you mailed your return. A new check will be issued in your name and mailed to you.

Line B

Check the box on line B **only** if you are the decedent's court-appointed personal representative claiming a refund for the decedent on **Form 1040X,** Amended U.S. Individual Income Tax Return, or **Form 843,** Claim for Refund and Request for Abatement. You **must** attach a copy of the court certificate showing your appointment. But if you have already sent the court certificate to the IRS, complete Form 1310 and write "Certificate Previously Filed" at the bottom of the form.

Line C

Check the box on line C if you are not a surviving spouse claiming a refund based on a joint return **and** there is no court-appointed personal representative. You must also complete Part II. If you check the box on line C, you **must** attach the proof of death. But if you have already sent the proof of death to the IRS, complete Form 1310 and write "Proof of Death Previously Filed" at the bottom of the form.

The proof of death **must** be an authentic copy of **either** of the following:

- The death certificate, or
- The telegram or letter from the Department of Defense notifying the next of kin of the decedent's death while in active service.

Example. Your father died on August 25. You are his sole survivor. Your father did not have a will and the court did not appoint a personal representative for his estate. Your father is entitled to a $300 refund. To get the refund, you must complete and attach Form 1310 to your father's final return. You should check the box on line C of Form 1310, answer all the questions in Part II, and sign your name in Part III. You must also attach a copy of the death certificate or other proof of death.

Lines 1-3

If you checked the box on line C, you must complete lines 1 through 3.

Printed on recycled paper *U.S. Government Printing Office: 1997 - 417-677/60198

Glossary

A-B trusts: Credit shelter and marital deduction trusts.
Abatement: Process of selling estate property to pay debts.
Accounts receivable: Business asset consisting of funds due for goods or services sold.
Advance directives: Document that expresses the health care wishes of the signatory.
Ademption: Loss of testamentary gift because the testator no longer owns the property at his or her death.
Administrative control rule: Tax rule for short-term trusts making the trustor tax liable if he or she retains administrative control over the trust.
Administrator: Personal representative of an intestate.
Administrator cum testamento annexo (CTA): Personal representative appointed by the court when a will fails to name an executor, or the named executor fails to complete the estate administration.
Administrator de bonis non (DBN): Personal representative appointed by the court when a previous administrator fails to complete the estate administration.
Advancement: Inter vivos gift to children in anticipation of their share of a parent's estate.
Affinity: Relationship by marriage.
Alternative valuation: Rule permitting assets to be valued at date of death, or six months later, whichever is less.
Ancestor: Relative of a previous generation.
Ancillary administration: Estate administration established in state where property is located if outside the domiciliary state.
Annuity: Periodic payments of fixed sums of money.
Anti-lapse statute: State law providing that gifts to deceased heirs go to those person's heirs.
Ascendent: Lineal ancestor.

Attestation: Clause signed by witnesses to a will.
Beneficiary: Recipient of personal property under a will or the holder of the equitable title under a trust.
Bequest: Gift of personal property under a will.
Bond: Evidence of indebtedness secured by a specific piece of property, paying interest until the loan is repaid, or security posted with the court to insure a fiduciary's performance.
Certificate of deposit: Long-term bank savings account.
Cestui que trust: Trust beneficiary.
Charitable remainder annuity trust: Trust in which the income goes to a private person and the remainder goes to charity.
Charitable remainder unitrust: Trust in which private person and charity share the income.
Charitable trust: Trust created for a public, charitable purpose.
Chose in action: One form of intangible personal property.
Citation: Notice sent to parties with standing to contest a probate petition.
Civil commitment: Confinement of a person to a mental health facility.
Class: Group of persons identified by a common characteristic.
Clifford trust: Short-term trust.
Codicil: Formal document used to amend a will.
Collateral relative: Nonlineal blood relations.
Community property: Method of holding title to property acquired during marriage; each spouse owns one-half of the property.
Competency: The legal ability to make decisions for oneself.
Condominium: Type of ownership of real estate with some attributes of a tenancy-in-common.
Consanguinity: Relationship determined by blood ties.
Constructive trust: Implied trust used to right a wrong.
Conveyance: Transfer of real estate.
Conveyance in trust: Method of transferring realty to a trust.
Co-operative: Type of interest in realty evidenced by owning shares; considered personal property.
Copyright: Government grant of exclusive use of artistic and literary works.
Corpus: Trust property.
Creator: Trustor.
Cumulative Bulletin: Official publication of IRS Revenue Rulings and Revenue Procedures.
Curtesy: Old form of widower's right in property of deceased wife.
Death certificate: Official document proving a person's death.
Debenture: Unsecured evidence of indebtedness similar to a bond.
Declaration of trust: Instrument creating an inter vivos trust.
Deed: Document specifying title to realty.
Deed of trust: Method of transferring realty to a trust.
Defined benefit plan: Pension plan in which the amount of the pension is specifically determined by the employee's length of service and salary.

Defined contribution plan: Pension plan in which the pension is determined by the amount of the contributions made to the plan during the pensioner's period of employment.

Degrees of separation: Number of generations a person is removed from the decedent.

Demonstrative legacy: Testamentary gift of money from a particular source.

Department of Veterans' Affairs: Federal agency that administers veterans' benefits.

Dependent relative revocation: Court doctrine holding that if a later will is found invalid, an earlier valid will will be probated.

Devise: Testamentary gift of real property.

Devisee: Recipient of a testamentary gift of realty.

Discount: Present value of securities that have not yet matured.

Discretionary income: Disposable income.

Discretionary trust: Trust in which the trustee is given broad powers of discretion with respect to investments and distribution of income.

Distributee: Intestate inheritor of personal property.

Divested: Losing a legal right.

Domicile: Legal home.

Donee: Recipient of a gift.

Donor: Person who gives a gift.

Do-Not-Resuscitate Directive: Document indicating that the signatory does not wish to be resuscitated or kept on a life support system.

Dower: A widow's interest in deceased husband's property.

Durable power of attorney: Power of attorney that takes remains in effect even if the principal becomes incapacitated.

Duration rule: Tax rule stating that trusts that exist for less than ten years and a day, or the life of the beneficiary, make the grantor tax liable.

Employee Retirement Income Security Act (ERISA): Federal statute that imposes fiduciary duties on managers of private pension plans.

Endowment policy: Short-term life insurance policy in which proceeds are paid to the insured if alive at the end of the term, or to a beneficiary named in the policy if the insured is deceased.

Enjoyment control rule: Tax rule for short-term trusts making the trustor tax liable if he or she may enjoy the income from the trust.

Equitable title: Title giving the beneficiary the right to enjoy trust property subject to limitations imposed by the trustor.

Escheat: Process by which the state inherits the property of an intestate who has no living blood relatives.

Estate: Interest in land; property of a decedent.

Estate administration: Process of collecting assets, paying debts, and distributing a person's property after his death.

Estate planning: Process of accumulating assets during life and planning its distribution after death.

Execution of a will: Formal signing and witnessing of a will.

Executor(trix): Personal representative named in a will.
Exordium: Introductory paragraph of a will.
Express trust: Trust created by the voluntary and deliberate act of the trustor.
Face value: Redemption value of a bond or debenture.
Failed trust: Trust that terminated because its objective cannot be accomplished.
Fee: Estate in land.
Fertile octogenarian: Doctrine stating that a person is capable of bearing children until death.
Fiduciary: Trustee, a person held to a standard of care higher than ordinary care.
Final return: Last income tax return of the decedent.
Financial plan: Strategy to help a person acquire assets.
Fixture: Property permanently affixed to real estate.
Foreclosure: Ability of a mortgagee to repossess the land.
Forced share: Statutory entitlement of a surviving spouse.
Form 706: Federal estate tax return.
Form 1040: Federal income tax return.
Form 1041: Federal fiduciary tax return.
Fraud: Misrepresentation to induce a person to sign a will.
Freehold: Estate in land for an indefinite period.
Fully insured: Having worked at least 40 quarters to be qualified to receive Social Security benefits.
General administrator: Personal representative appointed by the court for an intestate.
General enrollment period: Yearly period during which persons may enroll in Medicare Part B.
General revocatory clause: Will provision revoking earlier wills and codicils.
Generation skipping transfer: Transfers of property that benefit persons two or more generations removed from the grantor are subject to special tax rules.
Gift: Transfer of property without consideration.
Goodwill: Intangible business asset.
Grantee: Recipient of real estate.
Grantor: Transferor of real estate.
Guardian ad litem: Competent adult appointed by a court to represent persons under an incapacity during litigation.
Guardian of the estate: Guardian to manage the property of an incapacitated person.
Guardian of the person: Person legally authorized to manage the personal, non-financial affairs of an incapacitated person.
Health care proxy: Legal document authorizing someone other than the principal to make health care decisions for the principal should the principal be unable to speak for him or herself.
Heir: Intestate inheritor of real property.
Holographic will: Will written in the testator's own hand.

Illegitimate: Born out of wedlock.
Implied trust: Trust created by operation of law.
In terrorem clause: Anti-contest clause.
Incapacitated person: Current term for a ward.
Incidents of ownership: Control a person keeps over the rights of a life insurance policy.
Income in respect of a decedent (IRD): Income received by a beneficiary that was due the decedent but wasn't paid to the decedent while alive.
Incorporation by reference: External document included by specific mention in the document in question.
Indefinite class: Group identified by general characteristics, a charitable group of beneficiaries.
Individual account plan: Defined contribution plan.
Individual retirement account (IRA): Private pension plan given favorable tax treatment.
Individual retirement account-plus (Roth): Form of IRA that permits withdrawal without tax penalties.
Informal probate proceedings: Probate permitted in certain jurisdictions for small estates in which no notice is required.
Inheritance tax: Tax imposed in some states on the transfer of property from a decedent.
Initial enrollment period: Period during which an eligible person can enroll for Medicare.
Injunction: Court order to stop engaging in specified activity.
Intangible: Personal property that represents something of value but may have little intrinsic value itself.
Internal Revenue Code: Federal tax statute.
Internal Revenue Service: Federal agency that administers the tax laws.
Inter vivos trust: Trust created during the life of the trustor to take effect during the trustor's life.
Intestate: Person who dies without a valid will.
Intestate succession: Persons who are entitled to inherit property of a person who dies without a valid will.
Issue: Direct lineal descendents.
Joint ownership: Two or more persons holding title to property with rights of survivorship.
Joint tenancy: Title to property held by more than one person with a right of survivorship.
Joint will: One will used for two persons.
Landlord: Person who leases real estate.
Lapse: Provision in a will indicating that if a recipient of a gift under the will predeceases the testator the gift forms a part of the testator's residuum.
Laws of descent and distribution: Statutes indicating a person's intestate heirs.
Laws of succession: Statutes indicating a person's intestate heirs.
Leasehold: Tenancy in real estate for a fixed period of time.

Legacy: Testamentary gift of money.
Legal list: Statutory group of safe and risk-free investments.
Legal title: Title held by a trustee enabling him to preserve, protect, and defend the trust property.
Legatee: Recipient of money under a will.
Lessee: Tenant.
Lessor: Landlord.
Letters of administration: Court authorization to act granted to an administrator.
Letters testamentary: Court authorization to act granted to an executor.
License: Grant of use of intellectual property given by the holder of the exclusive right to the property.
Lien: Creditor's attachment of real and personal property.
Life estate: Tenancy for a period of the tenant's life.
Life estate pur autre vie: Tenancy for the life of another person.
Limited guardianship: Guardianship for a limited purpose.
Lineal relations: Blood relatives directing ascending or descending.
Living trust: Trust created to take effect during the trustor's life.
Living will: Instrument indicating a person's wishes with respect to life support should he be unable to speak for himself at the time life support may be needed.
Look-back period: Period of time the government will review to determine whether an applicant for Medicaid has improperly divested him or her self or his or her assets.
Marital deduction: Tax provision permitting property that goes to a surviving spouse to pass tax free.
Marshalling assets: Collecting and categorizing the estate of a decedent.
Maturity date: Date on which debtor repays the bond or debenture.
Medicaid: Federally funded program providing medical care to low-income persons.
Medicare: Federally funded health insurance for persons who receive Social Security.
Medi-gap Insurance: Supplemental insurance designed to provide payment for items not covered by Medicare.
Menace: Threats used to induce a person to sign a will.
Mortgage: Security interest in real estate.
Mortgagee: Person who gives a mortgage to purchase real estate.
Mortgagor: Person who takes a mortgage to purchase real estate.
Mortmain statute: Law limiting charitable gifts under a will.
Mutual will: Identical wills executed by two persons.
Next of kin: Closest intestate blood relation.
Nonmarital children: Children born out of wedlock.
Non-service related disability: Disability resulting from an occurrence that did not take place during military service.
Nuncupative will: Oral will permitted in limited situations.
Operation of law: Actions having certain legal consequences regardless of the wishes of the parties involved.

Overendowed trust: Resulting trust with income greater than is needed to accomplish the trust purposes.

Partition: Method of dividing the interests of multiple owners of real estate.

Passive trust: Trust in which trustee is given no active duties.

Patent: Government grant of exclusive use of a scientific invention given to the inventor.

Pension benefit plan: Pension plan that provides for retirement income.

Per capita: Equally to each person in his or her own right.

Per stirpes: Taking property by right of representation.

Personal property: Property that is moveable and intangible, not real estate.

Personal representative: Fiduciary responsible for administering a decedent's estate.

Petition for a family allowance: Request to the court to permit the family to use estate funds pending probate.

Petition for interim letters: Request to the court to authorize a person to act on behalf of the decedent until final letters are granted.

Petition for letters of administration: Request for a court order appointing the personal representative of an intestate.

Petition for letters testamentary: Request for a court order appointing the personal representative of a testate.

Petition for preliminary letters: Petition for interim letters.

Petition for temporary letters: Petition for interim letters.

Petition to open safe deposit box: Request to the court to allow safe deposit box to be opened to locate a will.

Petition to search: Request to the court to allow property to be searched to locate a will.

Plenary guardian: Guardian of both the person and the property of an incapacitated person.

Pour-over trust: Property being added to the corpus of a separate trust.

Power of appointment: Legal right to select a successor beneficiary.

Power of Attorney: Legal document authorizing someone to act on the behalf of the signatory.

Premium payment rule: Tax rule for short-term trusts making the grantor tax liable if the trust can be used to pay the trustor's insurance premiums.

Pretermission: Omitting mention of a child or issue in a will; the omitted child or issue is entitled to an intestate share of the estate.

Principal: Trust property of cash.

Private trust: Trust designed to fulfill a private purpose of the trustor.

Probate: To prove a will is valid.

Publication 559: IRS publication listing tax forms to be filed by executors and administrators.

Public trust: Charitable trust.

Purchase money resulting trust: Resulting trust in which a person holds property for the benefit of the person who paid for the property.

Qualified terminable interest property (QTIP): Property given to a surviving spouse that qualifies as a marital deduction even though the spouse's interest is not absolute ownership.

QTIP trust: Special trust that qualifies for the marital deduction.

Quiet title: Action to settle title to real estate.

Real property: Land and anything permanently affixed to the land.

Recapture rule: Tax rule taxing the trustor of a short-term trust.

Remainderman: Person in whom legal and equitable titles merge.

Rent: Fee paid by a tenant to a landlord.

Representative payee: Person authorized by the Social Security Administration to receive benefits on behalf of the recipient of Social Security benefits.

Res: Trust property consisting of personalty.

Resulting trust: Implied trust in which trust property reverts to the trustor.

Revenue Procedure: Official IRS procedure for complying with the tax laws.

Revenue Ruling: IRS internal case decision having precedential value.

Reversion: Legal and equitable title merging in the trustor.

Reversionary interest: Remainder interest of a trustor.

Revocable trust: Trust in which the trustor retains the power to revoke.

Right of election: Right of the surviving spouse to elect to take by the will or by statutory share.

Risk aversion: Degree of risk a person is willing to undertake in selecting an investment.

Royalty: Fee paid to holder of a copyright for use of the copyright.

Rule Against Perpetuities: All interests must vest, if at all, within 21 years after the death of a life in being plus the period of gestation.

Salvage doctrine: State laws used to help trusts avoid violating the rule against perpetuities.

Secured debt: Debt to which specific property has been pledged in case of default.

Secured interest: Creditor's right to specific property that has been set aside to satisfy the creditor in case of default.

Securities: Contractual, proprietary interests between an investor and a business, evidenced by stocks, bonds, etc.

Self-dealing: Breach of fiduciary obligation in which trustee makes a benefit for himself instead of the trust.

Self-proving will: Will with an affidavit of attesting witnesses attached.

Settlor: Trustor who creates a trust with personal property.

Share: Stock.

Simultaneous death clause: Provision indicating how property is to be distributed if the testator and heir die in a common disaster.

Slayer statute: Law prohibiting a murderer from inheriting from his victim.

Social Security Act of 1933: Federal statute that provides for retirement income for qualified workers.

Social Security Administration: Federal agency that administers Social Security benefits.
Sovereign immunity: Legal inability to sue the government.
Special enrollment period: Time period in which the working elderly can enroll in Medicare.
Specific performance: Court order to perform a specified act.
Spend-down program: Method whereby a person divests him or her self of assets in order to qualify for Medicaid.
Spendthrift trust: Trust designed to prevent the beneficiary from alienating his interest.
Spray trust: Discretionary trust.
Springing power of attorney: Power of attorney that takes effect in the future.
Sprinkling trust: Discretionary trust.
SS-4: Federal tax form used to acquire a tax ID number.
Statute of uses: Feudal law concerned with trusts.
Statutory share: Forced share.
Statutory trust: Trust provided by specific state statute.
Statutory will: Form will appearing in some state statutes.
Stock: Evidence of ownership in a corporation.
Straw man: Method of changing title held by multiple owners.
Summary proceeding: Shortened probate proceedings permitted in certain jurisdictions for small estates.
Supervised administration: Court scrutinizing every aspect of the estate administration.
Supplemental insurance: Health care coverage designed to provide benefits for care not covered by Medicare or other insurance programs.
Supplemental Security Income (SSI): Government transfer payments to very low-income persons.
Surplus income: Income above the limit to qualify for Medicaid.
Tangible property: Personal property that is moveable or touchable.
Tax credit: Deduction from taxes owed based on other taxes paid.
Tax deduction: Amount reducing the value of taxable property.
Tenancy: Right to real property.
Tenancy in common: Multiple ownership of property with divisible interests.
Tenancy by the entirety: Joint ownership of property by legally married couples.
Tenancy in partnership: Multiple ownership of property by business partners; property passes to surviving partners, heirs of deceased partner receive the value of the deceased partner's interest in the property.
Tenancy in severalty: Ownership by just one person.
Term life insurance: Life insurance in which premiums increase periodically, the insured has no cash surrender value, and the face amount decreases over time.

Testamentary capacity: Knowing the nature and extent of one's property and the natural bounty of one's affections.
Testamentary trust: Trust created by a will.
Testator: Person who dies with a valid will.
Testimonium: Last clause in a will.
Tickler: Checklist or deadline reminder.
Title: Evidence of ownership or possession of property.
Totten trust: Bank account "in trust for" another party.
Trust instrument: Document creating a trust.
Trustee: Person who holds legal title to trust property.
Trustor: Creator of a trust.
Trust property: Property held in trust.
Undue influence: Ability of a person in a close relationship to the testator to use that position to cause the testator to make a particular testamentary disposition.
United States Code: Published source of federal statutes.
Unsecured debt: General obligation for which no specific property has been pledged in case of default.
Unsupervised administration: Estate administration not scrutinized by the court.
Use: Feudal term for a trust.
Venue: Physical location of the court of competent jurisdiction.
Vested: Moment at which a person has a legally enforceable right.
Ward: Former term for an incapacitated person.
Welfare benefit plan: Employee benefit plan that provides for medical care and benefits other than retirement income.
Whole life insurance: Life insurance in which premiums and face amount remain constant and the insured has property rights in the policy.
Will: Document used to dispose of a person's property after death.
Will contest: Legal challenge to the validity of a document presented as a will.
Wrongful death: Action to recover for the willful or negligent death of a person.

Index

A-B trust, 84
Abatement, 119
Ademption, 118-119
Administration. *See* Estate administration
Administrator cum testamento annexo, 12
Administrator de bonis non, 12
Advance directives, 160
Advancements, 129
Affinity, 50
Ancestor, 51
Ancillary executors, appointment of, 123-124
Ancillary jurisdiction, 13
Annuity, 40
Anti-contest clause, 129
Ascendent, 51
Asset, 8
Attestation clause, 130

Bailment, 22
Beneficiary, 75-77
  indefinite class, 79
  life insurance, 6
Bequests, 126
Bonds, 37-38
Business property, 42

Capacity, 161
Cash surrender value, 7
Certificate of deposit, 9
Charitable remainder annuity trust, 79
Charitable remainder unitrust, 79
Charitable trust, 78
Civil commitment, 164
Claims and benefits, 40-42
Clifford trust, 83
Co-operatives, 34
Community property, 28
Competency, 161-163
Concurrent ownership, 24-29
Condominiums, 34
Consanguinity, 50
Conservator, 163
Consideration, 4
Constructive trust, 82
Conveyance, 22, 24
Copyrights, 39
Corporate stock, 37
Credit shelter trust, 84
Curtesy, 33

Death certificate, 14
Debenture, 38
Debt, 41
Deed, 24
Defined benefit plan, 168
Defined contribution plan, 168
Demonstrative legacy, 126
Department of Veterans' Affairs, 166
Descendent, 50
Devises, 126
Discretionary income, 8
Discretionary trust, 78
Disposable income, 2
Domicile, 13
Donee, 4

Donor, 4
Do-Not-Resuscitate directive, 161
Dower, 33

Easement, 32
Elder, 155
Elective share, 33
Employee Retirement Income Security Act (ERISA), 168
Endowment policies, 7
Escheating, 50
Estate, 23
Estate administration, 11-15
  ancillary jurisdiction, 13
  compared with estate planning, 16-17
  death certificate, 14, 188-189
  domicile, 13
  executor, 12
  executrix, 12
  fiduciary, 13
  formal administration, 15
  general administrator, 13
  general administratrix, 13
  generally, 1, 12, 187, 188
  informal administration, 15
  letters, 14, 204-208
  letters of administration, 15
  letters testamentary, 14
  notice and waivers of notice, 209-216
  personal representative, 12, 13
  petition for family allowance, 194
  petition for guardian ad litem, 194
  petition for interim letters, 195-196
  petition for letters of administration, 204-205
  petition for letters testamentary, 205-208
  petition to open safe deposit box, 191-192
  petition to search, 193-194
  preprobate process, 188-196
  probate administration, 196-219
  probate authority, 12
  probate hearing, 216
  summary proceeding, 15
  testate, 12
  venue, 14
Estate law, jurisdictional comparison, 255
Estate planning, 2, 8-9
  compared with estate administration, 16-17
  generally, 1
Executor, 12
Executrix, 12
Exordium clause, 122-123
Express trust, 78-80

Family omissions, 129
Fee simple, 24
Fiduciary, 13
Fixtures, 34
Forced share, 33
Formal administration, 15
Freehold estate, 23
Fully insured, 165
Funeral and disposition of body, 125

General administrator, 13
General administratrix, 13
General revocatory clause, 130
Gift, 4
  bequests, 126
  charitable gift, 118
  demonstrative legacy, 126
  devises, 126
  lapsed gift, 119
  legacies, 126
  property, 22-23
  testamentary gifts, 126-127
Goodwill, 42
Guardian, appointment of, 124, 161
  limited, 164
  of the estate, 163
  of the person, 163
  of the property, 163

Health care proxy, 160
Heirs, 51, 55
Holographic will, 134

Illegitimate child, 50
Implied trust, 80-82
  constructive trust, 82
  resulting trust, 81
Incapacity, 162
In terrorem clause, 129
Incidents of ownership, 6
Individual Retirement Account, 167
Individual Retirement Account-Plus (Roth), 168
Informal administration, 15
Intellectual property, 39
Inter vivos trust, 86-87
Intestate, 13
Intestate administration, 55-57
Intestate heirs, 55

Intestate succession, 50-53
- collateral, 51
- degrees of separation, 51, 52
- lineal, 51
- situational analysis, 54

Irrevocable trust, 86

Joint tenancy, 5, 25-27
- partition, 26
- right of survivorship, 26
- straw man, 26

Landlord, 31
Lease, 31
Leasehold, 23
Legacies, 126
Lessee, 31
Lessor, 31
Letters, 14
Letters of administration, 15
Letters testamentary, 14
License, 39
Lien, 33
Life estate pur autre vie, 29
Life estates, 29
Life insurance, 6
- cash surrender value, 7
- endowment policies, 7
- limited payment, 7
- term, 6
- whole, 7

Life insurance trust, 85
Life tenant pur autre vie, 30
Limited payment life insurance, 7
Living trust, 6
Living will, 136
Look-back period, 159

Marital deduction, 126
- will, 7

Marital deduction trust, 84
Mark, 40
Medicaid, 159-160
Medicare, 156-159
Medi-gap insurance, 158
Minors clause, 126
Mortgage, 32
Mortgagee, 32
Mortgagor, 32
Mortmain statute, 118

Noncupative will, 134
Nonprobate assets, 4

Part A coverage, 156-158
Part B coverage, 158-159
Patent, 39
Pension, 40, 167-168
Per capita, 56
Per stirpes, 56
Personal property, 8, 21, 35
- intangibles, 36-42
- settlor, 66
- tangibles, 35-36

Personal representative, 12, 13
- appointment of, 123
- right and duties of, 124

Pets, 129
Pour-over trust, 85
Power of appointment, 41
Power of attorney, 135-136
Private trust, 78
Probate assets, 4
Probate authority, 12
Promissory note, 38-39
Public trust, 78
Publication clause, 122-123

Qualified Terminable Interest Property (QTIPs), 7, 84

Real property, 8, 21
- co-operatives, 34
- community property, 28
- concurrent ownership, 24-29
- condominiums, 34
- conveyance, 22, 24
- curtesy, 33
- deed, 24
- dower, 33
- easement, 32-33
- elective share, 33-34
- fixtures, 34
- forced share, 33
- freehold estate, 23
- joint tenancy, 25-27
- landlord, 31
- lease, 31
- leasehold, 23
- lessee, 31
- lessor, 31
- lien, 33
- life estates, 29-32
- mortgage, 32
- remainderman, 29
- rent, 31

Real property (*Continued*)
shares, 34
statutory share, 33
tenancy, 24
tenancy by the entirety, 27-28
tenancy in common, 24-25
tenancy in partnership, 28-29
tenancy in severalty, 24
tenant, 31
title, 24
Remainderman, 29, 76
Rent, 31
Residuary clause, 129-130
Resulting trust
failed trust, 81
overendowed trust, 81
purchase money, 81
Reversion, 76
Reversionary interest, 76
Revocable trust, 86
Right of survivorship, 26
Risk aversion, 9
Royalty, 39
Rule against perpetuities, 88-89

Self-proving will, 133
Service mark, 40
Share in realty, 34
Short-term trust, 83
Simultaneous death clause, 128-129
Social Security, 165-166
Sole proprietorship, 42
Spend-down, 160
Spendthrift trust, 82
Spray trust, 78
Sprinkling trust, 78
Statutory share, 33
Statutory trust, 86
Statutory will, 135
Stock, 37
closely held, 37
Straw man, 26
Succession, 49-59
effect of laws of, 57-58
Summary proceeding, 15
Supplemental needs trust, 83
Surplus income, 160

Tax deduction, marital, 7
Taxation
estate tax return, 234
federal tax forms, 234-247
federal tax law, 233-234
fiduciary income tax return, 232-233
generally, 231-233
generation skipping transfer, 96-97
individual income tax, 232
short-term trust, 95-96
trust, 94-97
Tenancy, 24
Tenancy by the entirety, 5, 27-28
Tenancy in common, 24-25
Tenancy in partnership, 28-29
Tenancy in severalty, 24
Tenant, 31
Term life insurance, 6
Testamentary capacity, 57
Testamentary trust, 87, 127
Testate, 12
Testator's signature, 130
Testimonium clause, 130
Tickler, 21
Title, 24
Title transfers, 5
Totten trust, 84
Trademark, 40
Trust, 6
A-B trust, 85
charitable remainder annuity trust, 79
charitable remainder unitrust, 79
charitable trust, 78
Clifford trust, 83
conveyance of trust, 86
corpus, 67
creation of, 85-87
creator, 66
credit shelter trust, 84
cy pres, 80
declaration of trust, 86
deed, 86
defined, 63
discretionary trust, 78
drafting, 97-100
express trust, 78-80
generally, 63-65
grantor, 66
implied trust, 80-82
inter vivos trust, 86-87
investments, 90
life insurance trust, 85
living trust, 6
marital deduction trust, 84-85
pour-over trust, 86
principal, 67

private trust, 78
public trust, 78
purpose, restrictions on, 91-92
requirements, 65-78
res, 67
restrictions, 87-92
role of parties, 90
rule against perpetuities, 88-89
settlor, 66
short-term trust, 83
spendthrift trust, 82
statute of uses, 87-88
statutory trust, 87
supplemental needs trust, 83
tax considerations, 94-97
termination, 92-94
testamentary trust, 87
totten trust, 84
trust instrument, 86
trust property, 67-68
trustee. *See* Trustee
trustor, 65-67
valid trust purpose, 68-70
Trustee, 70-75
invade the corpus, 77
legal list, 73
liability, 72-75
removal, grounds for, 73-74
sovereign immunity, 71

Venue, 14
Veteran's benefits, 166-167

Whole life insurance, 7
Will
abatement, 19
ademption, 118-119
advancement, 118
age, 112
amendment through codicils, 136-137
amendment through operation of law, 137-138
ancillary executors, appointment of, 123-124
antenuptial agreements, 117
anti-contest clause, 129
attestation clause, 131
changing, 136-139
charitable gifts, 118
clauses, 122-131
contest, 139-142
drafting, 120-131
executing, 131-134
exordium clause, 122-123
family omissions, 129
family status, 131
fraud, 114
funeral and disposition of body, 125
general revocatory clause, 130
generally, 7, 111-112
guardians, appointment of, 124
holographic will, 134
incorporation by reference, 117
intent, 114-116
lapsed gifts, 119
living will, 135
marital deduction, 7, 127
menace, 114-115
mental ability, 112-114
minors clause, 126
mortmain statute, 118
noncupative will, 134
omitted children, 117-118
personal representative
appointment of, 123
rights and duties of, 124-125
pets, 129
power of attorney, 135-136
preparation, 120-122
pretermitted, 117
publication clause, 122-123
residuary clause, 129-130
revocation, 138-139
sample will and accompanying documents, 142-149
self-proving will, 133
simultaneous death clause, 128-129
slayer statutes, 138
statutory will, 136
surviving spouse, 116-117
temporary incapacity, 116
testamentary capacity, 57, 112-116
testamentary gifts, 126
testator's signature, 130
testimonium clause, 130
undue influence, 115
witnesses, 130-131
witnesses' signatures, 130
Witnesses' signatures, 130
Wrongful death, 41